The Kenyon Critics

The Kenyon Critics

STUDIES IN MODERN LITERATURE FROM

THE Kenyon Review EDITED BY

John Crowe Ransom

KENNIKAT PRESS, INC./PORT WASHINGTON, N. Y.

THE KENYON CRITICS

Copyright 1951 by The Kenyon Review
Reissued in 1967 by Kennikat Press by arrangement with
The World Publishing Company

Library of Congress Catalog Card: 67-25258

Manufactured in the United States of America

Analyzed in the ESSAY AND GENERAL LITERATURE INDEX
under Main Entry: The Kenyon Review

CONTENTS

Essays

Book Reviews

Introduction

THE CRITICS included in this book are thirty-three in number, and each is represented by a single writing. They are Kenyon Critics at least for the moment, and in the sense that these writings of theirs are all taken from the twelve volumes of the *Kenyon Review* of which Volume xii is just now being concluded. The total content would fill about half of one volume, or two average quarterly issues.

The word average is slightly embarrassing. It must be confessed that issues of the magazine which have a uniform content of so high a grade as this do not actually occur in the run of periodical publication. And for a moment a familiar depression settles upon the editor's spirits. He remembers that an issue never did measure up with anything like evenness to the perfection which had been dreamed for it. The feeling is not really relieved by his being morally certain that other magazines also fail to sustain their own highest standards. Nor is there any advantage in his figuring that fifty authors might perhaps have been exhibited instead of the thirty-three here, without sacrifice in the quality; or that the size of the book might have been doubled but for the rule limiting the authors to one item apiece, regardless of how many top-grade authors may have contributed repeatedly to the magazine over the years, and even borne the reputation of being regular contributors. The book in its character of critical anthology, that is to say of extreme miscellany, demands a good deal of its readers as it stands already; so it is big enough. And the fact remains, mortifyingly, that we can issue no book of this sort without ransacking the whole house.

But a better moment succeeds presently to this one. It brings a great flare-up of pride in the achieved body of criticism however long that may have taken to accrue, and subdues every other thought; a suffusion of glory, such as an editor in these days cannot afford to reproach in himself, and would be mean if he disavowed publicly. These pieces are sponsored from one little corner of the American scene, yet they compose a body of work which seems excellent and trustworthy, possessing a kind of functional integrity, perhaps bearing a national importance. What is indicated by such an event, as it appears to me, is that one of the saving gifts of our age, against the many ways it has devised for being wretched, is its turn for literary criticism, and for a literary criticism evidently so enterprising and acute, and so grounded in good conscience, as can scarcely be predicated of the other periods of literary history. Perhaps it is compensatory, and makes some headway against the bad tendencies of the time, including its foul humors and reckless human strategies. The reader will judge that for himself.

It could be, if we might weigh all the intangible evidences, that the literary critic is one of the most responsible agents of our very best humanity. But of course I mean the good literary critic, the one who by temperament and practice is healthy in his feelings and habitually right in his judgments. The critic needs a great deal of wisdom; sometimes he achieves it. But he is exposed to his own impatiences, and to blind alleys which he has supposed to be the shortcuts of procedure. I think we do not trust the critic, at least the young critic, whose tone is too righteous; on the assumption that righteousness is defined for him by the doctrines of a "school" of literary theory, or a "position." Often the literary object is going to be too various for him, or too subtle. The doctrinal satisfactions have spoiled many a critical apparatus in our time, disposing it to shallow judgments; the harm is bad enough when the doctrine has to do with honest-seeming ideologies, but it is especially brutal when the critic is led to reject on the basis of supposed technical or formal requirements. But there is one risk which I am prepared to run. I am not constitutionally afraid of the critic who finds the human significance that is hidden in the marginal behaviors of a piece of literary plotting, or of a scene, or even a cluster of words, and develops it with a logical intelligence. Many of the critics here judge well because they are professionally sensitive to what is latent in the work, therefore likely to be difficult, and will not content themselves with what is manifest and for everybody to see.

Among the public registers of the infinite human spirit, we are compelled to believe that literature is the completest. But we would be callow and unformed, we would be romantic, to regard it as the most explicit. The register which is most explicit is literary criticism. And if we once consent to this, the public function of the literary critic becomes very clear. In the glorious ages, which were the ages of faith, perhaps even in the prosy stolid ages, the public must have possessed its literature with an immediacy which we cannot now understand. And the critic may well have been the mere àesthete who attached himself to the literary estate for his own pleasure, to bask in its sun; or he was the public herald, or the hired private retainer, being of a suitable sonority, and good at finding the right occasions; at any rate he was something of an expendable figure or supernumerary. In this age,—but how can the great changes be indicated quickly? By an anticlimactic turn of historical process we are all caught now at this late date in the sense of our human uncertainties; to know that we know nothing about the human situation, and the human fate, is the form of our secret consciousness. It is not the less painful for being slightly comical. We have lost our faculty, and to some extent we have lost our taste, for the rule of action which is positive and life-giving. And why not accept the confident voices of ancient authority? It is becoming better and better established that the one authority which is still universally reputable is literature. But literature is cryptic, it is Delphic, in its teasing obscurity. We need not suppose it has fancied this policy perversely; but literature competes with the explicit authorities which have gone out of fashion, and it takes unconscious guard of its own authority which must stay hidden. Indeed, the greater our faith in its authority, the more hidden is likely to be its rule of life and way of salvation. That which is manifest in it was manifest before literature took it up, so that upon reflection it goes back into the common disrepute. It is the critic who must teach us to find the thing truly authoritative but hidden; the critic trying and judging the literary work which has one content that is visible and another content which is not so visible.

This is said more stoutly than I can justify in haste. I must concede that there are many stages in the difficulty of literary works, and sometimes we will conclude that there is a kind of difficulty which is not intelligent; for example, when it does not become intelligible to the approved critic, or when the human good he recovers from it is trifling, and not worth the bother.

I supply a few observations about the book. In the *Kenyon Review* there appears in ordinary course some matter which is primarily literature and not literary criticism; I mean lyric poems, and short fictions. In justice to their authors I wish to say that some items in both kinds seem to us entirely worthy of republication, and indeed many of them have been republished, here or there. But the present book is dedicated to literary criticism.

The critical writings are furnished in two divisions headed Essays and Reviews, respectively. In each division the order is that of original publication.

It should not be taken for granted that, in being smaller than the essays, the reviews are critically inferior. Good reviews are likely to hold to an extreme economy, but sometimes are all the more wonderful in their easy deployment of critical principles and methods answering to the purpose. When the magazine was unable to pay any contributors what their writings were worth on the literary market, we adopted a differential word-rate in order to pay the slightly higher figure not to the essayists but to the reviewers.

A bibliography at the end of the book lists the contents under the authors' names, and supplies a key to the dates of original publication.

JOHN CROWE RANSOM

Gambier, Ohio
January 15, 1951

Essays

John Peale Bishop   THE SORROWS

OF THOMAS WOLFE

THOMAS WOLFE is dead. And that big work which he was prepared to write, which was to have gone to six long volumes and covered in the course of its narrative the years between 1781 and 1933, with a cast of characters whose numbers would have run into the hundreds, will never be finished. The title which he had chosen for it, *Of Time and the River*, had already been allowed to appear on the second volume. There its application is not altogether clear; how appropriate it would have been to the work as a whole we can only conjecture. No work of such magnitude has been projected by another of his generation in America; Wolfe's imagination, it appears, could conceive on no smaller scale. He was, he confesses, devoted to chance; he had no constant control over his faculties; but his fecundity was nothing less than prodigious. He had, moreover, a tenacity which must, but for his dying, have carried him through to the end.

Dying, he left behind him a mass of manuscript; how much of it can be published there is now no knowing. Wolfe was the most wasteful of writers.

His aim was to set down America as far as it can belong to the experience of one man. Wolfe came early on what was for him the one available truth about this continent—that it was contained in himself. There was no America which could not be made out—mountains, rivers, trains, cities, people—in the memory of an American. If the contours were misty, then they must be made clear.

3

It was in flight from a certain experience of America, as unhappy as it had been apparently sterile, it was in Paris, in an alien land, that Wolfe first understood with hate and with love the horror and the wonder of his native country. He had crossed the seas from West to East only to come upon the North Carolina hills where he had been born. "I had found out," he says, "during those years that the way to discover one's own country was to leave it; that the way to find America was to find it in one's own heart, one's memory, and one's spirit, and in a foreign land. I think I may say that I discovered America during those years abroad out of my very need of her."

This is not an uncommon experience, but what made it rewarding in Wolfe's case was that his memory was anything but common. He could—and it is the source of what is most authentic in his talents —displace the present so completely by the past that its sights and sounds all but destroyed surrounding circumstance. He then lost the sense of time. For Wolfe, sitting at a table on a terrace in Paris, contained within himself not only the America he had known; he also held, within his body, both his parents. They were there, not only in his memory, but more portentously in the make-up of his mind. They loomed so enormous to him that their shadows fell across the Atlantic, their shade was on the café table under which he stretched his long American legs.

"The quality of my memory," he said in his little book, *The Story of a Novel,* "is characterized, I believe, in a more than ordinary degree by the intensity of its sense impressions, its power to evoke and bring back the odors, sounds, colors, shapes and feel of things with concrete vividness." That is true. But readers of Wolfe will remember that the mother of Eugene Gant was afflicted with what is known as total recall. Her interminable narratives were the despair of her family. Wolfe could no more than Eliza Gant suppress any detail, no matter how irrelevant; indeed, it was impossible for him to feel that any detail was irrelevant to his purpose. The readers of *Look Homeward, Angel* will also remember that Eugene's father had a gift, unrivalled among his associates, of vigorous utterance. Nobody, they said, can tie a knot in the tail of the English language like old W. O. But the elder Gant's speech, for all that it can on occasion sputter into fiery intensity, more often than not runs off into a homespun rhetoric. It sounds strong, but it has very little connection with any outer reality and is meaningless, except in so far as it serves to convey his rage and frustration. We cannot avoid supposing that Wolfe drew these two characters after his own parents. At the time he began writing *Look Homeward, Angel,* he stood far enough apart from them to use the endlessness of Eliza's unheard discourses, the exaggerated violence of old Gant's objurgations, for comic effect. He makes father and mother into something at once larger and less than human. But in his own case, he could not, at least so long as he was at his writing, restrain either the course of his recollections or their outcome in words. He wrote as a man possessed. Whatever was in his memory must be set down—not merely because he was Eliza's son, but because the secret end of all his writing was expiation—and it must be set down in words to which he constantly seems to be attaching more meaning than they can properly own. It was as though he were aware that his novel would have no meaning that could not be found in the words. The meaning of a novel should be in its structure. But in Wolfe's novel, as far as it has gone, it is impossible to discover any structure at all.

2

It is impossible to say what Wolfe's position in American letters would have been had he lived to bring his work to completion. At the moment he stands very high in the estimation both of the critics and of the common reader. From the time of *Look Homeward, Angel,* he was regarded, and rightly, as a young man of incomparable promise. *Of Time and the River* seemed to many to have borne out that promise and, since its faults were taken as due merely to an excess of fecundity, it was met with praise as though it were the consummation of all Wolfe's talents. Yet the faults are fundamental. The force of Wolfe's talents is indubitable; yet he did not find for that novel, nor do I believe he could ever have found, a structure of form which would have been capable of giving shape and meaning to his emotional experience. He was not without intelligence; but he could not trust his intelligence, since for him to do so would have been to succumb to conscience. And it was conscience, with its convictions of guilt, that he was continually trying to elude.

His position as an artist is very like that of Hart Crane. Crane was born in 1899, Wolfe in 1900, so that they were almost of an age. Both had what we must call genius; both conceived that genius had been given them that they might celebrate, the one in poetry, the other in prose, the greatness of their country. But Wolfe no more than Crane was able to give any other coherence to his work than that which comes from the personal quality of his writing. And he found, as Crane did before him, that the America he longed to celebrate did not exist. He could record, and none better, its sights, its sounds and its odors, as they can be caught in a moment of time; he could try, as the poet of *The Bridge* did, to absorb that moment and endow it with the permanence of a myth. But he could not create a continuous America. He could not, for all that he was prepared to cover one hundred and fifty of its years, conceive its history. He can record what comes to his sensibility, but he cannot give us the continuity of experience. Everything for Wolfe is in the moment; he can so try to impress us with the immensity of the moment that it will take on some sort of transcendental meaning. But what that meaning is, escapes him, as it does us. And once it has passed from his mind, he can do nothing but recall another moment, which as it descends into his memory seems always about to deliver itself, by a miracle, of some tremendous import.

Both Crane and Wolfe belonged to a world that is indeed living from moment to moment. And it is because they voice its breakdown in the consciousness of continuity that they have significance for it.

Of the two, Wolfe, I should say, was the more aware of his plight. He was, he tells us, while writing *Of Time and the River,* tormented by a dream in which the sense of guilt was associated with the forgetting of time. "I was unable to sleep, unable to subdue the tumult of these creative energies, and, as a result of this condition, for three years I prowled the streets, explored the swarming web of the million-footed city and came to know it as I had never done before. . . . Moreover, in this endless quest and prowling of the night through the great web and jungle of the city, I saw, lived, felt and experienced the full weight of that horrible human calamity. [The time was that of the bottom of the depression, when Wolfe was living in Brooklyn.] And from it all has come as a final deposit, a burning memory, a certain evidence of the fortitude of man, his ability to suffer and somehow survive. And it is for this reason now that I think I shall always remember this black period with a kind of joy that I could not at that time have believed possible, for it was during this time that I lived my life through to a first completion, and through the suffering and labor of my own life came to share those qualities in the lives of the people around me."

This passage is one of extreme interest, not only for what it tells us of Wolfe at this time, but for the promise it contains of an emotional maturity. For as far as Wolfe had carried the history of Eugene Gant, he was dealing with a young man whose isolation from his fellow men was almost complete. Eugene, and we must suppose the young Wolfe, was incarcerated in his own sensibility. Locked in his cell, he awaits the coming of every moment, as though it would bring the turning of a releasing key. He waits like Ugolino, when he woke uncertain because of his dream and heard not the opening, but the closing of the lock. There is no release. And the place of Wolfe's confinement, no less than that of Ugolino, deserves to be called Famine.

It can be said of Wolfe, as Allen Tate has said of Hart Crane, that he was playing a game in which any move was possible, because none was compulsory. There is no idea which would serve as discipline to the event. For what Wolfe tells us was the idea that furiously pursued him during the composition of *Of Time and the River,* the search for a father, can scarcely be said to appear in the novel, or else it is so incidentally that it seems to no purpose. It does not certainly, as the same search on the part of Stephen Dedalus does in *Ulysses,* prepare a point toward which the whole narrative moves. There was nothing indeed in Wolfe's upbringing to make discipline acceptable to him. He acts always as though his own capacity for feeling, for anguished hope and continual frustration, was what made him superior, as no doubt, along with his romantic propensity for expression, it was. But he was wrong in assuming that those who accept any form of discipline are therefore lacking in vigor. He apparently did not understand that there are those who might say with Yeats, "I could recover if I shrieked my heart's agony," and yet like him are dumb "from human dignity." And his failure to understand was due to no fault of the intelligence, but to a lack of love. The Gant family always strikes us, with its howls of rage, its loud Hah-hahs of hate and derision, as something less than human. And

Eugene is a Gant. While in his case we are ready to admit that genius is a law unto itself, we have every right to demand that it discover its own law.

Again like Crane, Wolfe failed to see that at the present time so extreme a manifestation of individualism could not but be morbid. Both came too late into a world too mechanic; they lacked a wilderness and constantly tried to create one as wild as their hearts. It was all very well for them, since both were in the way of being poets, to start out to proclaim the grandeur of America. Such a task seemed superb. But both were led at last, on proud romantic feet, to Brooklyn. And what they found there they abhorred.

They represent, each in his way, a culmination of the romantic spirit in America. There was in both a tremendous desire to impose the will on experience. Wolfe had no uncommon will. And Crane's was strong enough to lead him deliberately to death by drowning. For Wolfe the rewards of experience were always such that he was turned back upon himself. Isolated in his sensations, there was no way out. He continually sought for a door, and there was really none, or only one, the door of death.

3

The intellectual labor of the artist is properly confined to the perception of relations. The conscience of the craftsman must see that these relations are so presented that in spite of all complications they are ultimately clear. It is one of the conditions of art that they cannot be abstractly stated, but must be presented to the senses.

What we have at the center of all Wolfe's writing is a single character, and it was certainly the aim of that writing to present this character in all his manifold contacts with the world of our time. Eugene has, we are told, the craving of a Faust to know all experience, to be able to record all the races and all the social classes which may be said to exist in America. Actually Eugene's experience is not confined to America.

But when we actually come to consider Eugene closely, we see that, once he is beyond the overwhelming presence of his family, his contacts with other people are all casual. The perfect experience for Eugene is to see someone in the throes of an emotion which he can imagine, but in which he has no responsible part. From one train, he sees people passing in another train, which is moving at a faster speed than his own.

"And they looked at one another for a moment, they passed and vanished and were gone forever, yet it seemed to him that he had known these people, that he knew them far better than the people in his own train, and that, having met them for an instant under immense and timeless skies, as they were hurled across the continent to a thousand destinations, they had met, passed, vanished, yet would remember this forever. And he thought the people in the two trains felt this, also: slowly they passed each other now, and their mouths smiled and their eyes grew friendly, but he thought there was some sorrow and regret in what they felt. For having lived together as strangers in the immense and swarming city, they had now met upon the everlasting earth, hurled past each other for a moment between two points of time upon the shining rails; never to meet, to speak, to know each other any more, and the briefness of their days, the destiny of man, was in that instant greeting and farewell."

He sees from a train a boy trying to decide to go after a girl; wandering the streets of New York, he sees death come to four men; through one of his students at the university, he comes in contact with an old Jewess wailing a son dead for a year. Each of these moments is completely done; most of them, indeed, overwrought. From the country seen from a train he derives "a wild and solemn joy—the sense of nameless hope, impossible desire, and man's tragic brevity." He reacts to most circumstances, it must seem to us, excessively. But to men and women he does not really answer. The old Jewess's grief fills him "with horror, anger, a sense of cruelty, disgust, and pity." The passion aroused returns to himself. And it is precisely because his passions cannot attain their object, and in one person know peace, that he turns in rage and desire toward the millions. There is in Eugene every emotion you wish but one; there is no love.

The most striking passages in Wolfe's novels always represent these moments of comprehension. For a moment, but a moment only, there is a sudden release of compassion, when some aspect of suffering and bewildered humanity is seized, when the other's emotion is in a timeless completion known. Then the moment passes, and compassion fails. For Eugene Gant, the only satisfactory relationship with another human creature is one which can have no continuity. For the boy at the street corner, seen in the indecision of youthful lust, he has only understanding and pity; the train from which he looks moves on and nothing more is required of Eugene. But if he should approach that same boy on the street, if he should come close enough to overhear him, he would hear only the defilement of language, words which would awaken in him only hate and disgust. He would himself become lonely, strange and cruel. For emotions such as these, unless they can be used with the responsibility of the artist, must remain a torment to the man.

The only human relationship which endures is that of the child to his family. And that is inescapable; once having been, it cannot cease to be. His father is still his father, though dying; and his brother Ben, though dead, remains his brother. He loves and he hates and knows why no more than the poet he quotes. What he does know is that love has been forbidden him.

The only contemporary literary influence on Wolfe which was at all strong is that of Joyce. I shall consider it here only to note that while we know that Joyce could only have created Stephen Dedalus out of the conflicts of his own youth, we never think of Stephen simply as the young Joyce, any more than we think of Hamlet as Shakespeare. He is a creation. But in Wolfe's novels it is impossible to feel that the central figure has any existence apart from the author. He is called Eugene Gant, but that does not deceive any one for a moment; he is, beyond all doubt, Thomas Wolfe. There is, however, one important distinction to be made between them, and one which we should not allow ourselves to forget: Eugene Gant is always younger, by at least ten years, than Thomas Wolfe.

Wolfe described *Of Time and the River* as being devoted to "the period of wandering and hunger in a man's youth." And in it we are meant to take Eugene as every young man. The following volume would, Wolfe said, declare "a period of greater certitude, which would be dominated by a single passion." That, however, still remains to be seen. So far, Eugene has shown no capacity as a lover, except in casual contact with whores. When for a moment he convinces himself that he is in love with Ann, who is a nice, simple, conventional girl from Boston, he can only shriek at her and call her a bitch and a whore, which she certainly is not. The one contact which lasts for any time—leaving aside the blood ties which bind him to the Pentlands, his mother's people, and the Gants—is that with Starwick. Starwick is the only friend he makes in his two years at Harvard, and in Paris, some years later, he still regards his friendship with Starwick as the most valuable he has ever known.

It ends when he discovers that Starwick is a homosexual. And it has usually been assumed that the violence and bitterness with which it ends are due to disillusionment; the sudden turn in Eugene's affections for the young man may well be taken as a natural reaction to his learning, first that Ann is in love with Starwick, and only a little later how hopelessly deep is Starwick's infatuation with the young tough he has picked up, by apparent chance, one night in a Paris bar. But that is, I think, to take too simple a view of the affair. There is more to it than that. What we have been told about Starwick from his first appearance in the book is that, despite a certain affection and oddity of manner, he is, as Eugene is not, a person capable of loving and being loved. What is suddenly revealed in Paris is that for him, too, love is a thing the world has forbidden. In Starwick's face Eugene sees his own fate. Just as in his brother Ben's complaint at his neglect, he had looked back through another's sight at his own neglected childhood and in his brother's death foremourned his own, so now, when he beats Starwick's head against the wall, he is but raging against his own frustration and despair.

In his father's yard, among the tombstones, stood for years a marble angel. Old Gant curses it, all hope he thinks lost that he will ever get his money back for it. It stands a magnificent reminder of the time when as a boy, with winged ambition, he had wanted to be not merely a stone cutter but a sculptor. Then, unexpectedly, a customer comes for it. The one symbol of the divine in the workshop is sold to adorn the grave of a prostitute; what the boy might have been the man lets go for such a purpose. It cannot be said that Thomas Wolfe ever sold his angel. But the faults of the artist are all of them traceable to the failures of the man. He achieved probably the utmost intensity of which incoherent writing is capable; he proved that an art founded solely on the individual, however strong his will, however vivid his sensations, cannot be sound, or whole, or even passionate, in a world such as ours, in which "the integrity of the individual consciousness has been broken down." How far it has broken down, I do not believe he ever knew, yet all that he did is made of its fragments.

Philip Rahv PALEFACE AND

REDSKIN

VIEWED historically, American writers appear to group themselves around two polar types. Paleface and redskin I should like to call the two, and despite occasional efforts at reconciliation no love is lost between them.

Consider the immense contrast between the drawing-room fictions of Henry James and the open air poems of Walt Whitman. Compare Melville's decades of loneliness, his tragic failure, with Mark Twain's boisterous career and dubious success. At one pole there is the literature of the lowlife world of the frontier and of the big cities; at the other the thin, solemn, semi-clerical culture of Boston and Concord. The fact is that the creative mind in America is fragmented and one-sided. For the process of polarization has produced a dichotomy between experience and consciousness—a dissociation between energy and sensibility, between conduct and theories of conduct, between life conceived as an opportunity and life conceived as a discipline.

The differences between the two types define themselves in

every sphere. Thus while the redskin glories in his Americanism, to the paleface it is a source of endless ambiguities. Sociologically they can be distinguished as patrician vs. plebeian, and in their aesthetic ideals one is drawn to allegory and to the distillations of symbolism, whereas the other inclines to a gross, riotous naturalism. The paleface is a "highbrow," though his mentality—as in the case of Hawthorne and James—is often of the kind that excludes and repels general ideas; he is at the same time both something more and something less than an intellectual in the European sense. And the redskin deserves the epithet "lowbrow" not because he is badly educated —which he might or might not be—but because his reactions are primarily emotional, spontaneous, and lacking in personal culture. The paleface continually hankers after religious norms and tends toward a refined estrangement from reality. The redskin, on the other hand, accepts his environment, at times to the degree of fusion with it, even when rebelling against one or another of its manifestations. At his highest level the paleface moves in an exquisite moral atmosphere; at his lowest he is genteel, snobbish, and pedantic. In giving expression to the vitality and to the aspirations of the people, the redskin is at his best; but at his worst he is a vulgar anti-intellectual, combining aggression with conformity and reverting to the crudest forms of frontier psychology.

James and Whitman, who as contemporaries felt only disdain for each other, are the purest examples of this dissociation. In reviewing *Drum Taps* in 1865 the young James told off the grand plebeian innovator, advising him to stop declaiming and go sit in the corner of a rhyme and meter school,[1] while the innovator, snorting at the novelist of scruples and moral delicacy, said "Feathers!" Now this mutual repulsion between the two major figures in American literature would be less important if it were mainly personal or aesthetic in reference. But the point is that it has a profoundly national and social-historical character.

James and Whitman form a kind of fatal antipodes. To this, in part, can be traced the curious fact about them, that, though each has become the object of a special cult, neither is quite secure in his repu-

---

[1] In *A Backward Glance* Edith Wharton relates that in his old age James liked to recite Whitman's poetry. But if he changed his mind about Whitman he certainly kept it a secret so far as any public expression is concerned.

tation. For most of the critics and historians who make much of Whitman disparage James or ignore him altogether, and vice versa. Evidently the high valuation of the one is so incongruous with the high valuation of the other that criticism is chronically forced to choose between them—which makes for a breach in the literary tradition without parallel in any European country. The aristocrat Tolstoy and the tramp Gorky found that they held certain values and ideas in common, whereas James and Whitman, who between them dominate American writing of the nineteenth century, cannot abide with one another. And theirs is no unique or isolated instance.

The national literature suffers from the ills of a split personality. The typical American writer has so far shown himself incapable of escaping the blight of one-sidedness: of achieving that mature control which permits the balance of impulse with sensitiveness, of natural power with ideological depth. For the dissociation of mind from experience has resulted in truncated works of art, works that tend to be either naive and ungraded, often flat, reproductions of life, or else products of cultivation that remain abstract for the reason that they fall short on evidence drawn from the sensuous and material world. Hence it is only through intensively exploiting their very limitations, through submitting themselves to a process of creative yet cruel self-exaggeration, that a few artists have succeeded in warding off the failure that threatened them. And the later novels of Henry James are a case in point.

The palefaces dominated literature throughout the nineteenth century, but in the twentieth they have been overthrown by the redskins. Once the continent had been mastered, with the plebeian bourgeoisie coming into complete possession of the national wealth, and puritanism had worn itself out, degenerating into mere respectability, it became objectively possible and socially permissible to satisfy that desire for experience and personal emancipation which heretofore had been systematically frustrated. The era of economic accumulation had ended and the era of consummation had arrived. To enjoy life now became one of the functions of progress—a function for which the palefaces were temperamentally disqualified. This gave Mencken his opportunity to emerge as the ideologue of enjoyment. Novelists like Dreiser, Anderson, and Lewis—and, in fact, most of the writers of the period of "experiment and liberation"—rose against social conventions that society itself was beginning to abandon. They helped to "liquidate" the lag between the enormous riches of the nation and its morality of abstention. The neo-humanists were among the last of the breed of palefaces, and they perished in the quixotic attempt to re-establish the old values. Eliot forsook his native land, while the few palefaces who managed to survive at home took to the academic or else to the "higher" and relatively obscure forms of writing. But the novelists, who control the main highway of literature, were and still are nearly all redskins to the wigwam born.

At present the redskins are in command of the literary situation, and seldom has the literary life in America been as intellectually impoverished as it is today. The political interests introduced in the nineteen-thirties not only have strengthened their hold but also have brought out their worst tendencies; for the effect of the popular political creeds of our time has been to increase their habitual hostility to ideas, sanctioning the relaxation of standards and justifying the urge to come to terms with semi-literate audiences.

The lowbrow writer in America is a purely indigenous phenomenon, the true-blue offspring of the western hemisphere, the juvenile in principle and for the good of the soul. He is a self-made writer in the same way as Henry Ford is a self-made millionaire. On the one hand he is a crass materialist, a greedy consumer of experience, and on the other a sentimentalist, a half-baked mystic listening to inward voices and watching for signs and portents. Think of Dreiser, Lewis, Anderson, Wolfe, Sandburg, Caldwell, Steinbeck, Saroyan: all writers of genuine and some even of admirable accomplishments, whose faults, however, are not so much literary as faults of raw life itself. Unable to relate himself in any significant manner to the cultural heritage, the lowbrow writer is always on his own; and since his personality resists growth and change, he must constantly repeat himself. His work is ridden by compulsions that depress the literary tradition, because they are compulsions of a kind that put a strain on literature, that literature more often than not can neither assimilate nor sublimate. He is the passive instead of the active agent of the *Zeitgeist*, he lives off it rather than through it, so that when his particular gifts happen to coincide with the mood of the times he seems modern and contemporary, but once the mood has

passed he is in danger of being quickly discarded. Lacking the qualities of surprise and renewal, already Dreiser and Anderson, for example, have a "period" air about them that makes a re-reading of
their work something of a critical chore; and one suspects that
Hemingway, that perennial boy-man, is more accurately understood as a descendant of Natty Bumppo, the hero of Fenimore
Cooper's Leatherstocking tales, than as the portentously disillusioned
character his legend makes him out to be.

As for the paleface, in compensation for backward cultural
conditions and a lost religious ethic, he has developed a supreme
talent for refinement, just as the Jew, in compensation for adverse
social conditions and a lost national independence, has developed
a supreme talent for cleverness. (It might be pertinent, in this
connection, to recall T. S. Eliot's remark about Boston society,
which he described as "quite uncivilized, but refined beyond the
point of civilization.") Now this peculiar excess of refinement is
to be deplored in an imaginative writer, for it weakens his capacity
to cope with experience and induces in him a fetishistic attitude to
tradition; nor is this species of refinement to be equated with the
refinement of artists like Proust or Mann, as in them it is not an
element contradicting an open and bold confrontation of reality. Yet
the paleface, being above all a conscious individual, was frequently
able to transcend or to deviate sharply from the norms of his group,
and he is to be credited with most of the rigors and charms of the
classic American books. While it is true, as John Jay Chapman put
it, that his culture is "secondary and tertiary" and that between him
and the sky "float the Constitution of the United States and the traditions and forms of English literature"—nevertheless, there exists the
poetry of Emily Dickinson, there is *The Scarlet Letter,* there is *Moby-
Dick,* and there are not a few incomparable narratives by Henry
James.

At this point there is no necessity to enter into a discussion of
the historical and social causes that account for the disunity of the
American creative mind. In various contexts a number of critics have
disclosed and evaluated the forces that have worked on this mind and
shaped it to their uses. The sole question that seems relevant is
whether history will make whole again what it has rent asunder.
Will James and Whitman ever be reconciled, will they finally dis-

cover and act upon each other? Only history can give a definite reply to this question. In the meantime, however, there are available the resources of effort and of understanding, resources which even those who believe in the strict determination of the cultural object need not spurn.

Robert Penn Warren PURE AND

IMPURE POETRY

CRITICS are rarely faithful to their labels and their special strategies. Usually the critic will confess that no one strategy —the psychological, the moralistic, the formalistic, the historical —or combination of strategies, will quite work the defeat of the poem. For the poem is like the monstrous Orillo in Boiardo's *Orlando Innamorato*. When the sword lops off any member of the monster, that member is immediately rejoined to the body, and the monster is as formidable as ever. But the poem is even more formidable than the monster, for Orillo's adversary finally gained a victory by an astonishing feat of dexterity: he slashed off both the monster's arms and quick as a wink seized them and flung them into the river. The critic who vaingloriously trusts his method to account for the poem, to exhaust the poem, is trying to emulate this dexterity: he thinks that he, too, can win by throwing the lopped-off arms into the river. But he is doomed to failure. Neither fire nor water will suffice to prevent the rejoining of the mutilated

Delivered as one of the *Mesures* Lectures at Princeton in 1942.

members to the monstrous torso. There is only one way to conquer the monster: you must eat it, bones, blood, skin, pelt, and gristle. And even then the monster is not dead, for it lives in you, is assimilated into you, and you are different, and somewhat monstrous yourself, for having eaten it.

So the monster will always win, and the critic knows this. He does not want to win. He knows that he must always play stooge to the monster. All he wants to do is to give the monster a chance to exhibit again its miraculous power.

With this fable, I shall begin by observing that poetry wants to be pure. And it always succeeds in this ambition. In so far as we have poetry at all, it is always pure poetry; that is, it is not nonpoetry. The poetry of Shakespeare, the poetry of Pope, the poetry of Herrick, is pure, in so far as it is poetry at all. We call the poetry "higher" or "lower," we say, "more powerful" or "less powerful" about it, and we are, no doubt, quite right in doing so. The souls that form the great rose of Paradise are seated in banks and tiers of ascending blessedness, but they are all saved, they are all perfectly happy; they are all "pure," for they have all been purged of mortal taint. This is not to say, however, that if we get poetry from one source, such a single source, say Shakespeare, should suffice us in as much as we can always appeal to it, or that, since all poetry is equally pure, we engage in a superfluous labor in trying to explore or create new sources of poetry. No, for we can remember that every soul in the great rose is precious in the eyes of God. No soul is the substitute for another.

Poetry wants to be pure, but poems do not. At least, most of them do not want to be too pure. The poems want to give us poetry, which is pure, and the elements of a poem, in so far as it is a good poem, will work together toward that end, but many of the elements, taken in themselves, may actually seem to contradict that end, or be neutral toward the achieving of that end. Are we then to conclude that, because neutral or recalcitrant elements appear in poems, even in poems called great, these elements are simply an index to human frailty, that in a perfect world there would be no dross in poems which would, then, be perfectly pure? No, it does not seem to be merely the fault of our world, for the poems include, deliberately, more of the so-called dross than would appear necessary. They are not even as pure as they might be in this imperfect world. They mar themselves with cacophonies, jagged rhythms, ugly words and ugly thoughts, colloquialisms, clichés, sterile technical terms, head work and argument, self-contradictions, clevernesses, irony, realism—all things which call us back to the world of prose and imperfection.

Sometimes a poet will reflect on this state of affairs, and grieve. He will decide that he, at least, will try to make one poem as pure as possible. So he writes:

> Now sleeps the crimson petal, now the white;
> Nor waves the cypress in the palace walk;
> Nor winks the gold fin in the porphyry font:
> The firefly wakens: waken thou with me.

We know the famous garden. We know how all nature conspires here to express the purity of the moment: how the milk-white peacock glimmers like a ghost, and how like a ghost the unnamed "she" glimmers on to her tryst; how earth lies "all Danaé to the stars," as the beloved's heart lies open to the lover; and how, in the end, the lily folds up her sweetness, "and slips into the bosom of the lake," as the lovers are lost in the sweet dissolution of love.

And we know another poet and another garden. Or perhaps it is the same garden, after all:

> I arise from dreams of thee
> In the first sweet sleep of night,
> When the winds are breathing low
> And the stars are shining bright.
> I arise from dreams of thee,
> And a spirit in my feet
> Hath led me—who knows how?
> To thy chamber window, Sweet!

We remember how, again, all nature conspires, how the wandering airs "faint," how the Champak's odors "pine," how the nightingale's complaint "dies upon her heart," as the lover will die upon the beloved's heart. Nature here strains out of nature, it wants to be called by another name, it wants to spiritualize itself by calling itself another name. How does the lover get to the chamber window? He refuses to say how, in his semi-somnambulistic daze, he got there. He blames, he says, "a spirit in my feet," and hastens to disavow any knowledge of how that spirit operates. In any case, he arrives at the chamber window. Subsequent events and the lover's reaction toward them are somewhat hazy. We only know that the lover, who faints and fails at the opening of the last stanza, and who asks to be lifted from the grass by a more enterprising beloved, is in a condition of delectable passivity, in which distinctions blur out in the "purity" of the moment.

Let us turn to another garden: the place, Verona; the time, a summer night, with full moon. The lover speaks:

> But soft! what light through yonder window breaks?
> It is the east . . .

But we know the rest, and know that this garden, in which nature for the moment conspires again with the lover, is the most famous of them all, for the scene is justly admired for its purity of effect, for giving us the very essence of young, untarnished love. Nature conspires beneficently here, but we may chance to remember that beyond the garden wall strolls Mercutio, who can celebrate Queen Mab, but who is always aware that nature has other names as well as the names the pure poets and pure lovers put upon her. And we remember that Mercutio, outside the wall, has just said:

> . . . 'twould anger him
> To raise a spirit in his mistress's circle
> Of some strange nature, letting it there stand
> Till she had laid it and conjured it down.

Mercutio has made a joke, a bawdy joke. That is bad enough, but worse, he has made his joke witty and, worst of all, intellectually complicated in its form. Realism, wit, intellectual complication— these are the enemies of the garden purity.

But the poet has not only let us see Mercutio outside the garden wall. Within the garden itself, when the lover invokes nature, when he spiritualizes and innocently trusts her, and says,

> Lady, by yonder blessed moon I swear,

the lady herself replies,

O, swear not by the moon, the inconstant moon,
That monthly changes in her circled orb.

The lady distrusts "pure" poems, nature spiritualized into forget-fulness. She has, as it were, a rigorous taste in metaphor, too; she brings a logical criticism to bear on the metaphor which is too easy; the metaphor must prove itself to her, must be willing to subject itself to scrutiny beyond the moment's enthusiasm. She injects the impurity of an intellectual style into the lover's pure poem.

And we must not forget the voice of the nurse, who calls from within, a voice which, we discover, is the voice of expediency, of half-measures, of the view that circumstances alter cases—the voice of prose and imperfection.

It is time to ask ourselves if the celebrated poetry of this scene, which as poetry is pure, exists despite the impurities of the total composition, if the effect would be more purely poetic were the nurse and Mercutio absent and the lady a more sympathetic critic of pure poems. I do not think so. The effect might even be more vulnerable poetically if the impurities were purged away. Mer-cutio, the lady, and the nurse are critics of the lover, who believes in pure poems, but perhaps they are necessary. Perhaps the lover can only be accepted in their context. The poet seems to say: "I know the worst that can be said on this subject, and I am giving fair warning. Read at your own risk." So the poetry arises from a recalcitrant and contradictory context; and finally involves that context.

Let us return to one of the other gardens, in which there is no Mercutio or nurse, and in which the lady is more sympathetic. Let us mar its purity by installing Mercutio in the shrubbery, from which the poet was so careful to banish him. You can hear his comment when the lover says:

> *And a spirit in my feet*
> *Hath led me—who knows how?*
> *To thy chamber window, Sweet!*

And we can guess what the wicked tongue would have to say in response to the last stanza.

It may be that the poet should have made his peace early with Mercutio, and have appealed to his better nature. For Mercutio seems to be glad to cooperate with a poet. But he must be invited; otherwise, he is apt to show a streak of merry vindictiveness about the finished product. Poems are vulnerable enough at best. Bright reason mocks them like sun from a wintry sky. They are easily left naked to laughter when leaves fall in the garden and the cold winds come. Therefore, they need all the friends they can get, and Mercutio, who is an ally of reason and who himself is given to mocking laughter, is a good friend for a poem to have.

On what terms does a poet make his peace with Mercutio? There are about as many sets of terms as there are good poets. I know that I have loaded the answer with the word *good* here, that I have implied a scale of excellence based, in part at least, on degree of complication. I shall return to this question. For the moment, however, let us examine a poem whose apparent innocence and simple lyric cry should earn it a place in any anthology of "pure poetry."

> *Western wind, when wilt thou blow*
> *That the small rain down can rain?*
> *Christ, that my love were in my arms*
> *And I in my bed again!*

The lover, grieving for the absent beloved, cries out for relief. Several kinds of relief are involved in the appeal to the wind. First there is the relief that would be had from the sympathetic manifestation of nature. The lover, in his perturbation of spirit, invokes the perturbations of nature. He exclaims,

> *Western wind, when wilt thou blow*

and Lear exclaims,

> *Blow, winds, and crack your cheeks! rage! blow!*

Second, there is the relief that would be had by the fulfillment of grief—the frost of grief, the drouth of grief broken, the full anguish expressed, then the violence allayed in the peace of tears. Third, there is the relief that would be had in the excitement and fulfillment of love itself. There seems to be a contrast between the first two types of relief and the third type; speaking loosely, we may say that the first two types are romantic and general, the third type realistic and specific. So much for the first two lines.

In the last two lines, the lover cries out for the specific solace of his case: reunion with his beloved. But there is a difference between the two lines. The first is general, and romantic. The phrase "in my arms" does not seem to mean exactly what it says. True, it has a literal meaning, if we can look close at the words, but it is hard to look close because of the romantic aura—the spiritualized mist about them.[1] But with the last line the perfectly literal meaning suddenly comes into sharp focus. The mist is rifted and we can look straight at the words, which, we discover with a slight shock of surprise, do mean exactly what they say. The last line is realistic and specific. It is not even content to say,

And I in bed again!

It is, rather, more scrupulously specific, and says,

And I in my *bed again!*[2]

All of this does not go to say that the realistic elements here are to be taken as cancelling, or negating, the romantic elements. There is no ironical leer. The poem is not a celebration of carnality. It is a faithful lover who speaks. He is faithful to the absent beloved, and he is also faithful to the full experience of love. That is, he does not abstract one aspect of the experience and call it the whole experience. He does not strain nature out of nature;

---

[1] It may be objected here that I am reading the phrase "in my arms" as a twentieth-century reader. I confess the fact. Certainly, several centuries have passed since the composition of the little poem, and those centuries have thickened the romantic mist about the words, but it is scarcely to be believed that the sixteenth century was the clear, literal Eden dawn of poetry when words walked without the fig leaf.

[2] In connection with the word *my* in this line, we may also feel that it helps to set over the comfort and satisfaction there specified against the bad weather of the first two lines. We may also glance at the word *small* in the second line. It is the scrupulous word, the word that, realistically, makes us believe in the rain. But, too, it is broader in its function. The storm which the lover invokes will not rend the firmament, it will not end the world; it will simply bring down the "small" rain, a credible rain.

he does not over-spiritualize nature. This nameless poet would never have said, in the happier days of his love, that he had been led to his Sweet's chamber window by "a spirit in my feet"; and he certainly would not have added the coy disavowal, "who knows how?" But because the nameless poet refused to over-spiritualize nature, we can accept the spirituality of the poem.

Another poem gives us another problem.

> *Ah, what avails the sceptered race,*
> *Ah, what the form divine!*
> *What every virtue, every grace!*
> *Rose Aylmer, all were thine.*
>
> *Rose Aylmer, whom those wakeful eyes*
> *May weep, but never see,*
> *A night of memories and of sighs*
> *I consecrate to thee.*

This is another poem about lost love: a "soft" subject. Now to one kind of poet the soft subject presents a sore temptation. Because it is soft in its natural state, he is inclined to feel that to get at its poetic essence he must make it softer still, that he must insist on its softness, that he must render it as "pure" as possible. At first glance, it may seem that Landor is trying to do just that. What he says seems to be emphatic, unqualified, and open. Not every power, grace, and virtue could avail to preserve his love. That statement insists on the pathetic contrast. And in the next stanza, wakefulness and tearfulness are mentioned quite unashamedly, along with memories and sighs. It is all blurted out, as pure as possible.

But only in the paraphrase is it "blurted." The actual quality of the first stanza is hard, not soft. It is a chiseled stanza, in which formality is insisted upon. We may observe the balance of the first and second lines; the balance of the first half with the second half of the third line, which recapitulates the structure of the first two lines; the balance of the two parts of the last line, though here the balance is merely a rhythmical and not a sense balance as in the preceding instances; the binders of discreet alliteration, repetition, and assonance. The stanza is built up, as it were, of units which are firmly defined and sharply separated, phrase by phrase, line by line.

We have the formal control of the soft subject, ritual and not surrender.

But in the second stanza the rigor of this formality is somewhat abated, as the more general, speculative emphasis (why cannot pomp, virtue, and grace avail?) gives way to the personal emphasis, as though the repetition of the beloved's name had, momentarily, released the flood of feeling. The first line of the second stanza spills over into the second; the "wakeful eyes" as subject find their verb in the next line, "weep," and the *wake-weep* alliteration, along with the rest after *weep,* points up the disintegration of the line, just as it emphasizes the situation. Then with the phrase "but never see" falling away from the long thrust of the rhetorical structure to the pause after *weep,* the poem seems to go completely soft, the frame is broken. But, even as the poet insists on "memories and sighs" in the last two lines he restores the balance. Notice the understatement of "A night." It says: "I know that life is a fairly complicated affair, and that I am committed to it and to its complications. I intend to stand by my commitment, as a man of integrity, that is, to live despite the grief. Since life is complicated, I cannot, if I am to live, spare too much time for indulging grief. I can give *a* night, but not all nights." The lover, like the hero of Frost's poem "Stopping by Woods on a Winter Evening," tears himself from the temptation of staring into the treacherous, delicious blackness, for he, too, has "promises to keep." Or he resembles the Homeric heroes who, after the perilous passage is made, after their energy has saved their lives, and after they have beached their craft and eaten their meal, can then set aside an hour before sleep to mourn the comrades lost by the way—the heroes who, as Aldous Huxley says, understand realistically a whole truth as contrasted with a half-truth.

Is this a denial of the depth and sincerity of the grief? The soft reader, who wants the poem pure, may be inclined to say so. But let us look at the last line to see what it gives us in answer to this question. The answer seems to lie in the word *consecrate*. The meter thrusts this word at us; we observe that two of the three metrical accents in the line fall on syllables of this word forcing it beyond its prose emphasis. The word is important and the importance is justified, for the word tells us that the single night is not merely a lapse into weakness, a trivial event to be forgotten when the weakness is overcome. It is, rather, an event of the most extreme and focal importance, an event formally dedicated, "set apart for sacred uses," an event by which other events are to be measured. So the word *consecrate* formalizes, philosophizes, ritualizes the grief; it specifies what style in the first stanza has implied.

But here is another poem of grief, grief at the death of a child:

> *There was such speed in her little body,*
> *And such lightness in her footfall,*
> *It is no wonder that her brown study*
> *Astonishes us all.*
>
> *Her wars were bruited in our high window.*
> *We looked among orchard trees and beyond*
> *Where she took arms against her shadow,*
> *Or harried unto the pond*
>
> *The lazy geese, like a snow cloud*
> *Dripping their snow on the green grass,*
> *Tricking and stopping, sleepy and proud,*
> *Who cried in goose, Alas,*
>
> *For the tireless heart within the little*
> *Lady with rod that made them rise*
> *From their noon apple dreams, and scuttle*
> *Goose-fashion under the skies!*
>
> *But now go the bells, and we are ready;*
> *In one house we are sternly stopped*
> *To say we are vexed at her brown study,*
> *Lying so primly propped.*

Another soft subject, softer, if anything, than the subject of "Rose Aylmer," and it presents the same problem. But the problem is solved in a different way.

The first stanza is based on two time-honored clichés: first, "Heaven, won't that child ever be still, she is driving me distracted"; and second, "She was such an active, healthy-looking child, would you've ever thought she would just up and die?" In fact, the whole poem develops these clichés, and exploits, in a backhand fashion, the ironies implicit in their inter-relation. And in this connection, we may note that the fact of the clichés, rather than more original or profound observations, at the root of the poem is important; there is in the poem the contrast between the staleness of the clichés and the shock of the reality. Further, we may note that the second cliché is an answer, savagely ironical in itself, to the first: the child you wished would be still *is* still, despite all that activity which your adult occupations deplored.

But such a savage irony is not the game here. It is too desperate, too naked, in a word, too pure. And ultimately, it is, in a sense, a meaningless irony if left in its pure state, because it depends on a mechanical, accidental contrast in nature, void of moral content. The poem is concerned with modifications and modulations of this brute, basic irony, modulations and modifications contingent upon an attitude taken toward it by a responsible human being, the speaker of the poem. The savagery is masked, or ameliorated.

In this connection, we may observe, first, the phrase "brown study." It is not the "frosted flower," the "marmoreal immobility," or any one of a thousand such phrases which would aim for the pure effect. It is merely the brown study which astonishes—a phrase which denies, as it were, the finality of the situation, underplays the pathos, and merely reminds one of those moments of childish pensiveness into which the grown-up cannot penetrate. And the phrase itself is a cliché—the common now echoed in the uncommon.

Next, we may observe that stanzas two, three, and four simply document, with a busy yet wavering rhythm (one sentence runs through the three stanzas), the tireless naughtiness which was once the cause of rebuke, the naughtiness which disturbed the mature goings-on in the room with the "high window." But the naughtiness has been transmuted, by events just transpired, into a kind of fanciful story-book dream-world, in which geese are whiter than nature, and the grass greener, in which geese speak in goose language, saying "Alas," and have apple dreams. It is a drowsy, delicious world, in which the geese are bigger than life, and more important. It is an unreal (now unreal because lost), stylized world. Notice how the phrase "the little lady with rod" works: the detached, grown-up primness of "little lady"; the formal, stiff effect gained by the omission of the article before *rod*; the slightly unnatural use of the word *rod* itself, which sets some distance between us and the scene (perhaps with the hint of the fairy story, a magic wand, or a magic rod—not a common, every-day stick). But the stanzas tie back into the premises of the poem in other ways. The little girl, in her naughtiness, warred against her shadow. Is it crowding matters too hard to surmise that the shadow here achieves a sort of covert symbolic significance? The little girl lost her war against her "shadow," which was always with her. Certainly the phrase "tireless heart" has some rich connotations. And the geese which say "Alas!" conspire with the family to deplore the excessive activity of the child. (They do not conspire to express the present grief, only the past vexation— an inversion of the method of the pastoral elegy, or of the method of the first two garden poems.)

The business of the three stanzas, then, may be said to be two-fold. First, they make us believe more fully in the child and therefore in the fact of the grief itself. They "prove" the grief, and they show the deliciousness of the lost world which will never look the same from the high window. Second, and contrariwise, they "transcend" the grief, or at least give a hint of a means for transcending the immediate anguish: the lost world is, in one sense, redeemed out of time, it enters the pages of the picture book where geese speak, where the untrue is true, where the fleeting is fixed. What was had cannot, after all, be lost. (By way of comparison—a comparison which, because extreme, may be helpful—I cite the transcendence in *La Récherche du Temps Perdu*.) The three stanzas, then, to state it in another way, have validated the first stanza and have prepared for the last.

The three stanzas have made it possible for us to say, when the bell tolls, "we are ready." Some kind of terms, perhaps not the best terms possible but some kind, have been made with the savage underlying irony. But the terms arrived at do not prevent the occasion from being a "stern" one. The transcendence is not absolute, and in the end is possible only because of an exercise of will and self-control. Because we control ourselves, we can say "vexed" and not some big word. And the word itself picks up the first of the domestic clichés on which the poem is based—the outburst of impatience at the naughty child who, by dying, has performed her most serious piece of naughtiness. But now the word comes to us charged with the burden of the poem, and further, as re-echoed here by the phrase "brown study," charged by the sentence in which it occurs: we are gathered formally, ritualistically, sternly together to say the word *vexed*.[3] *Vexed* becomes the ritualistic, the summarizing word.

I have used the words *pure* and *impure* often in the foregoing pages, and I confess that I have used them rather loosely. But perhaps it has been evident that I have meant something like this: the pure poem tries to be pure by excluding, more or less rigidly, certain elements which might qualify or contradict its original impulse. In other words the pure poems want to be, and desperately, all of a piece. It has also been evident, no doubt, that the kinds of impurity which are admitted or excluded by the various little anthology pieces which have been analyzed, are different in the different poems. This is only to be expected, for there is not one doctrine of "pure poetry"—not one definition of what constitutes impurity in poems—but many. And not all of the doctrines are recent. When, for example, one cites Poe as the father of *the* doctrine of pure poetry, one is in error; Poe simply fathered *a* particular doctrine of pure poetry. One can find other doctrines of purity long antedating Poe. When Sir Philip Sidney, for example, legislated against tragicomedy, he was repeating a current doctrine of purity. When Ben Jonson told William Drummond that Donne, for not keeping of accent, deserved hanging, he was defending another kind of purity, and when Dryden spoke to save the ear of the fair sex from metaphysical perplexities in amorous poems, he was defending another

---

[3] It might be profitable, in contrast with this poem, to analyze "After the Burial," by James Russell Lowell, a poem which is identical in situation. But in Lowell's poem the savagery of the irony is unqualified. In fact, the whole poem insists, quite literally, that qualification is impossible: the scheme of the poem is to set up the brute fact of death against possible consolations. It insists on "tears," the "thin-worn locket," the "anguish of deathless hair," "the smallness of the child's grave," the "little shoe in the corner." It is a poem which, we might say, does not progress, but ends where it begins, resting in the savage irony from which it stems; or we might say that it is a poem without any "insides," for the hero of the poem is not attempting to do anything about the problem which confronts him—it is a poem without issue, without conflict, a poem of unconditional surrender. In other words, it tries to be a pure poem, pure grief, absolutely inconsolable. It is a strident poem, and strident in its rhythms. The fact that we know this poem to be an expression of a bereavement historically real makes it an embarrassing poem, as well. It is a naked poem.

kind of purity, just as he was defending another when he defined
the nature of the heroic drama. The eighteenth century had a doctrine of pure poetry, which may be summed up under the word
sublimity, but which involved two corollary doctrines, one concerning diction and the other concerning imagery. But at the same time
that this century, by means of these corollary doctrines, was tidying
up and purifying, as Mr. Monk and Mr. Henn have indicated, the
doctrine derived from Longinus, it was admitting into the drama
certain impurities which the theorists of the heroic drama would
not have admitted.[4]

But when we think of the modern doctrine of pure poetry, we
usually think of Poe, as critic and poet, perhaps of Shelley, of the
Symbolists, of the Abbé Brémond, perhaps of Pater, and certainly
of George Moore and the Imagists. We know Poe's position: the
long poem is "a flat contradiction in terms," because intense excitement, which is essential in poetry, cannot be long maintained; the
moral sense and the intellect function more satisfactorily in prose
than in poetry, and, in fact, "Truth" and the "Passions," which are
for Poe associated with intellect and the moral sense, may actually
be inimical to poetry; vagueness, suggestiveness, are central virtues,
for poetry has for "its object an *indefinite* instead of a *definite*
pleasure"; poetry is not supposed to undergo close inspection, only
a cursory glance, for it, "above all things, is a beautiful painting
whose tints, to minute inspection, are confusion worse confounded,
but start out boldly to the cursory glance of the connoisseur"; poetry
aspires toward music, since it is concerned with "indefinite sensations, to which music is an *essential,*, since the comprehension of
sweet sound is our most indefinite conception"; melancholy is the
most poetical effect and enters into all the higher manifestations of
beauty. We know, too, the Abbé Brémond's mystical interpretation,
and the preface to George Moore's anthology, and the Imagist
manifesto.

But these views are not identical. Shelley, for instance, delights
in the imprecision praised and practiced by Poe, but he has an enormous appetite for "Truth" and the "Passions," which are, except

---

[4] Samuel Holt Monk, *The Sublime: a Study of Critical Theories in XVIII-
Century England,* and T. R. Henn, *Longinus and English Criticism.*

for purposes of contrast, excluded by Poe. The Imagist manifesto, while excluding ideas, endorses precision rather than vagueness in rendering the image, and admits diction and objects which would have seemed impure to Poe and to many poets of the nineteenth century, and does not take much stock in the importance of verbal music. George Moore emphasizes the objective aspect of his pure poetry, which he describes as "something which the poet creates outside his own personality," and this is opposed to the subjective emphasis in Poe and Shelley; but he shares with both an emphasis on verbal music, and with the former a distaste for ideas.

But more recently, the notion of poetic purity has emerged in other contexts, contexts which sometimes obscure the connection of the new theories with the older theories. For instance Max Eastman has a theory. "Pure poetry," he says in *The Literary Mind,* "is the pure effort to heighten consciousness." Mr. Eastman, we discover elsewhere in his book, would ban idea from poetry, but his motive is different from, say, the motive of Poe, and the difference is important: Poe would kick out the ideas because the ideas hurt the poetry, and Mr. Eastman would kick out the ideas because the poetry hurts the ideas. Only the scientist, he tells us, is entitled to have ideas on any subject, and the rest of the citizenry must wait to be told what attitude to take toward the ideas which they are not permitted to have except at second-hand. Literary truth, he says, is truth which is "uncertain or comparatively unimportant." But he assigns the poet a function—to heighten consciousness. But in the light of this context we would have to rewrite his original definition: pure poetry is the pure effort to heighten consciousness, but the consciousness which is heightened must not have any connection with ideas, must involve no attitude toward any ideas.

Furthermore, to assist the poet in fulfilling the assigned function, Mr. Eastman gives him a somewhat sketchy doctrine of "pure" poetic diction. For instance, the word *bloated* is not admissible into a poem because it is, as he testifies, "sacred to the memory of dead fish," and the word *tangy* is, though he knows not exactly how, "intrinsically poetic." The notion of a vocabulary which is intrinsically poetic seems, with Mr. Eastman, to mean a vocabulary which indicates agreeable or beautiful objects. So we might rewrite the orginal definition to read: pure poetry is the pure effort to heighten consciousness, but the consciousness which is heightened must be a consciousness exclusively of agreeable or beautiful objects—certainly not a consciousness of any ideas.

In a recent book, *The Idiom of Poetry,* Frederick Pottle has discussed the question of pure poetry. He distinguishes another type of pure poetry in addition to the types already mentioned. He calls it the "Elliptical," and would include in it symbolist and metaphysical poetry (old and new) and some work by poets such as Collins, Blake, and Browning. He observes—without any pejorative implication, for he is a critical relativist and scarcely permits himself the luxury of evaluative judgments—that the contemporary product differs from older examples of the elliptical type in that "the modern poet goes much farther in employing private experiences or ideas than would formerly have been thought legitimate." To the common reader, he says, "the prime characteristic of this kind of poetry is not the nature of its imagery but its obscurity: its urgent suggestion that you add something to the poem without telling you what that something is." This omitted "something" he interprets as the prose "frame," to use his word, the statement of the occasion, the logical or narrative transitions, the generalized application derived from the poem, etc. In other words, this type of pure poetry contends that "the effect would be more powerful if we could somehow manage to feel the images fully and accurately without having the effect diluted by any words put in to give us a 'meaning'—that is, if we could expel all the talk *about* the imaginative realization and have the pure realization itself."[5]

---

[5] F. W. Bateson, in *English Poetry and the English Language,* discusses the impulse in contemporary poetry. Tennyson, he points out in connection with "The Sailor Boy," dilutes his poetry by telling a story as well as writing a poem, and "a shorter poem would have spoilt his story." The claims of prose conquer the claims of poetry. Of the Victorians in general: "The dramatic and narrative framework of their poems, by circumventing the disconcerting plunges into *medias res* which are the essence of poetry, brings it down to a level of prose. The reader knows where he is; it serves the purpose of introduction and note." Such introduction and notes in the body of the poem itself are exactly what Mr. Pottle says is missing in Elliptical Poetry. Mr. Bateson agrees with Poe in accepting intensity as the criterion of the poetic effect, and in accepting the corollary that a poem should be short. But he, contradicting Poe, seems to admire precise and complicated incidental effects.

For the moment I shall pass the question of the accuracy of Mr. Pottle's description of the impulse of Elliptical Poetry and present the question which ultimately concerns him. How pure does poetry need to be in practice? That is the question which Mr. Pottle asks. He answers by saying that a great degree of impurity *may* be admitted, and cites our famous didactic poems, *The Faerie Queene, The Essay on Man, The Vanity of Human Wishes, The Excursion.* That is the only answer which the relativist, and nominalist, can give. Then he turns to what he calls the hardest question in the theory of poetry: what kind of prosaism is acceptable and what is not? His answer, which he advances very modestly, is this:

> . . . the element of prose is innocent and even salutary when it appears as—take your choice of three metaphors—a background on which the images are projected, or a frame in which they are shown, or a thread on which they are strung. In short, when it serves a *structural* purpose. Prose in a poem seems offensive to me when . . . the prosaisms are sharp, obvious, individual, and ranked coordinately with the images.

At first glance this looks plausible, and the critic has used the sanctified word *structural*. But at second glance we may begin to wonder what the sanctified word means to the critic. It means something rather mechanical—background, frame, thread. The structure is a showcase, say a jeweler's showcase, in which the little jewels of poetry are exhibited, the images. The showcase shouldn't be ornamental itself ("sharp, obvious, individual," Mr. Pottle says), for it would then distract us from the jewels; it should be chastely designed, and the jewels should repose on black velvet and not on flowered chintz. But Mr. Pottle doesn't ask what the relation among the bright jewels should be. Apparently, not only does the showcase bear no relation to the jewels, but the jewels bear no relation to each other. Each one is a shining little focus of heightened consciousness, or pure realization, existing for itself alone. Or perhaps he should desire that they be arranged in some mechanical pattern, such a pattern, perhaps, as would make it easier for the eye to travel from one little jewel to the next when the time comes to move on. Structure becomes here simply a device of salesmanship, a well arranged showcase.

It is all mechanical. And this means that Mr. Pottle, after all, is himself an exponent of pure poetry. He locates the poetry simply in the images, the nodes of "pure realization." This means that what he calls the "element of prose" includes definition of situation, movement of narrative, logical transition, factual description, generalization, ideas. Such things, for him, do not participate in the poetic effect of the poem; in fact, they work against the poetic effect, and so, though necessary as a frame, should be kept from being "sharp, obvious, individual."[6]

I have referred to *The Idiom of Poetry,* first, because it is such an admirable and provocative book, sane, lucid, generous-spirited, and second, because, to my mind, it illustrates the insidiousness with which a doctrine of pure poetry can penetrate into the theory of a critic who is suspicious of such a doctrine. Furthermore, I have felt that Mr. Pottle's analysis might help me to define the common denominator of the various doctrines of pure poetry.

That common denominator seems to be the belief that poetry is an essence that is to be located at some particular place in a poem, or in some particular element. The exponent of pure poetry persuades himself that he has determined the particular something in which the poetry inheres, and then proceeds to decree that poems shall be composed, as nearly as possible, of that element and of nothing else. If we add up the things excluded by various critics and practitioners, we get a list about like this:

1. ideas, truths, generalizations, "meaning"

-----

[6] Several other difficulties concerning Mr. Pottle's statement may suggest themselves. First, since he seems to infer that the poetic essence resides in the image, what view would he take of meter and rhythm? His statement, strictly construed, would mean that these factors do not participate in the poetic effect, but are simply part of the frame. Second, what view of dramatic poetry is implied? It seems again that a strict interpretation would mean that the story and the images bear no essential relation to each other, that the story is simply part of the frame. That is, the story, characters, rhythms, and ideas are on one level and the images, in which the poetry inheres, are on another. But Miss Spurgeon, Mr. Knight, and other critics have given us some reason for holding that the images do bear some relation to the business of the other items. In fact, all of the items, as M. Maritain has said, "feelings, ideas, representations, are for the artist merely materials and means, still symbols." That is, they are all elements in a single expressive structure.

2. precise, complicated, "intellectual" images
3. unbeautiful, disagreeable, or neutral materials
4. situation, narrative, logical transition
5. realistic details, exact descriptions, realism in general
6. shifts in tone or mood
7. irony
8. metrical variation, dramatic adaptations of rhythm, cacophony, etc.
9. meter itself
10. subjective and personal elements

No one theory of pure poetry excludes all of these items, and, as a matter of fact, the items listed are not on the same level of importance. Nor do the items always bear the same interpretation. For example, if one item seems to be central to discussions of pure poetry, it is the first: "ideas," it is said, "are not involved in the poetic effect, and may even be inimical to it." But this view can be interpreted in a variety of ways. If it is interpreted as simply meaning that the paraphrase of a poem is not equivalent to the poem, that the poetic gist is not to be defined as the statement embodied in the poem with the sugar-coating as bait, then the view can be held by opponents as well as exponents of any theory of pure poetry. We might scale down from this interpretation to the other extreme interpretation that the poem should merely give the sharp image in isolation. But there are many complicated and confused variations possible between the two extremes. There is, for example, the interpretation that "ideas," though they are not involved in the poetic effect, must appear in poems to provide, as Mr. Pottle's prosaisms do, a kind of frame, or thread, for the poetry—a spine to support the poetic flesh or a Christmas tree on which the baubles of poetry are hung.[7] T. S. Eliot has said something of this sort:

The chief use of the "meaning" of a poem, in the ordinary sense, may be (for here again I am speaking of some kinds of

---

[7] Such an interpretation seems to find a parallel in E. M. Forster's treatment of plot in fiction. Plot in his theory becomes a mere spine and does not really participate, except in a narrow, formal sense, in the fictional effect. By his inversion of the Aristotelian principle, the plot becomes merely a necessary evil.

poetry and not all) to satisfy one habit of the reader, to keep his mind diverted and quiet, while the poem does its work upon him: much as the imaginary burglar is always provided with a bit of nice meat for the house-dog.

Here, it would seem, Mr. Eliot has simply inverted the old sugar-coated pill theory: the idea becomes the sugar-coating and the "poetry" becomes the medicine. This seems to say that the idea in a poem does not participate in the poetic effect, and seems to commit Mr. Eliot to a theory of pure poetry. But to do justice to the quotation, we should first observe that the parenthesis indicates that the writer is referring to some sort of provisional and superficial distinction and not to a fundamental one, and second observe that the passage is out of its context. In the context, Mr. Eliot goes on to say that some poets "become impatient of this 'meaning' [explicit statement of ideas in logical order] which seems superfluous, and perceive possibilities of intensity through its elimination." This may mean either of two things. It may mean that ideas do not participate in the poetic effect, or it may mean, though they do participate in the poetic effect, they need not appear in the poem in an explicit and argued form. And this second reading would scarcely be a doctrine of pure poetry at all, for it would involve poetic casuistry and not poetic principle.

We might, however, illustrate the second interpretation by glancing at Marvell's "Horatian Ode" on Cromwell. Marvell does not give us narrative; he does not give us an account of the issues behind the Civil War; he does not state the two competing ideas which are dramatized in the poem, the idea of "sanction" and the idea of "efficiency." But the effect of the poem does involve these two factors; the special reserved, scarcely resolved, irony, which is realized in the historical situation, is an irony derived from unstated materials and ideas. It is, to use Mr. Pottle's term again, a pure poem in so far as it is elliptical in method, but it is anything but a pure poem if by purity we mean the exclusion of idea from participation in the poetic effect. And Mr. Eliot's own practice implies that he believes that ideas do participate in the poetic effect. Otherwise, why did he put the clues to his ideas in the notes at the end of the *Waste Land* after so carefully excluding any explicit statement of them from the body of the poem? If he is regarding those ideas as mere bait—the "bit of nice meat for the house-dog"—he has put the ideas in a peculiar place, in the back of the book—like giving the dog the meat on the way out of the house with the swag or giving the mouse the cheese after he is in the trap. All this would lead one to the speculation that Marvell and Mr. Eliot have purged away statement of ideas from their poems, not because they wanted the ideas to participate less in the poetry, but because they wanted them to participate more fully, intensely, and immediately. This impulse, then, would account for the characteristic type of image, types in which precision, complication, and complicated intellectual relation to the theme are exploited; in other words, they are trying—whatever may be their final success—to carry the movement of mind to the center of the process. On these grounds they are the exact opposite of poets who, presumably on grounds of purity, exclude the movement of mind from the center of the poetic process—from the internal structure of the poem—but pay their respect to it as a kind of footnote, or gloss, or application coming at the end. Marvell and Eliot, by their cutting away of frame, are trying to emphasize the participation of ideas in the poetic process. Then Elliptical Poetry is not, as Mr. Pottle says it is, a pure poetry at all if we regard intention; the elliptical poet is elliptical for purposes of inclusion, not exclusion.

But waiving the question of Elliptical Poetry, no one of the other theories does—or could—exclude all the items on the list above. And that fact may instruct us. If all of these items were excluded, we might not have any poem at all. For instance, we know how some critics have pointed out that even in the strictest imagist poetry idea creeps in—when the image leaves its natural habitat and enters a poem it begins to "mean" something. The attempt to read ideas out of the poetic party violates the unity of our being and the unity of our experience. "For this reason," as Santayana puts it, "philosophy, when a poet is not mindless, enters inevitably into his poetry, since it has entered into his life; or rather, the detail of things and the detail of ideas pass equally into his verse, when both alike lie in the path that has led him to his ideal. To object to theory in poetry would be like objecting to words there; for words, too, are symbols without the sensuous character of the things they stand for; and yet it is only by the net of new connections which words throw over things, in recalling them, that poetry arises at all. Poetry is an attenuation, a rehandling, an echo of crude experience; it is itself a theoretic vision of things at arm's length." Does this not lead us to the conclusion that poetry does not inhere in any particular element but depends upon the set of relationships, the structure, which we call the poem?

Then the question arises: what elements cannot be used in such a structure? I should answer that nothing that is available in human experience is to be legislated out of poetry. This does not mean that anything can be used in *any* poem, or that some materials or elements may not prove more recalcitrant than others, or that it might not be easy to have too much of some things. But it does mean that, granted certain contexts, any sort of material, a chemical formula for instance, might appear functionally in a poem. It also may mean that, other things being equal, the greatness of a poet depends upon the extent of the area of experience which he can master poetically.

Can we make any generalizations about the nature of the poetic structure? First, it involves resistances, at various levels. There is the tension between the rhythm of the poem and the rhythm of speech (a tension which is very low at the extreme of free verse and at the extreme of verse such as that of "ulalume," which verges toward a walloping doggerel); between the formality of the rhythm and the informality of the language; between the particular and the general, the concrete and the abstract; between the elements of even the simplest metaphor; between the beautiful and the ugly; between ideas (as in Marvell's poem); between the elements involved in irony (as in "Bells for John Whiteside's Daughter" or "Rose Aylmer"); between prosisms and poeticisms (as in "Western Wind"). This list is not intended to be exhaustive; it is intended to be merely suggestive. But it may be taken to imply that the poet is like the jiujitsu expert; he wins by utilizing the resistance of his opponent—the materials of the poem. In other words, a poem, to be good, must earn itself. It is a motion toward a point of rest, but if it is not a resisted motion, it is motion of no consequence. For example, a poem which depends upon stock materials and stock responses is simply a toboggan slide, or a fall through space. And the good poem must, in some way, involve the resistances; it must carry something of the context of its own creation; it must come to terms with Mercutio. This is another way of saying that a good poem involves the participation of the reader; it must, as Coleridge puts it, make the reader into "an active creative being." Perhaps we can see this most readily in the case of tragedy: the definition of good or evil is not a "given" in tragedy, it is something to be earned in the process, and even the tragic villain must be "loved." We must kill him, as Brutus killed Caesar, not as butchers but as sacrificers. And all of this adds up to the fact that the structure is a dramatic structure, a movement through action toward rest, through complication toward simplicity of effect.

In the foregoing discussion, I have deliberately omitted reference to another type of pure poetry, a type which, in the context of the present war, may well become dominant. Perhaps the most sensible description of this type can be found in an essay by Herbert Muller:

> If it is not the primary business of the poet to be eloquent about these matters [faith and ideals], it still does not follow that he has more dignity or wisdom than those who are, or that he should have more sophistication. At any rate the fact is that almost all poets of the past did freely make large, simple statements, and not in their prosy or lax moments.

Mr. Muller then goes on to illustrate by quoting three famous, large, simple statements:

> *In la sua voluntade e nostra pace*

and

> *We are such stuff*
> *As dreams are made on; and our little lives*
> *Are rounded with a sleep.*

and

> *The mind is its own place, and in itself*
> *Can make a heaven of hell, a hell of heaven.*

Mr. Muller is here attacking the critical emphasis on ironic tension in poetry. His attack really involves two lines of argument. First, the poet is not wiser than the statesman, philosopher, or saint, people who are eloquent about faith and ideals and who say what they mean, without benefit of irony. This Platonic (or pseudo-Platonic) line of argument is, I think, off the point in the present context. Second, the poets of the past have made large, simple affirmations which have said what they meant. This line of argument is very much on the point.

Poets *have* tried very hard, for thousands of years, to say what they mean. But they have not only tried to say what they mean, they have tried to prove what they mean. The saint proves his vision by stepping cheerfully into the fires. The poet, somewhat less spectacularly, proves his vision by submitting it to the fires of irony— to the drama of his structure—in the hope that the fires will refine it. In other words, the poet wishes to indicate that his vision has been earned, that it can survive reference to the complexities and contradictions of experience. And irony is one such device of reference.

In this connection let us look at the first of Mr. Muller's exhibits. The famous line occurs in Canto III of the *Paradiso*. It is spoken by Piccarda Donati, in answer to Dante's question as to why she does not desire to rise higher than her present sphere, the sphere of the moon. But it expresses, in unequivocal terms, a central theme of the *Commedia,* as of Christian experience. On the one hand, it may be a pious truism, fit for sampler work, and on the other hand, it may be a burning conviction, tested and earned. Dante, in his poem, sets out to show how it has been earned and tested. One set of ironic tensions, for instance, which centers about this theme concerns the opposition between the notion of human justice and the notion of divine justice. The story of Paolo and Francesca is so warm, appealing, and pathetic in its human terms and their punishment so savage and unrelenting, so incommensurable, it seems, with the fault, that Dante, torn by the conflict, falls down as a dead body falls. Or Farinata, the enemy of Dante's house, is presented by the poet in terms of his human grandeur, which now, in Hell, is transmuted into a superhuman grandeur,

com' avesse l'inferno in gran dispitto.

Ulysses remains a hero, a hero who should draw special applause from Dante, who defined the temporal end of man as the conquest of knowledge. But Ulysses is damned, as the great Brutus is damned, who hangs from the jaws of the fiend in the lowest pit of traitors. So divine justice is set over against human pathos, human dignity, human grandeur, human intellect, human justice. And we recall how Virgil, more than once, reminds Dante that he must not apply human standards to the sights he sees. It is this long conflict, which appears in many forms, this ironic tension, which finally gives body to the simple eloquence of the line in question; the statement is meaningful, not for what it says, but for what has gone before. It is earned. It has been earned by the entire poem.

I do not want to misrepresent Mr. Muller. He does follow his quotations by the sentence: "If they are properly qualified in the work as a whole, they may still be taken straight, they *are* [he italicizes the word] taken so in recollection as in their immediate impact." But can this line be taken so in recollection, and was it taken so in its "immediate impact"? And if one does take it so, is he not violating, very definitely, the poet's meaning, for the poet means the *poem,* he doesn't mean the line.

It would be interesting to try to develop the contexts of the other passages which Mr. Muller quotes. But in any case, he was simply trying, in his essay, to guard against what he considered to be, rightly or wrongly, a too narrow description of poetry; he was not trying to legislate all poetry into the type of simple eloquence, the unqualified statement of "faith and ideas." But we have already witnessed certain, probably preliminary, attempts to legislate literature into becoming a simple, unqualified, "pure" statement of faith and ideal. We have seen the writers of the 1920's called the "irresponsibles." We have seen writers such as Proust, Eliot, Dreiser, and Faulkner, called writers of the "death drive." Why are these writers condemned? Because they have tried, within the limits of their gifts, to remain faithful to the complexities of the problems with which they were dealing, because they refused to take the easy statement as solution, because they tried to define the context in which, and the terms by which, faith and ideals could be earned. But this method will scarcely satisfy the mind which is hot for certainties; to that mind it will seem merely an index to lukewarmness, indecision, disunity, treason. The new theory of purity would purge out all complexities and all ironies and all self-criticism. And this theory will forget that the hand-me-down faith, the hand-me-down ideals, no matter what the professed content, is in the end not only meaningless but vicious. It is vicious because, as parody, it is the enemy of all faith.

Austin Warren MYTH AND

DIALECTIC IN THE LATER NOVELS

OF HENRY JAMES

THE general occasions of the "last period" are tolerably clear, if scarcely of the same order of being. There is, first, the gradual loss of the larger audience reached by *Daisy Miller* and the novels of Howells; then the judgment that country-house weekends and the "season" in London had already provided "saturation"; then, the shift, in compositional method, from writing to dictation; then the impetus of admiration from sympathetic younger writers, and the allied, induced, partial participation in the new literary movement of the "nineties," the "aesthetic" movement associated with the names of Pater, Wilde, Harland, *The Yellow Book,* and—by extension—of Stevenson, Conrad, Crane, Ford Madox Ford; then the just completed period of writing for the theatre, which produced not only *Guy Domville* but also a conception of the novel as drama; lastly, the influence, through Maeterlinck and especially the later Ibsen, of *symbolisme,* and the return thereby to Hawthorne and the "deeper psychology."

The retirement to Rye, which occurred in 1897, when James was fifty-four, distinguished between his life of experience and his life from "past accumulations" (as he once called it). His peregrinations over, he set himself, masterwise, to producing a world compact of all he had been able, coherently, to think and feel.

Then the process of dictation, beginning with *The Spoils of Poynton,* had its psychological and stylistic consequences. A timid, slow-speaking, stammering boy, Henry had rarely been able to make himself heard at the parental breakfast, at which the other males talked so opulently. Dictation offered dictatorship: his own voice, uninterrupted by those of more rapid speakers, enabled him to have his oral say in a style which is nearer to his father's than to William's, but slower than the father's. Henry's later manner is an Allegro slowed down to a Largo, the conversational in apotheosis. "Literally" as, all sprinkled with its commas of parenthesis, it looks on paper, it is an oral style; and, verifiably, it becomes clear, almost luminous, if recommitted to the voice.

This oral tone was certainly abetted by James's steady turn toward the drama. Rather early, Henry wrote his brother of having mastered the dramatic technique of those makers of the "well-made play," Augier and Sardou. He was, of course, an admirer of the Comédie Française and so, we may think, of Molière and Racine. To the French classical drama, as well as to Sardou, I should attribute his increasing use, in his later work, of structure fairly to be called neoclassical, geometrical: wing matching wing, and pilaster corresponding to pilaster, in designs sometimes monstrous in their regularity.

The drama of the nineties, Maeterlinck and especially Ibsen, had its effect on the later novels, in which, though the author proudly renounces his right of omniscience, he returns triumphantly in the mode of tonality, figuration, almost color scheme. The relation between Kate and Milly, in *The Wings of the Dove,* becomes, at one point, the "likeness of some dim scene in a Maeterlinck play; we have positively the image, in the delicate dusk, of the figures so associated, and yet so opposed, so mutually watchful: that of the angular pale princess, ostrich-plumed, black-robed, hung about with amulets, reminders, relics, mainly seated, mainly still; and that of the upright restless slow-circling lady of her court who exchanges

with her, across the black water streaked with evening gleams, fitful questions and answers. . . ." There is no question of wholesale
admiration. It is the slightly comic because immensely refined and
"cultural" Mrs. Susan Shepherd Stringham who "admires" Maeterlinck and Pater; but James respected both, and in the former could
find warrant for a kind of symbolist drama restricted in characters
and in action, and unified by tone. Ibsen, whose *Hedda* and *Master
Builder* he saw, about whom he wrote (in 1891 and 1893) with
regard and discernment, gave him examples of fictional work the
reverse of improvisation. "Wrought with admirable closeness is the
whole tissue of relations between the five people whom [in *Hedda*]
the author sets in motion and on whose behalf he asks of us so few
concessions." "The distinguished thing is the firm hand that weaves
the web, the deep and ingenious use made of the material." The
more one looks at an Ibsen play, the "more intentions" one sees.
The patterns of the two have a general parallel of early romanticism, middle realism, and a late maturity which attempts to create
what James attributes to the *Master Builder*—a "mingled reality
and symbolism."

In poetic drama—*The Tempest* (to which he wrote a poetic
introduction), the plays of Racine, Maeterlinck, and Ibsen—James
came nearest to finding precedence for his later novels. And in these
plays are adumbrated the two devices which dominate one's recollection of the later James: close conversation and the metaphor.

Prefacing *The Wings of the Dove,* James differentiated the
"picture" from the "drama" as two rival techniques of the novel,
a distinction corresponding (I take it) to that between the "fore-
shortened" (or narrated) and the presented. After his experiment,
in *The Awkward Age,* with the novel as a set of scenes or dialogues
uninterrupted by a unifying consciousness, he grew technically
aware, and systematically provident, of dialogue in alternation with
narrative, a narrative of consciousness and inner soliloquy.

This technical or structural distinction has its epistemological
and metaphysical counterpart. James distinguished two modes of
knowing: at the expense of grandiosity, I shall call them dialectic
and myth.

One is a cerebral process, pursued by two or more minds, in
contrapuntal movement of thesis, antithesis, synthesis. The topic is

attacked from without; the speakers circle around it. Like co-laboring detectives, they piece together their evidence; or, like attorneys for the defense and the prosecution, they proceed alternately on rival systems. There are examinations and cross-examinations. There are mutual misunderstandings, false clues, shifts of position.

James liked to read the reports of divorce trials and murders; he was a confessed admirer of Roughead's chronicles. But it is unnecessary to suppose any external incitation to such close, minute, unwearying analysis as James's people carry on. We know their kind. There are people who find a great dinner or ball or simpler occasion quite unsatisfactory unless before, and especially after, the event there is, in collaboration with another critical observer, an exhaustive analysis of the occasion—its persons, the shifts of relation between them, the discovery of unexpected relations, the probable motives of those present, the intent of speeches and interlocutions which baffled immediacy. James was obviously such a person in his talks with Howard Sturgis, A. C. Benson, Edith Wharton, or Paul Bourget.

By the closeness and intensity of the "dialectic" James commits himself: he really believes in the all but supreme importance of personal relationships; and because they are so important the proper interpretation of them becomes important. Yet relationships between civilized (deep and subtle) people involve concealments as well as avowals; the more developed, the more affectionally, socially, ethically complicated the people, the more precarious and elaborate their relations, and the more imperative the need of system and persistence in making them out.

Unlike the Socratic dialogues, these progress without the aid of a master mind to control. Nor are they the dialogues of Racine, though in those we grow near to James: Miss Gostrey, Mrs. Assingham, Mrs. Stringham are *ficelles,* are *confidantes,* like Phaedra's nurse, Hippolytus' tutor and Orestes' friend Pylades. But the characteristic dialogue in Racine pits a passionate protagonist against the background of a moderator: we might call it the struggle of judgment against passion. In James, however, the interlocutors are jointly concerned to understand a situation; their passion goes into their seeing. And the *confidantes* do not merely serve to transform soliloquies into dialogues or to draw out their principals; they confer with one another, and with other principals. Mrs. Stringham, for example, serves as "muse" and palace guard and tutor in the "higher and finer things," yet she is also a mind intent and alert for conference with Mrs. Lowder and Densher.

The characteristic dialogue of the later novels avoids the long speech—turns, indeed, almost to stichomythia. Even the short speeches are interrupted; and so close is the texture that words and phrases are taken up and returned. Sometimes a figure started by one is developed in turn, after the fashion of *bouts rimés*. In *The Ivory Tower* Gray and Horton so collaborate for four pages, as Horton tries to make his friend see the chances to marry, the amorous assailments, which await a rich young American.

The dialogues exhibit the conscious mind, working hard and critically scrutinizing all available facts, examining semantically the import of words. This work of intelligence is for James a social act. There is much about ourselves and others which can be got at only in this way; there is a reality which is social, without participation in which we lose our sanity. James seems classical, French, in his whole attitude towards society, intelligence, communication. Unlike Hawthorne's, his people are not tempted by pride to isolate themselves from their fellows; even the shy protagonists are free from pride or inferiority: they reach out their hands to association.

But then there is another kind of truth not to be arrived at socially, intellectually, or analytically but personally, intuitively, imaginatively—through images and symbols. Origins and ends have to be put mythically—as Plato puts them in the *Phaedrus,* the *Gorgias,* the *Republic*. Our reasonings start from an intuition, a total feeling of the nature of the world, or the nature of a person; they return constantly to check themselves by that intuition; and it is an intuition upon which, finally, we act. The Jamesian equivalent of myth lies, I think, in the metaphors which, much increasing in *The Wings* over *The Ambassadors,* reach their high richness in *The Bowl* and *The Ivory Tower*.[1]

---

[1] The three completed masterpieces, *The Ambassadors, The Wings of a Dove,* and *The Golden Bowl,* were written between 1900 and 1904, when James went to America for ten months. The order in which these novels were published does not match the order of their production: a letter written to Howells in August, 1901, makes clear that *The Ambassadors,* though pub-

Here we must distinguish two modes of figuration in the later James. The first is the "extended conceit" made by prolonging an image, commonly an image proverbial, trite, conventionally "beautiful." Instances are frequent in the later novels; in revising the texture of his earlier work for the New York edition, James became aware of buried metaphors and resurrected them. In the following sequence, from *The American* (written in 1877, revised thirty years later) the italicized prelude, anticipating the "sacred fire," was added in 1907: Mrs. Tristram is *"interesting from this sense she gave of her looking for her ideals by a lamp of strange and fitful flame.* She was full—both for good and ill—of beginnings that came to nothing; but she had nevertheless, morally, a spark of the sacred fire." These regalvanized figures, a kind of wit-work, suggest minor "metaphysical" poetry—that of King or Joseph Beaumont.

The second mode is an emblematic perception, a symbolized intuition—in form an original image, sometimes comic, sometimes horrendous, often grotesque. It is these which offer the mythic. The "expressionism" of the later novels makes it difficult to locate, psychologically, all these emblematic perceptions. Some of James's people—his favorite heroines, certainly—are repeatedly asserted to "image" a situation—that is, instinctively to conceive of it in metaphorical terms. But there is perhaps no character—even to Colonel Assingham—who is not occasionally given a metaphor; and I conclude that James thinks of all his characters as having an Unconscious, as having a world of instinctive, feeling reactions, reactions which in art must express themselves (even if by intermediation of the novelist) in metaphoric terms.

Recollected images become metaphors. For years, James had travelled diligently in France and Italy, written conscientious commentaries on cathedrals, chateaux, and galleries. Now people remind

---

lished the year after *The Wings,* was composed before it; and this discrepancy explains why *The Wings* is stylistically nearer to *The Bowl.*

Nearly ten years elapse, years occupied by *The American Scene,* the autobiographical volumes, the revision of the earlier novels, and a return to the writing of plays. Finally, in 1914, when he is seventy, he returns to the novel, first with *The Ivory Tower,* and then, when the War makes a contemporary subject unmanageable, with *The Sense of the Past,* a manuscript begun at the period of *The Wings.*

him of art, become indeed works of art. His heroines, almost without exception, are thus translated. The auburn-haired Milly Theale is a Bronzino; Aurora Coyne becomes "an Italian princess of the *cinque-cento*: Titian or the grand Veronese might . . . have signed her image." Nan, the modernist and un-British daughter of *The Sense of the Past,* recalls "some mothering Virgin by Van Eyck or Memling. . . ." For Maggie, there is evoked some slim draped statue from the Vatican, "the smoothed elegant nameless head, the impersonal flit of a creature lost in an alien age. . . ." Mme. de Vionnet's head could be found on "an old precious medal, some silver coin of the Renaissance," while her daughter is a "faint pastel in an oval frame . . . the portrait of an old-time princess. . . ." Some embarrassment prevents similar translation of the heroes into paintings or statues; but the Prince (who is bought, after all, as a work of art and appraised by his father-in-law with the same taste which appraises a Luini) can scarcely be described except out of art history: by way of representing the superior utility and weight of the male, James renders him in architecture. His eyes, for example, prompt the *concetto* of their being "the high windows of a Roman palace, of an historic front by one of the great old designers, thrown open on a feast day to the golden air." And his union to the Ververs, the new "relation" which it establishes, suggests to Adam Verver that "their decent little old-time union, Maggie's and his own, had resembled a good deal some pleasant public square, in the heart of an old city, into which a great Palladian church, say—something with a grand architectural front—had suddenly been dropped. . . ."

The obvious errand of these analogies is honorific; they belong to the high and hallowed world of "culture." But in the decorative and the "beautiful," James's taste (like his taste in poetry) was conventional. He had to come to the poetic by misapprehension, one might say—by the way of the unlovely.

Unlike his Prince, who "never saw . . . below a certain social plane," James had looked observantly, in his days of "notation," at zoos and aquariums and circuses; and he remembered the crowded perceptions of "A Small Boy" in a remote America. Having neither children nor wealth Mrs. Assingham confronted "two great holes to fill, and she described herself as dropping social scraps into them as she had known old ladies, in her early, American time, drop morsels of silk into baskets in which they collected the material for some eventual patchwork quilt." For regression to the "good old," there are the childhood images: Adam Verver, indulging in a tiny holiday from responsibility, seems "caught in the act of handling a relic of infancy—sticking on the head of a broken soldier or trying the lock of a wooden gun. . . ." In their continued intimacy after both have other mates, father and daughter were "at times, the dear things, like children playing at visits, playing at 'Mr. Thompson and Mrs. Fane'. . . ."

The chief occasions for "imaging" are perceptions of persons and personal relations. In *The Bowl* and the unfinished novels, the characters are not visualized analytically but felt for us, rendered in terms of the total impression they make. Book I of *The Ivory Tower* is constantly metaphorical, moving into dialectical prose only to chronicle the Bradhams' large, busy tea. Rosanna, her father, the Bradhams, and Cissy Foy, their protegee, appear in poetry. Rosanna's massiveness and heroic stature and indomitability are rendered by the recurrent image of the ship in full sail; her voice rings out like that of Brünnhilde at the opera; her parasol is the "roof of some Burmese palanquin or perhaps even pagoda"; her presence is apprehended by Cissy as that of "some seated idol, a great Buddha perched upon a shrine."[2] Though he owns the literal stage property of a rocking chair on a vacant Newport piazza, Rosanna's father is also "a ruffled hawk, motionless but for his single tremor"; he broods "after the fashion of a philosopher tangled in some maze of metaphysics." When he makes his single shift of gear, from business to his daughter, he passes from his "market" into "some large cool dusky temple, a place where idols other than those of his worship vaguely loomed and gleamed."

The zealous exegete of meanings studies his companions' faces. He sees, for example, that Davy Bradham's "good worn worldly face, superficially so smooth," has "the sense of it lined and scratched and hacked across much in the manner of the hard ice of a large pond at the end of a long day's skating." Densher notes

---

[2] James's Oriental figures are relatively frequent and always to be attended; they habitually betoken the strangeness of that East which is East and hence incommunicable to the West.

it "an oddity of Mrs. Lowder's that her face in speech was like a lighted window at night, but that silence immediately drew the curtain."

Our recollection of Mrs. Lowder, James's massive rich British matron, is almost entirely compounded from the imagings of Densher, through whose at once admiring and hostile and amused consciousness we chiefly see her. The master metaphor is metallic. We first view her in her cage—all "perpetual satin, twinkling bugles and flashing gems, with a lustre of agate eyes, a sheen of raven hair, a polish of complexion . . . ," encased in the hard glittering surface of armor. Later, at the dinner table, managing a conversation, she becomes a steamboat, "steering a course in which she called at subjects as if they were islands in an archipelago,"—resumes, "with a splash of the screw, her cruise among the islands." Still later she has "something in common, even in repose, with a projectile, of great size, loaded and ready for use."

Mrs. Midmore, briefly presented in *The Sense of the Past*, and Mrs. Newsome, indirectly presented, never seen, belong, by their analogical treatment, to the same category with Mrs. Lowder: they are women as massive as, ultimately, menacing. . . . It is never quite clear how far Strether understands his feeling toward Mrs. Newsome (or how completely James understands it): Mrs. Newsome is not, like Mrs. Lowder, an obvious case of Philistinism; indeed, regards herself as an apostle of Culture—of the higher and finer and rarer and newer thought; and James apparently wants to represent Strether as making a sacrifice in renouncing Mrs. Newsome (as well as the more suitable Miss Gostrey). Yet, though the Lady of Woollett represented maternal protection as well as maternal domination, Strether's chief sense, upon losing her, must, like Lewes' upon losing the great Eliot, have been Relief.[3] Mrs. Newsome is massive because she has no imagination, she rests, sits, is—a fact without resilience. Others, the imaginative, must adjust, accommodate. As he thinks of her Strether's "eyes might have been fixing some particularly large iceberg in a cool blue northern sea."

---

[3] I am remembering the anecdote of James told by Stephen Spender in *The Destructive Element,* a book to which I am indebted.

If Philistines are to be "imaged" as inflexibly massive, metallic (unimaginative), the children of light owe their erect posture, their equilibrium, to their flexibility. They summon up recollection of ballet dancers, show people, brave ritualists who perform, upon exhibition, feats of persistence and agility: figures proper to Degas, Goya, Toulouse-Lautrec. Assingham watches his wife engaged at her favorite social analysis "much as he had sometimes watched at the Aquarium the celebrated lady who, in a slight, though tight, bathing suit, turned somersaults or did tricks in the tank of water which looked so cold and uncomfortable to the non-amphibious." When Maggie, courageously, undertakes a grand dinner at Portland Place, Mrs. Assingham assists "like one of the assistants in the ring at the circus, to keep up the pace of the sleek revolving animal on whose back the lady in short spangled skirts should brilliantly caper and posture." Throughout most of her half of *The Golden Bowl*, Maggie is the "overworked little trapezist girl." The novel rehearses her progress from being a child to being the lady in spangled skirts who can keep her balance while she capers on the back of a circus horse.

There are other fresh aspects of Maggie to be celebrated—for one, her resourceful Americanism—in contrast to her husband's ancient, aristocratic lineage. By virtue of this difference, Maggie must be expected to do most of the "adjustment": she must act like a "settler or trader in a new country; in the likeness even of some Indian squaw with a papoose on her back and barbarous bead work to sell." But without question there are governing images. As Maggie is the trapezist, so Charlotte, through the corresponding second half of *The Bowl,* is some wild creature, tormented by the gadfly; she is a caged creature which, bending the gilt bars, has escaped to roam; she wears "a long silken halter looped round her beautiful neck."

In the later novels, the chief thing, after all, is the structure. The characters exist in relations, and we are unbidden to information about them irrelevant to the fable and the relations. A character might almost be defined as the situs at which a given number of relations join: the Prince, for example, is the total of his relations to Mrs. Assingham, Mr. Verver, Charlotte, and Maggie:

though he has to be preliminarily posited as a classic instance of the aristocratic European, James presents that datum as summarily as possible.

One who, like Gray Fielder and his creator, is "critico-analytically interested" in people, gives inevitable attention to defining relationships. His skilled attention delights in the idea of a little set or group (like Mrs. Brook's), capable of developing its own vocabulary of allusions and words; but he specializes on the relation as between two. Hawthorne was James's great predecessor in this study, especially in those masterly chapters of *The Scarlet Letter* describing Chillingworth's sadistic operations on Dimmesdale. Relationships are not static and are never so represented by James; and the change in one relationship affects a corresponding change in another. "Critico-analytical" people do not take fixity of relationship for granted, but are constantly attempting to name the new state into which a relationship has entered, the new quality which has emerged. The relations most "imaged" are likely to be those which can least be talked out. Maria Gostrey and Strether don't image one another because the relation between them is dialectical; but, since Chad (for all his wonderful renovation) is neither dialectical nor imaginative, Strether has strenuously to use his own intuitive instrument. When Strether first encounters the Paris Version, Chad's "attitude was that of a person who has been gracefully quiet while the messenger at last reaching him has run a mile through the dust. . . ." And much later, Strether perceives that Chad "puts out" his excitement or whatever emotion "as he put out his washing. . . . It was quite for Strether himself in short to feel a personal analogy with the laundress bringing home the triumphs of the mangle."

The relation between Merton Densher and Kate Croy particularly rewards study, for Densher at least (whom we see more from within than Kate) is not only dialectically clever but also passionate. We wonder how he can tolerate Kate's plan or Kate for her plan; but, granting that his conscious mind found it "something so extraordinarily special to Kate that he felt himself shrink from the complications involved in judging it," we discover him, none the less, transcending his complicity. He is drawn to her by desire, yet repelled as well as fascinated by her calculations. As he looks at her, in the Gallery, the sight plays on his pride of possession, "as a hidden master in a great dim church might play on the grandest organ"; yet this sense of possession is more than matched by apprehension of her calculating power: more than once he said to her, "You keep the key of the cupboard, and I foresee that when we're married you'll dole me out my sugar by lumps."

In *The Sense of the Past*, the most "imaged" relation is between Ralph Pendrel, American introspective, and the blunt, massive, extroverted Perry Midmore, his contrary. When the other Regency and British Midmores are puzzled by the visitor, Perry has the advantage of not being "cultured": he trusts, animal-like, to his instincts, scents the presence of the clever and alien "as some creature of the woods might scent the bait of the trapper"; "like a frightened horse," he "sniffs in the air the nearness of some creature of a sort he has never seen." It is Perry, in turn, who most makes Ralph aware of his general peril, the precariousness of sustaining his rôle—how he must always use *manner* as a weapon, always "work from *behind* something—something that, look as it would, he must object to Perry's staring at in return as if it were a counterfeit coin or a card from up his sleeve."

The most powerful, most inclusive figure in this novel sums Ralph's sudden awareness of his 1820 Midmores in their historic, their psychic distance from him. In a somewhat similar moment of perception, Alice saw her companions as nothing but playing-cards; Ralph sees his as waxworks or statues: "an artful, a wonderful trio, some mechanic but consummate imitation of ancient life, staring through the vast plate of a museum." This perception marks the turn from Ralph's desire to live in the past to his counter-movement: James's hero, who disappoints his robust lady by his passionate love of the past, his desire to catch "the very tick of the old stopped clocks," is cured of his wish by its fulfillment, and at the end escapes, happily, to the modern world.

The second half of *The Golden Bowl*, supreme among the later novels for the density and richness of its symbolism, is dominated by Maggie's sense of the relations in which she stands, of which the most stable is with her father, the most precarious and menacing that with her rival, the Dark Lady.

The imagings—fear-images, many of them—which crowd the

later chapters arise from Maggie's inability to talk out her apprehensions except, and scantily, to Mrs. Assingham. Her relations with her father, the Prince, and Charlotte cannot, by the very nature of her problem and her project, be socially articulated: she must fight soundlessly and in the dark.

When the "little trapezist girl" tries to envisage her plight she often does so in architectural mode. The strangeness which she suddenly stumbles over—Charlotte's affair with the Prince—is an "outlandish pagoda, a structure plated with bright porcelain, colored and figured and adorned at the overhanging eaves with silver bells that tinkled," a pagoda set down in her own familiar, blooming garden. Later, in Book V, she feels the whole horrible situation to constitute the central chamber of a haunted house, "a great overarched and overglazed rotunda where gaiety might reign, but the doors of which opened into sinister circular passages." What Maggie must take in is the possibility of an evil which can appear in a Garden, or in the Home—which is not the villain of a melodrama or the Devil replete with horns. Evil met her, now, "like some bad-faced stranger surprised in one of the thick-carpeted corridors of a house of quiet on a Sunday afternoon." The sense of imprisonment is impossible to avoid, even when it is an enclosure allegedly therapeutic. Shut off from responsibility by the social gifts of her husband and his mistress, Maggie, coming to, finds herself locked up "in the solid chamber of her helplessness as in a bath of benevolence artfully prepared for her. . . . Baths of benevolence were all very well, but at least, unless one was a patient of some sort, a nervous eccentric or a lost child, one usually wasn't so immersed save by one's own request."

These oppressive claustric figures give way, as Maggie turns active, to more agile figures. In Book V, Maggie, feeling like a scapegoat, goes off into the darkness. From the terrace, looking in through the window, she sees her companions glassed, separated off like actors on a stage. Equipped with this perspective, she begins to fight; and even though images of frustration continue, they are intermitted with those of triumph; she overcomes her fear of Charlotte, lies boldly, kisses her with magnanimous treachery, and begins to "image" Charlotte's defeat; psychically hears, emitted from beneath her elegant mask, the "shriek of a soul in pain." Now out of prison, Maggie sees her companions caught: her husband strikes her as "caged" in his room; and our final view of Charlotte, consigned for shipment to American City, is that of a once living creature now petrified into "some colored and gilded image."

There are *données* of *The Bowl* which are perverse and scarcely to be accepted. Since James can't really bring himself to "realize" a union at once sexual and "good," the loves of the book are the passion of Charlotte for the Prince and of Maggie for her father. Dialectic, managed by another than James, might usefully have made these presuppositions explicit. But, to the saving of the novel's balance, the violent relation is between two women; and, whatever the pretext or the booty, Maggie becomes aware that evil may meet one garbed as an urbane friend, and learns how so to fight evil as to save what she prizes. James's sense of the good is, one might say, temperamentally conditioned; his sense of evil is normal and sound. And the great theme of *The Bowl* is the discovery that evil exists in the forms most disruptive to civilization: in disloyalty and treason.

In spite of the predominance of myth over dialectic in the novel, especially its second half, *The Bowl* does not represent James's escape into a defeatist Unconscious, the collapse of his system of values. Unlike many of his protagonists, Maggie is concerned not only to understand her situation but to will, savingly, and to act, successfully. Her dreams are, ultimately, those not of a patient but of a victor.

The tension in James between the dialectic and the mythic is an epistemological way of naming that rich interplay and reconciliation of impulses which constitutes his great achievement. As a person and as a writer, he matured slowly; he had to confront the long, slow business of synthesizing his impulse to emerge and the impulse to withdraw, his shyness and his sociability, his romanticism (his literary mode) and his realism, his humanism and his mysticism.

If there is the Henry James who speaks of dining out a hundred and seven times in a winter, who is to be "imaged" in the ritual garments—the silk topper, the morning coat, the fawn-colored waistcoat, the gloves folded in hand—there is also the inner James who never leaves the sanctuary, where are the altars of literature, the dead, and the Good.

One mustn't talk, here, of Appearance and Reality, for that is not the relation between this pair. In terms from the characterology (or perhaps hagiography) of James's youth, one can say that the outer self was modelled on Norton or Russell Lowell, while the inner self remained not remote from Emerson—if one may add, from Hawthorne, what James found deficient in Emerson, a "sense of the dark, the foul, the base . . . certain complications in life . . . human perversity." The outer James is an urbane humanist, an intelligent if precise defender of convention, usage, social discrimination and social intelligence; the inner James is an intuitionist, possessed of a deep non-utilitarian, non-traditional faith in goodness for goodness' sake, loyalty to loyalty, "pure love."

Because James was a "thinker" only on the theory of fiction, he did not schematize, still less adjust, his levels. He reported, honestly, whatever material, social or spiritual, he saw. He liked breeding, culture, taste; he perceived that these were the products (even if not the necessary products) of leisure, and leisure in turn of money. Yet from youth to age, he gives unpleasant pictures of the merely intelligent and cultivated—of the elder Bellegardes, of Osmond and Mme Merle, of Mrs. Gereth, Mrs. Newsome, Mrs. Brookenham. They are all "wonderful" specimens—expensive to produce and engaging to study; but they don't give us our scale. High exalted above the bright and cultivated are the good.

To be sure, he finds it difficult to work out his sum. His "good people" are generally poor, like Fleda Vetch and Strether; when, like Milly Theale and the Ververs, they are rich, it is by fabulous endowment: Adam's alleged power of making money remains unconvincing. By the time he wrote *The Ivory Tower,* James seems to have agreed with the Gospels that the salvation of the rich is precarious. Yet he as clearly believed that salvation—or total salvation—is, any way, rare. If riches can prevent one, so can envy, brutality, and stupidity, the vices of the poor, or complacency and hypocrisy, the vices of the bourgeois.

It is this range of standards in James which makes him both "rich" and "difficult." James's irony (which is pervasive) can be most readily detected in his act of praising people for having a virtue or two, virtues on which they plume themselves, when his criterion is a pluralistic perfection.

The danger of such a philosophy is that, in its awareness, its inclusiveness, it shall turn finally sceptical, or regard ambiguity and complexity as final virtues. This seems, in practice, not to have happened to James: though he probably had his confusions (his, in the pejorative sense, "ambiguities") he was not consciously proud of them. The general view of him, till fifteen years ago, simply scaled him down to a caricature of his "humanism"—namely, snobbery and aestheticism and Anglophilism, though equal evidence can be collected for his disapproval of "high society," for his Americanism and his moralism. But he was emphatically not a sceptic nor a believer in mutual cancellations. He had a clear hierarchy of values or, better, a hierarchy of value-series, which he applied with almost equal realism and rigor.

The distinctive, masterly achievement of Henry James in his maturity is a series of "metaphysical" novels in which, working as a poet, not a philosopher, he incarnates the interrelations between the conscious and the unconscious, between the social and the subjective. His fictional formalism and his incapacity for "ideas" must not lead us to forget that he belongs with Dostoievsky, Proust, and Mann.

Eliseo Vivas KAFKA'S DISTORTED

MASK

ONE need not read very far into *The Kafka Problem*[1] to see how grievously Kafka has suffered at the hands of some of his critics. Mr. Flores has thrown together, unembarrassed by any controlling criterion, a large number of articles, reviews and appreciations of Kafka, of diverse value and gathered from many European languages. A few essays, like that of the French critic Miss Claude-Edmonde Magny, are penetrating studies worthy of their subject. But the problem which most of these pieces raise is as to why the editor should have wanted to rescue them from discreet obscurity. Fortunately, if you want to check for yourself the validity of the various interpretations which have been foisted on Kafka, you are no longer obstructed by the difficulty which has confronted his slowly growing public during the last four or five years. For recently both his German publishers, now established in this country, and his various American publishers, have reprinted —although sometimes at fantastic prices—books of Kafka which it has been hitherto impossible to find. One of these publications is the indispensable biography by Max Brod which has been translated into English.

If one may judge by Flores' volume and by a few other essays which for some reason were left out of this democratic collection, "the Kafka problem" arises from the confused demands made by

---

[1] *The Kafka Problem*, edited by Angel Flores (New York: New Directions Press, 1946).

the readers and not from any unusual difficulty inherent in Kafka's work. This is most clearly seen in those egregious compounds of home-made psychoanalysis and facile sociology of art of a purely speculative nature, which without any inductive evidence to support them find Kafka's meaning in his psychological or political history and in so doing explain it utterly away. The sociological critic takes Kafka's fables to be the expression of the social conditions which allegedly motivated them. For him the question is not, What does the author say? but rather, Why does he say what he does? The psychoanalytic critic shares with the sociological the assumption that the content of Kafka's vision of the world is of no importance, but differs in that what he considers of importance is the way in which the work of art expresses an allegedly pathological condition of the author. Neither sociologist nor psychoanalyst finds the answer by reading the objective, public content of the work; they find it by applying to it a theory devised prior to the reading of it, regarding the relation said to hold between either social or psychological conditions and artistic expression. Now even granting that this kind of genetic analysis of art is valid, and that artistic symbols may indeed point to psychic conditions or to social determinants, it is nevertheless at least possible that the objective traits to which they refer are of interest to the reader as they are without doubt to the artist (or the latter would not have struggled as he did with the problem of choosing them and organizing them into the artistic work). This does not deny the therapist's right to use the work of art as diagnostic evidence. Psychoanalytic criticism is, however, seldom practised by properly trained therapists for their purposes; it is as a rule written by amateur psychoanalysts whose insensibility to the aesthetic values and indifference to the philosophic content of the work is hardly camouflaged by their pseudoscientific interest in it.

The reader who considers that the critic's most urgent task is to lead attention to those aspects of the world which are expressed by his subject is justified in passing by these highly speculative psychologistic or pseudosociological constructions. He must devote his efforts to exhibiting his subject's objective contribution and to essaying an evaluation of it. Inadequately supported speculations about the causes of the complicated difficulties which Kafka had with his father or his women or his job must necessarily be relegated to a relatively unimportant place until the work of objective criticism is finished and a working consensus obtains as to what is to be found in Kafkas' fables. But when at last we turn our attention to psychogenetic questions we should do so with a greater respect than the majority of these fanciful speculations show for the demands of inductive verification. The biographical data that we have on Kafka is inadequate because Brod, who was its chief gatherer, interprets Kafka in his own terms and seems incapable of distinguishing his own personal interest in his gifted friend and his interest in the objective meaning of his friend's fables. Brod's book does not enable us to check our fanciful psychoanalytic constructions against reliable and sufficient facts. But even if it did, it would still leave us with the chief problems of Kafka on hand, with the question of Kafka's aesthetic achievement and of the objective meaning and validity of his vision of the world. We have Freud's word, although we do not need it, for the insight that the analysis of aesthetic values is not within the reach of his analytic method. But psychological and sociological criticism —and Freud's own is to be included in it—systematically rides the genetic fallacy when it assumes that the discovery of the complete psychological or social sources of the artist's experience invalidates the objective meaning which is expressed by his art.

Although a large number of Kafka's critics avoid the fanciful constructions of his psychological or his sociological interpreters, they share with these the inability simply to take Kafka seriously as an artist at the objective level. Aware that art performs a very important function in elucidating objective experience but not clear as to how it does it, they have in one of two ways assumed that the key to his work is to be found, not within it, but beyond it. Some find it in some ready-made philosophical conception of the world, usually in Kierkegaard, as if all the artist had to do was to dress up in a dramatic costume a philosophic skeleton. Others, taking Kafka to be merely an allegorical writer, consider the task of criticism accomplished when the more or less superstructural allegorical features of his fables are translated into that for which they stand—or, as I shall call it, employing I. A. Richard's convenient terminology, into the "tenor" of the extended metaphor that is the allegory. The objective of these critics becomes then the translation of what Kafka meant by the Castle, or the Court, or by an advocate conveniently called "Grace," or by the Chinese emperor and his wall, or by the elaborate burrow built by the digger obsessed with a need to seek safe refuge from a predatory world. Although the difference in practice between these two modes of interpretation is important enough to notice, in principle they share the same assumption, namely, that the meaning of Kafka's work is to be found beyond the fables themselves and can therefore be better expressed in other terms than those which Kafka himself used.

Sharing the same assumption, these two modes of extrinsic interpretation also share a basic error consisting of a misconception of what the artist does and how he does it. The philosophic interpreters ignore the fact that the creative process involves a complete digestion of all the material on which the artist feeds so that what he finally produces is essentially different from what went into its make-up. They also ignore the fact that the poet, in the measure in which he is indeed a maker, does not seek to "imitate" or "represent" a reality which, independently of his poetic activity, possesses already a formal structure which anyone can discover. If this is true, it should be easy to see why the assumption that Kafka's meaning is to be found in a ready-made system of philosophy such as Kierkegaard's or anyone else's or even in a more or less systematic set of abstract ideas of his own, is a disparagement of his achievement. Artistically Kafka failed to a considerable extent. But his was the failure of a man who was an artist of major pretensions. His meaning is something not to be better stated abstractly in terms of ideas and concepts, to be found beyond the fable, but within it, at the dramatic level, in the interrelationships thus revealed to exist among the characters and between them and the universe. The fallacy of finding his meaning in abstract ideas inverts the relationship between philosophy and art, for it is the philosopher who must go to art for the subject matter which the poet has organized at the dramatic level, in order to abstract from it the systematic relationships which it is his business to formulate.

The allegorical interpreter fails for a similar reason. He translates the allegory into its "tenor" by supplying, not Kafka's own grasp of reality in dramatic terms, but a more or less commonplace version of it in abstract terms, and one which does not possess any of those traits which, in the fable, we discern to be the most distinctively Kafkan. But if Kafka had a contribution to make it was not to be found in the ingenuity of his allegorical "vehicle" (again in Richard's terminology) nor even in a version of a cock-eyed world whose absurdity at the human level had its source in the unqualified irrationality of transcending factors lying beyond human reach and beyond human comprehension. These conceptions of existence had already been expressed in one way or another in literature and in philosophy. What Kafka had to say was something else involving as much freshness and originality as one has a right to expect in literature. It is something which, so far as I know, he could not have borrowed from philosophy, for no thinker one hears of in standard histories of philosophy has ever viewed the world in quite the way in which Kafka viewed it. There are, undeniably, allegorical features in Kafka's vision of the world but they are obvious and relatively unimportant. What is important is the concrete dramatic world exhibited in his fables under the allegorical "vehicles" which he uses to capture it. Kafka, as Brod points out, even when trying to think conceptually, thinks in images and not in conceptual structures. But his vision has a coherence and meaningful interrelatedness lacked by the vision of the non-artistic mind, since the latter is distracted by the multifarious demands made on it and it is not driven by the need to organize and unify its experience. The picture of the world as it presented itself to Kafka was a mythopoetical one and if it is our business as readers to discover its meaning for us, in our own terms, we cannot do so until we are reasonably clear as to what was its own intrinsic meaning. Miss Magny puts the point so effectively that it is worth transcribing her own words:

> we ought not to . . . provide dialectical constructions for the unfolding of events which should be taken as a *real* account. Otherwise Kafka is quickly converted into a kind of frustrated

philosopher who needs to be explained to himself and to others for lack of sufficient power of analysis and abstraction . . . That would imply a gratuitous insult.

In spite of her depth and acuity, however, I believe that Miss Magny's interpretation of Kafka's conception of existence can be objectively shown to miss a very essential element. She says:

> the world for Kafka is essentially *turmoil*, something that is not *rational* and whose essence therefore only a fantastic tale can express. . . . Only the gratuitousness of the event itself, of the *contingit*, can reveal the essential absurdity of things.

At another place Miss Magny speaks of "Kafka's predilection for the infraconceptual, the infrarational." But Kafka's world was not merely absurd. Indeed what constituted for him the problem which he sought to resolve through his art—and of course the only manner in which an artist resolves his problem is through a statement of it in mythopoetic terms—was that certain transcending aspects of the universe envisaged through experience and seen to be those on which normal visible existence depends, blatantly proclaimed an irrationality which, upon the most casual glimpse, appeared to be at the same time rational.

But the Magny essay has at least this value, that it poses the Kafka problem correctly and reveals one aspect of our author without a grasp of which no understanding of him is possible. In Kafka, as she puts it, "the irrational . . . the horrible . . . the grotesque . . . are never induced for the sake of literary effect . . . but to express a depth of reality." Our problem therefore is to inquire as to what conception of existence is found in Kafka's fables. The answer must of course be couched in abstract terms, but it is not to be taken as a translation of Kafka's meaning but as a means of pointing to it within the fables themselves. The validity of the interpretation is to be judged by checking to see whether what I claim to be found in Kafka is indeed there and whether I do not neglect important factors which are there. The allegorical features must of course be translated into their "tenors" but this goes without saying and rather than constituting a difficult task—as in fact it does for critics like Rahv when they try to translate Kafka into Kierkegaardian philosophy—it is a relatively easy one. The labor of criticism however begins at that point and what it has to accomplish is a reading of Kafka. After that one may express one's opinion as to whether Kafka's conception of existence is valid or not.

2

In order to offer inductive evidence in favor of the preceding argument we must turn to an analysis of Kafka's works in search of his conception of existence. But since an exhaustive analysis of all of his works is not here possible, I propose that we turn our attention to *The Trial* and *The Castle* which embody his most ambitious efforts to integrate his various discoveries about the world. Let us first turn to *The Trial*.

We must first remember that Joseph K.'s arrest is sudden and seems to him so unjustified that never between the period of this arrest and of his execution does he admit his guilt. But while verbally denying it, unconsciously Joseph K. betrays his sense of guilt from the very first day of his arrest in numerous small ways. Let only one instance suffice: During the preliminary examination that took place the morning of his arrest Joseph K. said to the Inspector in anger and seemingly irrelevantly, "But this is not the capital charge yet." In a more important way Joseph K. gives evidence of his sense of guilt: The outward circumstances of his life do not at first change very radically but gradually Joseph K. gets more and more absorbed in his case and finally finds out that his job is suffering from his preoccupation with it. If he truly were convinced of his innocence he would have laughed at the whole absurd business, as he tried to do the first Sunday at the preliminary investigation when he told the Magistrate that his could not be a trial unless he recognized it as such. To the reader it is quite clear that Joseph K. did not want to admit to himself when he made that statement that he had already through action eloquently yielded the recognition that his lips withheld.

Remember next that while Joseph K. realizes that the Court is a formidable organization he insists nevertheless on his belief that its purposes are absurd, and the evidence for that is to be found, as he believes, in all that he discovers about it at the lower level.

Thus Joseph K. seems to be justified in his conviction, expressed angrily to the Magistrate, that the organization is interested in condemning innocent victims and doing so while keeping them in ignorance of what action is brought against them. This belief is strengthened by the result of his efforts to gain information about the higher officials of the Court.

But is Joseph K. really justified in his belief that the Court is an utterly aimless, absurd institution? A formidable organization with a code of Law and with such a large number of employees, with traditions and equipment, an organization that will punish its employees on occasion upon the complaint of a man under arrest—such an organization is simply not aimless. Its aims may not be knowable or may not seem to be intelligible to us but the evidence, without denying Joseph K.'s conviction of its absurdity, points, at the very same time, to a rationality all its own. Joseph K. does not want to admit this to himself and insists on judging the organization and its charges against him by his own criterion of rationality. But all his actions proclaim that he is not altogether ignorant of the limitations of his own criterion. In view of his stiff-necked attitude towards the evidence, the counsel which Joseph K. gives himself on the way to the execution has a tremendous ironic force. "The only thing for me to do now . . . is to keep my intelligence calm and discriminating to the end." He therefore resigns himself. But it has been precisely the failure of his discriminating intelligence that led him to the impasse in which he found himself. For it was not resignation that the situation required of him; what is required was admission of his guilt and genuine contrition. This is precisely what the priest tried in vain to tell him in the Cathedral. But Joseph K. was too discriminatingly intelligent and too proud of the primacy of his intelligence to listen.

The Castle is a much more complex book than *The Trial*. Indeed it represents the most ambitious effort on Kafka's part to gather together all the important aspects of his vision of the world into one coherent fable. For this reason the unfinished condition in which it was left suggests a radical criticism of the validity of Kafka's conception of existence. In this book his preoccupations are given a different organization from that which he gave them in *The Trial*. A problem with which *The Trial* is concerned only obliquely is here brought forward, namely the problem of man's place in the scheme of things and, as a corollary of this more comprehensive problem, the question as to the nature of the bond between man and his follow beings. In *The Trial* that bond, after the crisis of the arrest, is somehow unhealthy; for instance, for the normal relationship between his mistress and himself Joseph K. substitutes the relationship with Huld's maid, Leni, which does not involve either the fulfillment of genuine love or even the gratification which purely sexual relations can yield. In *The Castle* the emphasis seems to change but both the human and the merely sexual relations result in the same vague frustration. Again the question of guilt which is central in *The Trial* is subordinated in *The Castle* by being presented through the episode of Barnabas and his family. But the cause of the guilt, which in *The Trial* is only indirectly and ambiguously suggested, is in the latter explicitly traced to Amalia's refusal of Sortini's invitation to visit him in his room at the Inn; the guilt is caused, that is, by the pride of those who will not serve and is thus connected with the most ancient of guilts, the guilt that led to the fall before man's. The cause is brought out with sufficient clarity by the contrast between Amalia's attitude towards Sortini and the attitude of the Landlady and of Frieda towards Klamm. K. is himself relatively free from a sense of guilt but he is dominated by a need to find a place for himself in the scheme of things. The need, baffled, develops into anxiety as his efforts lead him to discover the nature of the organization that he has to contend with.

From Olga and from the superintendent who receives K. in bed, the Land Surveyor gains important information about the organization of the Castle. K. tries to make his informants admit that the organization is quite absurd and leaves much to be desired. But the superintendent does not admit that the organization lacks order or is subject to error. The apparatus works with great precision; in the Castle nothing is done without thought and the very possibility of error on the part of the Head Bureau must be ruled out. The superintendent admits that he is convinced that in respect to K. an error has been committed. But who can tell what the first Control Officials will say and the second and third and the rest? However, if there has been one, the error is not established by the evidence K. has from Klamm, for Klamm's letter to K. is not official, and as to the telephone calls, these mean nothing. If Huld in *The Trial* is an advocate without legal standing, Klamm in *The Castle* is a protector seemingly helpless to protect his man —that is, if there is a Klamm and if it is K. and not someone else in whom Klamm is interested.

I have purposely said in a vague way that K. was trying "to find his place in the scheme of things" because I do not find that K. is anxious about obtaining a livelihood or solving any other purely secular problem but only about finding a place in the village which would give him status not only in respect to the village itself but, more importantly even, in respect to the inaccessible powers of the Castle. K. wants an unambiguous statement of his position before the authorities of the Castle. This involves documents, proofs, something to which he could refer that could not be gainsaid, like the letters from Klamm, but containing of course an official appointment and a definition of his place. He starts with large demands and ends up by offering to take anything that will be given him so long as it brings him the needed nod of recognition for which he craves. But his efforts to get into direct touch with the officials of the Castle are no less pathetically useless than those of Barnabas' father who wants his crime defined. No one can be certain of anything beyond the elementary fact that there must be a Castle which is visible above the village and from which officials and servants constantly come and go. One also suspects that it must have its method, no matter how absurd that method may seem and how deeply it may outrage the feeling of what we take to be fitness or justice or rationality. But beyond that all is doubt and incertitude.

Between *The Trial* and *The Castle* there are important differences, but to me none seems as important as the fact that Joseph K. never learns anything whatever about the invisible Judges, while K. knows the name of the Lord of the Castle, Count West-west, and receives indications, however unsatisfactory, that between the Castle and himself there is some sort of nexus. He first tries to get into touch with the Count, then with the Castellan and, when he sees the impossibility of his ambition, he tries to reach Klamm. K.'s relations with Klamm are more baffling than those of Joseph K.

with his Judges in *The Trial* because there is more teasing evidence of Klamm's existence and therefore the evidence is more unintelligible. K. thinks he once saw Klamm but it turns out later that that is very doubtful. Was it Klamm who wrote the letter to K.? The signature is illegible and Olga later tells K. that the letters that her brother Barnabas has brought him were not received from Klamm but from a clerk. Even if they were from Klamm it is doubtful whether Klamm is well enough posted on K. really to be his patron or protector as the second letter that K. receives from Klamm clearly shows. The question is even more difficult since, if you press it, it turns out that there are all kinds of contradictory reports about Klamm, and some people go so far as to say that Momus, the Secretary, is Klamm. Who then is Klamm? Some sort of fluctuating image of him has been constructed but, as Olga tells K., perhaps it does not fluctuate as much as Klamm's real appearance does. However, in *The Trial* not even such a deceptive hope ever urges Joseph K. on and he conducts his defense in a state of unrelieved and increasing enervation.

It is not necessary to demonstrate in detail that the various aspects of the conception of existence that were integrated in these two novels are separately expressed in a large number of his stories and sketches: in *Investigations of a Dog*, *The Great Wall of China*, *The Burrow* and *The Giant Mole,* for instance, as well as in some of his shorter pieces like *The Problem of Our Laws.* But it is necessary to state frankly that there are a number of more or less important stories which could not be susceptible of this interpretation, for example, *Josephine the Songstress, Blumfeld, An Elderly Bachelor, The Penal Colony* and *The Judgment.* In some of these what Kafka was trying to do is not difficult to guess. He was exploring psychological reality strictly at the human level. The result of Kafka's psychological exploration, it seems to me, contradicts the purely hedonic conception of man which is found deeply imbedded in the liberal, secularistic tradition of our western world and which is true only of what Kierkegaard called the "aesthetic stage" of human development. Kafka's discoveries ally him with the tradition which Freud himself joined as a result of his metapsychological speculations and to which Dostoievsky and Kierkegaard belong—men who repudiate the shallow optimism which controls the conception of human destiny at the "aesthetic stage." For Kafka's psychological conceptions we must go to stories like *Metamorphosis, The Judgment* and *The Penal Colony*. With some diffidence I venture the opinion that an analysis of his contributions to the understanding of the purely psychological problems of contemporary men would hardly be worth the trouble it would involve.

Amerika, begun only a few months before *The Trial,* seems to represent, as I read it, an unsuccessful experiment of Kafka's, for in it he views his problem as imbedded in a purely social context. *Amerika* seems therefore to constitute very little more than social criticism of his temporal world and we find in it only faint and incomplete indications of the insights into the transcending aspects of experience which we identify as Kafka's central focus of interest and the elucidation of which constitutes his contribution.

3

We are now able to put together Kafka's conception of existence. Note first that what Kafka undertook was a stubbornly empirical exploration of experience, beyond which he discovered a constellation of factors for which evidence is found within the texture of experience itself. For this reason allegory must be employed to point to these factors not directly revealed. But the "tenor" of the allegory, being itself beyond direct grasp, must be expressed in mythopoetic terms drawn from ordinary life. Kafka, with whom Brod read Plato in his university days, could have invoked Plato as precedent for his use of myth, for the Greek used it to elucidate the structure which he glimpsed as lying beyond experience through evidence found within it. Kafka's discovery involves an ordered process which we can more or less adequately capture in the following formula: A crisis leads either to a sense of guilt or to a condition of alienation. In either case the crisis generates a struggle which expresses itself, among other ways, in the arrogant demands made by the hero. As he begins to feel the effects of the crisis the hero gradually trims his demands but he never altogether ceases to press them. The reduction of demands results from the hero's gradual discovery of a transcending organization which seems beyond his power either to look into, control or understand. His discovery is based not upon unwarranted assumptions or gratuitous hypotheses but on more or less direct empirical evidence, and although what is discovered seems unintelligible to him, the evidence is ambivalent and points not only to the irrationality of the organization but to its rationality as well. The anguished doubt into which the victim of the crisis is plunged is the result of the fact that the antinomy he faces cannot be resolved since it does not occur to him to transcend his perspective or go beyond his empirical method. But what other method is there? For Kafka's heroes there seems to be no other.

It is of the utmost importance, however, to note that Kafka's "empiricism" differs radically from that which is fashionable today—that which constitutes the foundations of scientific naturalism—since the latter has been devised in order to deny the evidence which experience presents of its lack of self-sufficiency, while Kafka through an empirical examination of human existence is led to assert its dependence on transcending factors.

We do not find in Kafka an assertion of a world made up of two aspects such as we find in the traditional dualism of Western philosophy; for in these the two terms, the visible and the transcending, are said to bear certain intelligible relations towards one another and in the major tradition the transcending term is taken as the ground of the rationality of the other. Nor do we have in Kafka a dramatized version of Schopenhauerian dualism in which a pure irrational factor is taken to be the ground of our world of experience. What we find is something quite different, something to a large degree fresh and original, expressing in challenging terms the novel conditions and predicaments of modern man. These predicaments generate anguish. But unlike Kierkegaard, who mastered his "sterile anguish" through faith, or Dostoievsky, who suggested that it could be mastered through faith and love in the way in which the Russian monk, Father Zossima, mastered it, Kafka's man never succeeds in surpassing human anguish. Face to face with what many of his critics recognize as a metaphysical problem—in a vague sense of this conveniently ambiguous word—Kafka tried to solve it empirically. But what he was up against was the problem of theodicy and not in the Leibnizian sense but in the fuller, in the Cartesian sense. The problem that Kafka faced was not primarily the conventional need to find a satisfactory human account of evil once it has been discovered that its roots lie beyond the human level.

Neither was it the problem of discovering what attitudes we may be expected to take towards an invisible agent on which we depend and which we know to be infinite—this was the Kierkegaardian problem. Rather it was the problem of discovering the ground of rationality. He went so far as to grasp clearly that that ground transcends human experience. But he could not go beyond this relatively elementary discovery because the stubborn empirical attitude which he assumed is helpless before questions of the magnitude he was raising.

This is not to say, however, that personally Kafka resigned himself to the monstrous predicament into which his discoveries plunged him. And least of all is it to say that the reader must himself be plunged into a pessimistic attitude by contemplating Kafka's picture of the world. Those readers who find him merely depressing have not read him carefully. Brod quotes a trenchant statement in his *Biography* which suggests the precise way in which Kafka himself avoided a purely enervating pessimism and in which the reader may also avoid it. "Our art," it reads, "consists of being dazzled by Truth. The light which rests on the distorted mask as it shrinks from it is true, nothing else is." The light is Truth but the mask on which it shines, the artifact of the maker, is "distorted"—and the rich contextual ambiguities of the statement are precisely what give it density of suggestive meaning and confirm the reader's hunch that in the ambiguities which Kafka systematically exploits is to be found the comic dimension of his picture of the world and the means of purging oneself from effects generated by its arbitrariness and irrationality. Kafka's artistry makes this comic feature compatible with the sense of anguish and even of terror that is the defining quality of existence in it. But it is not merged with or sacrificed to the latter. And in the reader its perception generates enough detachment to enable him to assimilate all the absurdity and pervasive anguish presented without surrendering to it.

The comical quality of Kafka's world is expressed in the way in which he treats the antinomous nature of existence. Generally speaking, a comic grasp of the world rests on the perception by the writer of a moral duality which elicits from the reader a "comic" response as the only means of freeing himself from the conflict towards values to which he is attached and yet towards which he cannot justify his attachment satisfactorily. It is not merely a moral duality but, if you will allow it, a cosmological duality that we find in Kafka's world, and its perception involves a disparagement of the means which reveal it, a disparagement of the mind as a rational tool of analysis. There is no gaiety in Kafka's irony as there is in Rabelais' satire; nor a deep sense of moral outrage and the bitter laughter arising from the fact that at least you know you cannot be fooled which we find in Swift. But there is nevertheless the essential element of the comic in Kafka: the transparent error involved in any statement that can be made of the world. Such a world, a world about which nothing can be said that cannot in the same breath be as plausibly contradicted, is a quintessentially comic world. You cannot of course expect its victims to find it so but you cannot, either, be expected by them to take them at their own asking value and in your mind you are ready with a discount. A world toward which one cannot develop any kind of attachment, however ideal and prospective, is a world in which the pain it creates, the terror it inspires, the cruelty it shows is not utterly crushing pain or terror or cruelty, because it crushes with its absurdity the piety it generates. The only response to it therefore is the ironic.

In the light of the foregoing it is not difficult to see in concrete terms that the differences between Kierkegaard and Kafka are essential and the affinities superficial. For the one thing one could not impute to Kierkegaard is the empirical attitude. He starts with it but he soon soars away into a region where intuition and faith, free from the demands of empirical evidence, allow him to ignore the insoluble problems which for the thorough-going empiricist stand in the way of accepting a historical or even a personal religious view of man and the world. Kierkegaard is therefore not at all baffled by the nature of those elements which he found to transcend experience. He does not claim that he is able to "know" them; but the proper response towards them is not for him that of the pure knower, the abstract ratiocinator in search of verified "truth." The existentialist is a man of flesh and bones—as Unamuno put it—who, disregarding the artificial limitations and restrictions of the pure knower, makes a total human decision and wills the act of belief; and not in the pragmatic sense of William James, either, but in a passionate, affirmative, plenary manner. For this reason Kierkegaard would have pooh-poohed the parallelism which has been found to exist between himself and Kafka. A man who tries to reach a plenary conviction as to the transcending structure that subtends human experience by "cognitive" means places himself at the very opposite pole of Kierkegaardian existentialism. Furthermore, because for Kierkegaard the object of faith was infinite, man must be in the wrong and as a result must endure anguish. But this is his highest condition. By contrast, the anguish that at times almost chokes Kafka's characters—the stagnant, the oppressive atmosphere of Barnabas' home or the claustrophobiac closedness of Tintorelli's room, the terrifying searches, the endless corridors—is the result of insecurity which arises from lack of knowledge. In Kafka anguish issues from doubt, in Kierkegaard from certitude.

There is, however, a modicum of justification for the coupling of the Danish philosopher with the Jewish novelist, since the reading of the former does make us aware of the importance of anguish, of the crisis and of absolute disjunctions in human experience. Without a full appreciation of these factors as inherent in the human situation, the effort to understand Kafka turns into a diagnostic hunt for signs of neuroses. It is important to keep in mind however the different way in which these factors function in philosopher and poet although it is impossible to undertake here specifications of the differences.

4

There is need to make explicit some hints I have given about what I take to be the validity of Kafka's conception of existence. Let us disregard the fact of his failure to bring any of his major works to completion, although such a failure may legitimately be taken as a basis for the most devastating criticism that may be leveled against Kafka's version of reality. Still it must be noted that Kafka's conception of existence is defective because it is inherently unstable. It seems to me that Kafka's picture constitutes a decided advance over that given us by contemporary naturalism, for Kafka has no desire to deny the evidence of experience which points to dimensions of existence which transcend it. But he could not or would not surrender his method to the demands of rationality and left us with a vision of the world which both artistically and philosophically represents an impasse. The change of attitude generated by the crisis opens to the subject large ranges of hitherto unsuspected possibilities as to the nature of existence. But these cannot be realized unless the new attitudes brought about by the crisis are accepted as revealing factors which experience itself cannot explore, but in which one must believe nevertheless even without a basis that those who have not gone through the crisis would be willing to accept as adequate evidence. And this is what the empiricist will not, cannot do. I believe it would be relatively easy to prove from his work that Kafka saw clearly the root of the difficulty. But his intellectual grasp of his perplexity was useless since his difficulty arose precisely from his insistence on the use of the intelligence beyond its legitimate range.

There is therefore a profound justification to Kafka's own remark that he expressed the negative tendencies of his age. Note however that he does so in the sense that he grasped clearly the meaning of certain phenomena as constitutive of normal human development in its break from what Kierkegaard called the "aesthetic" stage. But he was not able to concede what is demanded in order to reach the "ethico-religious" stage. Having been thrust from the aesthetic his heroes stop before they reach the next stage. And they stop because they refuse—or are unable to bring themselves—to solve their problems by the only means that such problems can be solved; in the manner in which Plato solved his, through the recognition of the valid claims of religious intuition in certain ranges of experience; or in the manner in which Kant did, by supplying the terms required to complete a rational picture of the world as postulates made necessary by the objective demands of practical reason. It is this leap, taken by the greatest number of the major philosophers of our West, that Kafka, faithful to the limitations of his empiricism, will not take. In that refusal Kafka is at one with the negative tendencies of his age and remains impaled on the horns of a brutal antinomy.

Adrienne Monnier JOYCE'S

ULYSSES AND THE FRENCH PUBLIC

Translated by Sylvia Beach

IT WAS on the 7th of December, 1921, that Valéry Larbaud introduced the Irish writer, James Joyce, to the "Amis des Livres." He spoke particularly of *Ulysses,* which had not yet been published in book form. This lecture, which appeared later in the *Nouvelle Revue Française,* now serves as a preface to *Gens de Dublin,* the French translation of *Dubliners,* and is unique in the history of literary criticism. It is the first time, I believe, that an English work has been revealed by a French writer before anything has appeared on the subject in English-speaking countries.

Of course, the presence of Joyce somewhat explains the phenomenon, but when one considers the difficulties to be met with in the text of *Ulysses,* one is amazed at the "tour de force" Larbaud accomplished. How did he produce, unprepared as he was, and at such short notice, so clear, so condensed and so jolly an interpretation of *Ulysses?*

Far be it from me to compete with such a master. My knowledge of English is but slight; moreover, I am not erudite. My aim is more modest, and, perhaps, more ambitious. I am going to try to express some of the essential summings-up of *Ulysses* by its French readers, and I shall add from time to time a few personal views on the subject. Before becoming the first publisher of the French translation of *Ulysses,* I was its first French reader. I have thought about it a great deal. My reflections, to begin with, were

75

not other than those of an ordinary reader, but as they were more abundant, and as I took more trouble to examine it carefully, my conclusions were probably a trifle more just.

In the first place, I must admit that we had a good appetite for the big book that was set before us. Since Larbaud had made our mouths water for it, we had been waiting eight years. He had warned us, it is true, that a reader who was not well-read, or only moderately well-read, would abandon *Ulysses* at the end of the third page, but we felt, and perhaps were right, that we were well-read readers, and that the light Larbaud had already thrown on the subject guaranteed us against any misunderstandings. But I must confess that if we read the book all the way through, it was not without a frequent temptation to abandon it on the way.

Let us start with a short account of the journey.

The first chapter we liked very much—in fact we had read it before as it had appeared in *Commerce*. It is a lively tale told with excellent realism and its poetic passages are surprisingly vivacious. One or two lines about the sea or the old milkwoman strike a new note and enchant us.

Second chapter: it begins to go uphill. Stephen has been our hero, so far; now he resolutely turns his back on us. The tone is no longer that of the narrative, there is not a path, sentences are more and more chopped-up, with references to a lot of things about which we know little or nothing, such as the history of Ireland, ancient history, philosophy, scholastic theology, early English poetry.

Third chapter: we are completely lost. It is the part that appeared in the *N.R.F.* under the title *"Protée."* The references are getting more and more obscure—insupportable. And now, Stephen not only turns his back on us, but he murmurs unintelligibly to himself, and we feel we are intruding. The book falls from our hands for the first time.

After at least one day off, we pick it up again, those of us who are stout-hearted, and lo! we are rewarded, for a title indicates that this is the second part of the work, and at last we have the real hero, Leopold Bloom—"Ulysses," Larbaud tells us. Reading on, we can find no connection whatsoever with the *Odyssey*; on the other hand, here scrupulously noted are the thoughts and acts of a man. The little choppy sentences with their exaggerated use of allusions—it is the famous "interior monologue"—still exasperate us a good deal, but we are beginning to get accustomed to this manner now, and at least the main character is no longer bookish, smug Stephen.

Mr. Bloom is very attractive. He is essentially a man of good intentions. His mind circulates easily among things of even the most trivial nature, without lowering itself; not that his thoughts are really elevated, but the way he has of communicating with the event, first deriving pleasure from it and then applying to it his entire little knowledge always in the hope of some slight improvement, ought to win a tender smile from the Goddess of Wisdom. He is the twentieth-century primitive, the man born of science, nurseling of vulgarization. One day we shall say "Bloomism" as we speak of "Don Giovannism."

Thus we follow this excellent Mr. Bloom in his many comings and goings, as he walks in the streets of Dublin, goes to the bath establishment, a funeral, drops in at a newspaper office—and this continues for five chapters which we find to a certain extent very satisfactory. It is curious, indeed, what pleasure the picturing of familiar things gives us—that ever-known country which we know so well. It is quite lifelike, we say, meaning that we have attempted to recreate and to restore to the Gods their gift to us: Art: the give-and-take with the powers above; admission to the Immortals.

But let us return to Mr. Bloom, whom we left coming out of the museum where he had been verifying a curious little matter.

In the next chapter, the ninth in the book, we lose sight of him and once more find Stephen.

We are in the library with some young intellectuals. This chapter is difficult to follow. Here again, Joyce doesn't take much trouble to initiate us into the mysteries of the discussion they are having, which, I imagine, is plain enough to the Irish, particularly to those who, like Joyce, were connected with Dublin's literary life in 1904. We do our best to follow them in their concern over such problems as the Celtic Renaissance, Symbolism and the esoteric. All these young men have read Mallarmé, Villiers de l'Isle Adam, Mrs. Blavatsky's *Isis Unveiled;* they know and thoroughly appreciate classic and modern English writings. The immediate elders are Yeats, George Moore, Synge, George Russell. Some of them are founding the Gaelic League and are making an effort to restore the ancient Irish tongue. The glory of the "swan" Shakespeare comes into their reveries. Among the group, which includes James Stephens and Padraic Colum, Stephen, who is Joyce himself as an adolescent, is already conspicuous for the extent of his culture and the originality of his mind. The conversation now going on between himself and his comrades deals almost entirely with the life and works of Shakespeare, and particularly with *Hamlet*. The discussion makes us feel deeply our ignorance. We knew—Buck Mulligan in the first chapter had ironically informed us—that Stephen possessed certain theories on the subject of Hamlet: we are at this moment present at the exposing of these theories, which lead to a definition, one that is already familiar to us, of the idea of Paternity. "Paternity," he says, "as conscious begetting, does not exist for man. It is a mystic state of being, an apostolic transmission by the only begetter to the only begot. Upon this mystery, and not on the Madonna, thrown as a sop to the western masses by Italian astuteness, the Church is founded, and founded unshakably because founded like the world, macro and microcosm, on the void. On uncertainty, improbability, 'Amor Matris,' genitive objective and subjective, the only reality in life." This definition invites endless discussion.

But let us continue on our way, for if we stop we might never reach the end of it. Now we come to a chapter that is very restful, and that is made up of a series of little Dublin scenes. The tone of these pieces is given us by the first of the characters to enter, the very reverend Father Conmee, S.J., a benevolent man, of a calm spirit, for whom the world has its explanation clearly and once for all. We have here, instead of Stephen's anxiety and Bloom's incessant problems, an outlook voluntarily superficial, where things, lightened of their burden of inner problems, appear in simple outline, color, sound, movement, and viewed thus, in passing, are clearer and perhaps truer than when they are used in support of an individual interpretation. Thus, we witness the lack of strength of Simon Dedalus' character—he is Stephen's father—and the poverty in which his family live. Joy in the street, sorrow in the house.

Again we meet the light-hearted Dedalus, Senior. He is at the Osmond Hotel with the singer Ben Dollard, Mr. Bloom and several other companions. Two charming barmaids, Miss Douce and

Miss Kennedy, bronze and gold, rule over this world. Music, particularly singing, forms the background of the episode. Everything gravitates around Mr. Dedalus and Ben Dollard who are asked to sing and who have been singing. The two first pages of the chapter appeared very "surrealistic" to most of our readers owing to the manner in which it is composed at random without any logical connection between ideas. In reality, these pages constitute an overture, such as that of an opera; the acts which are to follow are foreshadowed by short calls, repeated and growing louder as the piece goes on. In this episode, dedicated to the art of sound, imitative harmony occupies, naturally, a big place.

The episode that follows is very puzzling for the non-initiated reader. The scene takes place in Barney Kiernan's Bar and the persons present are only dimly perceived. A certain "Citizen," accompanied by his dog, plays, we presume, an important role in this part, but he never fully manages to emerge from the prevailing obscurity. Every page, however, has its admirable burlesque and lyrical inventions, and though we don't understand anything we are enchanted nevertheless. The most obvious feature of the method employed here is the alternation of popular slang with the jargon of the archaic legend, the daily paper, society columns, law, science, politics. Events are told in a vulgar and an idealistic manner in turn; sentiments are brought down to the lowest level, then exalted to unbelievable heights. Each detail, taken separately, can be understood without too great difficulty, but to grasp the meaning of the composition as a whole is out of the question. This is a chapter where initiation is indispensable. We have only to learn that it corresponds to the Cyclops in the *Odyssey* and it is quite simple. We see that the slang represents the trivial, earthy aspect of Ulysses' companions, tied underneath the bellies of the beasts, while the emphatic language is that of the Giants. The Giants, one might say, are the social body, the commonplace tradition; they are heroes raised by the people to the dignity of demigods. The outlook of the people, themselves, taken as individuals, is limited by their ignorance and their state of submission, which is only relieved by the freedom of their tongue, and it is the man who barks with his dog.

Luckily this piece with all its difficulties is followed by a diversion. We are carried to the beach in the company of three young girls; two of them are in charge of an infant and two little boys, and play "mamma," the third, Gertie, is absorbed in her dreams. Mr. Bloom is seated not far off, and not one of their gestures nor futile words escape him. The chapter up to the final monologue of Bloom maintains the tone of the items and the wonderful correspondence columns of the fashion papers. Everything that the ordinary woman lays at her own feet, the flattering murmur produced in herself by a crowd of herself, all the beauty hints, dictates of fashion, harmless poetry, tamed mystery, religion-of-all-work, kitchen recipes, advice about how to get on in the world, and above all, permeating every detail, be it ever so insignificant, love as its atmosphere. Yes, everything is here; that devil of a Joyce has left nothing out. The male public has much enjoyed this chapter.

Now we come to an episode that is no less arduous than that of the Cyclops, and if we are going to understand it, we shall need to know something of what the author meant. The "Oxen of the Sun" takes place in a maternity hospital. Mr. Bloom has come to inquire about Mrs. Purefoy, and finds himself among a number of his friends including Stephen Dedalus.

This episode is composed of a series of parodies of prose from the Anglo-Saxon, down through the fifteenth, sixteenth, seventeenth, eighteenth, and nineteenth centuries to the present day and the latest American slang. The method adopted here is an attempt to represent the development of the embryo by the development of English prose. The following, according to Joyce's own hints, are the writers whose style he has imitated each in turn: Mandeville, Malory, Bunyan, Defoe, Swift, Sterne, Addison, Goldsmith, Junius, Gibbon, Walpole, Lamb, De Quincey, Landor, Macaulay, scientific reviews of the first half of the nineteenth century, Dickens, Thackeray, Carlyle. This means, as we see, a terrifying virtuosity. If the episode were not, in some places, exceedingly licentious, it would make an excellent school exercise.

The chapters which follow, though they are the most admirable, I think are not really difficult, and one doesn't have to be initiated to enjoy their beauty. The long episode in dramatic form, that takes place in the brothel quarter, and terminates the second part of the work, is, in itself, an undoubted masterpiece.

Certain critics have compared this episode to the "Walpurgis

Night" and also to "The Temptation of Saint Anthony," but these works seem primitive beside Joyce's "Circe." Here phantasmagoria is no longer on the surface, borrowed, but has its inner truth, logic, according to the mind of each one of the characters. In the state of hallucination induced by drink, they create their own demons that spring from what is residual or larval in themselves. Every possible object of the senses and emotions and more or less repressed desires become flesh and play an episodic role while idea association like a "compere" calls forth the procession of them. A swarm of creatures, as lewd, as repugnant and as terrible as those invented by the people or the poet when inclined to deviltry, form the spectacle; but we have here, besides, an admirable psycho-physiological study. It is a scientifically established hell with all the most modern improvements.

The third part of the work opens with a chapter that does not generally get all the attention it deserves. We are in a small bar, "The Cabman's Shelter," to which Mr. Bloom conducts Stephen, after picking him up drunk outside the brothel. This chapter is written entirely—with the exception of the sailor's speech—in the style of Mr. Bloom's "exterior" conversation. One really hears him talk, with his carefully chosen commonplaces, his superabundant politeness, the best of his views on various questions, the whole effort of a man who is concerned with his fellows and who does not wish to be merely one of the common herd. This is a piece that is supremely successful, and shows, perhaps best, the mastery of the writer, the power of his effort, his close observation. Such a piece will be counted among literary exploits of the twentieth century.

The following chapter, written in the form of questions and answers, has not, it seems to me, been sufficiently admired, considering its merits. No doubt, the form, when first approached, is disconcerting, and the long enumerations are sometimes wearisome, but it is, perhaps, from a strictly Joycean viewpoint, the peak of the work. Personally, I find it very difficult to understand the reluctance of certain readers to admit this. It seems to me that he has discovered here a sort of stylization that might be an approach to Egyptian hieratism, science being substituted for religion. This produces, at times, in a most unexpected manner, prodigious emotional and comic effects. The rapidity of the sentences, their entirely scientific development, the immense forces called forth and utilized, result, at some points, in a sort of luminous condensation, which, by a doubly inverted action, magnifies the particular and diminishes the general. The slightest shades of feeling or of thought are projected immeasurably, while the earth with its myriads is reduced to a tiny point in the heavens.

The last chapter—what need be said of it? It is the famous monologue of the woman. Everyone has read and reread it. Some, indeed, seem to have read only that. Its peculiar style has no surprises for us; one knows that Joyce omitted the punctuation in order to give the impression of a continual unrolling, or, rather, a rotation like that of the Earth, the Earth being Goddess-Mother, essential femininity. It is matter, "chaos of irrationality" according to Bruno, "insensitive subject around which the vicissitude of forms is produced," forms (and their vicissitudes) being contributed by the male principle.

May I be pardoned for so summary and incomplete a commentary on these episodes that should be studied at great length and with vast learning. To tell the truth, I have made no attempt to do a criticism of *Ulysses*, M. Valéry Larbaud, Stuart Gilbert, Jean Cassou, René Lalou, Marc Chadourne and particularly Marcel Thiébaud having already done so admirably. Nor have I attempted to go into the human aspect of the book, rightly deemed the most important by Philippe Souppault.

So far, my principal effort has been to bring out, to the best of my abilities, a few ideas, oriented as much as possible towards literature. I have tried to throw some light on the means of expression used by Joyce, and the resulting effects. I have purposely avoided comment on the "interior monologue," however important, and perhaps of all the techniques employed the one that has attracted the most attention.

In fact, my aim was to record some of the reflections made by the French reader after a first, patient, attentive reading of *Ulysses*. Let us suppose that this reading is taking place in March 1929, just after the book has appeared, and the various authors from whom I have quoted not having published their articles yet—excepting of course Valéry Larbaud.

We are somewhat like the traveller returning from a long and often hard journey; we have gone a great distance, have barely seen anything, are dead-tired, have suffered in turn from thirst, giddiness in high altitudes, the sting of insects. But we have had moments of pleasure; we have been shown scenes as unforgettable as the arrival at Lhassa, the forbidden city.

On reflection, we concluded that *Ulysses* is a notable literary enterprise. It has many a time been described as a *Summa,* an encyclopedia. All science, every manner and method are here; none of the resources of expression is neglected in the conquest of every possible object of expression. And now, the first criticism that we, as Frenchmen, would be expected to make: does its encyclopedic breadth radically affect its artistic value? Rather than a masterpiece, have we not a pile of works that evokes Babel and might suffer the same fate? Certainly we are in the presence of a monster, "distended, deformed in every direction by a vain emulation of the universe's immensity," as Jules Romains would say. Adding, "we forget too often that if life is the material of art, the work of art is in itself a living body. The miracle in art is not so much the absorption as the organization of matter."

Does the famous "interior monologue," for example, constitute an appreciable literary gain? No, on reflection, for if it registers completely the cerebral mechanism, its value is purely a scientific one; if it means a new convention, there is no reason why it should be preferred to ordinary analytic methods. Besides, as M. Auguste Bailly justly observed, the integral psychic unfolding, with its layers of planes, cannot be reduced to the linear transposition to which handwriting obliges us. The interior monologue, as used by Joyce, cannot avoid the arbitrary, and analysis, in freeing the currents that are essential to consciousness, exposes the springs of an act or a feeling still more adequately.

And now another criticism: why the devil have there been established so many useless and haphazarded parallels with the *Odyssey?* And why, if the author must have these parallels, has he given us his book with no titles to the chapters, nor preface, nor anything that might serve as a guide? Nobody, to tell the truth, is capable of finding out the meaning with which his book is stuffed; the best works that have been done on the subject are, it must be confessed, almost entirely based on his own suggestions; initiation always comes from himself. We admit the fact that obscurity may be the result, as Valéry says, of "an accumulation of work," but not of the deliberate intention to be obscure.

The composition of *Ulysses*, if one thinks it over, seems a maniacal, senseless, teasing thing. It constantly requires, on the part of the reader, an immense effort that is not always rewarded. One gets nothing but riddles, obstacle-jumping, mortification. Life does not treat us otherwise, it is true, but art is opposed to brute nature, according to its own definition, is it not? It belongs to nature, but represents essentially the elements in their order and hierarchy, dispensing harmony and contemplation. Where in *Ulysses* shall we find a passage such as that in *War and Peace* when Prince André, alone and wounded, looks at the sky? Where is that fine weather air, that temperature of great works that brings peace once and always to the tormented heart of man, that justifies his hope?

Curtius says: "One can call geniuses, properly speaking, only those men whose production reflects something of the divine sense of the world, whose creation marks the uplifting of life. A light and a force emanate from the work of genius. It gives light to the spirit and to reflection, it purifies and ennobles the passions, it raises up images that inform our lives. The highest intensity of mind, the highest degree of power in invention and description do not yet constitute genius, if a work lacks the power that brings light and is fruitful. The work of Joyce is born of a revolt of the spirit and leads to the destruction of the world." He adds: "*Ulysses* unmasks, exposes, demolishes and degrades humanity with an acuity and completeness that, in modern thought, have no equivalent."

Though coming from a German, these reflections express the essential grievances of French idealists. It is, in fact, a great French idealist, M. Charles Du Bos, who quoted from them in a criticism published in the *Nouvelle Revue Française*.

Yes, have we not suffered ourselves, in reading *Ulysses*, not only from its literary obscurity but from its moral obscurity as well? Are not the most kindly pictures in the book those depicting filth, drunkenness, and debauch? Is not everything that we surround with respect and poetry: love, death, religion, degraded? for this is really the word, in this cruel work?

But I do not wish to dwell any further on the defects of *Ulysses*, they are innumerable. Before ending, however, we must not leave out M. André Maurois' criticism in which he wrote that *"Ulysses considered as a novel was a failure."*

Well, there you are; *Ulysses* is not a work of art, neither is it a success as a novel, nor is it an elevated production. It is not beautiful, clever nor sublime at all. And yet, when this is said, we are uneasy, we feel that we have not rendered a judgment and that this book towers over us and is our judge.

"A *Summa* of humanity" it has been called. In reality, it is indeed a human summing-up, that is to say, the possible total of that which in man, as Rimbaud defined it, is "of the world," opposed to that which is "not of the world."

Confucius said to his disciples who were questioning him on the mystery of death: "When one doesn't yet know what life is, how could one know death?" He said also to those who asked him how one could serve the spirits and the genii: "When one is not yet ready to serve men, how could one serve the spirits and the genii?"

Joyce appears to have assumed the task of serving men by helping them to attain complete self-knowledge.

It is a stranger enterprise than it seems; when this is attempted, one never fails to make use of God and the mysteries. It is believed that God can explain man, while it is perhaps man who can explain God. The Earth and all its works have never appealed very much to our species; it has always appeared to the best among us as a place one passed through, of exile. The spirit contained in this bit of matter of which we are composed draws us beyond and above, evaporates us, converts us to cloudy ease. And, no doubt, where there is such a tendency, it points to a real goal. Our aspiration to God and to a state of harmony, pure and eternal, is something as true as the need of eating. But before attaining that state, which is, perhaps, like all things, ideally contained in the expectation of it, ought we not to find out exactly what the situation is in which we are plunged? If there be a happy issue from this passage, does it not depend on the good life, that is to say, living conscientiously and consciously? Why not accept, esteem, that which is "given"? Are the discontented foredoomed to be always unsatisfied, and does not joy always spread like a flame, from joy?

It may seem strange to use the word "joy" in reference to Joyce, whose work, some people feel, is based on pessimism, the spiritual remaining improbable and the material the only certainty. But this is far from pessimistic, it is primarily a question of good sense. To be sure, men have always placed their confidence in the spiritual, a bank supposed to pay 100 per cent. So far, it does not seem to have been a great success, except, no doubt, in the case of saints and sages who expect no returns from a material world, convert all their assets into spiritual securities which they leave unclaimed. These, however, are a minority, valuable and unforeseen, on whom one cannot depend in matters of currency. They must not be used as a foundation. We must do without them as they do without us. A man like Joyce does without them, has made his choice of the immensity of others. I have always thought that at the root of his work a profound charity was present. The crushing task that he has set himself: this inventory of the sentient world—inventory that assumes order—has no relation to traditional saintliness, but nevertheless has something saintly about it, even in the Christian sense of the word, distinguishing it from ordinary philosophical and literary undertakings. Is it not a proof of humility, abnegation, courage, patience to the highest degree? Its aim is not perfection, which is impossible, contrary to every rule in life, and obtained by convention or fraud alone. Its aim is integrity of conscience. It practices the virtues of a scientific age, of which the asceticism is not easier than that of religious ages.

I do not agree with Curtius that Joyce's work is born of the spirit's revolt, but would say that it was born of submission of the spirit. Yes, submission of the spirit to nature, to matter; matter in its philosophical definition as *all physical or mental given facts ready made and worked out subsequently*.

Furthermore, if matter, even as we understand it in the current sense of the word, is drawn towards spirit as towards a superior state, is not spirit therefore drawn to matter, its only consecration? Ideas, at the highest limit of their evolution, become embodied. Divine principles are clothed in flesh in order to make themselves manifest, certain, sentient.

"That which is above is like that which is below, and that which is below is like that which is above." This is the real epigraph of *Ulysses*. With Joyce as with all mystics—he is a mystic in humanity—all is in all, the lesser reveals the greater, each thing produces its opposite, everything is held together by connections, visible or secret, and sometimes the most visible are the most secret. But this state of truth, of unity, that mystics express by the most beautiful and the purest pictures, Joyce wants to express by no matter what, the evil as well as the good. He chooses, when he does choose, what has been sacrificed, shamed, trimmed, made-over, what one had never dared to present just as it was, what had always been outlawed, unloved. For him, nothing is useless or unworthy. Everything only makes the belly of Our-Lady-under-the-Earth rounder.

It is also through submission of the spirit to reality, to all physical or mental facts, that he possesses and utilizes so much book learning. With him, the importance lies, not in formulating a personal interpretation of Ideas, of God, which seem to him, perhaps, to defy all reasonable interpretation, but to know what has been expressed about them, what, drawn from their eternal essence, has become incorporated with an act, a doctrine, a tradition or a book, what has become material for observation, experiment, what has begotten the present. He is not concerned with the possibility of truth in a belief, but with the power it may have gained by twenty centuries of accumulated authority. That is a part of the inventory, of the potential evaluation of the resources and reserves of this world. With him, there is a kind of "unanism" in time, as may be seen even in the plan of *Ulysses*. It is not indeed from Joyce that we are to expect a criticism of systems in force, a shaking of established customs. The purely passive resistance with which he confronts them at times, serves rather as a flying buttress to consolidate them. His mockery, seldom manifested, he reserves for the pretensions of the passing moment.

Yes, contrary to what it seems, he does not seek to reform nor to satirize. He never places himself above what he describes, he doesn't draw up a report showing an unfavorable balance of effort and result, he doesn't "pile it on," never blames at all, nor uplifts anything. He is only true, terribly true, and that is indeed the reason why he offends us.

Certainly, as Curtius says, Joyce exposes humanity, but he does not degrade it. It is humanity that is often itself degraded, less through its dependence on the laws of nature than owing to its ignorance and presumption. What he appears to demean, we have let fall in attempting to place it too high. If love, religion and death, seen through his work, are ugly and dirty, it is because we have smirched them endlessly. He has given us a mighty auto-vaccination.

Donat O'Donnell THE PIETIES OF

EVELYN WAUGH

MR. EVELYN WAUGH'S seventh and latest novel, *Brideshead Revisited,* was fortunate in earning the approval both of the reading public and of the theologians. In England, *The Tablet* saw in it "a great apologetic work in the larger and more humane sense," and in the United States, where it sold over half a million copies, the critics of the leading Catholic journals concurred in this judgment. One of them, however—H. C. Gardiner, in *America,* January 12, 1946—complained with justice that all the non-Catholic reviewers, including those who made it the Book of the Month Club selection, had missed the religious point of the book. It seems probable therefore that most of Mr. Waugh's readers, in America at any rate, did not know that they were reading a great apologetic work, and that, if they paid any attention to the Catholicism of *Brideshead Revisited* at all, they valued it as part of the general baronial decorations around a tale of love and high-life.

In this, of course, they were wrong, but their mistake was not entirely due to "secularist" stupidity and indifference. *Brideshead Revisited* is, in its author's words, "an attempt to trace the divine purpose in a pagan world"; men and women try to escape from the love of God, to find human happiness, but God destroys their human hopes and brings them back with "a twitch upon the thread." This is the central theme, austere and theological, but obscured (for those whose approach to religion is different from Mr. Waugh's) by bulky memorials of devotion to other gods. These alien pieties, some of them hardly compatible with strict Catholicism, were perhaps for Mr. Waugh the forerunners of a more articulated faith—as, in *Brideshead Revisited,* Sebastian Flyte's affection for a teddy-bear was the forerunner of a vocation. They appear in varying degrees and shapes in all his work, and now mingle with Catholicism in a highly personal system of belief and devotion, well worth analysis.

The main emotional constituent of Mr. Waugh's religion—using the term in a wide sense—is a deep English romanticism. His earliest work, *Rossetti,* betrayed a pre-Raphaelite affinity; and his first "serious" novel, *A Handful of Dust,* deals with the injury inflicted by modern flippancy and shallowness on a romantic mind. The hero, Tony Last, lives in a great ramshackle country house of nineteenth-century Gothic which he dearly loves, and which his wife's friends sneer at; his wife betrays him, and when he realizes the extent of her treachery his disillusionment shows us in a blinding flash his imaginative world:

> A whole Gothic world had come to grief . . . there was now no armour glittering through the forest glades, no embroidered feet on the green sward; the cream and dappled unicorns had fled. . . .

We should of course be wary of too easily attributing similar fantasies to the author—although he takes his hero's side so bitterly as to mar what is in many ways his best novel—but it is significant that Captain Ryder, the hero of *Brideshead Revisited,* lives in the same sort of climate. "Hooper," he says, referring to a member of the lower classes, "was no romantic. He had not as a child ridden with Rupert's Horse or sat among the camp-fires at Xanthus. . . . Hooper had wept often but never for Henry's speech on St. Crispin's day, nor for the epitaph at Thermopylae. The history they taught him had had few battles in it. . . ." And Captain Ryder hoped to find "that low door in the wall . . . which opened on an enclosed and enchanted garden, which was somewhere, not overlooked by any window, in the heart of that grey city." This persistence and intensity of youthful romanticism are remarkable, so also is the fierce conviction that the romantic dream is directly menaced by some element in modernity. Tony Last's Gothic forest is withered by the cynicism of smart and up-to-date people in London; Captain Ryder's enchanted garden is trampled by the mechanized Hooper.

Closely allied with this romanticism is a nostalgia for the period of extreme youth. Tony Last was an adult, but his bedroom "formed a gallery representative of every phase of his adolescence—the framed picture of a dreadnought (a colored supplement from Chums) all guns spouting flame and smoke; a photographic group of his private school; a cabinet called 'the Museum' filled with the fruits of a dozen desultory hobbies." The only card game he can play is "animal snap," a bout of which is made to occupy him during an evening of agony and suspense. Captain Ryder during part of his undergraduate life with the beautiful and charming Sebastian Flyte felt that he was "given a brief spell of what I had never known, a happy childhood, and though its toys were silk shirts and liqueurs and cigars, and its naughtiness high in the catalogue of grave sins, there was something of nursery freshness about us that fell little short of the joy of innocence." And amid all this he is conscious of "homesickness for nursery morality." Sebastian himself is described as being "in love with his own childhood." He carries with him everywhere a teddy-bear called Aloysius, which he occasionally threatens to spank. Mr. Waugh's preoccupation with youth even permeates his more or less cynical comic novels (*Decline and Fall, Vile Bodies,* etc.). There is no display of emotion in these, nor much analysis of states of mind, but sophisticated young people play "Happy Families" (*Black Mischief*) and a Communist journalist concentrates on working a toy train (*Scoop*). More important is the schoolboy delight in cruelty which marks the earlier books especially, and gives an almost hysterical tempo to their farce. One of the funniest scenes in *Decline and Fall* deals with the brutal murder of an inoffensive old prison chaplain. The convicts, in chapel, take advantage of the hymn-singing to pass on the news:

Old Prendy went to see a chap
  What said he'd seen a ghost
Well he was dippy and he'd got
  A mallet and a saw.

Who let the madman have the things?
  The Governor: who d'you think?
He asked to be a carpenter,
  He sawed off Prendy's head.

Time like an ever-rolling stream
  Bears all its sons away
Poor Prendy 'ollered fit to kill
  For nearly 'alf an hour.

Vile Bodies is rich in unregarded death; a drunken young
woman kills herself by swinging out of a chandelier; a titled
gossip writer puts his head in the gas oven; a Bright Young Thing
expires after a lively party in the room in the nursing-home where
she is recovering after a car accident. The comedy of *Black
Mischief* is ingeniously designed to lead up to a gruesome piece
of cannibalism. ("You're a grand girl, Prudence, and I'd like to
eat you." "So you shall, my sweet, anything you want." And,
as a result of later accidents, he does.)

"In laughter," according to Bergson, "we always find an
unavowed intention to humiliate and consequently to correct, our
neighbor." One of the secrets of Mr. Waugh's comic genius was
his keen interest in humiliation. Basil Seal, the adventurer-hero
("insolent, sulky and curiously childish") of *Black Mischief* and
Put Out More Flags, "rejoiced always," we are told, "in the
spectacle of women at a disadvantage." Mr. Waugh is a great ex-
ploiter of human disadvantages, and his unscrupulous adolescent
cruelty in this is the common quality of his two most obvious
characteristics: his humor and his snobbery. Two of his comic
novels, *Black Mischief* and *Scoop*, are largely based on a sly
appeal to the white man's sense of racial superiority; much of
the best fun in *Decline and Fall* comes from the exploitation of
the manners of Captain Grimes who, although he claimed to be
a public school man, was not really a gentleman and did not

often have a bath; in *Put Out More Flags* the purest comedy lies in lurid descriptions of the appearance and behavior of three proletarian evacuee children. Examples of his deft use of the snob-joke could be multiplied almost indefinitely. It can be said indeed that if he were not a snob, if he were not the type of man who refers frequently to "the lower orders" (as he does in *Labels*) and objects to the presence of natives in first-class railway carriages (as he does in *Waugh in Abyssinia*) he could not have written such funny books. This is an unpleasant fact; it means that the countless liberal newstatesmanish people who have laughed over these books share unconsciously these prejudices. Mr. Edmund Wilson, in the *New Yorker*, condemned the snobbery of *Brideshead Revisited*, but he had swallowed with delight the snobbery implicit in the earlier novels, from *Decline and Fall* to *Scoop*. Snobbery was quite acceptable as an attitude: the critic objected only when it was formulated as a doctrine.

It is true that in his later books Mr. Waugh's snobbery has taken on a different emphasis. As he becomes more serious, his veneration for the upper classes becomes more marked than his contempt for his social inferiors. This almost mystical veneration, entirely free from any taint of morality, may be discerned in a slightly burlesque form in his early books. Paul Pennyfeather, the drab hero of *Decline and Fall*, was cast into prison through the fault of the woman he loves, Mrs. Beste-Chetwynde, the rich, beautiful and aristocratic white-slave-trader. He forgave her however because he believed "that there was in fact, and should be, one law for her and another for himself, and that the naïve little exertions of nineteenth-century Radicals were essentially base and trivial and misdirected." *Decline and Fall* was, of course, published before Mr. Waugh's conversion to Catholicism, which took place in 1930; no doubt he would not now express his thought in the same way. But his almost idolatrous reverence for birth and wealth has not been destroyed by the Faith; on the contrary, *Brideshead Revisited* breathes from beginning to end a loving patience with mortal sin among the aristocracy and an unchristian petulance towards the minor foibles of the middle class.

As might be expected, Mr. Waugh's political outlook is the expression of his social prejudices. In the introduction to his book on Mexico, *Robbery Under Law*, he has set out his political creed in general terms. "I believe that man is by nature an exile and will never be self-sufficient or complete upon this earth . . . men naturally arrange themselves into a system of classes . . . war and conquest are inevitable." From these pessimistic premises he has drawn important practical conclusions; the propriety of strike-breaking; the justice of Mussolini's conquest of Abyssinia. As the title of his Mexican work indicates, his quarrel with the Mexican government concerns not so much their acquiescence in the persecution of the Church, as their encroachment on British oil interests. Taking Abyssinia from its Emperor is "inevitable" but taking Mexican oil from British investors is plain robbery. So phrased the argument appears dishonest, but Mr. Waugh's sincerity is beyond all doubt. Indeed his conservatism is so intensely emotional that he is a sort of Jacobite by anticipation. In his imagination the class he loves is already oppressed; the king has taken to the hills. Already in *Decline and Fall* Lady Circumference and her friends were "feeling the wind a bit"; in *Vile Bodies*, the Bright Young People gad about gallantly, touched by the fever of impending doom, to be blasted in the final prophetic chapter by war and inflation. In *Black Mischief*, Basil's friends are impoverished by the Depression and in the later works the shadow deepens (brightened by the brief rally of the Churchillian renaissance 1940-41) into the midnight of *Brideshead Revisited*. "These men," reflects Captain Ryder, contemplating the fate of some relatives of Lady Marchmain's, "must die to make a world for Hooper; they were the aborigines, vermin by right of law, to be shot off at leisure so that things might be safe for the travelling salesman with his polygonal pince-nez, his fat wet hand-shake, his grinning dentures." The Prison Governor in *Decline and Fall* whose ideas on occupational therapy had such unfortunate consequences for the Chaplain is, in Mr. Waugh's eyes, the typical reformer. He turns the full battery of his satirical power against "progressive" thinkers and workers, for he sees them as working to hand over power to a slavering mob of criminals, communists and commercial travellers.

An interesting sidelight on all this is shed by the autobiography of his father, Arthur Waugh (*One Man's Road*, 1931). Mr.

Waugh, senior, a well-to-do publisher, recounts that Evelyn, as a little boy, arranged theatricals in the nursery and "marshalled a 'pistol troop' for the defense of England against Germans and Jews."[1] He edited a magazine about this troop, and his fond father was able to have it bound for him "in full morocco." *One Man's Road* also contains a photograph of the house in Hampstead in which Evelyn was reared, with the legend printed beneath: "No doubt it was never anything more than an ordinary suburban villa. But it was a great deal more to me."

The Gothic dream, nostalgia for childhood, snobbery, neo-Jacobitism—this whole complex of longings, fears and prejudices, "wistful, half-romantic, half-aesthetic," to use a phrase of Mr. Waugh's, must be taken into account in approaching the question of Mr. Waugh's Catholicism. In Catholic countries Catholicism is not romantic, not invariably associated with big houses, or the fate of an aristocracy. The Bordeaux of M. Mauriac and the Cork of Mr. Frank O'Connor are not Gothic cities nor objects of wistfulness. But the Catholicism of Mr. Waugh, and of certain other English converts, is hardly separable from a personal romanticism and a class loyalty. Is Lord Marchmain's soul more valuable than Hooper's? To say in so many words that it was would be heresy, but *Brideshead Revisited* almost seems to imply that the wretched Hooper has no soul at all, certainly nothing to compare with the genuine old landed article. And *Brideshead Revisited* is the most Catholic of his novels. Mr. Waugh's religion, even before his conversion, abounded in consolation for the rich. That obliging and ubiquitous priest, Father Rothschild, S. J. (of *Vile Bodies*), refuses to censure the goings on of the Bright Young People: "It seems to me that they are all possessed with an almost fatal hunger for permanence. I think all these divorces show that. People aren't content just to muddle along nowadays. . . . And this word 'bogus' they all use. . . ." The paradoxes of the wealthy Jesuit are not perhaps intended to be taken very seriously, but the same sort of spiritual consolation, this time with no perceptible trace of irony, may be derived from *Brideshead Revisited*. Lady Marchmain confesses that once she thought it wrong "to have

---

[1] He also "placarded Boscastle harbour with home-made labels championing 'Votes for Women.' " This is less easy to reconcile with his later activities.

so many beautiful things when others had nothing," but she over-
came these scruples, saying: "The poor have always been the
favourites of God and his saints, but I believe that it is one of the
special achievements of Grace to sanctify the whole of life, riches
included." In Mr. Waugh's theology, the love of money is not only
not the root of all evil, it is a preliminary form of the love of God.

After the publication of *Brideshead Revisited* in America, a
certain Mr. McClose, of Alexandria (Va.), wrote a postcard to
Mr. Waugh saying: "Your *Brideshead Revisited* is a strange way
to show that Catholicism is an answer to anything. Seems more
like the kiss of Death to me." Mr. Waugh in an article in *Life*
(April 8, 1946) dismisses this criticism with a sneer about halitosis.
And yet it is much more to the point than are *The Tablet's*
eulogies. The death-bed conversion of Lord Marchmain is the
decisive crisis of the book; the death of an upper class and the
death of all earthly hope are two of its principal themes. The
lovers are forced apart by a sense of sin; the house is deserted;
the family scattered; the only child that is born is dead. Mr.
Waugh's political forebodings and the form of his private myths
(of which a sense of exile is the main constituent) make his
Catholicism something that is, in earthly affairs, dark and defeatist,
alien to the bright aggressive Catholicism of the New World,
as well as to the workaday faith of the old Catholic countries.
Out of all the tragedy, and justifying it, one good is seen emerging
—the conversion of the narrator. In Brideshead chapel he has
seen "a beaten copper lamp of deplorable design relit before the
beaten doors of a tabernacle," and he rejoices; but when he leaves
the chapel, he leaves it empty of worshippers.

This rearguard Catholicism is not indeed "an answer to anything," nor intended to be, any more than Tony Last's Gothic
city or Proust's rediscovered time is an answer to anything. The
funeral is strictly private, and salvation also. There was once an
Irish priest who refused to pray for the conversion of England,
and Mr. Waugh, I fear, might refuse to pray for the conversion
of Hooper.

And just as snobbery and adolescent cruelty gave edge and
tension to his early work, so now the intense romantic and exclusive
piety of his maturer years gives him strength and eloquence.

The clear focussing of remembered detail, the loving reconstruction of youth, and the great extension of metaphor in *Brideshead Revisited* all recall Proust more than any living writer, and the texture of Mr. Waugh's writing is both finer and stronger than is usual in Proust.[2] Mr. Waugh has evidently read some Proust —indeed in *A Handful of Dust* he twice pays him the tribute of misquotation—and there are passages in *Brideshead Revisited*, notably the opening of Book Two, that seem to paraphrase *Remembrance of Things Past.* "My theme is memory," says Mr. Waugh, "that winged host that soared about me one grey morning of war-time. These memories which are my life—for we possess nothing certainly except the past—were always with me. Like the pigeons of St. Mark's, they were everywhere, under my feet singly, in pairs." He continues in this strain for much longer than I can quote, and we recall Proust whose theme was the same, whose metaphors were equally exuberant, and who developed his theme from a recollection of feeling, under his feet, two uneven paving-stones in the baptistery of St. Mark's.

The resemblance is neither accidental nor merely superficial and it has nothing to do with plagiarism. The outward lives of the two men are very different—one can hardly imagine Proust in the Commandos—but their mental worlds are, up to a point, surprisingly similar. Proust was tenacious of childhood, with a feverishly romantic mind capable of turning a common seaside town into an enchanted city. This romantic sensitivity to names, and perhaps also his social position (he belonged, like Mr. Waugh, to the upper middle class), led him to a veneration for the aristocracy. For him the name of the Duchess of Guermantes could evoke the Patriarchs and Judges on the windows of the cathedral of Laon, as well as the ancient forests in which Childebert went hunting, and it was in pursuit of these things that he entered the salons of the Faubourg St. Germain. There he acquired a sense of social distinction as marked as Mr. Waugh's, and much more delicate. So far the resemblance is striking, but there it ends. Proust never raised a political or religious superstructure on

---

[2] This is not to imply that *Brideshead Revisited*, as a totality, comes within measurable distance of Proust's tremendous achievement in *Remembrance of Things Past.*

these foundations. Once he remembers wondering, in a fashionable restaurant, "whether the glass aquarium would always continue to protect the banquet of the marvellous beasts," but he does not make an issue out of it. He shows Parisian society decaying and breaking up under the pressure of the war, but he writes as a spectator, even as a connoisseur, not as a partisan. More than this, his mind is able at last to disentangle the Duchess of Guermantes from Childebert's forest, and to regard fashionable snobberies as not different in kind from disputes on precedence among green-grocers' wives. Mr. Waugh has not yet taken this decisive step. And Proust's religious experience, if we may call it so, is confined to the discrepancies of mortal life in time. He never took Mr. Waugh's decisive step, from romanticism to the acceptance of dogma.

The difference between the two men may be in part explained by their historical setting. Proust lived and wrote at a time when the upper classes were menaced, but not severely damaged. They had suffered an infusion from the classes below, but their money was still safe enough. It was easy for Proust—especially as his health was bad—to feel that "society" would last his time. As he had no children and did not believe in immortality he did not have to worry what happened after that. He could therefore cultivate an easy and speculative detachment. In our time, however, the upper classes, even in England, are not merely menaced; they have been gravely damaged. They feel not merely frustrated or irritated but actually oppressed by the high level of modern taxation; they see their equals levelled all over Europe and their hold on their own masses almost gone. Proustian detachment and sense of nuance tend to perish in this atmosphere, and the wistful romantic easily develops, as Mr. Waugh has done, into an embattled Jacobite.

It would, however, be a simplification to insist too much on the direct influence of economic history. Even if the two men had been born contemporaries their evolution would have differed widely, because of the great difference in the manners of their education. The efforts of Proust's parents to "harden" him were neither consistent nor successful, and no one else seems to have made the attempt at all. This easy upbringing did not produce an ideal citizen or soldier, but it did ensure a continuity of emotional life, with, in this case, a certain lucidity and calm. The young Waugh, on the contrary, was subjected to the discipline of an English public school, and a religious one at that.[3] Captain Ryder speaks sadly of "the hard bachelordom of English adolescence, the premature dignity and authority of the school system." Mr. Waugh endured these things and emerged an English gentleman, with slight symptoms of hysteria. Cream and dappled unicorns have clearly no place at a public school, and an interior life which includes such creatures will feel itself menaced. If it does not die it will take on a new intensity, becoming a fixed intolerant mythology. Such is Mr. Waugh's private religion, on which he has superimposed Catholicism, much as newly-converted pagans are said to superimpose a Christian nomenclature on their ancient cults and trees and thunder.

Richard Ellmann ROBARTES AND

AHERNE: Two Sides of a Penny

SINCE Yeats's death in 1939 he has faded, as he would have wished, into a group of myths. Critics, friends, and biographers have built up a variety of unconnected pictures of him. We are given the nervous romantic sighing through the reeds of the eighties and nineties and the worldly realist plain-speaking in the

---

[3] His father tells us that "We chose Lancing for Evelyn . . . because he had always shown a deeply religious temperament" (*One Man's Road*, page 367).

twenties; we have the businessman founding and directing the Abbey Theatre in broad day, the wan young Celt haunting the twilight, and the occultist practicing nocturnal incantations; we can choose between the dignified Nobel Prize winner who was also Senator of the Irish Free State, and his successor, the libidinous old man who translated the Upanishads. Some of his acquaintances describe him as shy and modest, others as arrogant and domineering; some say he was a moonstruck dreamer, others that he was a practical man with a keen eye on the box office. These portraits are not easily reconcilable, and the tendency has been, instead of reconciling, to prove certain of them inessential or to split up the poet's life into dozens of unrelated episodes.

No period of his life is more confused in biographical accounts than that from 1887, when in his twenty-first year he went to London, to 1896, when at the age of thirty-one he first stayed with Lady Gregory at Coole Park. During these years his writings varied from Irish folk ballads and dialect stories to the most elaborate Pre-Raphaelite verse and prose; he joined all manner of societies, from occult groups to Irish and English literary coteries to the revolutionary Irish Republican Brotherhood. He has so many interests and activities during this period, with so little obvious relation between them, that a strictly chronological account would give the impression of a man in frenzy, beating on every door in the hotel in an attempt to find his own room. But the maze was not without a plan, and in searching it out we may find a clue to the chameleon-like transformations which occur so frequently in his life.

We should not expect an easy explanation. Yeats grew up with no simple view of his own character; even as a boy he had begun to pose before the world as something different from what he was, and by late adolescence he had come to think of himself as divided into two parts. This sense of a bifurcated self was not, as he then thought it, unique, and if we consider the tendency as a general one we can avoid regarding Yeats as an anomaly, or his writings as a manifestation of the divided consciousness common in cases of hysteria.

We tread here on perilous ground, for what seems to be involved is a subtle change in mental climate during the nineteenth century. The nature of the change suggests itself if we take note of the different conceptions of personality held by Byron at the century's beginning and by Oscar Wilde at its close. The Byronic hero, Manfred or the Giaour, was a man outwardly calm but preyed upon by passions which he could not keep his fiery eyes from showing, and by a secret sin which eventually destroyed him by its intensity. He scorned societal values, his life welled up within him as an uncontrollable force, driving him to incest, revolution, murder, suicide.

In the course of the century this hero fell out of favor. To Wilde the true hero was not this man of unrestrainable passions, but the man whose passions had been tempered and refined into another self which was consciously fabricated, *posed*. "Create yourself," he said, "be yourself your pose." Wilde's view is that a man is really two men: the natural man and the manufactured man. One evidence of this split, which goes beyond literature, is the verbal distinction that becomes common towards the end of the nineteenth century between personality and character, the former as in some way the conscious product of the latter. Wilde, because he was compelled by his sexual abnormality to lead a double life, felt the split acutely and founded much of his art upon the tension between the pose and the real self, the importance of being and of not being earnest, between Dorian Gray and his picture. But his contemporaries understood the divided self too. Dr. Jekyll and Mr. Hyde and Beerbohm's *Happy Hypocrite* have much in common with Dorian Gray. The last decade of the century is thronged by extravagant poseurs like Lionel Johnson and Aubrey Beardsley; even James Joyce, growing up in this age, says he felt compelled to "cultivate the enigma of a manner." An extreme example is William Sharp, who wrote some of his books under the pseudonym of Fiona Macleod, and became so obsessed with his dual personality that he almost collapsed under the strain.

Yeats came to maturity in this atmosphere of doubling and splitting of the self, but his mental growth was parallel to that of other writers and did not derive from them. His own divided consciousness had its origin in his attempt as a child to revolt against the rationalist, scientific, materialist world of intellectual Dublin with which he associated his father; he tried desperately,

but not very successfully, to ally himself instead with the spontaneous, instinctive, unself-conscious life which his mother's family
lived in Sligo on the west coast of Ireland. Terrified by his father's
religious scepticism, of which his mother also disapproved, he
still could not escape it; he would have liked to dream the days
away in Sligo, but he wanted also to be a success in the world.
The inner struggle was dramatized in adolescence by his difficulties
with sexual desire; he had a continual battle with his senses and
was filled with self-loathing at what he thought was an unnatural
and horrible state of mind. Thus many personal factors, and beyond
these the spirit of the times, made him see his life as a quarrel
between two parts of his being.

As early as his nineteenth year he was already formulating a
theory about his divided consciousness. At that time he was greatly
excited by a friend's drawing which showed a man on a mountain,
terrified by his own gigantic shadow in the mist. The theme appears
in many of the poems which he wrote at the age of twenty-one
or twenty-two; the birds in one poem, for example, ponder on their
own shadows in the water; the dewdrops listen for the sound of
their own dropping; the parrot rages at his own image in the
enamelled sea. He began work on a play which was to have as
its hero a wanderer who travelled over all the world in a fruitless
effort to escape from *himself*.

When Yeats went to London in May, 1887, his sense of internal
division was made more complex and intense. He was then almost
twenty-two, painfully turned inwards, self-conscious and aware
of the vast gulf between what he was in actuality and what he
was in his dreams. Inordinately conscious of his own clumsiness,
he remembered all his life how Oscar Wilde sneered at the color
of his yellow shoes, and thought that he was constantly committing
gaffes. To a poor Irishman, longing for recognition, London
seemed alien and hostile. Yeats often dreamed of beating a retreat
to Sligo, and did in fact continually go to stay with his uncle there.
His early letters give a remarkable picture of maladjustment. "This
hateful London," he says again and again, "is always horrible
to me."

Yeats's father feared lest his son, in this dreary mood, abstract
himself too far from life, and therefore urged him to write a story

about real people. The young man accordingly wrote *John Sherman*. He took the personal problems which beset him and used them as material for fiction; in *John Sherman* it is easy to see that his real subject matter is himself, and that he has cut himself definitely into two parts. His dreamy nature is symbolized by Sherman, a young man who prefers his little town in the west of Ireland to every other place, and is empty of all ambition except to marry a rich woman so that he need do nothing but dream his life away. The counterpart to Sherman is the energetic William Howard, a High Church curate, a lover of cities and man of the world. In the story Sherman, like Yeats, is lured off to London for a time and works as a clerk in an office there. He at last has the opportunity to marry a rich girl, but knows that with her his dream life is impossible. He therefore cleverly manages to turn his fiancée over to Howard, while he himself goes back to a childhood sweetheart in the west of Ireland. There he will settle down to farming and dreaming.

The antithesis between Sherman and Howard was fairly completely worked out, with Yeats's sympathies obviously very much on Sherman's side. He knew that he must either go back or go forward: Sligo meant rest and peace, which he loved, while London meant turmoil and constant endangerment of his dreams. The traits of the two characters show the nature of the choice as it looked to Yeats at the end of 1888, when he was twenty-three: Sherman is rude and unconventional, while Howard is elegant and decorous; Sherman is vaguely heterodox, Howard is a High Church curate; Sherman is devious, Howard conscientious and candid; Sherman self-conscious, Howard self-possessed; Sherman escapist, Howard worldly.

When we remember that Yeats is both characters, we see that he himself had made no choice. He was aware of the fact and in the story symbolized it in a chess game that Sherman plays against himself, right hand against left. Yeats had in fact come to the stage which he later described in *A Vision*, where man "is suspended; he is without bias," and "only a shock resulting from the greatest possible conflict can make the greatest possible change."

The shock came on January 30, 1889, when Maud Gonne knocked on the door of the family's house. Yeats immediately fell in love with the beautiful young patriot, and the question became, which of his two selves should he show her? He could not use duplicity, he had to reveal to her his inmost heart, so with her he was John Sherman, the wild yet timid dreamer. Yet at the same time he knew that this ambitious beauty would be satisfied only if he were a master of men as well, who could carry her over a mountain in his arms. He could not hope to attract her to a farm life in the west of Ireland; no turning back to Sligo was possible any more. To win her he would have to be a revolutionary, organizing and building for his country.

But this would be to deny his dreamy, ineffectual self and to play the part of another. Can true love be secured through artifice? So long as love is unsuccessful it satisfies his dreaming nature; once successful, it is no longer wholly honest. Had Maud Gonne returned his love, as she did not, he would have feared that she loved him for qualities superimposed upon his natural ones. For underneath he knew that he was far from perfect; he thought of himself as full of weaknesses, and felt that if she loved him, unaware of his weaknesses, she would be deceived. The only solution was to love her in vain. That intermediate state suited him, and he glorified during the nineties all indeterminate things. He would choose finally neither one state nor the other, neither dream nor act, but the crepuscular state between spirit and sense where he was *not committed*. The twilight demanded no decision. He filled his poems with dim, pale things, and longed to return to an island like Innisfree, because an island was neither mainland nor water, but something of both, and because the return to Sligo would be a return to the pre-pubertal stage when his consciousness had not yet been split in two.

One wonders how a young man in this state of mind could act at all. Would not dream cancel out action and action dream? As a matter of fact, during this period his father remarked that Yeats was spending a great deal of time in bed. But the poet had also evolved a stratagem which prevented him from being inert; he could, when necessary, leave the dreaming Sherman behind and take over the active role of Howard. Under the pressure of his new love he did this more and more often. Tentatively but with increasing assurance, he adopted the role of Irish revolutionary and political organizer. To guide himself when he played this part he had the twin doctrines of passion and failure. The great thing in life, he thought, was to express one's whole passionate self; hence the active man throws himself with the utmost energy into what he does, and expresses himself always with reckless vehemence and confidence. But life does not reward the man of action with success; he must try to change Ireland or the world, or to win his mistress' favor, and fail, and in failure find apotheosis. Yeats makes a cult of frustration, and courts defeat like a lover. Even as he spurs himself and his friends on to preparing for the Irish revolution, he tells them that they will not attain their goal; and in his love poems he predicts his own defeat. His flaming desires are mixed with asbestos.

So much a part of him did his theories of unsuccessful action and unsatisfied love become that in his thirtieth and thirty-first years, when a beautiful married woman fell in love with him, he spent the first year in idealized chastity; and then, when they finally consummated their passion, he kept expecting love to end until finally it did, and he returned to his former hopeless adoration of Maud Gonne and to his twilit state between chastity and unchastity.

But his life was changing. Maud Gonne was a public figure, and to meet her on her own ground he had to spend far more time on public activities, so that the dream life, even though reinforced with the support of occult lore, became harder to keep intact. In view of the persistent parallelism between Yeats's life and works we should expect to find some reflection of this change in his writings. When he next separates himself into two parts, in some stories written in his thirtieth year, the antinomies are not the same as Sherman and Howard. Now he calls his two characters Michael Robartes and John Aherne, symbolic personages who recur in his writings during the rest of his life. Robartes is described as having features that are "something between" those of "a debauchee, a saint, and a peasant." He thus reflects Yeats's love affair with the married woman, then well under way, his occult bent and idealism, and his affection for the simpler life of Sligo. Robartes' counterpart, sometimes represented as simply the author, sometimes as John Aherne, is a pious Catholic on the verge of becoming a Dominican monk. Aherne is greatly tempted by Robartes, who tries to draw him into his Order of the Alchemical Rose, and thus into a world which fills him "with terror." That Aherne is a Catholic is not to be understood as meaning that Yeats himself was strongly attracted to Catholicism; he used that faith as a convenient dramatic symbol of conventional and prudent belief.

Aherne is always on the verge of giving way to Robartes' temptations, but always draws back in time. He is the conventional man, the refusing, abstract self which is counterposed to the daring mysterious Robartes. Aherne has "never looked out of the eye of a saint / Or out of drunkard's eye." He is the public man, as Robartes is the private one. Where in *John Sherman* the title character is obviously the more essential to Yeats's personality, in these stories about Robartes and Aherne it is difficult to know which is primary. While Robartes in many ways resembles Sherman, he is addicted to that ceremonialism and ritualism which Yeats had previously attributed not to Sherman but to Howard. In other respects, too, the characters are different. Robartes is more active and aggressive, and yet more full of dreams than Aherne, who is contemplative and withdrawn and yet favorable to worldly faiths and ways. The distribution of characteristics is more complex than in the earlier tale.

While this change could be interpreted as merely an elaboration of the storyteller's art, Yeats's almost constant use of autobiographical material suggests that it reflects the change which had taken place in his life between 1889, when he met Maud Gonne, and 1896, when he wrote the stories about Robartes. He was less certain now that he was by nature an escapist like Sherman, for dreaming and writing poetry had become more difficult for him now that he had begun to demonstrate his ability to organize nationalist groups and to play a part in Irish politics. He had become much more independent, too, of his father, for late in 1895 he moved away from the family and took rooms of his own. The change is apparent in his letters to his father, which in 1894, when he was twenty-nine, still begin, "My dear Papa," but in 1895 begin, "My dear Father." The alteration within was reflected by an alteration without, in manners and clothes. His manners, it is true, were still far from perfect; when he and Arthur Symons visited a wealthy Irish landowner in 1896, Yeats to Symons' horror proposed that they toss a coin to see who should get the better room. But in general he was much more at ease. He began to wear more conventional clothes and to dress with fastidiousness and care, and his friends noted a sudden increase in posing and posturing.

Yeats had now a considerable reputation, but where most men as they become successful become inwardly harmonious, he continued to see himself as the divided man. He functioned in two very separate spheres: on the one hand he was a prominent public figure in the Irish nationalist movement; on the other he was, like Robartes, a member of a secret order of occultists called the Golden Dawn. In this opposition, and its many variants, is the solution to many of the difficulties of the poet's biography. As he grew older he gave up the twilight where he was uncommitted, and began to commit himself violently, now on the side of Aherne, now on the side of Robartes. He evolved new terms for the antinomies, and theorized for years about the relations between face and mask and between self and anti-self. He felt justified in swinging from one end of the pendulum to another, and found nothing inconsistent in translating the Upanishads at the same time as he was writing unpublishable obscene verse. Both were legitimate expressions of his divided self. In the same way he developed a haughty, commanding demeanor, but always thought of himself, even when he had immortality in his pocket, as a timid man.

The effect upon his verse was to generate tremendous overtones of conflict. Thus in "Sailing to Byzantium," he celebrates life even as he rejects it, while in "A Dialogue of Self and Soul," he reviles life even as he accepts it. We feel that every poem is a battleground, with the sounds of gunfire audible throughout, and victory is won by one side or the other only after the fiercest struggle. Yeats's life may be read as a progressive reformulation of his inner conflict through the medium of lyrical verse.

For him this was no mere feat of intellectual gymnastics. It required courage and will to descend "into the abyss of himself" and perpetually re-examine the postulates of his being. The struggle to fix into a pattern the writhings and twistings of his mind was for him desperate and all-important, yet no pattern sufficed him for long because it was too forcible an arrest of the changing world. In the light of new experience every formulation had to be destroyed and a new one attempted. Few poets have found mastery of themselves so difficult or have sought it, through conflict and struggle, so unflinchingly.

W. H. Auden YEATS AS AN

EXAMPLE

ONE drawback, and not the least, of practicing any art is that it becomes very difficult to enjoy the works of one's fellow artists, living or dead, simply for their own sakes.

When a poet, for instance, reads a poem written by another, he is apt to be less concerned with what the latter actually accomplished by his poem than with the suggestions it throws out upon how he, the reader, may solve the poetic problems which confront him now. His judgments of poetry, therefore, are rarely purely aesthetic; he will often prefer an inferior poem from which he can learn something at the moment to a better poem from which he can learn nothing. This gap between his evaluations and those of the pure critic is all the wider in the case of his immediate predecessors. All generations overlap, and the young poet naturally looks for and finds the greatest help in the work of those whose poetic problems are similar to his because they have experiences in common. He begins, therefore, with an excessive admiration for one or more of the mature poets of his time. But, as he grows older, he becomes more and more conscious of belonging to a different generation faced with problems that his heroes cannot help him to solve, and his former hero-worship, as in other spheres of life, is all too apt to turn into an equally excessive hostility and contempt. Those of us who, like myself, have learned, as we think, all we can, and that is a good deal, from Yeats, are tempted to be more conscious and more critical of those elements in his poems with which we are not in sympathy than we ought to be. Our criticisms may sometimes be objectively correct, but the subjective resentment with which we make them is always unjust. Further, as long as we harbor such a resentment, it will be a dangerous hindrance to our own poetic development, for, in poetry as in life, to lead one's own life means to relive the lives of one's parents and, through them, of all one's ancestors; the duty of the present is neither to copy nor to deny the past but to resurrect it.

I shall not attempt, therefore, in this paper, to answer such questions as, "How good a poet is Yeats? Which are his best poems and why"—that is the job of better critics than I and of posterity—but rather to consider him as a predecessor whose importance no one will or can deny, to raise, that is to say, such questions as "What were the problems which faced Yeats as a poet as compared with ours? How far do they overlap? How far are they different? In so far as they are different, what can we learn from the way in which Yeats dealt with his world, about how to deal with our own?"

Let me begin with the element in his work which seems most foreign to us, his cosmology, his concern with the occult. Here, I think, is a curious fact. In most cases, when a major writer influences a beginner, that influence extends to his matter, to his opinions as well as to his manner—think of Hardy, or Eliot, or D. H. Lawrence; yet, though there is scarcely a lyric written today in which the influence of his style and rhythm is not detectable, one whole side of Yeats, the side summed up in the *Vision,* has left virtually no trace.

However diverse our fundamental beliefs may be, the reaction of most of us to all that occult is, I fancy, the same: How on earth, we wonder, could a man of Yeats's gifts take such nonsense seriously? I have a further bewilderment, which may be due to my English upbringing, one of snobbery. How *could* Yeats, with his

great aesthetic appreciation of aristocracy, ancestral houses, cere-
monious tradition, take up something so essentially lower-middle
class—or should I say Southern Californian—so ineluctably associated with suburban villas and clearly unattractive faces? A. E.
Housman's pessimistic stoicism seems to me nonsense too, but at
least it is a kind of nonsense that can be believed by a gentleman—
but mediums, spells, the Mysterious Orient—*how* embarrassing.
In fact, of course, it is to Yeats's credit, and an example to me, that
he ignored such considerations, nor, granted that his Weltanschauung was false, can we claim credit for rejecting what we have
no temptation to accept, nor deny that the poetry he wrote involving it is very good. What we should consider, then, is firstly, why
Celtic mythology in his earlier phases, and occult symbolism in his
later, should have attracted Yeats when they fail to attract us;
secondly, what are the comparable kinds of beliefs to which we
are drawn and why; thirdly, what is the relation between myth,
belief, and poetry?

Yeats's generation grew up in a world where the great conflict
was between the Religion of Reason and the Religion of Imagination, objective truth and subjective truth, the Universal and the Individual.

Further, Reason, Science, the general, seemed to be winning
and Imagination, Art, and the individual on the defensive. Now
in all conflicts it is the side which takes the offensive that defines
the issues which their opponents have to defend, so that when scientists said, "Science is knowledge of reality, Art is a fairyland," the
artists were driven to reply, "Very well, but fairies are fun, science
is dull." When the former said, "Art has no relation to life," the
latter retorted, "Thank God." To the assertion that "every mind
can recognize the absolute truths of science, but the values of art
are purely relative, an arbitrary affair of individual taste," came
back the counterclaim, "Only the exceptional individual matters."

Thus, if we find Yeats adopting a cosmology apparently on
purely aesthetic grounds, i.e., not because it is true but because
it is interesting; or Joyce attempting to convert the whole of existence into words; or even a dialectician like Shaw, after the most
brilliant and devastating criticism of the pretensions of scientists,
spoiling his case by being a crank and espousing Lamarckism, we

must see their reactions, I think, if we are to understand them, in terms of a polemical situation in which they accepted—they probably could do nothing else—the anthithesis between reason and imagination which the natural sciences of their time forced upon them, only reversing, with the excessive violence of men defending a narrow place against superior numbers, the value signs on each side.

Our situation is somewhat different. The true natural sciences like physics and chemistry no longer claim to explain the meaning of life (that presumption has passed to the so-called Social Sciences) nor—at least since the Atom Bomb—would any one believe them if they did. The division of which we are aware is not between Reason and Imagination but between the good and evil will, not between objectivity and subjectivity but between the integration of thought and feeling and their dissociation, not between the individual and the masses but between the social person and the impersonal state.

Consequently the dangers that beset us are different. We are unlikely to believe something because it would be fun to believe it; but we are very likely to do one of two things, either to say that everything is relative, that there is no absolute truth, or that those who do not hold what we believe to be absolute reject it out of malice.

When two people today engage in an argument, each tends to spend half of his time and energy not in producing evidence to support his point of view but in looking for the hidden motives which are causing his opponent to hold his. If they lose their tempers, instead of saying, "You are a fool," they say, "You are a wicked man."

No one now asserts that art ought not to describe immoral persons or acts; but many assert that it must show those on the right side as perfectly moral and those on the wrong as completely immoral. An artist today is less likely than his predecessors to claim that his profession is supremely important but he is much more likely to sacrifice his artistic integrity for economic or political reward.

No private citizen today thinks seriously, "Here is superior me and there are all those other people"; but "Here are we, all in

the same boat, and there is It, the Government." We are not likely
to become snobs—the great houses have become state institutions
anyway—but we can all too easily become anarchists who, by pas-
sively refusing to take any part in political life, or by acting blindly
in terms of our own advantage alone, promote the loss of that very
individual liberty we would like to keep.

To return from life to poetry: any poet today, even if he deny
the importance of dogma to life, can see how useful myths are to
poetry—how much, for instance, they helped Yeats to make his
private experiences public and his vision of public events personal.
He knows, too, that in poetry all dogmas become myths; that the
aesthetic value of the poem is the same whether the poet and/or
the reader actively believe what it says or not. He is apt then to
look around for some myth—any myth, he thinks, will do—to
serve the same purpose for himself. What he overlooks is that the
only kind of myth which will do for him must have one thing in
common with believed dogma, namely, that the relation of the former to the poet, as of the latter to the soul, must be a personal one.
The Celtic legends Yeats used were woven into his childhood—he
really went to seances, he seriously studied all those absurd books.
You cannot use a Weltanschauung like Psychoanalysis or Marxism
or Christianity as a poetic myth unless it involves your emotions
profoundly, and, if you have not inherited it, your emotions will
not become involved unless you take it more seriously than as a
mere myth.

Yeats, like us, was faced with the modern problem, i.e., of
living in a society in which men are no longer supported by tradition without being aware of it, and in which, therefore, every individual who wishes to bring order and coherence into the stream of
sensations, emotions, and ideas entering his consciousness, from
without and within, is forced to do deliberately for himself what
in previous ages had been done for him by family, custom, church,
and state, namely the choice of the principles and presuppositions in
terms of which he can make sense of his experience. There are, of
course, always authorities in each field, but which expert he is to
consult and which he is to believe are matters on which he is
obliged to exercise his own free choice. This is very annoying for the
artist as it takes up much time which he would greatly prefer to

spend on his proper work, where he is a professional and not an amateur.

Because Yeats accepted the fact that we have lost the old nonchalance of the hand, being critics who but half create,

> *Timid, entangled, empty and abashed*
> *Lacking the countenance of our friends,*

accepted it as a working condition and faced its consequences, he is an example to all who come after him. That is one reason why he may be called a major poet. There are others.

The difference between major and minor poetry has nothing to do with the difference between better and worse poetry. Indeed it is frequently the case that a minor poet produces more single poems which seem flawless than a major one, because it is one of the distinguishing marks of a major poet that he continues to develop, that the moment he has learnt how to write one kind of poem, he goes on to attempt something else, new subjects, new ways of treatment or both, an attempt in which he may quite possibly fail. He invariably feels, as Yeats puts it, "the fascination of what's difficult"; or, in another poem,

> *I made my song a coat*
> *Covered with embroideries*
> *Out of old mythologies*
> *From heel to throat;*
> *But the fools caught it,*
> *Wore it in the world's eyes*
> *As though they'd wrought it.*
> *Song, let them take it,*
> *For there's more enterprise*
> *In walking naked.*

Further, the major poet not only attempts to solve new problems, but the problems he attacks are central to the tradition, and the lines along which he attacks them, while they are his own, are not idiosyncratic, but produce results which are available to his successors. Much as I admire his work, I consider Hopkins a minor poet, and one of my reasons for thinking so is that his attempt to develop a rhetoric to replace the Tennysonian rhetoric is too eccentric, the proof of which is that he cannot influence later poets in any fruitful way; they can only imitate him. Yeats on the other hand has effected changes which are of use to every poet. His contributions are not, I think, to new subject matter, nor to the ways in which poetic material can be organized—where Eliot for instance has made it possible for English poetry to deal with all the properties of modern city life, and to write poems in which the structure is musical rather than logical. Yeats sticks to the conventional romantic properties and the traditional step-by-step structure of stanzaic verse. His main legacies to us are two. First, he transformed a certain kind of poem, the occasional poem, from being either an official performance of impersonal virtuosity or a trivial *vers de société* into a serious reflective poem of at once personal and public interest.

A poem such as *In Memory of Major Robert Gregory* is something new and important in the history of English poetry. It never loses the personal note of a man speaking about his personal friends in a particular setting—in *Adonais,* for instance, both Shelley and Keats disappear as people—and at the same time the occasion and the characters acquire a symbolic public significance.

Secondly, Yeats released regular stanzaic poetry, whether reflective or lyrical, from iambic monotony; the Elizabethans did this originally for dramatic verse, but not for lyric or elegiac. Thus:

> *What youthful mother, a shape upon her lap*
> *Honey of generation had betrayed,*
> *And that must sleep, shriek, struggle to escape*
> *As recollection or the drug decide,*
> *Would think her son, did she but see that shape*
> *With sixty or more winters on its head,*
> *A compensation for the pang of his birth,*
> *Or the uncertainty of his setting forth?*

Or take this:

> *Acquaintance; companion;*
> *One dear brilliant woman;*
> *The best endowed, the elect*

All by their youth undone,
All, all, by that inhuman
Bitter glory wrecked.

But I have straightened out
Ruin, wreck and wrack;
I toiled long years and at length
Came to so deep a thought
I can summon back
All their wholesome strength.

What images are these
That turn dull-eyed away,
Or shift Time's filthy load,
Straighten aged knees,
Hesitate or stay?
What heads shake or nod?

In spite of all the rhythmical variations and the half-rhymes which provide freedom for the most natural and lucid speech, the formal base, i.e., the prosodic rhythms of iambic pentameter in the first, and iambic trimeter in the second, and the rhyme patterns which supply coherent dignity and music, these remain audible.

The magazine *Vogue* once prepared, I believe, two series of photographs, one called Contemporary Great, the other Contemporary Influences, a project calculated to cause considerable ill-feeling. Does a man feel prouder of what he achieves himself or of the effect he has on the achievements of posterity? Which epitaph upon a poet's grave would please him more: "I wrote some of the most beautiful poetry of my time" or "I rescued English lyric from the dead hand of Campion and Tom Moore"? I suspect that more poets would prefer the second than their readers would ever guess, particularly when, like Yeats, they are comfortably aware that the first is also true.

Richard Chase THE STONE AND

THE CRUCIFIXION: Faulkner's

Light in August

WITHOUT ado I wish to direct attention to the symbolic texture of *Light in August*. This texture is very much a matter of mechanics and dynamics—a poetry of physics. Repeatedly Faulkner presents appearance, event, and even character in the images of stasis, motion, velocity, weight, lightness, mass, line, relative position, circle, sphere, emptiness, fullness, light, and dark. The phrase "light in August" has at least two meanings. As Mr. Malcolm Cowley informs us in his *Portable Faulkner*, the phrase means "light" as opposed to "heavy" and refers to a pregnant woman who will give birth in August. And it also means "light" as opposed to "dark"—an affirmation of life and human spirit. *Light in August* may be described, in Faulkner's own words (though he is describing something else), as "the mechanics, the theatring of evil." This is not a complete or fully fair description of Faulkner's novel, but it is complete and fair enough to demand that we look at the novel from this point of view—and that we finally ask, How successful is the author in extending his account of the mechanics and theatring of evil into an account of the human situation?

The reader of *Light in August* will be puzzled in the first few pages by what may be called "the string of beads image." We read that the wagon in which Lena Grove rides through the August afternoon is like "a shabby bead upon a mild red string of road" and that the village beside the railroad, from which she begins her long journey is like "a forgotten bead from a broken string." Later our attention is called to the row of iron bars in the fence which surrounds the orphanage of Joe Christmas' childhood, to the identical windows of a street car, to a picket fence, and to the rows of identical white houses in which the lower-middle-class whites live. To these images of linear discreteness Faulkner opposes images of the curve. Lena Grove—searching for Lucas Burch, the father of her unborn child—passes through "a long monotonous succession of peaceful and undeviating changes from day to dark and dark to day"; but her mode of action and of consciousness is not of the order of the "string of beads." She is "like something moving forever and without progress across an urn." For her the road is not linear but like a string "being rewound onto a spool." These images of linear discreteness and curve are extended into one of the central images of the book: flight and pursuit.

We have already encountered the symbolic representation of two realms of being which are counterposed throughout the novel. The linear discrete image stands for "modernism": abstraction, rationalism, applied science, capitalism, progressivism, emasculation, the atomized consciousness and its pathological extensions. The curve image stands for holistic consciousness, a containing culture and tradition, the cyclical life and death of all the creatures of earth. Throughout the novel, Lena retains her holistic consciousness and she is strong, enduring, hopeful. All the other characters in one way or another are victims of the linear delusion. For Joe Christmas, in whom the linear consciousness becomes pathological, the curve image is a "cage" or a "prison" to be broken out of. Or it is something to be gashed from the outside so that whatever it contains will be spilled meaninglessly out. Joe gashes the whisky tins he and Burch have buried in the woods as he has a vision of trees in the moonlight, standing like "a row of suavely shaped urns," each one cracked and extruding "something liquid, death-colored, and foul." At the end, when Joe can no longer perform this symbolic act of even smashing, the curve image becomes the fateful circle of repetition which he has never really either escaped or broken and which is the only path to the only kind of holism he will ever find: death. "I have never got outside that circle. I have never broken out of the ring of what I have already done and cannot ever undo." The tragic irony of the linear consciousness, Faulkner seems to say, is that it is an illusion; all consciousness is holistic, but it may be the holism of life (Lena) or of death (Joe). The remarkable symbol of the wheel in the passage describing the final madness of the Reverend Mr. Hightower presumably coincides with Joe's circle of doom, though here it may symbolize the completion in death of a cycle of legendary family history.

Faulkner's counterposing of motionlessness and motion seems to imply a fairly consistent deploying of polarity of character. Lena, Joe, and Hightower each has a certain kind of motionlessness. Lena, "her voice quite grave now, quite quiet," sitting "quite still, her hands motionless upon her lap," has the inner quiet of the wheel's axle, a stillness within movement. The stillness behind Joe's cold, contemptuous mask is the abstract stillness of separation, a schizoid disengagement from outer action. The motionlessness of Hightower, sitting "rigidly" behind his desk, his "forearms parallel upon the armrests of the chair," is the negation of the will and action by fear, "denial," and impotence.

The quality of Joe's action is simply a willed translation of his separateness. Whenever he is in motion, in fantasy or actuality, he is in flight; and this is true even of his many connections with women—these also he must turn into the pattern of flight whenever they threaten to bring him too close to the kind of central and holistic place represented by Lena. Although Burch is throughout the book in a sense in flight from Lena, Byron Bunch, or the sheriff, his movements entirely lack Joe's willed abstract control. He is pure aimless motion, a rural poor white uprooted and cast adrift in an industrial-urban society. "He puts me in mind," says Byron Bunch, "of one of these cars running along the street with a radio in it. You can't make out what it is saying and the car ain't going anywhere in particular and when you look at it close you see that there ain't even anybody in it." A friend of Bunch's replies, "Yes, he puts me in mind of a horse. Not a mean horse. Just a worthless horse." This rude progression of metaphors will serve to indicate that Faulkner's imagination very frequently ap-

proaches the level of human character and consciousness beginning
with the mechanical, and proceeding to the animal level through
an intermediate level of dynamics.

The denouement of the novel can be conceived as the final
resolution of several kinds of motion. Byron Bunch separates
himself from his spiritual kinship with Hightower and his hitherto
meaningless life finds its repose in Lena. Burch moves away from
Lena, dooming himself, as it were, to aimless perpetual motion.
The final flight of Joe to Hightower's house may seem too little
explained as part of the plot. But it has a symbolic significance,
since Joe, turning away for the last time from the realm of being
which is represented by Lena and which he has tried to find in
his various women, finds his ultimate refuge in the castration
and death vouchsafed to him by Percy Grimm (only the last of
all the symbolic castrations and deaths he has first sought and
then endured). Hightower himself had turned away from the
Lena-holism when years earlier he had in effect pursued his wife
out of existence by believing in his fantasy that his "seed" had
died with his grandfather in the Civil War.

2

Mr. Robert Penn Warren suggests that Faulkner's objection
to the modern world is that it lacks the ability to set up "codes,
concepts of virtue, obligations" by which man can "define himself
as human" and "accept the risks of his humanity." In *Light in
August*, Faulkner seems to be concerned with showing that the
codes modern man *does* set up do *not* allow him to define himself
as human—that codes have become compulsive patterns which
man clings to in fear and trembling while the pattern emasculates
him. Byron Bunch, wondering why he lives to the split second
by his big silver watch and works alone in the planing mill every
Saturday afternoon and why the Reverend Mr. Hightower has
refused to leave Jefferson, the scene of his ruin and disgrace,
reflects, "It is because a fellow is more afraid of the trouble he
might have than he ever is of the trouble he's already got. He'll
cling to trouble he's used to before he'll risk a change." Byron
and Hightower have for years been sustaining one another in
their "patterns." Their relationship ends over the question of

Bunch's aiding and courting Lena, pregnant with another man's child. The dilemma for each is whether to stick to a pattern of behavior which prohibits accepting "the risks of his humanity" or becoming involved responsibly in a human situation. Byron chooses to break the pattern and accept the consequences of intervention. Hightower remains in the pattern (though he makes certain senile excursions from it), choosing to conspire in closing the circle of his destiny, choosing separation and madness. It is not true, as has been said, that all of Faulkner's characters are rigidly controlled by fate: Byron, for one, is left free to choose his own fate.

Joe Christmas is in many ways a masterful portrait of a man whose earliest years have been spent in an institution—an experience, as the psychiatrists show, which definitively affects not only the emotional centers of the victim but also the character of his conceptual thinking. In the forbidding orphanage (a true symbol of the conditions of modern life) Joe finds a surrogate mother—a cynical, suspicious and indeed almost paranoiac dietitian, a mockery of the Nursing Mother of the myths. His surrogate father is an obscenely fanatical inquisitor and peeping tom who functions as the janitor of the orphanage and who later turns out to be Joe's grandfather. The pattern of Joe's life is inexorably formed when the dietitian finds that he has been hiding in her closet eating toothpaste while she has been entertaining an interne on her bed (the tube of toothpaste is another urn symbol). The definitive event is not that Joe has seen the dietitian in the act but that she fails to punish him and instead offers him money not to tell. Having felt terribly guilty, having expected and even wanted to be punished, and having had no idea of giving away the secret, he is irretrievably shocked when she offers him the money. He had wanted the woman to engross him in her life, if only by beating him. Instead she denies him this engrossment and gives him a silver dollar, whose shining circumference forms a circle Joe will never break through. Joe's homosexualism is another theme symbolized by the "string of beads" image. The relationship between Joe and his guardian, McEachern, a fanatical apostle of a parochial and degenerate Presbyterianism who beats Joe with the impersonal violence of a machine, has for both McEachern and Joe the uneasy satisfaction of an abnormal but vehemently pure sexual alliance. McEachern has succeeded with Joe where the dietitian failed. Joe finds the relationship "perfectly logical and reasonable and inescapable," and he quickly learns to hate Mrs. McEachern because her proffered feminine kindnesses always threaten to taint an abstract and predictable relationship—just as the food she offers him makes him sick (all the women in Joe's life try to feed him; one of them is a waitress in a restaurant).

Joe's many adventures with women are attempts to escape the abstract quality of a latently homosexual life. As Joe pauses outside Miss Burden's house before keeping a tryst with her, Faulkner says, "The dark was filled with the voices, myriad, out of all time that he had known, as though all the past was a flat pattern. And going on: tomorrow night, all the tomorrows, to be part of the flat pattern, going on." "Then," says Faulkner, "it was time"—which seems to be a pun (the same one occurs in *The Sound and the Fury*) meaning that now Joe's existence can be measured by time (the urn consciousness) rather than by the abstraction of eternity. But the connection with Miss Burden, like all of Joe's connections with women, turns into a ritual reaffirmation that no such connection is possible, a circular path back to the compulsive pattern—as we see when after various ingenious phases of sexual flight and pursuit, Miss Burden, before Joe kills her, is transmuted in appearance and behavior into a mocking likeness of McEachern. The sexual dilemma of Joe's life is nicely symbolized in the episode where he lolls in the woods (and gashes the whisky tins) reading a magazine "of that type whose covers bear either pictures of young women in underclothes or pictures of men shooting one another with pistols." He reads as a man "walking along the street might count the cracks in the pavement, to the last final page, the last and final word." He goes through life with this same attachment to his pattern, hating the women in underclothes, longing for a purely masculine annihilation.

In symbolic polarity to the compulsive pattern we have Lena, who does not need to flee from involvement in human life, and Lucas Burch. Distantly adumbrating all the polarities of *Light in August,* the gay, irresponsible, aimless Burch symbolizes pure Chaos. Perhaps through the child in Lena's womb, Burch symbolizes the undetermined possibility of a future the direction of which will be decided by the final resolution of forces among the other characters. If so, we may say that *Light in August* is a "hopeful" book. For the future is in the hands of Lena and Byron Bunch—a woman who endures and loves and a man who has decided to "accept the risks of his humanity."

3

Mr. Warren suggests that we ought not to think of Faulkner as an exclusively Southern writer but as a writer concerned with modern times in general. To this, one might add that Faulkner has many affinities with both Hawthorne and Melville. As Malcolm Cowley has said, the myth of a Southern society which emerges from Faulkner's work as a whole can be compared with Hawthorne's myth of New England. One might add that the dilemma with which Faulkner confronts Bunch and Hightower—whether to take the responsibility of moral intervention in human affairs—is the same dilemma which confronts many of Hawthorne's characters (for example, the painter in "Prophetic Pictures"). Joe Christmas would be recognized by Hawthorne; for he is frightened and obsessed by the inescapable stain on every human life. There is never any real proof that Joe is part Negro, but Joe's gratuitous assumption that he is tainted is at the root of all his actions. He becomes as obsessed with his stain as does Aylmer with the blemish on his wife's face in Hawthorne's "The Birthmark" and with a purpose as relentless and immoral as Aylmer's he goes about removing the stain—an impulse which arises in the central figures of both "The Birthmark" and *Light in August* from what is, in the final moral terms, simply their inability to bear the burden of being human. (The word "burden," by the way, seems to have the same significance for the Southern writers as the pack of the peddler had for Hawthorne and Melville: the "burden" of one's history or of one's continually self-annihilating humanity. Miss Burden, in *Light in August,* is not the only character in Southern fiction so named.)

Faulkner and Melville share a liking for physical, dynamic, and animal images. Both abound in images of light and dark. In Faulkner's novel there is a persistent reference to white "blood" and black "blood," and Joe's ambiguous character is symbolized by the dark serge trousers and white shirt he invariably wears. Both Ahab and Joe Christmas are seeking an elusive *purity*, symbolized by whiteness. Both shape their doom by their sharp rejections of their own humanity. Both are "unmanned," to use Melville's word, by fate or by their own moral acts. Faulkner's manner of handling symbols and themes is like Melville's. His downright spiritual vehemence often produces a wonderful lyric or epic sense of life; but sometimes the symbols are crudely imagined or imperfectly assimilated in context. For example, the uneasy connection of Joe Christmas with Christ: several of Joe's acts take place on Friday, or "on the third day"; Mrs. McEachern washes his feet; Burch betrays him for a thousand pieces of silver; Hines, his grandfather and the only father Joe knows, imagines that he is God. Faulkner seems not to sense exactly how the Christ theme should be handled, sometimes making it too overt and sometimes not overt enough. His attempts to enlarge Joe's character by adducing a willed mythology remind one of Melville's similar attempts in *Pierre*. It may finally seem to us that Faulkner and Melville are most in control of their work when they approach the epic form, as in *As I Lay Dying* and *Moby-Dick;* but that when they try novels of complex symbolic human relationships, their effort suffers from their uncertain power of grouping symbols into a close coherent statement.

4

It has been said of Faulkner that his rhetoric and the actions it expresses are so terrific that they annihilate his characters, that his characters become mere targets for violent emotive bombardments. The measure of truth in this criticism does not destroy Faulkner as an artist. It simply indicates that he is one kind of artist—surely he is not a novelist of manners in quite the way that such a phrase as "the Balzac of the South" would imply. As if in self-criticism, Faulkner writes of Hines and his fanatical sermons: "So they believed that he was a little crazy. . . . It was not that he was trying to conceal one thing by telling another. It was that his words, his telling, just did not synchronize with what his hearers believed would (and must) be the scope of a single individual." Yet in one of the utterances of the Reverend Mr.

Hightower we find this idea translated into a true definition of tragedy: "Too much happens. That's it. Man performs, engenders, more than he can or should have to bear. That's how he finds that he can bear anything. That's it. That's what is so terrible." In such a statement as this Faulkner begins to justify the overplus of superhuman and subhuman violence in his novels. Nevertheless there remains a discrepancy between the theoretical justification and the artistic practice. We cannot avoid phrasing the aesthetic implication of Hightower's words in some such way as this: "Faulkner attributes more action and emotion to his characters than can meaningfully be attributed to them."

The alienation of man *via* language is a common theme in *Light in August*. The people who have beaten and robbed Joe and left him on the floor of a cheap boarding house, speak "in a language which he did not understand." The sermons of Hightower seem to have been expressly contrived to separate him from his congregation. As for Lena, her separation-by-language is always maintained only to the degree necessary to her total purpose. When she asks along the road for Burch, people direct her to "Bunch," but to her they always seem to say "Burch." She is purposefully separated from irrelevance and relaxed in her vision of reality. Separation by language is surely a fact of human life. But is Faulkner entirely in control of this theme? In the orphanage the dietitian and Hines meet "calm and quiet and terse as two conspirators" and then proceed to discourse in some pseudo-Old Testament language which is anything but calm, quiet, or terse. But perhaps it is another form of dissociation which makes this putatively powerful situation seem defective. Perhaps—in order that the dissociation might be in *his* mind, for it needs to be in *someone's* mind—the five-year-old Joe should have been present, watching and listening in awe to the terrible creatures, his mythical father and mother. It is simply a novelist's mistake to present us with a sharp dislocation between his characters and what they say, without accounting in context for the dislocation. One feels that Faulkner has missed a chance in this scene to form a profound associative human situation.

This leads us to a general question: What is the quality of

consciousness displayed in *Light in August?* Surely, it is not a consciousness which broods over the whole range of action, associating people with each other or with a culture, establishing their manners and morals in a whole containment. It is a consciousness in flight and pursuit, wonderfully aware of fact, the physical and animal fact, wonderfully in possession of extreme emotions and the ecstasy of violence, cognizant too of the tender humorousness of love, and in general wonderfully fantastic and magical. *Par excellence,* it is the American folk-literary consciousness. When it seeks to interpret or enlighten the human situation, when Faulkner breaks off the humorous-tragical flow of rhetorical poetry and ventures an observation on human manners, he is likely to sound naive. He will speak in the manner of the folk proverb: "Yes, sir. You just let one of them get married or get into trouble without being married, and right then and there is where she secedes from the woman race and spends the balance of her life trying to get joined up with the man race. That's why they dip snuff and smoke and want to vote." Or he will attempt a more intellectually formulated observation, with the following unhappy result: "the faces of the old men lined by that sheer accumulation of frustration and doubt which is so often the other side of the picture of hale and respected full years"—What a piece of philosophy! One can hardly help sensing an uncomfortable hiatus between Faulkner's poetic portrayal of manners and his explicit consciousness of them.[1]

Probably the episodes of family and cultural history which accompany Faulkner's account of Miss Burden and Hightower would mean more to a Southerner than they do to me. But especially in the case of Hightower there seems to be a failure of consciousness precisely at the point where we should understand the quality of the association between Hightower and his own history. Hightower has projected his sexual and spiritual impotence back upon a myth of his grandfather. Faulkner goes along with Hightower on this point, assuming too much that a fantasy projected from some center of real causation is the cause itself. He nearly allows Hightower to determine the quality of his (Faulkner's) conscious-

---

[1] But the observations I have made in this paragraph would be substantially less true if applied to *The Sound and the Fury.*

ness. On the other hand, he is capable of involving Burch in a situation which calls for a degree of consciousness far above what seems possible, and then arbitrarily giving him the necessary consciousness; so that we have a dull country lout whose "rage and impotence is now almost ecstatic. He seems to muse now upon a sort of timeless and beautiful infallibility in his unpredictable frustrations" (the qualifiers "almost," "seems to," "a sort of" are significant). And a moment later we find Burch (so it seems) reflecting that a Negro he is talking with "does not appear to have enough ratiocinative power to find the town." In *Anna Karenina* a dog conducts a humorous and anxious conversation with himself. But unlike the Burch episode, this does not seem in the least out of place, because Tolstoy with his great associative consciousness always gives one the feeling that he knows exactly when and how much to withdraw or extend his mind in the universe of his novel. I do not mean to imply that Faulkner's novel *lacks* consciousness, but only that the consciousness it displays is sometimes unhappily biased, bardic, parochial, and, in the societal or cultural sense, unmannered. Davy Crockett still screams in the Southern wilderness.

But of course any discussion which compares Faulkner unfavorably with a writer like Tolstoy must not be guilty of the assumption that Faulkner's Southern culture is as cohesive and knowable as Tolstoy's Russian culture was; obviously it is not. And Faulkner's claim to be the novelist of a culture (if that is his claim) must be judged on the basis of his whole work. Nevertheless the evidence of *Light in August,* though it shows that Faulkner is capable of very fine and very extensive and complex fictional constructions, also seems to indicate that he can fail us exactly at that level of existence where the subtle complications of human behavior have to be established. Faulkner works inward from the extremities, from the mechanics and the ecstasy of life. And this relentless, bardic-American bias often makes us wish he would reverse the procedure, that his consciousness would work through human manners into the human character and then outward toward the extremities it can contain or fail to contain. Human life submits itself to die at the hands of the artist so that it may be reborn in art, somewhat as Joe Christmas submits himself to the beatings of McEachern: "The boy's body might have been wood or stone; a post or a tower upon which the sentient part of him mused like a hermit, contemplative and remote with ecstasy and selfcrucifixion." One wants to know finally, What manner of man is this *between* the stone and the crucifixion?

5

But it is only one's high estimation of Faulkner which raises these questions at all. Like the author of *Moby-Dick* Faulkner might say of himself, "I try everything; I achieve what I can." In these bad times, a serious venturesomeness must count heavily with us. But it is also a sense of Faulkner's achievement which makes me think him the equal of any American novelist of his generation. Perhaps *The Great Gatsby* is the only novel of the time which can be defended as superior to Faulkner's best work.

In the nineteen-thirties the liberal-progressive culture turned away from Faulkner for many of the same bad reasons which caused it, eighty years before, to turn away from Melville. If our liberal thought now begins to return from its disastrous wanderings of the last decades—that era of the great rejections—and to recover its vitality, it is because it grows capable of coming to terms with Faulkner, as it already learns again to come to terms with Hawthorne and Melville.

William Empson EMOTIONS IN

POEMS

I N THE Ogden-Richards *Meaning of Meaning*, the doctrine
that there are Emotive uses of language is prominent but does
not get much application to literary criticism. But in what might be
called the middle period of Professor Richards' books, from *The
Principles of Literary Criticism* to *Mencius on the Mind,* a series
of literary hints of this sort are dropped which I have come to think
actively misleading. The precise doctrine is hard to isolate, and
indeed I think the part which is wrong with it is a product of confusion; but there are a series of phrases to the effect that the Emotions given by words in poetry are independent of their Sense. It
seems to me that this doctrine, if taken at all simply, would be sure
to lead to bad criticism. However, on the whole Professor Richards
has succeeded in not giving definite examples of this effect; perhaps
this is partly because his most thoroughgoing speculations about the
Emotive functions of language were made in connection with texts
by Mencius which have remained obscure even to the Chinese. But I
think an example can be found in his defense of the last lines of the
Grecian Urn (Mencius page 116); Professor Richards says:

> Urns induce states of mind in their beholders; they do not
> enunciate philosophical positions—not in this kind of poetry—
> and *say'st* here is used as a metaphor which should not be over-
> looked.

I do not think poor Keats would have liked to be told he was
writing "this kind of poetry." Professor Richards goes on to show

that the range of meaning in Truth and Beauty overlaps at three points, so that there are three ways of making "Beauty is Truth" a mere tautology (not a sentence with any meaning). These possibilities, he says:

> account for its power *in the poem* (when, of course, it is not apprehended analytically) to convey that feeling of deep acceptance which is often a chief phase in the aesthetic experience.

Now it may well be that the lines are bad. But it seems to me that Professor Richards is not defending them; he is merely calling them bad in a complacent manner. And I should have thought, for that matter, that any word other than an exclamation or a swear-word has got to be apprehended as a meaning, giving room for a possible analysis of the meaning, if it is apprehended at all. A poet no doubt is not building an intellectual system; if you like the phrase, he feels the thoughts which are in the air (and here, I take it, the thoughts of Coleridge were in the air); or he is recording a time when his mind was trying out an application of the thoughts, not proving a doctrine about them. But all the same if he leads up with clear marks of solemnity to saying that Beauty is Truth he does not want to be told, any more than anyone else, that "of course" he meant nothing at all except to excite Emotion. It seems to me that a flat separation of Sense from Emotion would be merely a misreading here.

The question here looks like a verbal one, and yet it clearly brings in much larger issues. Apart from the doctrine that the Emotions of the words in poetry are independent of the Sense, Professor Richards maintains, and I take it is more interested in maintaining, that the function of poetry is to call out an Attitude which is not dependent on any belief open to disproof by facts. The two doctrines seem intimately connected, though I am not sure that they need be; and in both I think it needs a rather subtle analysis to get at the truth. Certainly I think it would be a worse heresy to maintain that poems are not concerned with Emotion, because they are Pure Art; but I hope it is clear from these examples that one needs more elaborate machinery to disentangle the Emotive from the Cognitive part of poetical language. Such at least is my excuse for offering my own bits of machinery; but as the second Richards doctrine is closely connected with the first it seems necessary to look at that as well.

The crucial belief here, which I take it he still holds, is that "awareness of the nature of the world and the development of attitudes which will enable us to live in it finely are almost independent" (*Principles of Literary Criticism*). It is clear that *almost* might become important here. The effects of the doctrine are complicated and far-reaching; he has been attacked for them on different grounds at different times, and indeed to recall them is rather a matter of digging up misunderstandings. Max Eastman wrote a very amusing book, *The Literary Mind*, some while ago, a great quarry for the background of this controversy, in which he attacked nearly everyone else for thinking that poetry ought to teach truths and attacked Professor Richards for thinking that, though not concerned with truth, it ought to convey valuable attitudes. Max Eastman himself thought that it ought to communicate experience, good or bad (because everyone likes to have plenty of experience); and the effect on him so far as he ventured into literary criticism, it seemed clear to me, was to make him prefer very trivial poems. He found it particularly absurd that the arts should be viewed as a socially important alternative to religion. As a writer of verse myself, I felt that Professor Richards' faith in the poets was a beautiful but rather unrealistic trait; the question was a more complicated one, about the taste of the public in general. Judging the theories in terms of the criticism they produced, I felt that Professor Richards was clearly less wrong than Max Eastman, but that a willful inhibition of all the truth-seeking impulses in poetry would make for a kind of bad criticism of its own. For example, the idea comes up again when we are told in the *Principles of Literary Criticism* that people who say "How True" when reading Shakespeare are wasting their time; it is suggested that they are comical old fogies anyway. This is not merely an attack on Bradley and other delvers into "character"; it is an attack on what almost everyone has felt, on what was most strikingly witnessed, with a sort of unwillingness, by Dr. Johnson, that in spite of all their faults the plays are somehow unescapably "like life." I do not think one can write any useful criticism of Shakespeare if one has succeeded in repressing this sentiment. Indeed I do not think that Professor Richards seriously meant to recommend that; the point is that when he claims to illustrate his doctrine he tends to use misleading language.

The reason why Tragedy was held to illustrate especially clearly the separation of Attitudes from Belief, if I follow him, was that a Christian audience has to drop the belief in Heaven, or tacitly confess that this belief is of a peculiar kind, because otherwise the death of the hero would not appear tragic. At least this is what an unbeliever is tempted to suppose; the believers seem to feel they can drop their habitual prop while seeing a tragedy, since they are being offered an alternative means to strength which will do as well for the moment. I think this does apply to *Lear*; the attempts to fit Christian sentiments onto it seem to me to falsify the play. But there is a great variety of tragedies, and it is hard to generalize about what Christians feel. *Faustus* is a tragedy which assumes that you believe the hero went to Hell, but it does not depend on that; indeed the author probably did not believe it himself. We are to envisage Hamlet as sung to his rest by flights of angels; Heaven appears as a state of peace, which he has been wanting to get to for some time; you may adopt so Christian a point of view as to wish he had died earlier, and the play is still tragic. Cleopatra says repeatedly that she expects some kind of happiness after her death, though in very metaphorical language; we seem meant to feel that her belief is pathetically untrue but has something profound about it. The atheist and the Christian presumably disbelieve her about equally, because the Christian consigns her to a very hot part of Hell. But on the other hand the pantheistic belief that we are somehow absorbed into Nature seems to have remained so natural to us that people of all opinions can follow the last act of the play without feeling positively that her assertions are wrong. Actually, if one reads straight ahead, I am not sure that she seems to assert anything, but the critics like Mr. Wilson Knight and Mr. Middleton Murry who have found a great deal in her speeches do not seem to be misreading them either. It is not so much (as Mr. Eliot pointed out) that Shakespeare is really thinking along the lines he has suggested; he is aware that the character might think along those lines, and leaves room for it. In this play, to use the woolly language of criticism, an "atmosphere of paganism" is what is wanted. Surely the audience is to do the same;

the solution of the "Problem of Belief," as to how we can enjoy the literary expression of beliefs which we don't hold, is not that we separate them from their consequences but that we imagine some other person who holds them, an author or a character, and thus get a kind of experience of what their consequences (for a given sort of person) really are.

But this whole question, though interesting, is a very minor one compared to the central generalization of Professor Richards. It seems clear that, even if your views about Heaven are in abeyance while watching Lear, you need to feel that the play is a true illustration of some part of human nature and the human situation; and indeed that you need to feel this about even the most unnaturalistic plays, if they are to be any good. Now there is no reason why Professor Richards should deny this; in fact the whole point of introducing the Theory of Value into the *Principles of Literary Criticism* was to give a means by which it could be maintained. The sort of truth we are shown, in which we find ourselves believing, is one about our own natures and the natures of the other people we have to deal with; perhaps it is essentially no more than the truth that to act in some ways would be good, and in others bad. Dr. Johnson, one can suppose, would have been ready to limit it to that. But if this is the truth in question, then according to Professor Richards' own theory of value, it is a real one and could eventually be tested by experience. No doubt the means by which this sort of truth can be verified or discovered are very different from those of scientific procedure, and this could give a basis for the distinction between emotive and cognitive uses of language. But it is a very different idea from saying that the belief-feelings are attached to nothing, like those induced by drugs (a parallel which he often uses). Indeed there is a curious footnote, on page 276 of the *Principles,* referring us back from the argument that Poetry does not depend on Belief to the argument that Art is not separate from Life; and this I think would have been enough to settle the matter if the confusion had not gone on creeping like a fog about the valleys of his later books, which have so much wild scenery.

The main theme of *Science and Poetry*, a moving and impressive pamphlet, is that the arts, especially poetry, can save the world from the disasters which will otherwise follow the general loss of religious and semi-religious belief; they can do this by making us experience what the higher kinds of attitude feel like, so that we adopt them of our own accord without needing to believe that we are repaid for them in Heaven or that they bring good luck on earth. I would be sorry to treat this as a mere false analysis of poetical language; the only objection that could be raised, I think, is that the plan is not strong enough for the purpose or is liable to excite an unreasonable expectation of quick results. The point I want to make, on the contrary, is that all this has almost nothing to do with the analysis of poetical language; when you come down to detail, and find a case where there are alternative ways of interpreting a word's action, of which one can plausibly be called Cognitive and the other Emotive, it is the Cognitive one which is likely to have important effects on sentiment or character, and in general it does not depend on accepting false beliefs. But in general it does involve a belief of some kind, if only the belief that one kind of life is better than another; so that it is no use trying to chase belief-feelings out of the poetry altogether. I am not sure how far to follow Professor Richards in his efforts to shoo them out, such as his plaintive remark that neither Yeats nor D. H. Lawrence "seems to have envisaged the possibility of a poetry which is independent of all briefs" (whereas they obviously needed to believe that good results would follow from what they were recommending); or his claim that:

> A good deal of poetry and even some great poetry exists (e.g. some of Shakespeare's Songs and, in a different way, much of the best of Swinburne) in which the sense of the words can be almost entirely missed or neglected without loss. Never perhaps entirely without effort, however; though sometimes with advantage. But the plain fact that the relative importance of grasping the sense of the words may vary (compare Browning's *Before* with his *After*) is enough for our purpose here.

The contrast here seems to me merely one of how far the interconnections of sense can be handled adequately while left in the subconsciousness, a region from which criticism can fish them up if it chooses. Many quite practical false beliefs can hang about in the dim suggestions of a word, for instance the belief that thirteen is unlucky. In any case, the idea of a puritanical struggle to avoid noticing the Sense of "Hark, hark, the lark," and still more the idea that if you succeeded in doing this you would have a substitute for puritanism, are I think obvious products of confusion. But rejecting this verbal part of the theory does not involve rejecting the main thesis of the book; and for that matter when first speaking of the two streams of experience in reading a poem, the intellectual and the active or emotional, Professor Richards remarks: "It is only as an expositor's device that we can speak of them as two streams. They have innumerable interconnections and influence one another intimately." Exactly: this interconnection is what I am trying to follow out; and my only objection to his other phrases on the subject is that they tend to imply that the interconnection had better be suppressed.

Looking back to *The Meaning of Meaning* (which of course was written earlier, with Mr. C. K. Ogden), I think the confusion there is only present in germ. The book often makes very reasonable admissions about the difficulty of separating the Emotive from the Cognitive parts; thus, "This subtle interweaving of the two functions is the main reason why recognition of the difference is not universal"; and it puts the main emphasis on whole passages not on single Emotive words:

> Very much poetry consists of statements, symbolic arrangements capable of truth or falsity, which are used not for the sake of their truth or falsity but for the sake of the attitudes which their acceptance will evoke. For this purpose it frequently happens, or rather it is part of the poet's business to make it happen, that the truth or falsity matters not at all to the acceptance.

Put in this way, the doctrine seems so reasonable that I must make a new set of admissions. Indeed it hardly says more than the old line of joke that the poets tell "excellent lies," or that the truest poetry is the most "faining"; but we still need to examine what kind of truth the joke enshrines. I do not feel there is much puzzle about pleasant lies (as that the mistress is perfect); the puzzle is rather over lies which are unpleasant and yet eagerly absorbed by the fit reader. Such a description, I think, applies to the Housman nettle poem (*More Poems* XXXII); after the first sentence (the lads are sowing) every one of the sentences contains an untrue assertion ('Tis little matter What are the sorts they sow, For only one will grow . . . The charlock on the fallow . . . will not twice arise. The stinging nettle only Will still be sure to stand . . . It peoples towns, and towers Above the courts of kings). Apart from the absurdity of the literal meaning, the metaphorical meaning seems to me plainly untrue; but I also think it is one of his finest poems, which is saying a good deal. Of course you may say that my optimism is naive, and that Housman is uttering the bitter truth which we recognize unconsciously but labor to ignore. It is also naive, I think I can retort, to imagine that in a "pessimistic" poem such as this one the despairing assertions are meant to be accepted quite flatly. The art-works which can be viewed as glorifying death-wishes cover a large field; T. E. Hulme seemed to regard all Byzantine art as of this type, Otto Ranke argued that the invention of portrait sculpture by the Egyptians derived from a sort of necrophily, Mario Praz in *The Romantic Agony* extended a solemn clinical disapproval over most of the nineteenth century literature. It seems to be a general rule, however, that if the effect is beautiful the lust for death is balanced by some impulse or interest which contradicts it. One might argue that the contradiction merely supplies the tension, and does not decide the note on which the string will vibrate—the resultant meaning may have very little to do with the apparent despair. I think the same applies to the nettle poem, so that, even supposing that its assertions are true, they are not really what it means to say.

At any rate, one must not be led aside into supposing that its merit depends on a belief that Housman was sincere. I think it does seem better if you know about Housman (who never published it) but it would still be a good poem if it had been written as a parody of him. But even then, it seems clear, the reader would be in effect asked to imagine a person who *was* in the "mood" expressed by the poem, who did believe these assertions, and who faced them with the pride, calm, and pity which the poem conveys. The point is not that their truth or falsity is irrelevant, but that you are asked to imagine a state of mind in which they would appear true. True perhaps within a particular world of experience, maybe a narrow one, but true somewhere. However, this kind of narrowing of the field might leave the claim still naive. The absurdity of the literal meaning is I think a positive help to the wilful pessimism of the metaphorical one, because (as well as making the supposed painful truth dramatic, astonishing, unnatural) it can suggest a slanging match—the speaker is spitting in the face of the blackguard who made the world, whatever tortures will follow; he is exaggerating because he thinks the facts deserve it, and perhaps to encourage his disciples. This kind of untruth (which need not be imputed) does not hurt the poem because you still have to imagine a person who is deeply convinced of the general case he is making out. And it seems clear that you can feel invigorated and deepened by the process of imagining this character, without agreeing with him at all.

I don't deny, at the other extreme, that you may simply agree with his assertions, but in that case I think the poems are merely harmful. I remember a Japanese class of mine reading Housman in 1931, when they were liable to be conscripted to fight in Manchuria (indeed a man had already been drafted from the class and killed in Shanghai), and they wrote down pretty consistently, "We think Housman is quite right. We will do no good to anyone by being killed as soldiers, but we will be admired, and we all want to be admired, and anyway we are better dead." To do the old gentleman justice, I fancy he would have been rather shocked by these bits of schoolwork. So I think Housman is about as pure a case as you can get of a poet using untruths to excite attitudes, and even here I think it would be a tedious flippancy to say that the truth or untruth of the assertions is simply irrelevant to the poem.

There is a distinction needed, I think, which becomes clearer if we go back to *Science and Poetry* and examine its idea of a "pseudo-statement." This is presented as an alternative to the idea that false statements in poetry belong to "a supposed universe of discourse, a world of make-believe, of imagination, of recognized fictions common to the poet and his readers." There is no such separate universe defined by a poem, Professor Richards truly pointed out, and he went on (wrongly, I think) to say that "except occasionally and by accident, logic does not enter at all." In any case

> The acceptance which a pseudo-statement receives is entirely
> governed by its effects upon our feelings and attitudes. . . .
> A pseudo-statement is "true" if it suits and serves some attitude
> or links together attitudes which on other grounds are desirable.

The objection I should want to make is that this account is liable
to be misunderstood so as to short-circuit the process. It seems to
me that the attitude recommended by the nettle poem, if we regard
its pseudo-statements as a series of stimuli imposed on the organism of the reader, is quite clearly a very *un*-desirable one. There
is merely a sullen conviction that no effort is worth making, a
philosophy for the village idiot; and the illogicality which we are
told to admire (as being typical of poetical language) is not any
"freedom" from logic but the active false logic of persecution
mania. On this theory the poem is very bad, whereas it seems clear
that an adequate theory would be able to admit its merits. It seems
enough to say that the experience ought to be "imaginative," in
that we imagine some other person in this frame of mind; we are
not simply worked upon, ourselves, as objects of a psychological
experiment. But as soon as you admit this, a good deal more
thinking has to go on in the background, and indeed a good deal
more logical consistency.

It can no doubt be objected that I am using truth in some
peculiar literary sense of the term here, and that scientific truth
is obviously not in question. The distinction seems to me extraordinarily hard to draw. The person we are asked to imagine believes that any efforts he makes will be frustrated, and surely
this idea (however remote) is entirely in the world of practical
experience. The Japanese students, to sum up the meaning of
such a poem, said that they would be better dead, a judgment of
value, and this I take it could be judged either true or false by
applying Professor Richards' Theory of Value to their cases. Of
course it is true that the connection of the attitudes with fact
is a very remote one, and furthermore that the attitude of the
nettle poem needs to be accepted in a peculiar way, neither as
completely right nor as inconceivably wrong; but I do not see that
the subtlety of the process detaches it from any connection with
fact, any more than the answer has free will if the sum is hard.

And in any case, of course, even if the meanings of the sentences were detached in this way, it would not make the meanings of the separate words Purely Emotive.

However, by the time Professor Richards came to write *The Philosophy of Rhetoric* and *Interpretation in Teaching*, he seems to have dropped the idea that a writer of poetry had better not worry about the Sense. I suspect this was because he had subjected himself to so much reading of bad criticism by his students in their "protocols" that his common sense revolted against a doctrine which they illustrated so frequently; and we now find him at the other extreme, writing as though the "somnial magic" were the natural enemy of "the sunshine comparative power," so that the only tolerable way to read poetry is to give the full Sense a very sharp control over the Emotion. This indeed had always been more in line with his temperament, so that the earlier doctrine might be regarded as a determined effort to give the emotions their due. Oddly enough the people influenced by him seem to have followed the beckoning of his style rather than his repeated instructions; the influence seems to me rather too anti-emotional and intellectualistic, without any reference to the doctrine that the Emotion can be practically independent of the Sense.

It may therefore seem unnecessary and disagreeable to write down lengthy objections to phrases by Professor Richards which are merely open to misunderstanding, or views which he probably no longer holds. But his books are still very much alive whether he agrees with them or not; and a mistake made by Richards, it has long seemed to me, is a great deal more illuminating than the successes of other writers in this line of country. I ought also to admit that, as I reread his books with these complaints in view, I was impressed by how often my own writing had repeated him unawares without acknowledgment, and how far beyond my own range his mind has habitually gone.

Eric Bentley MONSIEUR VERDOUX

AS THEATRE

"His [Chaplin's] great forte has been purely theatrical."—Parker Tyler

WHAT an achievement this film is! We don't have to compare it with other films: we don't have to compare it with the comedies or social dramas of Broadway: here is a work that can be taken seriously.

There are things to find fault with in *Monsieur Verdoux*. But I should say that there is something heartening even in Mr. Chaplin's faults—because they are faults of excess, not of deficiency. If some scenes in *Verdoux* are puzzling, is it not because they might mean several things, not that they might mean nothing? In the revolutionary act of making the screen say something, Mr. Chaplin has made it say too much. There is more material in his latest film than he is able to manage—which is to say, more than any living dramatic artist could manage. Had Mr. Chaplin been content to say something about capitalism, he could have done so with brilliant clarity. Actually, he blurred the edges of his main statement with perhaps incompatible and certainly irrelevant statements on other subjects no less enormous—such as the problem of evil and (what may be the same thing) the problem of women. It is hard to write a *Critique of Political Economy* and an *Apologia pro Vita Sua* at the same time; not all the psychological complexities of the latter seem relevant to the trenchant sociology of the former. Is it merely malicious of us to find Verdoux's attitude to some of his

This essay was originally a lecture read at the Kenyon School of English.

women less relevant to the story than to its author? Something in
the tone of scenes in Verdoux's real home, something in the tone of
his speeches in court and in jail, makes them hard to interpret and
hence harder to justify. To what extent is Mr. Chaplin critical of
Verdoux? And of his small-bourgeois conception of domestic
bliss? To what extent, in other words, is Verdoux Mr. Chaplin's
mouthpiece?

That such questions arise at all proves that the film—intended,
as it was, for mass audiences—is not as clear as Mr. Chaplin
must have wanted it to be. Nonetheless, most of the things I hear
said against it seem to indicate a limitation rather in the audience
than in Mr. Chaplin, seem to indicate—among other things—a
stubborn adherence to the theory of naturalism, a stubborn refusal
to allow any of the traditional devices and strategies of comedy.
The modern naturalist can destroy Shakespeare by the inordinate
demands he makes in the realm of motivation. Iago has no adequate motive. Neither have the comic villains of Jonson and
Molière. Neither has Monsieur Verdoux. Like Morose or Tartuffe,
he is a caricature, he is exaggerated. To complain of the exaggeration is silly. The question to ask is: does the exaggeration serve to
reinforce the truth as Mr. Chaplin sees it or does it weaken and
falsify?

Thus one does not ask: Is Verdoux's motive of making a living
under capitalism actually enough to make a man murder a large
number of women? or: Are these murders morally justified because
modern war kills an even larger number of women? That is, one
does not *end* by asking these questions. Had Mr. Chaplin wanted
to justify murder, he could easily have chosen a story and invented
a character that would be more sympathetic. Like Swift in his
Modest Proposal (I borrow the comparison from Robert Warshow),
he is *pretending* to justify murder in order to annoy everyone
back into a true humanity. Thus Mr. Chaplin's conception of a
Bluebeard has to be seen primarily as a satiric strategy of a traditional sort, a kind of devil's advocacy.

It may be that the modern mind has been so softened by
naturalism that we no longer understand the old, hardheaded, unrealistic comic strategies. Such, for example, as comic extension,
which is the theatrical form of the *reductio ad absurdum*. The

caricaturist takes a man's long nose and extends the line of it
until it not only is long but expresses, so to speak, the very idea
of length, of long-nosedness. This is comic extension. Mr. Chaplin
takes the familiar moral dichotomy between the private life and
the public, which in modern life has taken form as the dichotomy
between the solid citizen's respectable Christian home and his dirty
Machiavellian dealings in business. And he broadens the moral contrasts until they are expressible in terms of his own art which is,
if you like, slapstick. The strong contrast between the kind of
treatment the material suggests and the kind of treatment it
actually meets with at Mr. Chaplin's hands is likely to baffle the
solemn modern spectator whose imagination has been deadened
by naturalism. For Mr. Chaplin's purposes, however, the broader the
contrast the better. Like the classic comedians, he thrives on the
contrast.

When we complain that in all speeches commenting on the
action from outside, commenting on war and so forth, Mr. Chaplin
is destroying his art and is tumbling into mere propaganda, we are
again, I think, forgetting the methods of comedy and remembering,
say, Henry James. James told the writer to render his subject in
the round and not to report on it. More relevant, however, to Mr.
Chaplin than James on the novel is Pirandello on humor.

Pirandello concedes James's point that in literature generally,
the writer's reflection on the work must be concealed within it,
but he makes an exception of the kind of writing he calls humorous.
Our sense of humor, he says, is what forces us to press the analysis
of the comic situation to the point where we see that it is really a
pathetic situation. When we see a middle-aged lady overpainted
and overdressed we laugh. This is our sense of the comic. But if we
then learn that the lady has been driven into bedecking herself
ridiculously by her urgent need to keep her husband's affection
we tend to find her pathetic. Reflection turns the merely funny
into humor. The humorous work in literature is unlike the non-
humorous work in that reflection appears quite openly in it. Thus,
Pirandello argues, humor breaks up the normal form by interrup-
tion, interpolation, digression, and decomposition; and the critics
complain of lack of unity in all humorous works from *Don Quixote*
to *Tristram Shandy*—and we might add from *Little Dorrit* to

Monsieur Verdoux. It is not so much, of course, that the humorist is released from all obligation to unify his work, as that the unity he achieves must be a large one which has room for commentary. It seems to me that there are one or two superfluities in *Monsieur Verdoux,* but that it has an impressive approximate unity. Even if you will not grant me this, you will see some pertinence, I hope, in Pirandello's theory. For if Mr. Chaplin has something in common with Jonson and Molière, he is even more in the tradition of that different sort of comedy which Pirandello describes, the comedy of humor. The mixture of laughter and tears in *Monsieur Verdoux* is certainly no stranger than that in *Don Quixote.*

I mention the older traditions of comedy not with the idea of locking Mr. Chaplin up in an academic pigeonhole but with the intention of deflecting your minds from the somewhat bewildering façade of the film to the strong and time-honored buttresses that hold it up. I want *Monsieur Verdoux* to call forth, not your favorite utterance about art and propaganda, but your best appreciation of the comic spirit. We permit *Monsieur Verdoux,* as a work of Pirandellian humor, to turn hither and yon, but we are also pleased to find in it a certain backbone. In fact, if we may call everything up to the murder of Lydia a prologue, and everything after the wedding reception an epilogue, what we have in the very center of the film is fairly compact comic action. With his wife in the background, Verdoux is involved with two women. A familiar sort of triangle. One woman he is trying to get rid of, the other to add to his collection. In a sense, there are two actions here: parallel lines running in opposite directions. If we express the motif of Verdoux in a couple of infinitives, they are "to remove Annabella" and "to win Mme Grosnay." The two actions converge and explode in the wedding scene.

Such is the central comedy, a story at once classic, conventional, and low, on the standard comic theme of love and money—more explicitly, the distortion of love, which ideally would be the most disinterested of human impulses, by consideration of money. Verdoux is a thwarted idealist. He is a worse man than others because his intentions are better. He refuses to corrupt his own home, as others do not. But in order to keep his home absolutely uncontaminated he has to resort to measures more immoral than those

of the normally contaminated. The central comedy says all this—
up to a point. The rest of the film is a humorous agglomeration, an
agglomeration of details, comments, interruptions, that enrich and
elaborate the theme.

How, for instance, is the archetypal theme of love and money
given special reference to modern capitalist society? By Mr. Chaplin's filling in the portrait of Verdoux the great capitalist. Verdoux's mastery of the system is given to us in the assured phone
conversations with banks, in the expertness of his counting of bank
notes. The monstrous economy of profit makes its ultimate assault
on human value when it takes over human love, when, as with
Verdoux, it reduces marriage itself to economics. This is to push the
capitalist idea to its logical end. No one ever tried harder than
Verdoux to reduce capitalism to a principle. But he fails. That is
the hard fact. And why? Because the only principle of capitalism
is lack of principle. The unplanned economy hands destiny over to
pure chance, to luck. Thus Verdoux's is the tragedy of the rationalist who tries to reduce to principle what is essentially unprincipled.
In melodrama people pass unaccountably from rags to riches and
from riches to rags; so do they under the unplanned economy.
Thus at the same time as Verdoux moves from affluence to ruin, the
Girl moves from ruin to affluence: again Mr. Chaplin charts parallel
lines moving in opposite directions. Who then is successful under
capitalism? Perhaps nobody is, permanently. But for the time being
the vital vulgarian Annabella does very well. That is, she is consistently lucky. The maid comes home just as Verdoux prepares
his chloroform pad. The maid spills the poison just as Verdoux
is preparing it. In the rowing boat Annabella is saved by her own
good works and by divine intervention in the shape of a yodeller.
And so on.

What a comedian needs apart from words—and words are what
Mr. Chaplin needs least—is a piece of furniture, or some small
object that he can toy with and make a symbol of some aspect of
human fate. Now, for a great clown—and few would deny that
Mr. Chaplin is·that—the principal thing that he uses as furniture
is his own body and the principal objects are his limbs, his fingers,
his features. In *Monsieur Verdoux,* as in early movies, Mr. Chaplin
uses his body, his limbs, his fingers, and his face with an agility and

a precision, and at the same time a delicacy and a discretion, the like of which one has seen in nobody else. Every portion of his body is a field of action, and perhaps the best lecture on *Monsieur Verdoux* would be simply a commentary on Chaplin's many faces as they could be put before us in a series of stills. Even these would do him scant justice, however, since more remarkable than the faces themselves is the way they all move. To those who think that the best of Chaplin is exclusively in the earlier movies I would say: watch his face in *Verdoux*. We see many grave and sombre expressions that were never seen there before. Not to mention the very fine voice that this film is the first properly to display, a voice that might not make a Hamlet, certainly, but a voice that Mr. Chaplin can run hot or cold in very fine gradations.

A clown, of course, must not only be: he must do. He has his special routines, of which the most characteristic is to stumble and fall yet, the next instant, to pick himself up with a brave grin and proceed. Charlie the Tramp used to go through this routine again and again, and at the end of *Modern Times* the clown's brave recovery was given the sort of sentimental political meaning that Frank Capra's movies end with: there is hope for the future because the common man is undaunted. This is what Marxists call small-bourgeois idealism. By 1946 Mr. Chaplin had other thoughts. The clown may pick himself up after the first fall, or even after the twenty-first, or the two-hundredth, but the social system keeps knocking him down again and there comes a time when he gets up no more.

Thus the new movie is not about the Tramp, whose spirit in Mr. Chaplin is broken, but about his boss, the stockholder and speculator, polygamist and murderer, Henri Verdoux. The aspiration after a refined life, after courtesy and elegance, which the clowning always stood for has no longer any spontaneity. The hollow appearance of such an aspiration is brought into being for strictly business reasons by Henri Verdoux. But with no more consistency than Charlie the Tramp can Henri Verdoux simply be refined, courteous, and elegant. He too stumbles. He falls through the window when harassed. Does Verdoux's failure to be a flawless machine mean that after all he has retained a little humanity? That he will not quite succeed in his business efforts? It is hard to know how far it is proper to push psychological analysis of this realistic sort. There is a danger of treating art as life. What status, for instance, does our delight in Verdoux's clowning have? One would think that it was delight in Mr. Chaplin's workmanship, yet somehow it carries over into the life of the story and we do come to feel more sympathy for Verdoux than we otherwise would.

The clown's relation to the audience is always an ironical one, and I think Mr. Chaplin speaks for all clowns when he tells us he always begins by establishing a misunderstanding between himself and his public. When he walks the tightrope the clown fails to reach the opposite post. He falls off the rope in mid-career and executes a grotesquely confused double somersault in mid-air. The audience laughs as if it had never seen anything so clumsy and incompetent; the clown knows that what he did required more skill than merely to walk the tightrope from post to post. One can well understand why the clown has so often been represented as a man with a grudge. Is *Monsieur Verdoux* Mr. Chaplin's revenge? Will he no longer allow the audience its unearned superiority? By laughing at Verdoux's antics do we become accomplices in his crimes? I should think that some nervousness about this sort of thing is in our minds when we laugh at Mr. Chaplin in the new film. We watch the comic gags with admiration but also with horror because their usual meaning has been most shockingly inverted. That the clown lays the table for two when he is quite alone is funny, but in *Monsieur Verdoux* we know that he has removed his partner by cold-blooded murder; it makes a difference. At every turn devices that were quite lighthearted in early Chaplin movies become macabre in *Monsieur Verdoux*.

The general context effects a general inversion of meaning, and in addition Mr. Chaplin sometimes inserts particular inversions. The Pursuit of Charlie—an archetypal pattern of movie comedy—is ruthlessly inverted in the nightclub scene where Mr. Chaplin shows his old skill in leaping first to this side then to that while his pursuer rushes past. But the gymnastics are little more than futile virtuosity: Verdoux only wants time to say goodbye to the Girl. The Pursuit of Charlie cannot take place because Charlie is not running away.

When he got into hot water, the old Charlie used to say, as it were: "Appearances are against me but I love you and I'll be back." This is another archetypal pattern that is brilliantly inverted in the new film. Running at top speed, Verdoux wheels round, presses his hands to his heart, and passionately throws out the word "Beloved!" But he doesn't love her. And he won't be back.

Pursuit and flight or mock pursuit and mock flight: such cultural commonplaces, such comic turns and gags, are the bricks from which Mr. Chaplin constructs his edifice—and it is an edifice, not just a pile of bricks. To change the metaphor: *Monsieur Verdoux* is a network of continuities and cross-references. Some of these are matters of detail (but then every detail in a Chaplin movie is a studied effect). Verdoux thinks a girl is smiling at him, because he fails to look over his shoulder at her boy friend. Verdoux thinks a girl is not smiling at him because—at this later stage in the story—there seem so many others she would, more probably, smile at. The public prosecutor points at the mass-murderer but Verdoux who this time is quite sure he isn't being pointed at looks behind him—for the man who isn't there. Details: but they contribute subtly to Mr. Chaplin's treatment of confused identity. Cruder evidence, though just as true to Mr. Chaplin's vaudeville technique, is provided by Verdoux's twice mistaking his role. "Captain Bonheur," he says when re-introducing himself to Mme Grosnay. Then, remembering that she knows him by another name: "I said I have the honneur. . . ." Later, thinking he is dying, he shouts to Annabella "Telephone my wife" and Annabella replies "Here I am, pigeon."

Relations of size and shape have always been made much of in slapstick comedy. We often used to see Charlie and the big fat villain, Charlie and the big-busted lady, and there is a vestige of these relationships in Verdoux and Inspector Morrow, Verdoux and Mme Grosnay. More subtly effective in the new movie is the contrast between the rectilinear, taut, and artificial on the one hand and the curved, relaxed, and natural on the other. Perhaps the funniest dramatization of this contrast is the confrontation of Verdoux as the natty little Captain Bonheur with Annabella who winds her sinuous curves round a curtain or adds to them with an enormous loose-brimmed hat covered with grapes. Another central instance is the contrast between Verdoux as clown and Verdoux as man. The former—whether as Varnay, Bonheur, or whatever—is upright; his face is full of sharp lines; his movements are quick and assured.

The latter is seen rather as horizontal than vertical: in an armchair, hobbling along with bent shoulders, lying prone in his cell. The body of the real Verdoux is limp, the features rounded and loose.

I have spoken so far chiefly of Mr. Chaplin's use of human bodies, especially his own. But your conjurer, your acrobat, your vaudeville comedian needs also a few stage "props." Give Mr. Chaplin a few pieces of furniture, a few personal accoutrements, and he can make drama out of them. We all remember the oversize boots, the little bowler, the cane, the baggy trousers, and the undersize jacket of Charlie the Tramp. In *Monsieur Verdoux,* Mr. Chaplin uses his various costumes as fully as possible, and he retains all his old skill in the manipulation of props. A rose is delicately dangled under his nose during the first interview with Mme Grosnay. When effecting the precipitate persuasion of Lydia, he nonchalantly places a seashell to his ear. In the boating scene he has a rope, oars, a bottle, a handkerchief, a fishing-line, a worm, to play with—not to mention the little object whose loss provided the concluding line of the scene, "Where's my hat?" With the fantastic resourcefulness of a conjurer Verdoux produces a jeweller's glass from his pocket at the critical moment. In such a thing we are reminded of the fine appropriateness, in Chaplin's art, of symbol to thing symbolized. In having his jeweller's glass about him Verdoux is the successful practical man as much as when he applies his method of counting bank notes to finding a name in the phone book. Verdoux has constantly to be on the move. So Mr. Chaplin applies his comic technique with especial vigor to symbols of communication—the revolving of train wheels, the ringing of telephones and doorbells, the unlocking of doors, the running up and down stairs. Another of the fine hints provided in the opening sequences is the nervous jump Verdoux twice gives at the sound of a bell.

It is by stage properties—or at any rate by objects in the environment—that continuity is indicated in the two major affairs of Verdoux. In the courtship of Mme Grosnay roses are the *leitmotif*. Verdoux is carrying a rose when he first meets Mme Grosnay. He gives her the bunch of roses that we have seen him cut. He courts her exclusively with roses until she capitulates. The *leitmotif* in the courtship of Annabella is water. As a sea captain, Verdoux-Bonheur lives by water; Annabella enters upon speculations which, if successful, will make her ruler of the waves—"that's all," as she puts it. Finally Verdoux resolves that Annabella shall die by water. But Annabella has the capitalist virtue of luck and it is Verdoux who goes overboard.

I am not saying that all the groupings and parallels in *Monsieur Verdoux* are equally successful. Mr. Chaplin makes the parallel between Verdoux and the Girl a little too sentimental. She had had a wounded husband. He has a crippled wife. She is up against it; he has been up against it. Both are given a cat to be kind to. The music played for the sparing of the Girl is the music associated with the Verdoux home. And so on.

I am not praising Mr. Chaplin for the sheer number of parallels but for the degree of expressiveness achieved by most of them. To conceive of the parallels was something, no doubt; but it is in the individual "frame," the particular movement, that Mr. Chaplin's genius is manifest.

Consider the first sequence in which Verdoux appears. His appearance is carefully prepared by the photo of him in the possession of the Couvais family, and skilfully accompanied by quick discreet shots of the villa, the garden, the neighboring housewives, and the appalling column of smoke rising from the incinerator. The first glance gives us a good deal of Verdoux. We see an Adolphe Menjou, a "masher." We note the dapper figure, the dandified dress, the pursed lips, the overcontrolled features. I speak of this as if we were looking at a still portrait. Actually, from the moment we hear the jerky little Verdoux theme in the orchestra, the sequence has a swift staccato beat that is passed from one gesture or action to another. Many gestures, one rhythm. Verdoux snaps the scissors together two or three times, while his fingers stick out like piston rods. The soft voice, silky, rather dry, and thoroughly disciplined to the comic rhythm and tone, says very quickly: "Oh, la, la." A voice too can be a pair of scissors. Verdoux picks up a caterpillar. Such a kind gentleman, is he not? At least, so well under control? But then he shudders—with body and voice simultaneously. We now know a great deal about Verdoux. We shall not be surprised when he is nauseated by getting one of Annabella's feathers in his mouth.

How powerful a weapon Mr. Chaplin makes of the staccato effect throughout the movie! Think of the Hungarian Rhapsody as played by Verdoux and as extended into a rapping on the window-pane by the charwoman. Think of all the trips up and down stairs at lightning speed; think of them, not only as things seen but as things heard. Think of the repeated slaps on the face in Annabella's nightclub.

One speaks principally of Mr. Chaplin as a comic actor because that is what he, first and foremost, is, but after all he was the scenarist, composer, and director of *Monsieur Verdoux*. We must give him the credit for everything, including the performances of the other actors, many of whom were found to be doing much better work under Mr. Chaplin's direction than they have ever done before. Mr. Chaplin has not mastered words to the extent that he has mastered the non-verbal dramatic arts; yet even the words are much more intelligent words than we are used to these days; and when they are deliberately daft, they are very good. Verdoux's line of talk with each wife is quite in the vein of Chaplinesque comedy generally. To Mme Grosnay he pours out all the clichés of the gentleman lover: "deep pools of desire that can never be fulfilled or understood . . . ," "we can't help ourselves," etc. To Lydia he can talk of bridge-building, and to Annabella of standing on the poopdeck under a canopy of tropical stars. The vaudeville wordplay (like "glass, you silly ass, glass" or "you made a killing, didn't you?" as a question asked Verdoux about his business) is crude stuff but is adequately ironized by the context.

It is simply not true, in other words, that Mr. Chaplin is only an actor. What he does in *Verdoux* in the creation of characters shows an amazing creative talent. With the exception of two roles that are not very well acted—The Girl and the Flower-seller—every role in the film has a significant and well-defined identity, and, more-over, is sharply etched in the classic manner of dramatic characteriza-tion. For here at least one can agree with Professor E. E. Stoll: the playwright doesn't· have to put together detailed psychological portraits of complete human beings: he has quickly to bring into relief the relevant trait. This is exactly what Mr. Chaplin does with a whole gallery of people in *Monsieur Verdoux*: with the Couvais family, the druggist and his wife, the host and hostess at the wedding reception, with such a tiny part as the newspaper photographer outside the condemned cell. And of course Mr. Chaplin understands that comic characters more often exist in pairs than alone. Each of the principal women was obviously chosen to make the most interesting pairing with Verdoux, a kind of contrast that is redoubled by the fact that he is a different man with each wife. Mr. Chaplin understands also the specially cinematic way of portraying character. The cinema, need one say, is a visual art, and we find from *Monsieur Verdoux* that Mr. Chaplin has something of the talent of a great caricaturist.

I doubt, though, that character is the main thing in any important drama or film. I would rather follow Aristotle in his dictum that drama is "an imitation, not of men, but of an action and of life"— that is, an image not of individual psychology but of a developing situation which is representative of life. The comic dramatist's great task is to find an action which has the right shape and energy and at the same time is a perfectly adequate vehicle for his theme. Conceding that Mr. Chaplin's film is not perfect, one must marvel at the success with which he keeps his Bluebeard story in motion and uses it to express his vision of modern life.

As one who writes a good deal about drama, about comedy, I should like to record that, had I never seen Charles Chaplin, I would never have known what the possibilities of comic performance are—what the full realization of comic action is. I am much addicted to playgoing. I have seen Jonson and Molière competently and even expertly performed. But I wonder if the competence and expertness of a hundred different productions taught me more about the way comedy works than the film *Monsieur Verdoux*. I can now imagine what sort of a performance a Jonson or Molière play would require before it could fully exist.

I am addicted also to the *reading* of plays, and thus am fond of the art of dialogue, which in Mr. Chaplin's art is the least important and least impressive ingredient. I should defend the art of dialogue against such a theorist as Professor Erwin Panofsky, who thinks it of very minor importance in the movies. Nonetheless, what the movies can do without dialogue, or in addition to dialogue, is astonishing, especially perhaps in comedy, which, however spiritual its implications, has so much to do with the physical side of life, and in its manifestations is so grossly physical.

I think then that there is much in the dramatic arts that literary criticism—Old or New—does little to help us understand. Mr. Chaplin showed long ago that the comic spirit can find expression without words, without literature, altogether. Some extra-literary demands, surely, are made on the critic. But it is not only that dramatic art reaches out beyond literature into the territory of the visual and musical arts. It is also that the dramatic artist writes for actors. Literary critics often assume that this makes no difference. "You, the reader, are the actor," they say. But if you, the reader, don't know anything about acting you are likely to misread lines. In any case, what a great actor makes of a great role is not something that can be imagined: it has to be seen to be believed.

In any art which requires performance, the matter of perform-ance enters into the process of creation and modifies the nature of the art itself. Thus a composer does not compose music in general, he composes music for a particular instrument. Piano music is pianistic, and is specially adapted to every peculiarity of the human hands, such as the fact that the right hand is more agile than the left. In short, just as we are meant to appreciate the pianistic quality of piano music, so we are meant to appreciate the histrionic—or actorish —quality in dramatic art.

This is too bluntly and briefly said, but let anyone who is inclined to minimize the role of the actor see the film *Monsieur Verdoux*. And let him think of the things that, in reading the scenario, he would be inclined to set down as cliché. For instance, that Mr. Chaplin's elbow slips off the arm of a couch, or that Mr. Chaplin falls off the sofa without spilling a drop of his tea. The element of triteness which you might find in the scenario is entirely transcended by the deftness and delicacy of the performance. You need to know not only that a character falls off the couch. You need to know whether the actor is Charlie Chaplin or Red Skelton.

If one wanted a schoolbook conclusion for the dramatic theorist, one could understate it thus: *It is hard to judge the effectiveness and meaning of dramatic action from stage directions.* Or one could over-state it thus: *A play has two authors, the playwright and the actor.*

Robie Macauley THE GOOD

FORD

ALONG with G. P. R. James and Mrs. Oliphant, we have forgotten Ford Madox Ford. Some middle-aged book reader might remember that he collaborated with Joseph Conrad, changed his name from Hueffer to Ford, edited a magazine or two and wrote a series of somewhat baffling novels about the first World War. It would be hard to recall whether he was serious or not.

On some imaginery library shelf there are seventy-five books that carry his name; and three-fourths of them do it harm. For here is a case of literary dementia praecox if there ever was one. We can rearrange those books symbolically and the two enemies will become clear. On one side will be Ford the slipshod literary journalist, the smooth potboiler novelist, the peddler of suspect anecdotes, the author of *Thus to Revisit, The Rash Act,* and *Ring for Nancy.* He is a bad writer and a good riddance.

On the other side of the shelf there are a dozen or fifteen books in an unpopular eccentric style. They are superbly written, profoundly serious, and built with enormous skill. One of them is unlike any other novel in the English language. If they stand on the shelf with Henry James, Joseph Conrad, the Brontës, and Jane Austen, they do not suffer for it. Some of them are: the four Tietjens novels, *The Good Soldier, Women and Men.* But not all of them are novels.

When the reminiscent sentimentalist, the amateur verse-writer, dropped into oblivion, he pulled with him the sturdy author; but now that Ford is dead nine years we can trouble ourselves to divide them and, disentangling the good Ford, we shall have found something.

Beginning the process, I offer two examples. His most perfect miniature performance was *The Good Soldier,* a splendid novel written just before the first World War and published in 1915. It might be the lucky try of a gifted and fortunate minor novelist. It isn't.

It isn't, because of the evidence of the second example, which is the Tietjens series. This is Ford's achievement in size and scope. Here are four novels that are generally thought to be about the 1914-1918 World War and, superficially, they are. They are about it in the same way that *Madame Bovary* is about life in a small provincial French town and the way that *War and Peace* is about the Napoleonic invasion.

2

Reaching maturity late, Ford had dabbled in literature as a very young man. His poetry, his society novels and most of his literary essays we can forget. But he had been living in Germany and he saw war coming; for him it was now or never. Fifteen years after, in a preface to a later edition of *The Good Soldier,* he looked back to that time, saying:

> Until I sat down to write this book—on the 17th December 1913—I had never attempted to extend myself. . . . Partly because I had always entertained very fixedly the idea that—whatever may be the case with other writers—I at least should not be able to write a novel by which I should care to stand before reaching the age of forty. . . . I had never really tried to put into any novel of mine *all* that I knew about writing. I had written rather desultorily a number of books—a great number—but they had all been in the nature of *pastiches,* of pieces of rather precious writing, or of tours-de-force.

He considered at that time that this was his "Great Auk's egg," and he might as well die after finishing it. It was "something of a race that would have no successors," and it came from an idea that had matured for ten years in his mind. Ford survived the war

as it turned out. Then he went on to make the tremendous attempt
of the Tietjens series. But never again did he try for anything so
elaborately simple or so simply elaborate as *The Good Soldier*.

In a general sense it is like his other novels; in an explicit sense
it is very different. It is a novel that defies critical weighing and
measuring. It will not fall without protest into any type, category,
school, or genre.

There is only one literary parallel suggested by Ford himself.
"I had in those days an ambition: that was to do for the English
novel what in *Fort comme la Mort* Maupassant had done for the
French." This is misleading. The result was quite different. Very
broadly and generally, Ford took a style of language like that of
W. H. Hudson, whose naturalness and ease he much admired.
The expression is so closely allied to the matter of the plot and so
consistently a language of understatement that there are no spots
of fine writing, no metaphors that attach themselves to the memory,
no *pastiches,* not even any parts that are really quotable in themselves.

His narrator device recalls his apprenticeship with Conrad
when the two "wanted the reader to forget that he was reading . . .
to be hypnotized into thinking . . . that he was listening to a
simple and in no way brilliant narrator who was telling—not writing
—a true story." Ford's narrator, John Dowell, in many ways fits this
ideal better than Conrad's Marlow, being even less of an idiosyncratic observer. He is an ordinary American from Philadelphia;
and that is all we find necessary to know of him.

Finally, like most of Henry James's novels, *The Good Soldier*
is an intense story of interacting personal relationships. It is the
story of five people and two unhappy marriages unsystematically
told.

The phrase, "unsystematically told," of course applies only in a
very special sense to either James or Ford. It is more than "un-
chronologically told," because that does not suggest the extreme
artfulness of narration, the superb management of the story. The
time-shift is, actually, a structural device that is almost "poetic."
As the poet fits together images taken from widely-different areas
of knowledge and feeling to make a poem, the novelist ranges over
the whole field of memory, selecting events or sequences of events

from all the tenses of memory—the past, the perfect, the pluper-
fect and the "novelistic present"—and fits them together so that they
will supplement and comment on each other as images in a poem
do. Although step-by-step chronology will be violated, gradually the
events will fit into place and the reader will not be lost. A trial
example from *The Good Soldier* may affirm this.

> This is the saddest story I have ever heard. We had known the
> Ashburnhams for nine seasons of the town of Nauheim with an
> extreme intimacy—or rather an acquaintanceship as loose and
> easy and yet as close as a good glove's with your hand. My wife
> and I knew Captain and Mrs. Ashburnham as well as it was
> possible to know anybody, and yet, in another sense, we knew
> nothing at all about them.

In an easy anecdotal way the teller then goes on to sketch in Leonora Ashburnham, the clean, active, efficient Irishwoman and her
husband Edward, the good soldier, the handsome gentleman with
the brick-pink complexion and the blue eyes that were "perfectly
honest, perfectly straightforward, perfectly, perfectly stupid." But
beneath these conventional sketches there is an intimation that they
are not all they appear to be to the naked eyes, that they are capable
somehow of violences of good and evil.

And beneath the quiet tenor of the first part of the story—
Nauheim, the dining room at the Kur, outings and polo games,
walks and gossip—there is a suggestion of tenseness and caged
emotions.

Leaving this for a little while, Ford returns to the earlier life of
the teller. When his story has been suggested and a counterpoint
established, he returns to Bad Nauheim to relate some incidents
that serve to deepen and develop the characters of Leonora and her
husband. As we know them better, a second layer of their natures
is exposed—Ashburnham with his straightforward sentimentality
and honest self-deception and Leonora, whose look suggests that

> Certain women's lines guide your eyes to their necks, their
> eyelashes, their breasts. But Leonora's seemed to conduct your
> gaze always to her wrist. And her wrist was at its best in a black
> or doeskin glove. . . .

Having given us his people in the midst of daily life, Ford leads deceptively to his first climax with the beginning sentence, "So began these nine years of uninterrupted tranquility." Gradually the narrator begins to describe their excursion to the castle of St. Elizabeth of Hungary. There is a minor irritation and competition between the two wives. Florence chatters in a culture-conscious way. Leonora is cold and watchful as they pass through the village, the castle museum, the Rittersaal, and at last come to Martin Luther's bedroom and the glass case containing The Protest. Florence says, "It's because of that piece of paper that you're honest, sober, industrious, clean-lived. If it weren't for that piece of paper you'd be like the Irish or the Italians or the Poles, but particularly the Irish. . . ." Then she lays one finger on Captain Ashburnham's wrist. The narrator is aware of "something treacherous, something frightful, something evil in that day," but he cannot isolate it. Leonora is suddenly terror-struck. There is a moment of panic and she takes Dowell by the wrist and rushes out of the room. After a moment of agitation she says, "Don't you know that I'm an Irish Catholic?" It is, of course, not the real reason. The real reason stays concealed until later events reproduce it.

This is a sample of the book's technique. Ford will shift easily to a time far past in the lives of the Ashburnhams or the lives of the Dowells, gradually lead back to life at Nauheim, then slowly advance to some small explosive crisis. The apparent meaning of the crisis is there. As time goes on and more is told, it will take on a deeper and a greater one.

The book is a series of *progressions d'effet* of this kind. They are made possible by Ford's enormous skill in the use of transition. It is a difficult technical problem to shift scene—even for a novelist who uses the simple flashback. Too often the process is as awkward as an early movie with its fade-out, blank screen, scene-from-the-past sequence. Ford's transitions are almost imperceptible. We are with Leonora the day she broke down on the way back to Branshaw Teleragh. He calls our attention to her capability for deep feelings, her real passion for Edward with whom she had lived for years without uttering one word of tenderness. This, of course, was as fortuitous as her marriage to Edward—and before we know it we are in a run-down manor house in Ireland where Colonel Powys is wondering how to marry off his seven daughters, where Leonora and her sisters are getting ready for a family photograph. Going from particular surroundings to general ideas or generalized observation of his characters, Ford gently dissolves time and we again find ourselves in a particular landscape.

Once we have arrived at another time and place, the progression begins. Eventually we shall get back where we were, but meanwhile we learn something. The conversational disguise of the story, then, serves a real purpose. Ford can pretend that this is the ordinary sort of storyteller's memory—one that shifts things out of chronological place, forgets or undervalues certain events or scenes and later has to fill them in. Underneath the plausible deception is the master craftsman; the shifts, backtracking, omissions are closely calculated and remarkably managed. Ford wanted every possible bit of meaning and drama out of a scene or a fact; each one had to be interrelated and contrasted with the scenes before and the scenes after and yet still be part of a progression. So simple chronology, he said, is not art and won't do.

As the book goes on, the progressions become tenser, more dramatic, accumulating meaning. None reveals itself entirely.

Stripped to its bare essentials, the story is about two good people. Leonora and Edward Ashburnham are condemned by a chance marriage to a war that brings out the worst in each. In the course of that long combat each manages unknowingly to disintegrate the good character of the other and to make the other capable only of acts of hatred and violence.

I call this The Saddest Story rather than The Ashburnham Tragedy just because it is so sad, just because there was no current to draw things along to a swift and inevitable end. There was about it none of the elevation that accompanies tragedy; there is about it no nemesis, no destiny. Here were two noble people—for I am convinced that both Edward and Leonora had noble natures, drifting down life, like fire-ships afloat on a lagoon and causing miseries, heartaches, agonies of the mind, and death. And they themselves steadily deteriorated. And Why? For what purpose? To point what lesson? It is all a darkness.

Into the war between the two are drawn Florence Dowell, Mrs. Maidan and Nancy Rufford and each one is broken by it in turn. To reduce the sides, as they cannot satisfactorily be reduced, to certain terms: it is the struggle between an honest, generous, open, strong, animal and sentimental man with a precise, virtuous, vigorous, intellectual woman. Ford's strange powers of persuasion make us sympathize with both; both seem equally right and wrong, equally good and evil. The final tragedy of Edward Ashburnham's suicide is no more terrible than the sudden slackening of his wife's mind.

Like the Tietjens story, the superficial tragedy of *The Good Soldier* lies in this sexual tangle. More than that, it is a discussion of the natures of men and women, their eternal attraction and their eternal incompatibility. Edward Ashburnham loved only his wife. He loved her with an unconscious admiration for everything about her, but he could never reach her, touch her, or "see with the same eyes." For the woman he loves he takes one substitute after another. But they are not real and none can last.

So for a time if such a [substitute] passion comes to fruition, the man will get what he wants. He will get the moral support, the encouragement, the relief from the sense of loneliness, the assurance of his own worth. But these things pass away as the shadows pass across sundials. It is sad, but it is so. The pages of the book will become familiar; the beautiful corner of the road will have been turned too many times.

Leonora senses the gulf and even encourages the substitution with the hope that repeated failure will eventually bring her husband to her. The tragic paradox comes when Edward arrives at the last substitution and finds it impossible. (The girl is Nancy Rufford, their ward, and even his sense of honor revolts.) Then they know that the laws of their own natures divide them so inevitably that there never can be a question of either coming to the other. They can love each other only through a third person and finally no third person is possible.

The unhappy story has grown and reached out; with each attempt to use another woman as a temporary Leonora, Ashburnham has complicated and destroyed the lives of others. The narrator sees it involve his own wife and at last kill her. (At first it seems like a natural death.) It kills Mrs. Maidan when she is tossed aside as insufficient and it has the effect of insupportable tension in the mind of Nancy Rufford, who goes mad. Thus the major tragedy becomes surrounded by ancillary minor ones. At the end only the narrator is left. There is a sense that his preservation comes from having understood more of the story than any of the other people in it. When the book closes he is inhabiting the Ashburnhams' house in Southampton.

I have spoken of the nearly perfect union of language, style and narrative, the natural quality Ford worked for. It begins with his choice of words; "literary" words or sentences are rare and unobtrusive. He deliberately puts down the worn-out, the hackneyed, the simple turns of speech. But under his hand they come out new and strong. It is an amazing thing. There is one description of Nancy Rufford in which only the most common coin of language is used and yet in which she comes to life with clarity, with a sense of discovery: "She was very pretty, she was very young; in spite of her heart, she was very gay and light on her feet. . . ."

This note on language suggests the whole peculiar success of *The Good Soldier*. Ford has taken the most common materials and used them artistically: he has employed the wandering style of narration of an ordinary teller and used it for a series of brilliant *progressions d'effet;* he has used a commonplace vocabulary sensitively and precisely, making it sound fresh; he has taken the threadbare plot of unhappy marriage—even the "triangle"—and given it such new life and meaning that it becomes a passionate and universal story. During his period with Conrad (1897-1903) he learned to toil over every word, to write a book that was sustained from beginning to end, one in which every moment counted —which is the economy of great writing.

Ford (who was always bad at naming his books) wanted to call this novel *The Saddest Story,* but the publishers objected— it was too dreary a title for a wartime reading public. In despair and irony he suggested the present name and was surprised when it appeared. He meant to say, I think, that the saddest story is the perpetual story of love between man and woman, love than can never quite arrive at understanding and decays.

3

The Tietjens novel began with Arthur Marwood. Ford was thinking about him one day while he stood beside the roulette wheels at Monte Carlo, a broken-down officer of the Welsh Regiment convalescing at Menton.

Marwood had been dead a long time, but to Ford he had never really stopped living and around his symbolical memory ideas began to gather. Marwood's life had been all promises and no accomplishment. He was the son of a Yorkshire squire, a brilliant mathematician in the government office of statistics, a Tory, Ford's silent partner in *The English Review*. Ford called the quality of his mind "acute and scornful."

> He possessed the clear Eighteenth Century English mind which has disappeared from the earth, leaving the earth very much the poorer. It was not merely that his mind was encyclopaedic, it was that his information was all arranged.

The figure of Marwood became the center or fulcrum of the Tietjens novels Ford was conceiving.

> I seemed . . . to see him stand in some high place in France during the hostilities taking in not only what was visible but all the causes and all the motive powers of infinitely distant places. And I seemed to hear his infinitely scornful comment on those places. It was as if he lived again.

Thus, more or less given the character of Tietjens, Ford set out to involve him. The physical framework of the story was to be about love. Not love in the ordinary sense. Ford was incapable of simplicities and there is no literature more simple than the love story. Tietjens' relationship with two women throughout the books is the revealing clue for a critique of the whole moral-psychological shift in the relationships between men and women. It implies, symptomatically, a larger conflict.

Ford sensed that the world was deranged. England, specifically, seemed to be emerging from her Pyrrhic victory into social and intellectual chaos, a disorganization of personal lives and concepts. Something disastrous had happened to the whole cultural complex of the nation that had so confidently covered the world with her manners, morals and industrial goods during the last century. Even if it had been preparing for a long time, it seemed to have happened quickly.

Tietjens, who synthesizes in himself the bounded and settled past, undergoes the destructive experience of the present. That, essentially, is Ford's story. Tietjens is Christian, humane, educated in the classics, a Tory. His outlook is feudal and his temperament is chivalric. He represents the culture which the Middle Ages had prepared and the seventeenth and eighteenth century mind regularized. Imaginary as this may have been in fact, it was real as a belief and Tietjens stands for the balanced mind that knew its relation to other men, to nature, and to God.

At one point Tietjens tells himself a fable:

> The Almighty as, on a colossal scale, a great English landowner, a benevolently awful duke who never left his study and was thus invisible, but knowing all about the estate down to the last hind at the home farm and the last oak: Christ an almost too-benevolent land-steward, son of the Owner, knowing all about the estate down to the last child at the porter's lodge, apt to be got around by the more detrimental tenants: the Third Person of the Trinity, the spirit of the estate, the Game as it were, as distinct from the players of the game: the atmosphere of the estate, that of Winchester cathedral just after a Handel anthem has been played.

Almost Platonically, the supernatural world is an ideal image of the natural one. Every incident of life is governed by an appropriate law—moral, theological, or scientific. Then the laws seem to die out.

The shock of destruction when a system of human life and conduct gives way is never definable in purely historical terms. In *The Cherry Orchard,* for instance, it is concentrated in the dramatic break in the life of the Ranevskys. In *The Decline and Fall of the Roman Empire* we sense rather than see or feel the long slow crumbling of walls and character that passes almost without a marker into a new age. Ford tried to show it in the life of one man.

4

Like all of the Tietjens novels, *Some Do Not . . .* is scanty in events and rich in reflection. It is a tripartite introduction of themes and people. The first part takes Tietjens to Rye, where he plays a game of golf, has a brush with suffragettes, endures a strange breakfast at a clergyman's house, and takes a long ride in the fog with a young lady named Valentine Wannop. The next sequence gives us his estranged wife, Sylvia, in Germany in a long conversation with a priest. Tietjens' queer honesty is established in contrast with his wife's pride and recklessness. This beginning is understated and underwritten, all preparatory. Ford did not think in terms of one novel, but conceived the Tietjens story as an over-all pattern.

Roughly, the pattern to come is one of virtue, its trial and vindication. The irony lies in the fact that virtue is never recognized except by the reader and the vindication is only a personal one. Christopher Tietjens is condemned, publicly, as an anachronism. Privately he is to represent something truer and more intelligible than the world that has defeated him. This is an abstract of the theme; its development is rich and complicated.

The second part of *Some Do Not . . .* is the familiar *progression d'effet,* a psychological melodrama between Tietjens and his wife. He is back from France where the early battles of the war have produced in him a temporary amnesia. She attacks him. A desperate and neurotic woman, Sylvia is intent on reducing her husband to her own state of emotional anarchy. Tietjens' inner equilibrium is never better shown and in spite of all the tortures she can devise, he is forgiving, sane, courteous, and impassionate. She must make him show emotion, because any emotion will be a sign of weakness to their English minds. She lets him know how subtly she has blackened his character, spread rumors that he keeps a mistress and has had a child by another woman, how she has complicated his financial affairs to the verge of disgrace. She screams at him.

At last she discloses her final treachery: his father has been told of the scandals and, overcome by the thought that Christopher has got his oldest friend's daughter with child, has committed suicide. Tietjens answers, "Oh! Ah! Yes! . . . I suspected that. I knew it really. I suppose the poor dear knows better now. Or perhaps he doesn't. . . . It doesn't matter." This dramatization of the struggle between moral principle and neurosis is a good statement of the issues with which all four books are concerned. It will recur, be enlarged, developed, but essentially remain the same.

While the dialogue of the scene builds up the dramatic conflict, the mind of Tietjens is concurrently involved with other problems. One is his loss of memory resultant from the shock of war. But the greatest is the problem that hovers over the entire book, a synthesis of all the smaller ones. It is the problem of the meaning of the war.

If there is no human principle left, Tietjens asks himself, how can the war be anything other than a huge symptom of collapse? If the Sylvias, the MacMasterses and the Ruggleses of the story are human fragments belonging to no moral or metaphysical system, what hope is there? "We were fitted neither for victory nor defeat: we could be true neither to friend nor foe. Not even to ourselves!"

In the final sequence Christopher and his brother Mark come to an understanding as they walk to the War Office and meet Valentine. She is in love with Christopher and he has asked her to be his mistress. But in the end, she does not.

5

Though hardly "war books," *No More Parades* and *A Man Could Stand Up* occur in wartime France. Ford differs in every respect from those competent realists, Barbusse, Zweig, Remarque, Hemingway, Aldington, and Sassoon who went to war and wrote about it. Their books are lessons and the moral is familiar: war is a terrible thing. It is dull and deadly, exhausting and crippling; it destroys minds, bodies, and character. It must be treated cynically, seriously, realistically. Ford's war is an effect or a symptom, not a cause. While Sergeant Grischa or Winterbourne sees villages smashed up, Tietjens sees a civilization wrecked.

Now the need for the careful establishment of the hero in *Some Do Not* . . . becomes clear. We need no persuasion to believe that Aldington's protagonist is a young man from the British lower middle classes or that Sassoon's is a type from the upper. But Tietjens, if he is to see more widely and profoundly than they, must be of a philosophical order. Ford has tried to create a modern hero, not simply a protagonist. If the Greek or Romance heroes were of more than human strength or courage, Tietjens, the modern hero, must be taller intellectually. In this twentieth century Trojan War, Tietjens can detect and understand the broad designs of Hera, Zeus, or Aphrodite, but his gift of understanding is finally of no more use than was Hector's gift of strength.

No More Parades deals with the dull, wearing administrative part of modern warfare. Tietjens commands a base camp in France and has the duty of organizing drafts of troops to replenish weakened tactical units.

In *It Was the Nightingale,* Ford says:

A man at this point is subject to exactly the same disasters and perplexities as his temperament prepares him for in times of peace. If he is the sort of man to have put up with the treachery of others, his interests at home will suffer from treasons; if he is the man to incur burdens of debt, debts will unaccountably mass themselves; if he is a man destined to be betrayed by women, his women will betray him exaggeratedly and without shame. For all these vicissitudes will be enlarged by the strident note that in time of war gets into both speeches and events. . . . And he is indeed then *homo duplex*: a poor fellow whose body is tied in one place but whose mind and personality brood over another distant locality.

Psychologically, Tietjens is in a reflecting Hall of Mirrors. His anxieties, gross and distorted, appear in the men around him. There is a Welsh private with marital difficulties. There is McKechnie, an officer whose derangement mirrors Tietjens' temptation to insanity. The banging echoes in poor McKechnie's head imitate the times:

The memory seemed to burst inside him like one of those beastly enormous tin-pot crashes: the two came together, the internal one and the one outside. He felt that chimney pots were going to crash onto his head. You protected yourself by shouting at the damned infernal idiots; if you could outshout the row, you were safe.

The plot action centers around Sylvia's unauthorized visit to France. It is the breakfast scene over again—this time in action. She raises every kind of trouble—official, domestic, scandalous. Tietjens can ignore her because he understands her and he understands the nature of malice. But by this time he is beginning to realize that he is witness to the great crack-up. In 1914 he had gone into the War Office and had met a man who was devising a ceremony for the disbanding of troops (England was ready for one contingency at least, Tietjens reflects). At the end of the ceremony the band would play *Land of Hope and Glory* and the adjutant would then say, "There will be no more parades. . . ." Tietjens is almost inarticulate with irony. He says, "Don't you see how symbolical it was? . . . For there won't. There damn well won't. No more Hope, no more Glory, no more parades for you and me anymore. Not for the country. . . . Nor for the world, I dare say."

Sylvia's persecutions end in getting Tietjens sent to the front and that is the landscape of the third novel, *A Man Could Stand Up*. Again the book is in three parts. It opens with a long telephone call during which Valentine finds out that Tietjens, apparently out of his senses, has returned to London.

The long middle section is a day in the trenches, most of which takes place in Tietjens' consciousness. In the present tense it is concerned with duties, minor military matters. He jokes with the men of a new draft, he soothes the frantic McKechnie, he goes for a walk to inspect A Company's trenches. The memories and fragments of memories mingle with the real details. Ford's is different from any other battlefield of literature. The landscape is a visual focal point for the memory and imagination. Tietjens' new recruits remind him of music hall comedians; he creates an imaginary biography for his colonel; he remembers all the events of a day when a captured deserter broke down, he sees the figure of a Welsh officer caught in the barbed wire with one arm in the air like a rotting statue; he hears over again the voice from a German mine beneath his feet, "*Bringt dem Hauptmann eine Kerze*"; and, almost thematically conjures an image of George Herbert standing on a hill near Bemerton parsonage thinking of the line, "*Sweet day so cool, so calm, so bright, the bridal of the earth and sky. . . .*"

Again Tietjens sees the insanity and loss of purpose in all the

men around him encroaching on his own mind. McKechnie stares
madly, the Colonel raves, Lt. Aranjuez displays his irrational vanity.
And Tietjens even doubts himself. The voice from underground
calling for "a candle for the captain," was it real?

And again what carries him through is the structure of reference to which he can turn. He recognizes that an insane man has
no values, no principles, no logical frame of belief to provide
a power of acting consistently. (That Tietjens' system is feudal-
aristocratic-Anglo-Catholic is of no importance; the important thing
is that it is there.) Throughout the book Tietjens clings to his line
of George Herbert as a vision of sanity; it is not a charm or talisman
but a piece of evidence that there is or has been sometime a logical,
regular, beautiful order of nature. Sanity remains as long as you
know yourself to be part of that order.

The delirium ends with a tragi-comic incident. Tietjens is buried
by a German shell, succeeds in digging himself and another man
out, and carries the other away under fire. Immediately he is called
to present himself to an inspecting general who reprimands him
for not appearing, for appearing in a dirty uniform, for unsoldierly
conduct, and relieves him of command.

The third part returns to London as Valentine goes to see Tietjens. On the night of the Armistice they find themselves in his
empty house, at last ready to admit they love each other. One by
one the specters from the trenches wander in: the crazy colonel, the
vain lieutenant (with one eye gone now), the insane McKechnie.
But they have no power to alarm any more. Through understanding with Valentine, Tietjens has saved his equilibrium. He is out
of the madhouse world; his ordeal by psychosis over. They all sit
down to celebrate the end of the war.

Tietjens' dream-of-a-world-gone-mad seems past, but was it a
dream? *The Last Post* leads deceptively from a quiet rural scene
into a peacetime world as jumbled and disordered as the phantasmagoria of the trenches. The people are all non sequiturs, the furniture is pasted to the ceiling, no one ever answers anyone else in
conversation.

The book is an odd kind of oblique statement. Tietjens appears
for only one moment near the end, yet the novel is all about him.
In it are all the people who surround his life; their thoughts and

actions all seem to focus on the unseen center. It is organized into nine interrelated streams of consciousness, an elaborate pattern of psyches that needs some explanation. The action occurs within a few hours in which whole lifetimes are mentally examined. The several characters are given an opportunity to sort over the bric-a-brac of their memories as they move somewhere in the vicinity of the cottage to which the Tietjens brothers have gone with Valentine and Marie (Mark's mistress) after the war. Of the latter, Ford says, "Her mind was in fact like a cupboard, stuffed, packed with the most incongruous materials, tools, vessels and debris. Once you opened the door you never knew what would tumble out or be followed by what." But most of the incongruous material serves for direct or indirect comment on the life or character of Christopher Tietjens.

The arrangement and sequence of the interior monologues is carefully planned. Those belonging to Mark Tietjens, coming at the beginning, middle and end, supply the framework. He has been paralyzed by a stroke and lies out under a thatch roof where he can see a broad country landscape from his bed.

There is a simple series of events taking place in the "novelistic present" that relates the nine thought sequences. These actual events, as mirrored in each mind, overlap until there will have accumulated three or four different points of view on the same incident. Ford's method is to observe an event through one character, then find a point of coincidence by having another see the same thing from a different perspective, then to observe a second event through the second figure and a third. In this way he manipulates time present. But that is only one theme in the consciousness, and themes from the past appear and reappear, again furnishing points of time at which two or more minds coincide. Here it is a subjective rather than an objective time-shift.

Thus *The Last Post* becomes a rich multi-layered palimpsest of memory and impression. As each character mentally discusses an area of the Tietjens story, an extensive recapitulation is built up. The six minds serve as a chorus for an impressionistic narration of the events surrounding the life of the hero.

I have avoided comparisons with the Joyce, Proust, Dorothy Richardson, or Virginia Woolf "stream of consciousness" techniques.

There are both similarities and differences. However, at the time
he wrote these books, Ford had read none of their works except
Joyce's *Portrait of the Artist*.

Mark, as he lies paralyzed on his cot, supplies the first monologue. This leads into the reflections of Marie-Leonie, a French-
woman who has been his mistress for years and who is now his
wife. Cramp, a farmer employed by Tietjens, is third. Then comes
an American woman (her presence has to be accounted for later)
who bursts into the garden and addresses a long verbal monologue
to the helpless Mark. Mark's central thought sequence recovers
many of the events of Armistice night (some revealed now for the
first time). Following him again is Marie-Leonie, who is making
cider. Sylvia Tietjens herself comes next and at this place the reader
discovers that she is the cause of the commotion and the unwanted
visitors in the garden. Valentine Wannop, upstairs in the cottage,
has her turn. She comes down in time to observe a confused scene
when the small crowd pushes its way into the parlor of the cottage.

But Mark has the final word, a statement, at last, of the Tietjens
story from a clear and objective point of view. Since he is paralyzed
and near to death, his definition of the past takes on a curiously
removed and eternal character after the lies, the views and half-
views, the ambiguous impressions, and unreliable memories that
have been called upon before. Mark decides for the best. He realizes
the truth about his father's "suicide," finds that Christopher's son is
really Christopher's son, discovers that the curse is off the Tietjens
(it was to go when a certain ancient tree was cut down and the
estate again passed into the hand of a Catholic). He even decides on
his own entrance into heaven.

Unable to look, he hears the people in the garden as voices
from the past. "A lot of voices passing behind my head. Damn it
all, could they all be ghosts drifting before the wind?" Christopher
appears in front of him for a moment. He dies. With his death and
the crash of Groby great tree, the era of the Tietjens has ended.

In Mark's mind there cannot be any optimism for the future,
but all events of the past are reconciled. He presents the final summation of the Tietjens case and discovers that the whole strength
of it lies in the fact that they have been true to something. This is
their virtue. In an unconventional way, the whole story is a kind

of morality play—never between absolute good and absolute evil
but between one systematic theory of how men should lead a "good"
life in the world and no theory. Anarchy wins; but that is an historical fact, not an evaluation.

6

In his book called *The Critical Attitude,* published in 1911,
Ford has traced what he considered to be the finest fictional tradition in Western Europe—the intense study of human behavior that
began with Richardson and (with a few exceptions such as Jane
Austen) passed across the channel to France during the nineteenth
century. With the advent of James, Ford believed, it had come back
again to English literature and the Tietjens story was his own attempt to carry it on.

This might be defined as a kind of "inductive" psychological
novel. The writer explores the motives and feelings of a certain
group of characters with immense care and sensitivity. Simultaneously he examines the interaction and interpenetration of each
with the other. Since all society is a result of the way human beings
act in their relationships, the novel becomes an astute deductive
inquiry into the human world at that particular moment. Proust's
examination of ennui and decadence in a character will suggest the
symptoms of a common and contagious disease.

As a result, these novels become a type of allegory, penetrating,
as they do, further into the human complex than the superficial
Balzacian "man-as-a-product-of-his-environment" theory. They are
distinct from the novels in which characters play an assigned role in
a plot, become actors.

It was this kind of "Jamesian" novel that Ford attempted in
the Tietjens series. He tried to enlarge its scope by concerning it
with war. James (I quote a common objection) may have falsely
refined away too much of the incidental and non-contributory phenomena of ordinary life, purifying his stories to the essential emotional conflicts of their people, thereby losing "reality." Ford felt this
danger. He meant to give a broad view (but in the background
only) that would suggest the non-significant details of a real world;
yet in the foreground he would always keep the intense emotional-
psychological-moral study of characters and the interrelation of char-

acters. The war was his excuse for the "intensification." In addition
it served as a great outward symbol of the combat going on within
the center of the story.

The general "meaning" of the Tietjens books is a meaning
common to most of the important writers of the twentieth century.
It is a projection of disorder and breakup. Mann, Joyce, Eliot, and
Gide have perhaps dramatized it in different or larger ways, but
no more skillfully than Ford.

After an initial interest, Ford has been neglected by readers
and ignored by the critics. The Tietjens series has been wrongly
and accidentally classed with that type of ephemeral semi-journal-
istic "war novel" whose sudden popularity during the twenties soon
passed. A later generation will perhaps be able to make the separation and to recognize Ford's story as a concentrated examination of
human beings during a "time of troubles," an important psychological allegory that is more about a human era than an episode
labelled in history books as "World War I."

Vivienne Koch THE POETRY OF

ALLEN TATE

I SHOULD like to propose two revisions of the customary
valuation put upon the poetry of Allen Tate. First, it has become increasingly evident with each new work that Mr. Tate is a
fugitive from the Fugitives. The Fugitives were that talented group
of Southern writers who, finding the Northern poetic climate of
the early twenties too exacerbatingly modern, reaffirmed their alle-

giances with "tradition," a term they took some care to define. While we commonly think of the Southerners as a group, and while in a loose personal sense this may be so, it is my belief that in a veiled but not altogether deceptive fashion Mr. Tate has been seeking to free himself from the claims of group loyalty, claims which at one time had threatened the temper of his own sensibility.

Curiously enough, Tate's first symptomatic departure from his "tradition" came in what would seem, on the surface, to be the apotheosis of his conformance to it. It came in his translation of *Pervigilium Veneris* (1934), that neglected little classic never happily Englished, upon which he chose to exercise his powers, not so much as a Latinist, but as a poet of classical affiliations. Yet I think his choice of this delicately tinted but uninnocently erotic poem was perhaps motivated by the fact that, as Professor Mackail points out, it represents

> the first clear note of the new romanticism which transformed classical into mediaeval literature. . . . Nothing could be less like either a folk-song or an official ode. It touches the last refinement of simplicity. In the delicately running, softly swaying verses, that ring and glitter and return on themselves in interlacing patterns, there is germinally the essence and inner spirit of the whole romantic movement. All the motives of the old classical poetry survive, yet all have undergone a new birth.

The *Pervigilium Veneris* is Allen Tate's valedictory, from a safe distance, to the Fugitives, to the South, to the "classical" tradition, to his masters. The quickest way to get over the goodbyes is to say them in a strange language.

My second proposal flows from the historic process I have just described and is, at the same time and paradoxically, anterior to the whole development. I believe that Tate is a poet of romantic sensibility who has tried with varying success to compress his talents into a chastely classical form and that, in inverse degrees to his willingness or ability to do so, his best poetry has been written. Where his romanticism gets the better of him, or, to shift the metaphor, finds the classicist nodding, there we get the most enduring, vital and original poetry Tate is capable of writing. The *Pervigilium* was playing romanticism with the rules; with the publication of *The Winter Sea* it became clear that Tate was playing his own way.

In short, we have been assessing Tate too long in terms of his origins (the genetic fallacy) and his prose judgment (the doctrinal fallacy). It is time we began to follow the lead of the poems.

2

In Tate's *Selected Poems* (1937) it is possible to group together the work of the early twenties on several grounds. "Obituary," "Death of Little Boys," "Horatian Epode to the Duchess of Malfi," "The Subway," "Ditty," "Retroduction to American History," and "Mr. Pope," all bear the imprint of the Eliot of "Prufrock" in the characteristic quatrain (or aggregation of joined quatrains) with the typically anticlimactic, sometimes parenthetical usage of the fourth line. Similarly, the vocabulary is often derived from Eliot: "You have no more chance than an infusorian/ Lodged in a hollow molar of an eohippus./ Come, now, no prattle of remergence with the *ontos on*." All, without a single exception, whether the subject be Webster, Pope, the death of little boys, or their sleeping, reveal a bitter, angry and passionate rejection of the present, of contemporaneity where "you, so crazy and inviolate" are "hurled religiously/ Upon your business of humility/ Into the iron forestries of hell;/ . . . Dazed, while the worldless heavens bulge and reel/ In the cold revery of an idiot."

It is a present in which even "little boys grown patient at last, weary/ Surrender their eyes immeasurably to the night," and other "Little boys no longer sight the plover/ Streaked in the sky," while "men, who fail . . . will plunge, mile after mile of men, to crush this lucent madness of the face,/ Go home and put their heads upon the pillow. Turn whatever shift the darkness cleaves,/ Tuck in their eyes, and cover/ The flying dark with sleep like falling leaves." I hope it is excusable to resort to the kind of mosaic I have just composed in order to point a paradox: Allen Tate, at the start of his career in the early twenties, was affirming his allegiances with the classical past in the unsigned editorials of *The Fugitive* and, at the same time, betraying in every poem he was writing a frankly nihilistic temper which, in its alternating violence and absolution, was a romanticism of a somewhat more fiery brand than his criticism might have endorsed.

Perhaps the gauge of Tate's youthful romanticism may be best explored in his much-admired "Death of Little Boys" published in the *Nation* in 1925 when he was twenty-six years old:

> *When little boys grown patient at last, weary,*
> *Surrender their eyes immeasurably to the night,*
> *The event will rage terrific as the sea;*
> *Their bodies fill a crumbling room with light.*
>
> *Then you will touch at the bedside, torn in two,*
> *Gold curls now intricate with gray*
> *As the windowpane extends a fear to you*
> *From one peeled aster drenched with the wind all day.*
>
> *And over his chest the covers in an ultimate dream*
> *Will mount to the teeth, ascend the eyes, press back*
> *The locks—while round his sturdy belly gleam*
> *The suspended breaths, white spars above the wreck:*
>
> *Till all the guests, come in to look, turn down*
> *Their palms, and delirium assails the cliff*
> *Of Norway where you ponder, and your little town*
> *Reels like a sailor in his rotten skiff.*
>
> *The bleak sunshine shrieks its chipped music then*
> *Out to the milkweed amid the fields of wheat.*
> *There is a calm for you where men and women*
> *Unroll the chill precision of moving feet.*

The only "classical" element in this adventuresome poem is the plural in the title and the first line. The generalizing character of "boys" extends or is intended to extend an individual experience of death to a universal statement of it. But apart from this gesture (a successful one) there is no concession anywhere in the poem (unless it be in the rather diversified quatrains) to any poem I am familiar with in the "tradition" of English literature up to 1925. The poem is a consideration of the problem of identity or, more philosophically, the problem of permanence and change. The "you" of the second paragraph is not merely rhetorical address which seeks to involve the reader with the death of little boys, but it achieves exactly that.

The bedside is "torn in two" by the "event" of death, which, let us note, does not destroy the little boys but rather the room which crumbles with light. (The room, of course, may be everything which is contained in it.) The "gold curls" are "now deftly intricate with gray" because of the blinding vision of death in which "you" (the onlooker, father, or little boy grown up) must participate because you too feel the fear extended by the windowpane (night or death to which the little boys have in Stanza One surrendered their eyes). The emotional affects throughout are persistently ascribed to the landscape.

In Stanza Three the death is individualized in the singular pronouns (abandoning the universal), in the magnificently concrete, yet symbolic detail of the "sturdy belly" round which "gleam the suspended breaths" of the dead boy, or rather boy-in-man, and "you" (like another Hamlet, a questioning, dubious intellect) pondering on your cliff feel delirium (death, shifting identity) assailing it (just as, in a similar transfer of affects, it was the *room* and not the body which crumbled in Stanza One), and your little town (something built, *made*, the ego, perhaps) "reels like a sailor in his rotten skiff." Here the image of the dead boy as a wreck and the little town (the ego) about-to-be-wrecked converge in the sea symbolism. It is at this point (the crisis of the poem) that the fusion of meanings is consummated and the question of permanence (identity) arises like a lonely phoenix from the wreck of little boys (your wreck, of course). The last stanza is an anticlimax, and is so intended. The "bleak sunshine," the discordant shriek of its "chipped music," reaches out to the level of external quotidian existence (milkweed, etc.) where there are no more "events terrific as the sea" but only an ironic calm whose inevitable "precision of moving feet" implies an ultimately similar dissolution of the almost-wrecked ego.

Perhaps this explication will have seemed forced. In that event, I suggest returning to the sea metaphor introduced in Stanza One, picked up and developed in Three and consummated in the harsh despair of "reels," "drunk," and "rotten," to say nothing of the flimsy, useless phonetic fluff of "skiff." By that route, it seems to me, almost the same reading may be developed as the one I have got by the long way. Little boys die in men before men die. Man is torn in two by his past (his little boyhood) and his present. The agency of childhood is mysterious and terrifying in the personality of the man (the aster is man "peeled"—revealed—by his youth). The certainty of identity (integration of personality) is seriously threatened in Stanza Four. In Five there is a sick rebound: the world and its dull, mechanic inevitability must be met again. The let-down in diction, the clarity of the last stanza as opposed to the complexity of the others, is Tate's cold and disdainful bow to the outer world, to the nowness he *will* not recognize. This, then, is the kind of poetry Tate was writing when he was raging with youthful hauteur against the *nouveaux-arrivés* "experimentalists." To recapitulate: "Death of Little Boys" is a very good poem; it is revelatory of Tate's "original" temperamental bent (if learning had not already disguised the interior man); it is certainly as "experimental" as any poem I know of written at that time, including the "romantic" experimentalism of Tate's friend, Hart Crane.

The following five years, 1925-30, are crucial to the direction of Tate's growth. Some residence in England and France during that time leave superficial traces in his work. If Tate ever thought of himself as an exile (and at least one poem, "Message from Abroad," bears witness that he did) it was certainly not the kind of willed exile represented by Joyce's categorical imperatives for the artist, "Silence, exile and cunning," nor by Henry James's ambassadorial *rapprochements*, nor by Eliot's British repatriation. Europe merely reinforces for Tate the feeling he started out with in Kentucky. He is exiled not from a place, but from a condition. The present (and Europe is just as contemporaneous as the South) exiles him from the past. He is cut off *through no fault of his own* from a more meaningful condition of living. He will begin to try in these years to find, focus, and define the character of that past and so, perhaps, to possess it. . . .

Perhaps the most ambitious poem of this period, and one which summarizes Tate's intellectual situation in the early thirties, is "Causerie" (1925-31). The tone is again forensic but the vigor of the indictment is sustained throughout. Unlike his practice in "Meditation" Tate here depends on a rugged, irregular blank verse manipulated with great flexibility in terms of caesura to effect a swelling and urgent rhetoric. The poet is the prosecutor; yet he is himself among the accused:

> *I've done no rape, arson, incest, no murder,*
> *Yet cannot sleep . . .*

Through another means he asks the question of "Message from Abroad":

> *Where is your house, in which room stands your bed?*

In ironic answer comes a swift, Elizabethan-in-texture arraignment of the fate suffered by the South:

> *Have you a daughter,*
> *Daughters are the seed of occupations . . .*
> *Let her not read history lest knowledge*
> *Of her fathers instruct her to be a noted bawd.*

The argument proceeds by a kind of rhetorical casuality (note the force of "For" in the passage connecting with the above):

> *For miracles are faint*
> *And resurrection is our weakest point of religion.*

Later, the moral confusion of modern life is attributed to a loss of absolutes:

> *In an age of abstract experience, fornication*
> *Is self-expression, adjunct to Christian euphoria,*
> *And whores become delinquents; delinquents, patients;*
> *Patients, wards of society. Whores, by that rule,*
> *Are precious.*

The result is "a race of politic pimps" without "The antique courtesy of your myths." What Tate regrets is the loss of the principle of evil, a loss of which Wallace Stevens was to say fifteen years later: "the death of Satan was a tragedy / for the imagination. . . ." But, and I think this is a distinction which illuminates Tate's special quality as a moralist, he does not, like Stevens, relate this loss to its effect on art, but rather to its effect on conduct. This is a didactic poetry of such high order that the didacticism is (as in Blake) through the purest rhetorical fusion indistinguishable from the poetry. The control is sure and adult. The entirety of the loss is acknowledged; there is no longer an effort to reclaim the lost from "the province of the drowned." The poet is operating on a higher level of social "reality," but there is no acceptance—yet.

3

We can measure the range of Tate's later progress by a study of *The Winter Sea* (1944). Although containing less than a dozen poems, it yet projects an almost complete break with Tate's earlier work in the forthright abandoning of the tendency to allow "philosophic metaphors" about tradition to determine the structure and content of the poems. It is possible that his fine historical novel of the antebellum South, *The Fathers* (1938), had served Tate as a sieve for draining off this long-nourished interest into the more flexible formal unit of experience of the story. *The Fathers,* like "The Ode," is about those who were destroyed through what Hart Crane in a letter to Tate calls "an excess of chivalry." The only echo of the past to be found in the diverse emphasis of the poems in *The Winter Sea* is the concern with childhood guilt noted in "Sonnets at Christmas." This theme now advances into a more elevated symbolic use in "More Sonnets at Christmas" and in "Seasons of the Soul."

It would not be over-emphasizing the personal situation revealed by this volume to say that it releases in Tate the full force of the romantic strain which had seemed successfully inhibited during the preceding years. Still, the didactic impulse and conscious moral aim is too habitual to suffer serious diminution and courses along, a parallel stream of intention, with the revitalized romanticism. Tate's own critical prescription for this mode of moral inquiry is certainly met by his achievement in "Jubilo," in "Ode to Our Young Proconsuls of the Air," and in "Eclogue of the Liberal and the Poet." "The moral intelligence," he had written in 1940, "gets into poetry . . . not as moral abstractions, but as form, coherence of image, and metaphor, control of tone and rhythm, the union of these features." Tate's essays in the satire are vigorous, witty and, as in classical satire, full of honest prejudices. A prejudice, let it be noted in passing, is different from a *willed* belief. "Jubilo," using as refrain a phrase from a Negro popular song, is a tongue-in-cheek celebration of boys who "caress the machines they ride." The mock-heroic epic, while not at all a model, makes itself felt in "Ode to Our Young Proconsuls" in the deliberately heightened mock-allegorical language which raises the invective to dramatic irony.

"False Nightmare," a telling although not altogether just indictment of Whitmanism, is sure to be quoted by Tate's enemies as evidence of his "reactionary" views. It is a bitter poem but, carefully read, as reactionary as Jeremiah.

We become aware, then, that in Tate's recent poetry the traditional influences (whether of structure, idea, or both) operate only as qualities, not as models. Thus, one is barely conscious of the Dante influence in the impressive "Seasons of the Soul," but it is there in the deeply religio-ethical purpose of the poem as well as in the implied descent of the poet into his own hell. In the same poem the influence of the *Pervigilium Veneris* is felt in the erotic elements as well as in the subtle use of refrain. "Seasons of the Soul" can, I think, be thought of as the summation of Tate's present position. It is an instructive guide to his technical practice; it is a map to his present values, even though it merely poses a problem. But it is by the way in which a problem is framed that the nature of its solution is implied. Let us examine the frame.

The scheme of the poem is simple: the four seasons correspond to the four elements of the ancients. Thus the chronicle is of the four ages of man in relation to the four aspects of the universe he inhabits. More specifically, however, it is modern man whose spiritual biography Mr. Tate records. Summer is the first season; the background is now:

> *It was a gentle sun*
> *When, at the June solstice,*
> *Green France was overrun*
> *With caterpillar feet.*
> *No head knows where its rest is*
> *Or may lie down with reason*
> *When war's usurping claws*
> *Shall take the heart escheat—*

This suggests another summer (the summer of childhood which is identified with the summer of classical antiquity in its clarity and innocence) when "The summer had no reason;/ Then, like a primal cause/ It had its timeless day."

In Autumn, technically the most interesting section, the surrealist device of a dream is employed to enable the poet to prophesy, as it were, a vision of his own old age which is revealed to him as a trap. He is caught in a deep well, an empty house (the house of the past) peopled only by ghosts, his ancestors, who refuse to recognize him. The house of the past is not real, "The door was false—no key/ Or lock . . . yet I could see/ I had been born to it/ For miles of running brought/ Me back where I began." The failure of parents to recognize a son is another way of stating the problem of identity. We have seen how in his earliest writing this question engaged Tate. Now the dilemma is extended to the profoundest sort of personal epistemology: If your progenitors do not know you, if you are cut off from communication with your contemporaries ("I was down a well"), if, in short, there is no objective recognition of your identity, who are you? Along with this return to a study of his past, Tate also reverts to the more sensuous and concrete imagery of the early "romantic" poems, an imagery determined by inner, emotional connections and not by logical ones. I think especially of the father-mother imagery of Section II and the sea imagery of Section III.

From the frustration of this cyclical returning upon himself, the poet in "Winter," a strikingly beautiful section, pleads with Venus to return to her element. Christianity ("the drying God above/ Hanged in his windy steeple") is dead and "No longer bears for us/ The living wound of love." There is every reason to suppose that we must take this as Tate's mature view of the religious problem, a problem which he could not resolve with such brutal finality in the middle years. In "More Sonnets at Christmas," composed a little before "Seasons of the Soul," he had implied the dismissal:

> Ten years is time enough to be dismayed
> By mummy Christ, head crammed between his knees.

The violence of this image, its quasi-obscenity, even, is the measure of the distance Tate traveled in the ten dismaying years from the time when the question of anti-miraculism disturbed him. It is clear enough now that, as Tate once flippantly remarked, the question of Mr. Eliot's submission to the Thirty-nine Articles was never to be a live option in his own poetry.

But the pagan values are dead, too ("All the sea-gods are dead"). There is sex: The pacing animal who turns "The venereal awl/ In the livid wound of love." Again, a strange surrealist image connects the general with the poet's particular plight: In a grove under the sea the poet seizes the branch of a madrepore from which drips a "speaking blood/ From the livid wound of love":

> *We are the men who died*
> *Of self-inflicted woe,*
> *Lovers whose stratagem*
> *Led to their suicide*
> *I touched my sanguine hair*
> *And felt it drip above*
> *Their brother who, like them,*
> *Was maimed and did not bear*
> *The living wound of love.*

The "living wound" of love would seem to be suggested by the famous Proem to *De Rerum Naturae* in which Lucretius, looking on a war-torn Italy, calls upon Venus (as a fertility-principle) to inflict upon Mars the eternal wound of love (*aeterno volnere amoris*) and thus win peace and increase for the Romans. For Tate the "eternal wound" becomes the "living wound" and I take the implication to be that Love, growing from a "livid" wound into the "living" wound is the only possible power which can rescue man from his otherwise maimed existence. The passionate and suppliant address to Venus makes clear that she is the complex erotic symbol around which cluster the poet's hopes for various kinds of regeneration:

> *All the sea-gods are dead*
> *You, Venus, come home*
> *To your salt maidenhead.*

This reading, I think, is confirmed by the next section "Spring," a liturgical chant (still within the frame of the ten-line iambic trimeter stanza) to the Mother of Silences, a figure who simultaneously suggests the principle of the Virgin (the Mother, Life) and the principle of Death (the Mystery); the figure, significantly, never speaks. The symbol has a certain obscurity not altogether relieved by the following passage:

> *Come, mother, and lean*
> *At the window with your son*

And gaze through its light frame
These fifteen centuries
Upon the shirking scene
Where men, blind, go lame:

Now the mother appears to be Saint Monica as she appears in Book IX of St. Augustine's *Confessions*. Mother and son stand alone "leaning in a certain window, from which the garden of the house we occupied at Ostia could be seen"; cataloguing a set of earthly conditions, which, could they be "silenced," would enable them to arrive at an apprehension of the "hereafter." Soon after, Monica dies and leaves Augustine with a living wound "from having that most sweet and dear habit of living together suddenly broken off." Thus the Mother of Silences is a particular mother (St. Monica), the Virgin, the Mystery, and through Augustine's unmentioned wound she is identified further with the principle of Love. Love, then, is the luminous agency common to all the referents of the symbol. Yet, in the end, one feels that the hope of regeneration through Love is reluctantly abandoned and death is sought as the only certain "kindness" to which men can aspire.

"Seasons of the Soul" will stand as a major event in Tate's career as a poet. It is lyrical, sensuous and tragic. It is, for whatever meaning that chameleon term may still carry, romantic. In "Tension in Poetry," an interesting essay written some years ago, Tate distinguishes the metaphysical from the romantic poet in the following way:

> The metaphysical poet as a rationalist begins at or near the extensive or denotative end of the line. The romantic or Symbolist poet at the other, intensive end; and each by a straining feat of the imagination tries to push his meaning as far as he can toward the opposite end, so as to occupy the entire scale. . . .

But there is to be recommended a "poetry of the center," that is, "poetry of tension in which the strategy is diffused into the unitary effect." I am not sure after several rereadings how this strategy is implemented. Indeed, the concept of "tension" has been used by some critics, although not by Mr. Tate, to get around critical

problems more taxing to unravel than to designate as illustrative
of "tension."

However, if there is a poetry of tension and if there is a living
practitioner of this awesome and marvelous feat of poetic balance
between the classic and the romantic, the metaphysical and the
Symbolist among us, surely it is Tate himself. But it has become
increasingly evident that the idea of the poet as the daring young
man on the flying trapeze is giving way to a less perilous but more
fruitful enterprise: the paradoxical roles of suppliant and teacher
have lost their separate identities in a profound and humble appreciation of what de Unamuno calls "the tragic sense of life." In
"Winter Mask to the Memory of W. B. Yeats" (1943) Tate writes:

> *I asked the master Yeats*
> *Whose great style could not tell*
> *Why it is man hates*
> *His own salvation,*
> *Prefers the way to hell,*
> *And finds his last safety*
> *In the self-made curse that bore*
> *Him towards damnation:*
> *The drowned undrowned by the sea,*
> *The sea worth living for.*

R. P. Blackmur PARODY AND

CRITIQUE: *Notes on* Thomas Mann's *Doctor Faustus*

IN THIS country, at this time, our way of looking at our culture makes it difficult for us to look at a work of literary art
which announces itself in its title, in the motto on its title page, and
in the attributes of its hero as in intention a great work dealing
with a very great man. We do not take to great men unless they be
criminal or popular or fashionable or dead in some other way; we
resent claims to maximum attention and maximum response—we
like our great men to do our work for us, and we like to take up
their greatness on the side, without noticing it, and without pain.
The attitude is prudent, avoids risks and avoids snobbery, but it
leaves us at a loss before Thomas Mann's *Dr. Faustus,* the Life of
the German Composer Adrian Leverkühn as told by a friend—
and the sense of being at a loss is all the more acute when we see
that the rest of the title page is covered by nine lines of Dante's
Italian taken from the opening of the second Canto of the Inferno
where Dante pauses to take his first breath in the unutterable human
hell in which he found himself. Because I have now read this work
three times, and have been moved variously and incongruously each
time, it seems not only necessary but a good thing to risk both mistaken judgment and possibly snobbery—it seems good and necessary
to take this work in its asserted role and attempt to frame the maximum response which maximum attention can initially yield to this
image of greatness in our time. I have no fear I am alone in this

attempt; I know of others, though they do not crowd; but first of all I have as friend and companion him who tells and meditates upon the life of this modern Faust, I mean of course the Catholic humanist, Serenus Zeitblom, that serene flower of the hellish time, and it is because of him, and so much of faith as we share—we are both humanist though not both Catholic—that I understand how to begin.

I begin with the humanist's natural questions. I ask, in order to remind myself, what the name Dr. Faustus on a modern work might mean; and I ask what Dante's Italian is doing there under the title. What have a devil myth and an invocation of the Greek Muses got to do with contemporary bourgeois humanism? (We are still bourgeois, for the time being, if we are humanists at all.) Why should a work purportedly written by a humanist go so far back for its title and its motto—so far back that in each case it touches upon forces recognized, if at all, as prior to the human? Is it the predicament of the humanist that in order to combat the inhumanities of his own day he must get succor in remote forces that must seem at least as menacing as they are propitious? Or is it rather that he feels he must refresh in himself the stream of daemonic inspiration, of hidden and inexplicable strength, in order to combat not his enemies but his own weaknesses? I think both. But let us examine into title and motto for their own sakes.

What or who is Faustus? A medieval legend, an Elizabethan incantation, a German epic, a French opera, an attribute of the arrogance of the modern or experimental man; but in all cases combining the two traditions that inhabit us from our past and trouble us as to our future, the two traditions of light and darkness. There is on the one side the tradition of reason and revelation and inspiration, and on the other side the tradition of the daemonic, the chthonic, and the magical. Somehow in the image of Faustus the two traditions are combined; the things of darkness work into the broad day; and the combining agent is the devil, who offers us the pride of mastery of both traditions. All images of Faustus have to do with the mastery of absolute knowledge followed by the loss of it altogether. The devil tempts us by offering us knowledge of the truth about ourselves which, without the power of his temptation, we should not have the strength to bear; the knowledge refused to Adam in Paradise. How should we put it? It is a temptation to the absolute possession both in knowledge and of the substance of knowledge, so that we might know both our inspiration and what keeps us going: the knowledge both of what we love and of what we shun to think we are. The glorious and the sensual—neither of them "reasonable"—are in this image reconciled with the humiliating and the ascetic—which are not reasonable either. Faustus woos the Muses with the aid of the devil, the divine with the daemonic. Goethe was correcting nothing in the old legend when in the Second Part of his epic the marriage of Faustus and Helen serves for the reconciliation of the Greek and Christian worlds; he only developed the human necessity that was there to be declared, and to be created if it was not there. And it is on such an insight that Thomas Mann brings out his Faustian image; but because of this particular moment in time—our moment when so much has been taken away— he cannot proceed where Goethe left off; he has to begin behind Goethe in Dante, and he has to try to go further back still, not only into the old legend, but also into its roots in that country of the mind which is neither Christian nor Greek, to the country, in Mann's own phrase, of the naked human voice.

To do all this you have to be a little solemn and dedicated, but you have also to be passionate and exact. You have to believe and you have to wrestle with your belief in the flesh of the actual world around you. You have to be a humanist, not of the renaissance but of the bourgeois world—the bourgeois in that rebellion against both reason and flesh which constitutes his vitality; you have to be the bourgeois humanist seeking to rediscover, now that his order is failing, what all that turbulence was which he had put in order. You have to see, like James Joyce in *Ulysses,* the darkness that is in the light as well as the darkness that is all about us. You must look into two kinds of chaos, the mere disorder and the original black. Othello, you will remember, saw both kinds at once when looking after Desdemona in anguish of self-impalement he cried out:

> *Excellent wretch! Perdition catch my soul,*
> *But I do love thee! and when I love thee not,*
> *Chaos is come again.*

In short you have to deal with the devil in order to reach the daemonic, and as a humanist you will remember that, without the
human, the daemonic is the diabolic. The daemon is the indwelling
power, or spirit, or genius in things, whether for good or evil; the
daemon represents the basic conditions of human life; the devil is
their corruption, the temptation of finding means of not accepting
those conditions. Thus the devil in our psychology is a way-station
to the demon, providing by rebellion and denial and parody, the
incentive of remorse to go further. Look in the dictionary: Diabolos
is the slanderer, the calumniator, in Greek; in Hebrew, the tempter
and spiritual enemy of mankind—offering other than human conditions. One form of Christian tragedy is in the confusion of the two,
the merging of that which slanders with that which tempts; Greek
and Satanic pride here touch; and it is that confusion, that equiv-
ocalness, which inhabits the Dr. Faustus of Thomas Mann. So it
is that in the first chapter of that work, we find Serenus Zeitblom,
the Catholic humanist and son of the Muses, meditating the life of
his friend the great musician Adrian Leverkühn, and finding that
that life forces him, by its God-inflicted genius struggling with the
corrupt Faustian bargain, into the further meditation of the daemonic: in his friend's life and, above all, in his friend's music, both
of which he loved with tenderness and terror. There is the whole
theme of the work announced at once in terms of its title.

Now let us look at the motto or epigraph from Dante which
appears under the title. The motto is an appeal to the Muses, to
high Genius, to Memory, and the appeal is that of Dante, that rebel
of reason and liberty against the hardening of order into violence;
an appeal made between the middle age and the renaissance, between the beating of light and the spread over Europe of the odor
of death. The passage is worth looking at, in itself and for Dante,
and also because it is quoted to set going a Faustian work by this
last product of the northern renaissance and baroque reformation;
a human type so much more *aware* of the under-barbarism than
the Mediterranean world has ever been. It is we northerners, always,
who understand the *ground of appeal* to the resources of the Latin
and Catholic spirit; we need them more. I do not say this was so
for Dante's time; certainly not for Augustine's; but it is so for us.
We know what is corrupted, what corrupts, and how the relation

may become tolerable: we know what we must acknowledge although we do not wish to acknowledge it: the terms of an everlasting and vital predicament; and it is characteristic of our age that the acknowledgment should be attempted in works of art. And so, in the similar age of the fourteenth century, it was with Dante.

> Lo giorno se n'andava, e l'aer bruno
>   toglieva gli animai, che sono in terra,
>   dalle fatiche loro; ed io sol uno
>
> m'apparechiava a sostener la guerra
>   si del cammino, e si della pietate,
>   che ritrarrà la mente, che non erra.
>
> O Muse, o alto ingegno, or m'aiutate!
>   O mente, che scrivesti ciò ch'io vidi,
>   qui si parrà la tua nobilitate.

(The day was going off, and the brown air taking the animals that are on earth from their toil; and I, one alone, was working myself up to bear the war both of the journey, and of the pity, which memory that errs not shall relate [retrace]. O Muses, O high Genius, now help us! O memory, that has inscribed what I saw, here will be shown thy nobleness.)

Half the Graeco-Christian world is here, and very nearly all that remains of it: what is human and invocably human. The twilight is there, and the task: the journey from birth to death, and also the pity of the journey seen in itself; and so the war between the pity and the journey and the war in each. Then Memory, whose daughters are the Muses, is invoked as the image of the truth—the truth of the tradition and the truth of the actual experience; memory as the high or presiding genius of man—not man himself but his nobleness, the light that shines in him. What then does it shine on? What are the grounds on which it is appealed to?

This work of Thomas Mann, this discourse of an old humanist, this serene late bloom of spirit working through the discourse, is meant to stand for the possibility of an answer. The tireless spirit remains even after the most exhausted animals are gone. This is the spirit that was always there even in the worst moment of the war of the journey and the pity when the scum of the earth in each of us—Thomas Mann's phrase for the Nazi regime—put in power the dictatorship of the scum of the earth all the more scum for the memory it soiled, the tradition it debauched.

But what was the war; what extreme form of what perennial war? It is interesting that Dante did not have to ask that question. His memory knew that answer, and knowledge of it was implicit in his genius; but for us it must be made explicit, and it troubles us almost more than the question that we are driven to ask it. It is as if, by a change in the *phase* of consciousness (which we call self-consciousness or sometimes heightened consciousness) we had acquired a new possibility, however threatened, of choice: as if we had found some new way of tragic aspiration, some new perspective of intolerable failure, to compel us to new efforts of assent and dissent. The new occasion here—the extreme form of the perennial war—is the occasion when those so nearly without mind that their memories lie, take charge, like the Nazis in Germany, of those who still live and still woo—not the folk and the mob—but the Muses.

This is not a change—only a reversal of phase. We find in control what had been the object of control. We heighten the old techniques of imagination weighted by memory with the *élan* of our fresh freedom from purpose. The forces which we tried to understand overwhelm our understanding. Yet those forces, where they still move in the human animal, still crave to be understood—still crave to acquire the nobility of memory. The long human howl, the cry of infants, the naked human voice, will be music yet: though the whole world howl before it happen, and if in the process it seem to come to destruction.

So the humanist faced with the Faustian image must believe, and that is what the passage from Dante gave Serenus Zeitblom the strength to believe while he passed through the war of the journey—the Germany of the last sixty years—and the war of the pity—the life of his friend the great German musician, Adrian Leverkühn. So, as in the first chapter we found the whole theme of the work announced in terms of Faustus, in the second chapter we find that theme repeated and strengthened, counterpointed, with another strain. Here the Faustian image is put to music, and in that music we hear the classical tongues of human reason and dignity over against that other language of tones, a language not humanistic, not reliable: both living by contradiction in human nature; the one nobility of mind, the other peril of spirit, here joined in new service to the deities of the depths. It is as if the humanist insisted that it is the function of his culture, by piety to his memory, to regulate and propitiate the entrance of the dark and uncanny into the service of the gods.

It is in the service of the gods, then, that this life of a great musician is written under the double image of a new Faustus and old Memory; and it is the role of artist—that characteristic hero of the high literature of the last seventy years—and the music he creates which press together to combine the image. So much for the statement of the theme; interpretation may come later; meanwhile we remind ourselves of the material through which it is worked and of the techniques or forms to which it takes for expression.

The material is of several kinds. There is the immediate biography of the young genius capable equally, at twenty-one, of experience, of music, and of theology. He withdraws from experience and theology and dedicates himself to the composition of music which is a further reach of both: his withdrawal is perfected after a single sexual contact which leaves a secret syphilis to combine with a hereditary migraine, and after, also, a single hallucinated interview with the devil. He is by nature one not to be touched, to be adored not loved; and he becomes by consequence of his disease and his compact with the devil free, or almost free, of the obligations that go with human contact and love, and is bound only, and almost wholly, by the special obligation to mocking laughter— which is response pure, response without sharing. That is, he can sink unimpeded into what underlies all experience—what is in the self *no matter what* is taken away: the revelation of the equivocal without any control 'or standard except for those of the process of revelation. Thus, having no connection with experience, except through daemonism and disease, he can afford that ruthless irresponsibility of the artist which is in the end responsibility plain, full response *away from* the truth, *under* the truth, *without* truth. In other words, he is asserted to have in fact that absolute mastery of experience which every adolescent requires himself to see as the immediate, or at least the next possibility of his own genius: surely the oldest imagined role, older than Faustus, older than Memory. In his life itself he succeeds in his withdrawal, his dedication, and secret power till near the end, when life strikes him two blows. The first blow is the murder of his one personal friend which he brings on by expressing a desire for marriage. The second is the death of his darling and beautiful nephew Nepomuk or Echo—the echo in infant form of the life he never lived. From the second he never recovered except for the moment of his last composition. Finishing that—the lamentation of Dr. Faustus—he collapses into idiocy, his work done, and the life he never lived still to be begun, if at all, by those who are to come after him.

Against the biography of Leverkühn there are three critiques: the critique of the social history of the German haut-bourgeois from 1885 to 1940, the critique of German national history in the War from 1939 to 1945, and the critique of Adrian Leverkühn's principal compositions, all told in the increasingly desperate humanistic tones of Serenus Zeitblom. Altogether, the three make a single critique of Europe as the forced sell-out. Let us say that the critique of the Nazi war is of the ambience: it is the horror in our nostrils, and it is there in the book; and saying that let us have done, for it is only the holocaust of what had been long on fire. But let us think of the critique of society over against the figures of the composer and the scholar, each further ahead of his society and deeper in it than anyone, as the artist and humanist ought to be—and each misunderstood or ignored by the society he expressed. The artist expresses what the humanist must understand: man's disobedience to his own nature. Only here in this time, 1885-1940, instead of a tension, a precarious balance, between expression and understanding, which hold society together, we find society tearing itself apart. We get expressionism and authority, not balanced or related, but identified, confused, a matter of random because indistinguishable resort.

This we see wonderfully in the careers of the lesser characters, particularly in those of Clarissa and Inez Rodde, ending for the one in blackmail and suicide, for the other in drugs and murder, the one caused by shame and failure of talent, the other by distrust of suffering and cultivated infatuation. We see it in the aesthete who bought bad pictures and loved the beauty of bloodshed, and in the poet who wrote no poetry but invoked violence. It is in Schildknapp, the cadging translator and anglophile, who never got his own work done; in Rudi Schwerdtfeger, the fiddler, the victim of his own coquetry. Above all it is in the discussion club of the twenties where because all the horror of the thirties was seen as *possible* it was adopted and wooed as a *necessity*; but it is no less in the writhing reptilian eloquence of the impresario from Paris. What we see is the moral suicide—not simple viciousness or ordinary depravity—but such confusion of order with disorder—such failure of memory—as is tantamount to the moral suicide of bourgeois society. No wonder the chattering terror became the only mode, first of expression, then of action. And for final commentary there is the hideous and gratuitous death of little Echo. It is always the gratuitous that reminds us of the essential.

There remains the third critique which is of Adrian Leverkühn's music: *Love's Labours Lost*—a mocking opera bouffe of Renaissance Humanism; the *Gesta Romanorum,* a parody of the daemonic element in medieval Christianity; the Oratorio of the *Apocalypse,* where the howling glissando of the human voice, moving from the bestial to the sublime in mocking imitation parodies the musical styles of hell, reaching finally the "inaccessibly unearthly and alien beauty of sound, filling the heart with longing without hope"; and lastly the lamentations of Dr. Faustus, written after the death of Echo, which we now see was a parody of the life of Leverkühn and his society. Of this last piece, here is the humanist's description:

> We children of the dungeon dreamed of a hymn of exultation, a *Fidelio,* a Ninth Symphony, to celebrate the dawn of a freed Germany—freed by herself. Now only this can avail us, only this will be sung from our very souls: the *Lamentation* of the son of hell, the lament of men and God, issuing from the subjective, but always broadening out and as it were laying hold on the Cosmos; the most frightful lament ever set up on earth.

So the humanist, Serenus Zeitblom; and saying that, he forces himself a little beyond his humanism: out upon the base on which humanism is built, and which it denies and shuns, avoids and rediscovers at moments of outward catastrophe or inward "break-through." It is always the task of humanism to break through itself *again* to reality, whether by reason or image. That is what that early humanist, Marco Lombardo, whom Dante found untying the knot of his anger in Canto XVI of the Purgatorio—that is what Marco meant when he said Man has a mind of his own.

> *A maggior forza ed a miglior natura*
> *liberi soggiacete, e quella cria*
> *la mente in voi, che il ciel non ha in sua cura.*
>
> *Però, se il mondo presente disvia,*
> *in voi è la cagione, in voi si cheggia. . . .*

("Ye lie subject, in your freedom, to a greater power and to a better nature; and that creates in your mind which the heavens [i.e. the influence of the stars, mechanical law] have not in their charge. Therefore, if the world today goeth astray, in you is the cause, in you be it sought."—Temple Classics edition.) *The Divine Comedy* is among other things a great exemplary break-through by reason and image to the base of the human. Adrian Leverkühn's *Lamentation of Dr. Faustus* is an image, an idol, an invocation for such a break-through; a supplication which, if we could only hear it, might enact itself in our contemplation. It is the human voice at the crisis of phase: at the moment of reversal or renewal; and it is in this light that the remaining comments of Serenus Zeitblom ought to to read. He is asking us to hear. To hear all modern music as lament and *lasciatemi morire*. To hear *this* putative music as Echo, "The giving back of the human voice as nature-sound, and the revelation of it *as* nature-sound . . . essentially a lament: Nature's melancholy 'Alas!' in view of man, her effort to utter his solitary state." He asks us also to hear this music as complete, as saying "nothing and everything," as creating a universal identity of the blest and the accursed, in which the freedom is so wholly expressed that it is wholly subject to the form—*a maggior forza ed a miglior natura*. The intention is again Dantesque; for it is Dante who is the most deliberate and the most complete of all poets; it is in his work that everything is taken care of, and something else besides; and so we are meant to hear the evoked music of Adrian Leverkühn—both as to the deliberateness and as to what is deliberated: the liberation of maximum expressiveness in the condition of maximum control. The

Lament is written in twelve tones (the chromatic scale of Arnold Schoenberg) on the twelve syllables of the words "For I die as a good and as a bad Christian"—good by repentance, bad in that the devil will have his body. "It is the basis of all the music—or rather, it lies almost as key behind everything and is responsible for the identity of the most varied forms—that identity which exists between the crystalline angelic choir and the hellish yelling in the *Apocalypse* and which has now become all embracing: a formal treatment strict to the last degree, which no longer knows anything unthematic, in which the order of the basic material becomes total, and within which the idea of a fugue rather declines into an absurdity, just because there is no longer any free note." What this form controls in absolute liberation is the last change of mind—"a proud and bitter change of heart!"—in the "speaking unspokenness" of music, whereby final despair achieves a voice, and the consolation of the voice, the voice for the creature in its woe, and whereby "out of the sheerly irremediable hope might germinate . . . a hope beyond hopelessness, the transcendence of despair." . . . The end is the high G of a cello. "Then nothing more: silence, and night. But that tone which vibrates in the silence, which is no longer there, to which only the spirit hearkens, and which was the voice of mourning, is so no more. It changes its meaning; it abides as a light in the night."

That is how Serenus Zeitblom would have us hear "the most frightful lament ever set up on earth," and a little later, when before the final wail of his own voice, Leverkühn mangles and eviscerates himself in words ("one's fellow men are not meant or made to face such truth") Zeitblom makes the following observation: "Never had I felt more strongly the advantage that music, which says nothing and everything, has over the unequivocal word: yes, the saving irresponsibility of all art, compared with the bareness and baldness of unmediated revelation." And in this observation is clarified the mystery why it is music, in the absence of religion, that makes the break-through into reality tolerable as truth and viable as image. Dante would not have needed it, or would have used it— indeed he did so use it—as a compensatory weight; but this other age has need of it: "the saving irresponsibility of all art," clearest and most nearly credible in music.

It is this evoked, this putative music, its working presence to the good will of our belief, that transforms the critique and the anecdotes and the biography into something we can call a novel; of two composers whom I know, one insists he wrote Leverkühn's music, and the other hears it completely; as for myself, with less skill, I hear it incompletely; but I know how everything works into what I hear and do not hear. But if the novel is governed by the music, we must emphatically remember that all the music, except the last piece, is parody and that the medium of the parody is that echo of nature the naked human voice, and that it stands in analogy and parallel everywhere to a series of critiques of individuals in their history. The notions in these words, parody, critique, and the naked human voice, taken under the image of Faustus and Dante, represent the means by which the work was composed, and also both qualify and limit the meaning—the music—which goes on when the book has stopped.

Of these three notions, the naked human voice should be familiar: its presence, real or invoked, has always worked as a great force; it is the substance of poetry so far as we can read it and of music so far as we can play it; and it is the one daemonic force in which we all have some skill at heightening ourselves, by which, in ourselves, we call on something beyond ourselves. Parody and critique as serious means to artistic purpose, especially in the novel, are relatively new, and are without rules of thumb; and what makes them interesting here is the sense that Mann was driven to employ them by a combination of the limitations of his talent and the cultural conditions of our times. Parody is the form of this novel and critique one of its developments. Let us see.

If parody is the right name for the form of this novel it cannot be unique and is not likely without a common cause; which may well be some inability to create individuals along with an unwillingness to resort to type in the use of the age before our own. Gide, Kafka, Joyce, Eliot, Mann—even Yeats and Proust—have none of them had the gift of creating individuals or composing in sustained narrative. Each has lacked power of objective creation; each has depended in high particular upon his own biography. Individual character reached its height with Shakespeare and Rembrandt and Tolstoi, and, if you like, Beethoven. It may be that harmony is needed to create character, vital and cultural harmony, and that in a polyphonic age only parody of character and the individual is possible to express. Private life disappears either into public life or into itself and is in either case, when expressed, only a parody of itself. But if I am right I do not see that parody is any less expressive than the epic. And I suggest that "myth" in the lauding sense we use it of Joyce and Kafka can only be a parody, so self-conscious it is, of what we mean by myth in Greek drama.

A few claimers and disclaimers as to the meanings and uses of the word are in order. Parody is something sung beside the main subject. Parody is not caricature, not satire: it is a means of treating reality so as to come short of it either on purpose or through necessity. Parody emphasizes mechanics, especially prescriptive mechanics in executive technique, and greedily fastens on the merest possibilities in the material. In our day, every man is a parody of his moral self. Parody is our ordinary means of judging men and events. Music alone parodies the rest of humane culture: which is why it frightens us and how we put up with it: we know what is parodied. Because it involves, points at, and limits what it parodies, parody is a good name for a means of getting at material that—in our state of belief—does not submit to existing system. Parody is arduous, rigorous, and establishes relations in its own way. It makes possible the free use of dualisms—the oldest technique of Yin and Yan, Up and Down, for parody is free of single beliefs and is bent on the object.

In Mann's chapter of the corrupt bargain with the devil we have precisely an example of parody freely resorting to dualism, for here Mann parodies both his own book and the humanity the book was meant to re-discover. But I do not know that Mann parodies himself. For him parody is a way out, and he can be objective about it—as Leverkühn in his opera bouffe of *Love's Labours Lost*. He can submit all his desperate material to the arrogant, debasing parody of itself. That is the adventure of the bourgeois turned artist. It is the rebellion of the bourgeois against himself in a created self. Only the bourgeois understands Bohemia (his slipping) or needs the devil (his climbing); or at any rate, the bourgeois is in the gulf between his slipping and his pride—which is why he adapts to himself the notions of birth and breeding: that he may somehow reach irresponsibility and dishonor. He is like Pascal in this, who saw that birth and breeding save a man twenty years. And it is the devil who lets the bourgeois parody himself; the devil is always what happens to the ideal: the dishonor and irresponsibility of practice carried to an extreme.

What is the temptation to the young bourgeois composer, Leverkühn?—That the presumption of total and absolute guilt—of the sin so great mercy is impossible on it—gives absolute knowledge and with it the nearest approach to absolute redemption. It is the lust in the brain, not the lust in the flesh, that is tempted. As if, thus renouncing love, the human touch, the fraternal, and thus assuming the great human cold (that is, by deliberately parodying our inadequacies), we could somehow come on the elemental and the actual, and, however intolerable themselves, communicate through them a joyous life to those who come after: an ambition, surely, of love and touch and brotherhood. It is the temptation "within"; it has nothing of the temporal power about it. It is the right temptation for the time held to be sterile in its technics and techniques: in a time of asserted omniscience and the mechanization of crafts. Adrian Leverkühn strove for that illumination by which he could restore assent to the conditions of human life by himself, in his genius, first escaping or denying them; and to do this required a compact with the devil: at any rate a confusion between the daemonic and the diabolic. He parodied his humanity in order to find it: at once an affair of pride and force and a protean cheapening of himself: the lout, the merchant, the familiar—above all the lout—in which forms the devil made his apparitions. The parody points, terribly, at the reality, as the devil points at God; and it is one of the possibilities of the humanists in our time so to point.

It seems to be not a possibility but a necessity for the humanist to resort also to critique, to carry his critique along with him and make it a part even of his most imaginative works. Partly he does this to make present what he cannot create, partly to explain what his audience will not understand in what he has created, and partly in the effort to make up for the lack of a common background— the lack of the Great Memory which mothered the Muses—in even a small and select audience. As Shakespeare had to bed down his play about *Troilus and Cressida* with images of lechery and insurrection, a novelist like Thomas Mann has also to bed down his work with a critique of present history and character and surviving memory. If we can think of *Troilus and Cressida* as the train of its images, we can think of *Doctor Faustus* as the train of its critique; both trains are employed for the same purpose: to unite disparate elements, to order inchoate elements, and to mark the vitality of what is united and what is ordered. The image and the critique are what the works are about; and in the case of Mann this is what separates him from Fielding's Lucretian inter-chapters in *Tom Jones* and the essays on the theory of history in Tolstoi's *War and Peace*, where the critique was on a parallel intellection of the subject: In Mann's *Doctor Faustus*, as in *The Magic Mountain*, they are central to the subject and reveal it.

Thus, in *Doctor Faustus*, when we come to Leverkühn's next to last piece, *The Apocalypse*, we feel the excitement of a real thing in the critique by Zeitblom which alone presents it to us. We feel all three of our themes: the artist, the humanist, the naked human voice—together with their rigid correspondences in the world of history and the world of critique—all these themes have merged, or at any rate they give voice to one another in one organized place in time. We see, or hear, in the *Apocalypse*, that the music is about all these, and so makes the one "critique" that unites the intellect in the feeling, transforms the feeling in the intellect, and makes of the whole, as Croce would say, an instance of theoretic form. Art has itself become critique.

So it has with Gide: In the various journals for *The Counterfeiters*; with Joyce: in the polylingual multi-myth of *Finnegans Wake*; with Proust: in the "Place Names" and the "social history"; and, perhaps, with Kafka: in the creation and distension of a pseudomythical world to explain "K." It is merely because Mann is so much more explicit than these others, and wishes to make his critique stand for so much more of ordinary life in present history than they do, that he stands out as a novelist of critique, and has made more to do with it than they have. But he is not alone; and what he has done with critique, like what he has done with parody, is a reflection of the cultural conditions of the times. Granted that he intended great work, the resort to critique in the novel of the individual as humanist beyond himself was inevitable. For one thing, the horizon of the humanist had stretched enormously with the divisiveness of modern knowledges and their incongruous techniques; for another thing, even the best humanist finds his own Great Memory failing, let alone that of his audience: he must tell himself as well as his reader what he has in mind; and, for a third thing, the impulse to set the individual in his milieu, his history, and what Erich Auerbach calls his "moving background," has run out, along with its dividends, and there has been a renewal of the older impulse to create the individual in terms of his type, that is to say, in terms of the critique of the individual and his "moving background." But since the humanist here is imaginative, the critique itself must become art: which with Mann is the art of music.

There are many ways of saying it. We can think of the novel as the characteristic art of the modern individual and his world; and it may be that the world in which that individual is lodged has so changed that the art of the individual can no longer redeem the sense of the individual, nor the intellect that of the intellect. Critique would then be the last gasp: *Doctor Faustus* would then be the bonfire of the daemonic. Our great hope lies in our consciousness of terrible loss in our inability to portray the individual. Knowing the loss proves the individual still exists, we still hear his music and in the music his voice. In our sense of loss is our right to that music and our new sense that the music is somehow a critique of the reality. Critique is the mind turning to parody because it must; and music is the imperative of the turning.

Parody, then, is what art must do when it has become critique, when in it the individual becomes biography and anecdote; parody comes about because art can no longer be pious to either the journey or the pity in the old forms, and has not yet found the means to settle on new forms. Parody is a form for transition, and in the interim of transition can well lean on music for its models. If music is equivocal and is also the organization of sound, then it is the art both most apt to parody and the furthest from it. It parodies what it is and it reaches what it is through parody; as the later quartets of Bartók show more clearly than any music of Schoenberg. It reaches the naked human voice and—in that—the absolute irresponsibility of art.

Above all it is parody that rescues us from the curse—we cannot be rescued from the burden—of critique and the false escape of anecdote. It is parody that makes it possible, in such an age as ours, to seek what we must shun; makes it possible to see the elements of the substance of our ordeal not in logical or statistical but in organic opposition; and so, after the break-through, make something out of them. Parody brings us to the voice and the irresponsibility.

Let us return with all these provisional and, in all the old senses, disheartening terms to Thomas Mann's book itself. This great man and German and composer, Adrian Leverkühn, is above all a parody of the human. Standing between the dictatorship of the scum of the human race and the folk who threw up the scum; or, not standing, let us say bestriding them, Adrian Leverkühn is that parody of all the bourgeois humanist held dear which shall restore him: he is what is in the names of his principal works—*Love's Labours Lost, Gesta Romanorum, Apocalypse, Doctor Faustus*. He is that terrible parody of the bourgeois, the "break-through" by which he may yet be re-created, only in another image. Only the idol is dead. Parody is a means, no matter how hard to take still a means to touch the understanding, which might, for practical purposes, reach further than the everlasting mercy—at least when, like Leverkühn, we must pass through the daemonic to reach again the human.

If that is true—if in any sense we must pass through the daemonic to reach the human—we can take that truth as the clue to *Doctor Faustus* at its most serious level: which is the level where we identify Faust and Leverkühn. Adrian Faust Leverkühn is the daemonic scapegoat for humanity. He comes to his destruction, is absorbed by the devil, precisely at the moment when he has understood the sins of mankind by re-enacting them in that mood of the mind which is both most human, in that it stirs, or touches, the deepest human places, and, also, is most removed from the human in that it touches directly upon none of the ordinary concerns of men. Faust has sold his humanity in order to come upon understanding of the force which keeps humanity alive and perennially on the edge, in the maw, of suicide. And this Faust, this Leverkühn, achieves his understanding by creating its image in the most equivocal language available to man, which is the image of music: the naked human voice. But there is no redemption here, no Christ, no Cross, only destruction. Our Christian religion has at its heart the image of a perfectly good man who takes up the evil that breaks life into his goodness, taking it to salvation in a mystery. The image of Faust as Leverkühn is not a mockery of Christ but a reversal: it works back into the conditions from which Christ is the redemption. It reminds us in its own way, and in another language, what the European Christ is for. The devil is always the other thing than God, like God; the devil is God gone to the devil; the man possessed of the devil is the man stripped of everything human except the elementally human: those very elements out of which, after each catastrophic slump to gulf-bottom, the human can be re-born, re-made, re-created.

That is why Adrian Leverkühn is cold—the coldness of the human; why he is mathematical—the sequence of the heartbeat; why he is aloof—the loneliness of the human; and it is why he is proud—because of the great human pride, the temptation to re-create himself in his own fastness. He is cold, mathematic, aloof and proud; but he is neither a good man nor a bad man. He is neither above nor below good and evil; he is both good and evil in the culture of 1900 to 1950, and being both he is apart from either. He is the image—the idol or eidolon—to which good and evil happen, and he is required to be enough deprived of ordinary humanity to meet the truth of that image: the truth which he devoted himself, with a devotion constantly on the edge of infatuation, to create. And for this devotion, this infatuation, he must be the man without God; for if he thought he had God, if he felt he were the man-God, he would have been the god who gave in to the temptations on the mountain, he would have been the god become—as Hitler and the others—the dictatorship of the scum of the earth: the debasement of the divine, or the daemonic, in the human. No; Adrian Leverkühn is the man become the devil on behalf of the divine; the man become the devil insofar as the devil is a parody as a means of access to God: Thomas Mann's limit of human approach.

There is something absolutely irresponsible about any image which is perfectly evil, perfectly good, or perfectly apart from both;

but of the three images, the human imagination in our day, having too much experience of the first, and too little of the second, can attempt to create only the third. This is no time for Cervantes to create Don Quixote; and anybody who tried would make a worse failure of the perfectly good man than Dostoevsky did with that haunting failure Prince Myshkin in that great book *The Idiot*. Thomas Mann was right. In line with Cervantes and Dostoevsky, he yet followed Goethe, who struggled to make the very Europe live which we wish to recreate, and like Goethe Mann chose the image of Faust as his weapon. Only in the image of Faust can Thomas Mann's understanding, lacking the everlasting mercy and the living grace, come upon "the hope beyond hopelessness, the transcendence of despair" which may yet break through to mercy and grace because they are the naked human voice itself, the voice crying in the dark always there. But the voice is the voice of the Muses.

Philip Blair Rice EXISTENTIALISM

AND THE SELF

FRENCH Existentialism is a complex and, to the critic, a disconcerting product of the European agony. How shall we treat it? As a philosophy in the sense of an attempt at logically ordered discourse which tries to prove something, and hence can be argued with? Or as a kind of metaphysical tone poem, seeking to evoke or express something, and so to be studied as a psychological and sociological phenomenon and to be judged, if judged at all, by aesthetic rather than logical criteria? Some of its critics thus far have adopted one of these strategies and some the other. When viewed as a metaphysical tone poem, Existentialism has come out looking considerably more worthy of respect: one pays obeisance to it as expressing the ethos of the French Resistance, or perhaps more broadly as a cry of pain in the twilight of Western culture, together with a spasmodic heave of expiring life, heroically if frantically voicing against the encroaching atomic or totalitarian night some of the residual values of the Occident, and particularly its aspiration to absolute freedom.

At least the partial appropriateness of such an approach seems evident in the case of Jean-Paul Sartre's version of Existentialism. Sartre is a novelist and a playwright, a man of the Left Bank and the *avant-garde*; even his philosophical writings seem of the same epoch as expressionism and surrealism in the arts, and show a community in theme and feeling with the poems of his contemporaries, Michaux, Prévert, and Queneau. If his terminology and what passes for his "logic" are those of Hegel, his rhythms and his syntax are often suggestive of Gertrude Stein. Whether or not the logical positivists are right in holding that metaphysics in general is merely semantic confusion plus emotive utterance, it would appear that in Sartre they have a strong case in point. However Sartre has written not only fiction but books that in form more closely resemble philosophical treatises. His close associate in the development of Existentialism, Maurice Merleau-Ponty, writes a more classic—or at any rate a more conventional—prose, draws more widely than Sartre on history and recent experimental psychology, and uses generally, though not invariably, a logic closer to that of Aristotle and Russell than to that of Hegel and Heidegger.[1]

---

[1] Except where otherwise indicated the writings chiefly drawn upon in this essay are, by Sartre: *L'Être et le néant* (Gallimard, 1943), *Existentialisme est un humanisme* (Nagel, 1946), and *Situations I* (Gallimard, 1947); by Merleau-Ponty: *La Structure du comportement* (Presses Universitaires de France, 1942), *Phénoménologie de la perception* (Gallimard, 1945), *Humanisme et terreur* (Gallimard, 1947), and *Sens et non-sens* (Nagel, 1947); by Simone de Beauvoir: *Pyrrhus et Cinéas* (Gallimard, 1944) and *Pour une morale de l'ambiguïté* (Gallimard, 1947). Among the great mass of historical and critical writings recently produced in France I might mention especially: *Études Kierkegaardiennes,* by Jean Wahl (Aubier, 1938); *Le Cogito dans la*

It would seem then that a sufficient treatment of Existentialism, which this essay intends at most to suggest, would examine its pretensions to be logical discourse as well as aesthetic expression. When this has been tried—as by A. J. Ayer in *Horizon* and by Jean Wahl in *Deucalion* among others—several of the central doctrines of Existentialism have been shown to be extremely vulnerable: the arguments for them are revealed as flimsy paradoxes based on elementary logical fallacies, some of which were perpetrated by Parmenides and Zeno and exposed by Plato in his later writings, even before the birth of systematic logic.

But even if the Existentialists have not proved anything, it may be that they have conveyed something besides an emotion. They at least seem to be trying earnestly to tell how things are with them, to impart a representation of the human condition, and to show us what to do about it. Their philosophy is above all a philosophy of human existence: they wish to render in its immediacy what it feels like and otherwise seems like to enact the role of a person. This is their doctrine that the starting point for philosophy is subjectivity, and insofar as we can break out of subjectivity we do so by following the self in its movement of discovering a non-human world and a society in which the self is enmeshed. Although one of the Existentialist dogmas is that there is no "essence" of human nature, they offer, nevertheless, to point out to us certain characteristics of the human psyche and certain features of the human situation which are common to all men, actually or potentially—and these in any other philosophy would be taken to constitute man's essence. This concern is exhibited by their treatment of the self in four of its relationships: to inanimate existence, to the human body, to freedom, and to other persons in the context of society and history.

---

philosophie de Husserl, by Gaston Berger (Aubier, 1941); "Remarques sur les rapports entre Existentialisme et Marxisme," by Raymond Aron, in *L'Homme, le monde, l'histoire* (Arthaud, 1948); and "De la Phénoménologie à l'Existentialisme," by Alphonse de Waelhens, in *Le Choix, le monde, l'existence* (Arthaud, 1947). A few of the briefer Existentialist writings, and also *A Short History of Existentialism,* by Jean Wahl, have been published in English by the Philosophical Library, New York.

1. *The Self in the World*

French Existentialism claims as its ancestors several philosophers who wrote before the twentieth century, including Kierkegaard, Nietzsche, Pascal, and the early Hegel. More immediately the French movement derives from recent French Idealism and from two twentieth century German philosophers, the late Edmund Husserl and Martin Heidegger. Merleau-Ponty shows less stimulation and less befuddlement by Heidegger than does Sartre, and for the most part prefers to go directly to Husserl in acknowledgement of his sources. The two Germans, whatever their merits, are uncommonly cloudy thinkers and prolix writers, even for the tradition of German academic philosophy; and these qualities pass from bad to worse in going down the line from Husserl to Heidegger. But they are tidied up somewhat by the French, who even in their least lucid moments are never quite as opaque as these Germans.

Merleau-Ponty has written that Heidegger's Existentialism and the French movement stem from an "indication" in Husserl's later philosophy, which survives almost entirely through his unpublished manuscripts and through his students' recollections of his oral teaching. In fact, both Sartre and Merleau-Ponty seem originally to have preferred to be called Phenomenologists rather than Existentialists: witness the former's subtitle for *L'Être et le néant,* "Essay in Phenomenological Ontology," and the title of the latter's most substantial work, *Phénoménologie de la perception.* M. Alphonse de Waelhens, in an essay, "From Phenomenology to Existentialism," speaks of three phases in Husserl's philosophy. In the first of these Husserl deliberately excluded questions of existence and devoted himself to "descriptive phenomenology." The so-called phenomenological reduction, which was the first step in philosophical method for the school, involved "bracketing" the world, "putting it between parentheses" and dealing with meanings, intentions and essences in abstraction from the truth of their claims to represent objects not immediately given in experience. Phenomenology did not, like Subjective Idealism, deny the existence of a world transcending the individual experience; it did not even, like Phenomenalism, deny the possibility of knowing such a world: it simply chose to limit itself initially to discovering what could be learned about experience and the ideas that organize it, by suspending belief in a world outside experience and by describing or analyzing what is immediately given to consciousness, including its intentions of going beyond the given. In Husserl's second phase, typified by his *Méditations Cartésiennes,* he examined experience for indications of a transcendental self, or ego as subject, consisting in a set of functions active in constituting a world of meanings or essences and unifying the intentions found in the act of knowing. In the third and final phase of Husserl's philosophy, as Merleau-Ponty presents it, there is a return to the problem of existence. However much we may try to "bracket" the world, we cannot suspend belief in it for long; it is always breaking out of the parentheses into which we have put it. The world of existence is always welling up (*surgir*) or spurting up (*jaillir*) to assert itself. Essences cannot really be divorced from existence; existence is always claiming them. Our attempt to "refuse complicity" to the world is self-defeating; existence engages us, gears us into itself. So that "the greatest lesson of the phenomenological reduction is the impossibility of a complete reduction."

In order to get the feeling of existence, as Merleau-Ponty interprets Husserl, we must try to recapture the world before consciousness, the *Lebenswelt,* the *monde vécu.* "The world is not what I think, but what I live; I am open to the world, I communicate with it, but I don't possess it, it is inexhaustible." The truth about existence is not something to be grasped in abstract concepts: "we are inside the truth and evidence is experience of the truth." The existence of the world transcending the immediately given is therefore not something that we can prove by argument. It is an absurdity or a mystery and one that is on the "hither side of solutions," that is, the solutions of logical argument. The world forces itself on me as the "permanent horizon" of my perception, action and thought. In *L'Être et le néant* Sartre offers an "ontological proof" of the existence of the world, but it is so scanty and so weak that we are forced to take as the main Existentialist position that we know the world by revelation or disclosure. His best description of this, which amounts to a kind of mystical experience, is found in his novel *Nausea.*

"The true philosophy," as Merleau-Ponty puts it, is accordingly "to relearn to see the world," or to live it, and so, he adds, an anecdote can convey the sense of the world as profoundly as a philosophical treatise. It is then as no mere embellishment of their philosophy that several of the French Existentialists have written novels and plays.

It follows that there is not much we can put into words about being-in-itself or physical existence. Sartre lists three characteristics of it: it is, it is in itself, it is what it is. We can derive its existence neither from the possible, by purely *a priori* reasoning, in the fashion of traditional Rationalism, nor from consciousness as the Idealists tried to do. The world has no meaning in itself, but only such meaning as human beings give it. In an essay in *Situations I*, Sartre presents rhapsodically a version of naïve or direct realism according to which we know the qualities of the world, such as the shape and color of objects, as they are in themselves. But he has a short way of dealing with this epistemological problem, over which philosophers have wrangled so much, and he does not give any attention whatsoever to the methodology of physical science. Up to a point, at any rate, a liberal interpretation of his views might make them compatible with operationalism, which reduces the physical world to data and the human operations by which we assign them a meaning; though for him the physical world is more than this.

Merleau-Ponty's theory of the physical world in his *Structure du comportement* is a bit more extensive, but still meager. He professes to base his views on field theory and he holds that existence is made up of three "fields," the physical, the physiological and the mental, each consisting in a "system of tensions and currents." Yet elsewhere in his discussion he reverts to an old-fashioned type of mechanism. Nature is a "whole of *partes extra partes*," "a multiplicity of events external to each other and linked by causality," a view incompatible with the new physics of field theory. Each of the fields or *Gestalten* for Merleau-Ponty has its dominant characteristic: quantity for the physical, order for the organic, and value or meaning for the mental, but each of these categories is applicable in some degree to all. Between the three fields there are no causal relations; such tenuous connection as they have is "dialectical." The higher field or structure absorbs the lower into its system of meanings. The lower does not exert any causal action upon the higher but merely "releases" (*déclenche*) its otherwise autonomous activity. Laws of some sort hold within each field but they are dependent upon its concrete structure, and there are no laws linking the three fields to each other.

Nature appears to the Existentialist as simply the shadowy background of human activity and is discussed for the most part by contrast with it. Nature is inert and stable, whereas conscious existence is always changing, always negating itself. The Existentialists thus transfer from the world of space, time and motion to the human realm the puzzles of Parmenides and Zeno as to the difficulty of something becoming what it is not. The human reality is lack (*manque*). It exists only by pursuing an intention to become something else. "Consciousness is a being for which there is in its being a question of its being insofar as its being implies a being other than itself." This is Sartre's definition of consciousness or the human self, which is most fully expounded in his doctrine of freedom.

2. *The Self as the Body*

The basic human drive, to go beyond what one is and has, is found below the plane of logical and reflective thinking in those activities which, though they are conscious, we regard as primarily "bodily." The human body, in the most important sense of the term, is not an object of physical science. My body as it is for me is not my body as it is for the physiologist. "I have never seen, and never will see, my brain and endocrine glands." I can see and touch my leg, as other people do, and I can describe it as a part of the natural and physiological world, but *for me* my leg is primarily "a possibility that I am of walking, or running, or playing football." To look at my leg is to transform these into "dead possibilities"— being-in-itself or being-for-others. Awareness of the body-for-itself is an engaged consciousness of it. I know my body primarily through its involvement with the world. I am my body in act and my body is the world. I am my hand, and my hand is in turn what it does, e. g., the manipulation of my pen in writing. There is, however, something approximating passive awareness of the body even when it is regarded from within my consciousness. When I do catch an awareness of the body as something distinct from its acts, it is no longer a smoothly functioning instrument. If the body is functioning well I am not conscious of it as such; the body is the neglected, the "passed-over-in-silence." Only when something disrupts my smooth commerce with the world do I become explicitly aware of the body as having a kind of existence distinct from its acts—that is, in Sartre's language, do I "exist" it. Pain is precisely the eyes insofar as consciousness "exists" them. I also have awareness of my body as such in sexual desire. Sartre puts the matter strikingly by saying that sexual desire is incarnation; by means of it I exist as flesh. The body obtrudes its own nature, imposes itself as something felt, lived, in its *facticité* and not merely as an instrument. Hence, Sartre might have added, the perennial popularity of sex, which resists the effort of ascetic moralists to discourage it. The fundamental drive of man is to exist as an individual being: and sexual passion gives him assurance of this. Physical love is an effort at incarnation by force or violence—and as I am primarily concerned with myself becoming flesh, the primary mode of love is masochism, where I use the other to "exist" me. So far as I grasp the other person as object, he is initially just something for me to manipulate. "The totality of utensils is the exact correlate of man's possibilities." My body for another and another's body for me, *qua* objects, are then simply utensils, instruments to be used. When I seek to incarnate the other it is to give me assurance of my power, and in this way I pass from masochism to sadism. (Sartre uses both these terms to express the attitudes toward existence here defined, and not in their ordinary meaning of delight in suffering or inflicting pain.) Love, according to Sartre, is a vacillation between the two; the gap between selves is unbridgeable, and there is no middle ground by which we can avoid the extremes of masochism and sadism.[2]

In addition to the dramatic incarnations in pain and sexual experience, there is a continuing awareness of my body as datum, in the general coenesthesis, or background of somatic feeling, to which Sartre gives the sensational name of "nausea." It consists in

---

[2] This disposal of the sexual problem, as a final solution, has been repudiated by Simone de Beauvoir, who attributes it to the servile position traditionally imposed upon women (*Le deuxième sexe,* Gallimard, 1949).

"the perpetual grasp by my consciousness of an insipid taste, one without distance, which accompanies me even in my efforts to deliver myself from it, and which is *my* taste. A discrete and insurmountable nausea reveals my body to my consciousness perpetually; pain and pleasure reveal themselves against this background of nausea." Just why Sartre applies to this sense of "withness of the body," as Whitehead calls it, the term nausea, is not clear. Possibly variations in constitutional types have something to do with the question, and indeed a viscerotonic in reasonably good health, whose bodily mass frequently appears to him as a warm and agreeable glow, is likely to infer that M. Sartre is suffering from a chronic disorder of the liver. There is, however, another less cynical explanation, which sticks more decorously to metaphysical grounds, and this is that Sartre is such an activist, so much concerned with changing the world and asserting his freedom, that he regards with physical revulsion the passivity displayed in an attitude of enjoyment of the body.

But it is not in the body as a passive datum of consciousness that we find the body-as-the-self, or as expression of the true self. This is discovered, as we have seen, through the body in action, or through those functions of the body in which it is engaged with the world. Merleau-Ponty finds this best illustrated by the act of perception, which is a form of vital communication with the world, at the same time something more than a passive reception of sense data and something less than explicit reasoning. Perception always has a direction, and is imposing a meaning on the materials presented to it. "Sensations and images . . . never appear except in horizons of meaning," and in perception as distinguished from reasoning, this direction is spontaneously assumed by the bodily organism. Merleau-Ponty draws upon some of the familiar materials of Gestalt psychology to show how we fill out the clues presented to us in sensation. For example, we respond to a house seen from without as having an unseen roof, basement and interior, as falling into a system of "perspectives," which extends beyond what we see. There is then in perception much more than we can introspect, more than we can analyze into given parts. The horizons of meaning, which orientate us, are not given but assumed or implied in our attitudes and actions. Perceptual consciousness is not an "I think" but an "I can." An object is the whole of what it can do to us and of what we can do to it. When we try to put a finger on these horizons of meaning, they elude us, just as consciousness itself eludes introspection. If consciousness is not exactly, as Hegel called it, a "hole in reality," a pure nothingness, it is at any rate a "hollow," or a "fold," or "furrow." The awareness of an intention, as grasping something beyond the given, is attached to or hovers over the given, and therefore does not exhibit itself as a pure vacuum, but still it evades direct seizure. The meaning or intention is an invisible goal, or a set of unrealized possibilities, exerting an attraction on us. The body as agent rather than patient, then, is not the massive lump of feeling given in pain, sexual desire or "nausea," but a "nucleus of living significations."

In some of the more complicated forms of perception, including illusory perception, the direction is imposed by one's general "style of being," by the individual's "life-project." In support of this view Merleau-Ponty draws upon examples from pathology. The "phantom" arm of the amputated soldier is not to be explained mechanically, as Descartes did, by the stimulation of nerve-endings in the stump, but by the patient's refusal to accept his mutilation and the style of life that it would entail. Merleau-Ponty adduces similarly Stekel's explanation of feminine frigidity as a refusal of the feminine condition, based on rejection of the sexual partner and the destiny he represents. Sexuality in general is for Merleau-Ponty not the single basic drive of the Freudian libido, but rather a "privileged sign" of the fundamental drama of the individual—of his relationship to past and future, to the self and others, that is, to the principal dimensions of existence. Sexuality is so completely enlisted by the other elements in the personality, and at the same time it so permeates them, that it is impossible to say of a particular act that it is either sexual or non-sexual.

3. *The Self as Freedom*

As we have seen, conscious or personal existence, *être-pour-soi*, is distinguished from nonconscious existence, *être-en-soi*, by its capacity to negate itself. There is a nothing at the heart of man and man generates this nothing. Negation is not found outside the human reality and is the very stuff of it. Sartre proceeds to elaborate pseudological paradoxes, based upon ambiguities in the notions of being and of negation, which have been patiently exposed by Jean Wahl and A. J. Ayer in the articles I have previously cited. These paradoxes, however, can be conceived as decorations of Sartre's main conception of freedom which I shall try to treat without reference to them.

I learn my liberty through my acts, but Sartre holds that liberty is prior to the action: it is outside the organization "motive-intention-act-end." Our actions are not, strictly speaking, purely "gratuitous" or unmotivated, yet motives, as Sartre uses the term, are not causes of the act; they enter into it after the basic choice which gives it direction. This is the "global" choice of a style of life. Sartre has two words for the aspects of the act that would ordinarily be denoted in English—and, I believe, in French also—by the term motive: *motif* and *mobile*. The *motif* is the explicit reason that we give for an act, and the *mobile* is the desire or "drive" that is operating. But neither of these factors is ultimate. "Voluntary deliberation is always tricked": if I say that my reason for going to college is to seek an M.D., this expresses only a means to a style of life that I have already implicitly chosen. The *mobile* or desire that I may invoke as influencing my action—for example, the desire to relieve suffering—is also relative to the style of life that it expresses. Desires, furthermore, can either be indulged or resisted; freedom is found in the indulgence or resistance. My past as a whole cannot be conceived as the cause of my acts, for the past is that which I am always surpassing. Its meaning is unfixed until I determine the meaning by my further decision. The overthrow of the Bastille in itself was an undecisive event in the French Revolution; only when it was chosen as the symbol of a future goal did it acquire significance. The initial choice is always engaged and absurd. It grows out of a situation but is not determined by it, for human action consists in changing the situation, giving it new direction. I am constantly evaluating my past and present, and values spring up spontaneously "like partridges."

Now this doctrine of freedom does not lead Sartre to an optimistic view of human expectations. I can have no confidence in my ability to choose rightly, hence "I am *condemned* to be free." In fact, as we are given no operable criteria of the right choice,

choice reduces to luck. Hence the sense of freedom is accompanied by its constant witness, anguish. Ordinary or objective fear is directed toward external events over which I have no control; anguish is fear of myself, of my own freedom, of not finding myself on the other side of the rendezvous which I have made with myself. When on a mountain climbing expedition I skirt a precipice I may have an objective fear that the footing will crumble before me; but I have anguish when I contemplate the possibility that I will give way to vertigo and throw myself into the abyss. Anguish is ever-present and unconquerable. It cannot be reduced by forming habits of reliable action, or by achieving a progressive knowledge of myself and of the world—for these would require a reliance on law and causality which the Existentialists repudiate. The pathos of the human situation is found in the striving of being-for-itself to become being-in-itself, man's craving to be the cause of his own actions and to become something definite. Since this craving is doomed to frustration, "man is a useless passion."[3]

Particular ends are generated spontaneously by my involvement in situations, and are chosen by my intuition in the individual case. The only general end that Sartre appears to recognize as legitimate is freedom itself. The global choice wherein freedom resides consists in a decision to accept my status as a free being or to try to evade it. The chief moral evil, "bad faith," is accordingly refusal of freedom, or flight from freedom. I am guilty of bad faith when I try to keep from changing, to remain the same, like an inanimate thing, or when I renounce my right of individual choice and let others choose for me, as when I accept the ready-made values of my society or yield myself to an authoritarian church or an authoritarian political party. The attempted flight from freedom is self-defeating, for in these cases of bad faith I am choosing and changing myself by that choice—even though I am choosing to become a rock or a robot.

This ideal of Sartre's is too protean even for Merleau-Ponty. He agrees that, insofar as I am free, "I am a continual refusal to be

---

[3] In a footnote (*L'Être et le néant*, page 484) Sartre says that "these considerations do not exclude the possibility of an ethic of deliverance and salvation," based on a "radical conversion." But he gives no hint of how this is to be accomplished on the assumptions of his system.

anything definite," but he adds that this is "accomplished under the surface by a continual acceptance of a given way of character- izing myself. For even this refusal is among the styles of life and patterns in the world." In place of Sartre's dictum that we are either completely determined or completely free, Merleau-Ponty offers what he calls "semi-determinism." The free act, to be dis- coverable, must stand out against a background of life which is not free or is less free. Freedom rests upon a certain "sedimenta- tion of life"—this appears to mean that it is a modification of more or less stable structures of habits and values, and not a shooting- off of disconnected sparks in the void. I am a psychological and historical structure, and cannot shed this determinateness entirely. My ends are not purely spontaneous "spurtings-up," but are "determinate-indeterminate," continuous with my previous life but not wholly prescribed by it. For Merleau-Ponty my freedom is both limited and shaped by the possibilities of the historical and social situation.

4. *The Self in Its Social Relations*

To the French Existentialists, the engagement by which the self discovers itself is above all a social process. We learn this only gradually. At first I treat the other person as an object, which means to treat him as an instrument, to place him in the order of my utensils. But the other-as-object, Sartre says, is "an explosive instrument that I handle with apprehension." He is always blow- ing up in my face, belying my predictions about him, forcing his freedom on me. I first become aware of the other-as-subject by perceiving that he is looking at me. His gaze makes me realize that he is judging me, assigning to me a meaning-for-him, using his freedom to take account of me. I understand the other-as- subject when I grasp the order of his utensils, or his possibilities, and his capacity for choice. Henceforward my own "human space" is a pathway between selves, a social world whose inhabitants are personalities. Thus arises the third principal dimension of existence: besides being-in-itself and being-for-itself, there is also being-for- others (*être-pour-autrui*).

Consciousness of such solidarity with others as I am able to achieve arises similarly. Neither cooperation nor common suffering suffices to produce the sense of the "we," the *nous-sujet*. Common suffering or a prescribed common task may isolate individuals rather than unite them, for pain, as we have seen, makes us conscious of our passive individuality. The "us," the *nous-objet*, comes before the "we." When we the slaves realize that the master, the oppressor, is looking at us, exploiting us collectively for his purposes, then a bond is established between us and it is a short but not inevitable step to the awareness that we can act together as well as be acted upon; so that each man is responsible to all for everything. The mere fact that a group is exploited will not goad it to revolt. It must confer a meaning on its situation and must evolve a plan of action. Here cultural and intellectual factors are operating of a kind having a partial autonomy; in consequence the Existentialists reject the extreme forms of economic determinism.

Sartre seems to suggest that this human solidarity is very limited, and tends to be confined to crisis situations such as the Occupation in France or what Marxists call a revolutionary situation. When the crisis is past, people revert to their separateness. There is no way of closing the gap, the "nothingness" that exists between selves, for this is implicit in the very nature of individuality and freedom. So that when the crisis is over, the truth of Hegel's saying emerges again: "each consciousness exists by seeking the death of the other."

The doctrine that solidarity arises in crisis situations explains the fact that, despite the highly individualistic flavor of their philosophy, the French Existentialists call themselves revolutionary socialists, and in fact they carried on for several years a flirtation with the Communist Party. Sartre wasted a good deal of time trying to convince the Communists that Existentialism was a better philosophical basis for revolution than Marxism. Merleau-Ponty's strategy was somewhat different: Marx was an Existentialist, Merleau-Ponty's interpretation of Marx is the true Marxism and should replace the party-line philosophy, with its materialistic and deterministic dogmas. This attempted collaboration resulted from the common front of the Resistance movement, but soon after the War was made impossible by Communist spokesmen themselves, who sensed more quickly than the Existentialists the incompatibility between the French philosophy and the practices of the U.S.S.R. and world Communism, proceeding to heap upon Sartre and Merleau-Ponty their wonted vilifications. As a result of this rude rejection, the Frenchmen themselves have gradually become aware of the incompatibility and have retired into a kind of loaded neutrality: "on ne peut pas être communiste, on ne peut pas être anti-communiste" (Merleau-Ponty). Their later utterances, however, indicate that they still hate and fear the United States—about which they are, by the way, uncommonly ill-informed—more than Soviet Russia. In *Humanisme et terreur* (1947) Merleau-Ponty writes that "the United States, country of anti-semitism, racism, and the repression of strikes, is no more than in name the 'land of liberty.'" And he adds, "In the U.S.S.R., violence and ruse are official, humanity is in daily life; in the democracies, on the other hand, the principles are humane, ruse and violence are found in practice." The matter is just as simple as this Gallic antithesis.

However superficial his opinions on practical politics, Merleau-Ponty's political philosophy is somewhat more carefully thought out. Like Marx, he moves in a Hegelian atmosphere, as has already been indicated in the doctrine that the self is a "historical structure." Man exists "in situation" and his projects are responses to inter-personal relationships. "Man is a historical idea and not a natural species"; the meanings by which he guides his action are centered upon possible forms of life in a cultural milieu, and he is always oriented to social horizons. The Existentialists, however, wear both their Hegelianism and their Marxism with a difference. Holding their views on freedom, they cannot accept either the Hegelian conception of history as the rigorously predetermined self-realization of an Absolute Reason in history, or the fatalistic version of Marxism by which history, rigorously necessitated by changes in modes of industrial production, marches toward a classless society. The future is unfinished, ambiguous, and there is no science of it, in the sense of a body of knowledge affording predictive certainty. The human condition, furthermore, is such that there is no good solution. Politics is by its very nature immoral and violence is our lot insofar as we are incarnate. Some of Merleau-Ponty's best passages deal with the tragic character of man's political life, where he has to make irrevocable decisions in the dark, groping toward social goals whose nature can be only dimly foreseen, and where he is forced to use means that at best are pregnant with great evil. This outlook, however, is not altogether tragic. The unpredictability of history also has its consolations, and Merleau-Ponty treats the hero—for example, the hero of the French Resistance—as one who "takes arms against the probable." When the future is undetermined, there is room for hope: the desperate hope of the gambler at the roulette table.

The Existentialist theory of value, indeed, gives us no very detailed criteria by which to judge forms of society. A value is a leap in the dark, an intuitive choice which admits ultimately of no rational verification. Yet the doctrine of *engagement* offers some semblance of an objective criterion. Merleau-Ponty defends proletarian revolution, not as the road to Utopia, but as "the simple prolongation of a practice already at work in history, of an existence already engaged, which is that of the proletariat." The present situation both of Capitalism and of the democratic Socialist parties is contradictory, intolerable, and meaningless. Revolutionary Marxism, on the contrary, "is essentially this idea that history has a meaning—in other words, that it is intelligible and that it is oriented—that it goes toward the power of the proletariat which is capable, as the essential factor of production, of transcending the contradictions of Capitalism and of organizing the human appropriation of nature,—as 'universal class,' of transcending social and national antagonisms and the conflict of man with man." The problem of the U.S.S.R. versus the U. S. A., Merleau-Ponty says, is: whether one system is invested with a "historic mission" and if so, which? A few years previously Merleau-Ponty would have answered this question confidently; now that he has learned a bit more about how the Soviet system operates, he leaves us with the wistful question.[4]

In what precedes I have tried, with a minimum of interpretation, to let the Existentialists speak in their own terms, so as to sug-

---

[4] The uneasy "neutrality" of Sartre and Merleau-Ponty, relieved by occasional essays at flirtation, is still going on. They refused to sign an appeal for an investigation of Soviet forced-labor camps, circulated by David Rousset, for reasons given in a recent issue of *Les Temps Modernes,* where although they admit that as much as a tenth of the male population of Russia may be in such camps, they argue that "no matter what the nature of present Soviet society, the Soviet Union is . . . situated, in the balance of forces, on the side of those who fight against all forms of exploitation."

gest both the liveliness of their language and its imprecision. We must take their more brutal linguistic shock tactics, exemplified by their use of overcharged words like "masochism," "sadism," "nausea" and "anguish," as itself designed, or at any rate appropriate: the tactic is suited to the general strategy of their philosophy, which is to evoke a sense of the self's buffeting by mysterious dimensions of existence in which it finds itself both alienated and enlisted. Whether what they have to say is wise or foolish, they could not have conveyed it so fully by straight logical or functional prose.

The tactic is one familiar to poets and to critics who deal with the poetic uses of language—and indeed their tools of analysis could well be tried out on the Existentialist writing. Deplorably little attention has been given to the problem of philosophical style. We know of course what the logical positivists have to say on this score, but their alternatives are too neat, and would require us to dismiss as mere emoting too much of what the world still treasures as significant in philosophical writing.

The history of philosophy is capacious and tolerant: it preserves not only the great rigorous system-builders and the great lucid destroyers but also some of the muddleheads, the eccentrics, and even the stinkers, provided they can suggest possible styles of life or possible perspectives on reality. Philosophy must make its main advances on the high road of rationality trodden with some divagations by Aristotle, Aquinas, Spinoza, Hume, and Kant. But we need look not only to the myths of Plato and the dithyrambs of Nietzsche to be aware that rationality wins its battles on the frontiers of the irrational, beyond which it must make frequent scouting expeditions: there is also the most admirable of reasoners and the most lucid of clarifiers, David Hume himself, who in the Conclusion to Book I of his *Treatise of Human Nature* tried to give a sense of what his philosophy, or any philosophy, could not capture by the methods of deductive or inductive logic—the very movement of nature or existence itself, and the non-rational foundation of all rationality. Generally the rational and the non-rational are more scrambled together than in Hume. Every bright sophomore can detect the gilt-paper flimsiness of Descartes' superficially so lucid pages in behalf of rational method, and we are forced to defend him for his great half-formed perceptions of new avenues to knowledge, and for the obstinacy of his *intention* to doubt thoroughly and to think methodically—as a man who gives us the travail of thought rather than its deliverances; in short, as an "existential" thinker. To a mind with any respect for the semantic decencies, what could be more outrageous than Hegel's way of expressing himself? And yet, for better and for worse, how his progeny have transformed the course of thought and of history in the last hundred years!

Existentialism's vogue in France has been due not merely to its voicing a prevailing mood, and to its helping the stunned French to assure themselves that they existed and in some sense were free beings. It offered further a prospect of something more "profound" than the Cartesian pseudo-clarity which has usually characterized French philosophical writing, and something more contemporaneous than this writing through its kinship with *avant-garde* literary movements, to which the average literate Frenchman is more closely attuned than is the average educated American.

In some respects, however, the Existentialist way of philosophizing is less of a novelty to us in America than to the French. Our pragmatisms have always at least professed to start from the immediate life concerns of the individual. And our great philosophical names have not been especially remarkable for surface clarity nor for ostentation of logic. One could adduce the crabbed writing of our greatest logician, C. S. Peirce—to which James's characterization, "flashes of light against a Cimmerian darkness," is often just— or James himself, a short-winded reasoner but a writer with a delicate sense for the "flights and perchings" of experience. Although Dewey has raised a great outcry on behalf of "scientific method," he is notoriously fuzzy in argument, incapable of sharpening a definition or evading self-contradiction; his principal achievements may turn out to lie in such things as a voluminous evocation of the ambience of scientific inquiry, of the stresses and torments undergone by Nature in converting itself into Experience, and of the electric play of meanings as they emerge from a "situation" and give direction to human action.[5] On Whitehead in this connection I need not expatiate. Santayana has his Latin polish and a highly coherent set

---

[5] Cf. "John Dewey's Use of Language," by Virgil C. Aldrich, *Journal of Philosophy*, May 11, 1944.

of organizing principles, but the manner is that of a casual essayist moving jauntily through the Realms of Being, more concerned with painting the nuances of the ontological landscape than with making a surveyor's chart of it. In *Scepticism and Animal Faith* (1923) and the volumes to which it is a preface, he not only carried out the "phenomenological reduction" but passed through the realm of essence to a richer and more massive re-creation of the undergirding of consciousness in Nature and the psyche than any of his French or German counterparts have given us. Here are but a few samples from *Scepticism and Animal Faith*:

> The sense of existence evidently belongs to the intoxication, to the *Rausch,* of existence itself; it is the strain of life within me, prior to all intuition, that in its precipitation and terror, passing as it continually must from one untenable condition to another, stretches my attention absurdly over what is not given, over the lost and the unattained, the before and after which are wrapped in darkness, and confuses my breathless apprehension of the clear presence of all I can ever truly behold. . . .

> Existence, change, life, appearance, must be understood to be unintelligible: on any other assumption the philosopher might as well tear his hair and go mad at once. . . .

> There is an ever-present background felt as permanent, myself always myself; and there is a large identity in the universe also, familiar and limited in spite of its agitation, like a cage full of birds. Everything seems to be more or less prolonged; comfort, digestive warmth, the past still simmering, the brooding potentiality of things to come, shaping themselves in fancy before they have occurred.

Some time before the contemporary revival of Existentialism, Santayana wrote in *Soliloquies in England* (1920): "This world is contingency and absurdity incarnate, the oddest of possibilities masquerading momentarily as a fact." And in the essay "Ultimate Religion" (1933), he speculated that "Nature may be imperfectly formed in the bosom of chaos," and that it may contain regions to which the notion of rigorous law is inapplicable—in this supposition having been anticipated by Peirce's "tychism," as by the ancient Atomists. The Existential philosophers, from Kierkegaard on, have come out of a philosophical milieu so immersed in Idealist rationalism that they turned fey upon being confronted with the fundamental mystery in the nature of things: they are parvenus to absurdity. As a result, they have exaggerated the unintelligibility of the world, or misplaced it; our own philosophers, while acknowledging the brute "facticity" of existence and its properties, have gone on to explore the respects in which it does yield to rational inquiry. Santayana discerned a patient and even rather monotonous order of matter or substance behind the phantasmagoria of conscious experience, and Dewey and Whitehead in their different ways have been occupied with seeking out the continuities between levels of being.

If the Existentialists looked a little deeper into contemporary "field theory" in the sciences, they would have to soften their contrast between being-in-itself and being-for-itself. For the physical domain as it now reveals itself exhibits the same precarious and shifting equilibrium, the same "negation" of the already attained, the same restless impulse of vectorial forces toward new configurations, that they have discovered in the realm of mind. Since the Existentialists reject supernatural agencies, presumably they must hold that mind evolved out of life, and life out of the non-living, but we find in them no recognition of a genetic and functional continuity between these levels, nor anything like the sustained effort of post-Darwinian philosophy in America and Britain to square the fact of "emergence" or qualitative novelty with such continuity. Instead, Merleau-Ponty gives us dogmatic denials of causal relationships between the levels of being, admitting structural laws within each level but only capricious trigger-action between the levels.

Similar criticisms could be brought against the Existentialist theories of the relation of the self to the body and to freedom. Although I believe Sartre's and Merleau-Ponty's treatments of the role of the body, so far as they go, are valuable and suggestive, they reach hasty conclusions. For example, Merleau-Ponty was able to draw only upon the earlier writings of the Gestalt psychologists, produced when they were working in Germany under the spell of an Idealist atmosphere, and he would perhaps be led to modify his dogmatic repudiation of correspondences between the conscious or phenomenological field and the physiological field if he were acquainted with the neurological investigations of Köhler, and the theoretical revisions of Gestalt theory by Koffka and Lewin, carried out in this country.

The French philosophers took over from Phenomenology and its Idealist heritage a disposition to conceive "meanings" as ultimate and unique, almost occult, forces governing the mind by a kind of magnetic attraction and "expressing" themselves through the physiological organism without themselves in turn being dependent upon its functioning. But here likewise our semioticians from Peirce to Morris have preferred to work on the assumption that meanings have a natural habitat and a natural history, and as products of the interaction between a minded organism and a physical and social environment can be understood by patient empirical study. We shall, I believe, pursue this assumption further before yielding to the Existentialists' insistence that meanings and values come into being through a kind of virgin birth, begotten airily upon the self by its own spontaneous self-negations.

"Negation" itself, in the pre-logical or pseudological sense which the Existentialists give it, is not a unique property of consciousness. It has its inorganic paradigms, at least, in the repulsion of similarly charged electrons for each other and in a chemical solution's extrusion of heterogeneous matter in the process of crystallization. On the plane of life it appears in the amoeba's ejection of substances that will not nourish it; and, at the very core of the human propulsiveness, in the organism's "deficit conditions" of hunger and thirst which give us our primitive sense of *manque* and are registered in awakening consciousness long before we learn to symbolize our objectives in the manner that distinguishes conscious choice.

Sartre's version of the negative doctrine of freedom, perhaps the most extreme version known to the history of thought, is scarcely more seductive than his theory of negation. It is tonic to be reminded that man makes the meaning of his life, that the past is something to be surpassed, that we are open to the future, and that each life is a unique achievement like a work of art. It is well enough to have articulated—though of this just now we less need reminding—that man gropes in awful ignorance of himself and of his destiny, so that his power of decision is also a curse. But the curse weighs heavier than that of the House of Atreus—which according to Aeschylus was finally lifted through the pleading of Athene—in a doctrine that divorces freedom from self-knowledge and from knowledge of the human situation. If these fail us now, we dissolve into the nuclear vapors.

There is an old Hindu story that can convey the positive doctrine of freedom stated in Spinoza, Locke, Hume, and even in Hegel:

As a man was walking in the jungle one day, an enormous serpent dropped from a tree and coiled itself about him. His first impulse was to struggle, but the more he struggled the tighter the snake embraced him. Finally he relaxed his body and contorted it to follow the sinuous lines of the serpent's coils. As soon as he had done this, behold, he slipped free!

The coils of the serpent are the strands of Necessity in the nature of things. It is only so far as we gain knowledge of these and conform to this knowledge that we can become free, i.e., that we can live the good life within the potentialities of the world and of ourselves as the time offers them. What precise form self-knowledge can take—whether it can achieve the grasp of "laws" or must often be content to envisage tendencies and values—is a question for which we have not yet found a clear answer. But as Merleau-Ponty recognizes to some extent in his "semi-determinism," there is in us a more or less stable core of instinct, habit, personality and cultural inheritance that can only gradually be negated and transformed. And in *Pour une morale de l'ambiguïté,* the only sustained attempt so far at an ethics by a French Existentialist, Simone de Beauvoir has tried to conceive our freedom in such a way that it is compatible with either determinism or indeterminism: whether our uncertainty about the future springs from a radical contingency in the nature of things or simply expresses our subjective ignorance before a rigorous necessity, we never have complete evidence on which to act, so that we are always more or less in the shadows. Our "freedom," consequently, lies not in an assurance that we can evade the clutches of necessity but in the room that our incomplete knowledge leaves us for hope that our ends and values can be realized. Since we cannot know for certain that they are doomed, we are permitted to cling to them.

Such a view of freedom, Mme de Beauvoir urges, will keep us from sacrificing entirely the immediate and discernible decencies of life to an absolute value in the future, as a totalitarian program would have us do: ". . . An action which would serve man should be on guard against forgetting him along the way. . . . One of the ruses of Stalinist orthodoxy is playing on the idea of necessity, to put the whole revolution on one scale of the balance; in comparison, the other scale will always seem lightly weighted."

Mme de Beauvoir has given us a cautious and reasonable statement of the negative conception of freedom. But no more than her fellow-philosophers does she offer an ethics which can afford an articulated account of ends and values themselves. The Existentialist theory of the self, as we have seen, is incomplete, unanchored, at the nether end through its scanty recognition of the continuity of the self with nature; through its failure to look downward to the stability supplied the self by its subjection to natural processes. This doctrine of the self is likewise unfinished in the shortsightedness of its upward gaze toward values or norms of action.

Here again American empiricism has labored long and, I believe, not in vain, at a problem that the Existentialists have not yet faced—the slow crystallization of patterns of values from experience through the interplay of impulse and feeling with knowledge and reflection. In such writings as Santayana's *The Life of Reason* and Dewey's ethical treatises, we find that openness to the emergence of novel values that the Existentialists so cherish, and at the same time an analysis of the way in which such general norms as those of the classic ethical philosophies—happiness, satisfaction of needs, development of the capacities of the individual, respect for personality, fitness in performance of social functions—shape themselves out of the human situation. These norms offer us in the shadows of our partial ignorance more reliable beacons than the coruscations of Sartrian freedom, a child's sparkler in black darkness, or the ominous glow of Merleau-Ponty's mystical goal, a "historic mission." They also supply us with a positive content for freedom, to which the negative freedom of Existentialism at best can serve only as a means.

This analysis of the Existentialist conception of the self has its applications to the problem of philosophical style, a problem which in turn cannot be divorced from questions as to the methods and functions of philosophy. I have tried to indicate that both the French school and the American philosophers with whose approaches I have compared them practice styles that, up to a point, incorporate the poetic concern for the qualitative and affective particularities of experience. But I believe that the Americans come closer than these Frenchmen to achieving something similar to an "anagogic" level of meaning, of the sort that we ultimately demand of the philosophic vision. For the classic American philosophers have drawn widely upon the immediacy of experience—and from many areas of it that have escaped the notice of the Existentialists—and have further incorporated into their most comprehensive statements about the world the functional and operational meanings that can be attained only through science and logical analysis. There is perhaps only a difference of degree here between philosophy and poetry at their highest reaches, but we cannot give hearty assent to a philosophy that does not contain this second element in outstanding measure. The settlement at which philosophy aims would be one in which poetry and science have been allowed to fight their battles to a peace without victory, where both retain their tensions and their autonomy, and at the same time have abolished tariff barriers and achieved free trade.

Nevertheless, if we take the Existentialist movement as a whole from Kierkegaard onward, we should hesitate to deny it an important place in the stream of ideas. A great philosophy—if I may paraphrase Whitehead—is one after the shock of which human thought can never again be the same. Existentialism has at least forced on our attention the awful possibilities of fragmentation in human nature and the ever-present solicitations to anguish in the human predicament. Though anguish has not been lacking in American fiction and poetry, our major philosophers have been too well-organized to be deeply tinged with it. The British, who have not taken up Existentialism, seem still less capable of experiencing anguish, or at any rate of expressing it in any violent way—though their plight at present is as hazardous as that of the French—and our own cultural traditions are strong enough to keep us from yielding to it to the extent permitted by French theatricality. We have also the task of assimilating the insights of religious Existentialists from Kierkegaard to Tillich, who have something to offer besides fragmentation and anguish—a subtle if dislocated eye for the drama of moral struggle and of the religious yearning. What American philosophy can well do, by its own native genius, is to translate these concerns into operable and humanistic terms.

A final word is called for on French Existentialism's prospects for growth. Its leading philosophers are in their early forties, and a comparison of them with American thinkers who have rounded out a long life's work would be unfair if the object were to assess the respective talents of individuals. But there is room for doubt that Sartre, whatever his future as a novelist and playwright, will be able to carry farther the vein in philosophy to which he has given the most electric expression. The deviations of Merleau-Ponty and Beauvoir from Sartre have been in the direction of reasonableness: and if the school takes this tack it has a long way to go. Without being chauvinistic, it is possible to hold that the primary opportunity and responsibility for keeping philosophy afloat in the stormy waters ahead lies in this country (whose philosophers fortunately include many able thinkers of foreign birth, as they included Santayana and Whitehead). Even—or perhaps I should say especially— with the mushroom cloud on the horizon, Existentialism has not yet given us grounds for surrendering what can be salvaged in our heritage of meliorism and our faith that reflective intelligence can find a solution, if solution there be. Should there prove to be no solution, there is at least an accommodation. This is to set bounds to anguish:

Et la mort ancienne
Est de fermer les yeux sacrés et de se taire.

Parker Tyler NOVEL INTO FILM:

All the King's Men

ABOVE a line cut of his signature, Robert Penn Warren wrote a statement about the film version of his Pulitzer Prize novel, *All the King's Men*, which appeared in New York papers as an advertisement. After praising the independent authenticity of the screen characters and story, he says: "In this picture, I think, there is intensity without tricks and pretensions, and always a sense of truth: such a thing as this could happen in a world like this." With what a magnificent sideways motion Mr. Warren has pointed a steady finger at the dark mysteries of Hollywood—yes, "a world like this" is, and could be, nothing but the local spot, the very scene of the crime, where American movies are largely made and almost totally conceived.

If Mr. Warren, because of his peculiar position as the author of the novel, must be gingerly, there is no reason for me to be. I ask bluntly: If Jack Burden, the narrator of both film and novel, is caught in the mesh of an action which it takes dearly bought experience to induce him to believe he understands, isn't Mr. Warren under the same burden of compulsion with his novel in the stark hands of Hollywood? Mr. Warren's generous tribute to the Hollywood vision of things covers a multitude of modifications, big and little. These might appear slight or random to someone with reasons, but to someone without reasons, such as myself, who has respect for the novel but none at all for the screen version, they make all the difference, indeed, between a world like Hollywood's and a

world like Mr. Warren's. The major revision will indicate the degree
to which everything must newly conform: Judge Irwin of the
novel becomes Judge Stanton of the screen, an uncle of Adam and
Anne Stanton; as such, his secret paternity of Jack Burden, in
vanishing, disposes of one of the crucial elements of the novel's
plan.

On the silver screen, all adds up to a considerably solid deface-
ment. The casting of the character of Willie Stark himself is a key
to the web of artistic mayhem. The screen type is well-known: he
is a burly man with a flattened nose who, if cast strictly to Hollywood type, would appear as an ex-pug, possibly a strong-arm man
in the bodyguard of a big-city politician; he is not a Southern
hick lawyer or a surrogate for Huey Long, he is an old-fashioned
"gorilla." And he talks like one, straight from the boss's (not his)
mouth. The accent is East Side, moreover, not Deep South. I am
trying to say, more directly than did Mr. Warren, that Broderick
Crawford as Willie Stark is not in any respect convincing as the
character in Warren's novel, and scarcely even as a human being,
unless you find good, round, unpretentious Hollywood ham to your
taste in the theatre.

Some literary critics complained, I believe, that Mr. Warren
liked Huey Long's surrogate too much. But if he did, his novel
justified his extravagance to the hilt. If Willie has a certain essential
elusiveness to Jack Burden, who is Mr. Warren's mouthpiece, he
has the same for the reader. But this elusiveness has a suggestive
contour and a clear poetic substance. Willie talks with some of the
color of the Bible and the Elizabethans, and it sounds natural because, as Jack Burden believes, in a way he *means* it. (Mr. Crawford
has been told, of course, that Willie doesn't mean it; people only
think he does.) How did Burden know Willie meant it? He knew
because Mr. Warren conceived these passages of Willie's speech
in inspiration and they relate to a center of intelligence one couldn't
find in the film with a squad of detectives and a search warrant.
To what is Mr. Warren referring, then, with such perfect discretion
when he speaks of the film as "a world like this"? He refers to a
world without coherent ideas, but more than that, to a world without any intent to make ideas cohere, for it is a world whose

profession is to understate and if possible avoid the intellectual consciousness of the real world.

Whatever Mr. Warren accomplished in his novel, either as work of art or as social commentary, he took the real world for his inevitable setting, for he wanted to state something sincerely. Jack Burden's role as moral chorus for Willie's quasi-tragic career as demagogue, as well as Willie's own role of people's messiah, are stated succinctly in the film as truthfully as orthodox Hollywood can hope to say it. This statement occurs in miniature when a sort of "March of Time" newsreel within the film is made of Stark's career, and the commentator declaims at the end fortissimo: "Messiah or Dictator?" The conversion of supposed life into formal terms is scientifically accurate here if we accept, as the world of this film adaptation, the world we are in when we sit in a newsreel theatre. What happens to Willie Stark's life by way of the newsreel-short is the same as happens to the novel—to Jack Burden's continual struggle with himself and his search for Willie's true meaning—on a more elaborate scale in Robert Rossen's screen story. The latter is streamlined, consciously reduced in dramatic and intellectual stature, and converted, in brief, to the terms in which assiduous readers of *Time* and *Life* regard everything from the atom bomb to the writings of Gertrude Stein. These terms are those to which a state of goggle-eyed detachment is all-receptive.

A sure-fire system of reading the misreadings of the film is in respect to the screen's dialogue, where paraphrases and duplications of the novel's words have been used. Screen synopsis has a cute way of rejuggling situations, and thereby compliments itself on prodigious feats achieved in the interests of condensation as well as convenience. But everywhere that one may identify condensation in the film version one may just as clearly perceive falsification. Now Mr. Warren himself has opened the way (in gentlemanly manner) to considering the filmic *All the King's Men* a separate entity, perhaps as though it bore something of the relation of *Alice in Wonderland* to the life of a real little girl in Carroll's own era. If, by some curious move of fate, the *Iliad* were to be translated into Ojibway, I suppose there might be valid grounds for concluding that, so far as the Ojibways went, a very satisfying job had been done on the

Homeric epic. But I dare say not every soul who sits in a movie theatre is an Ojibway or first cousin to one.

Though I put myself in the position of one with a Homeric rather than a Hollywoodian attitude toward Mr. Warren's novel, let us be perfectly fair. Eric Bentley's criticism of the novel's short-comings should be studied and expanded.[1] For Mr. Bentley went so far as to place Mr. Warren's world grazingly close to what came to be Mr. Rossen's world: "The worst thing you can truthfully say about *All the King's Men*," observed Mr. Bentley, "is that the almost Hollywoodian thriller which is Warren's vehicle is all too easily separable from his theme." Indeed? Is Mr. Warren, one may wonder, trying to dissociate himself from the very deed he helped to perpetrate? The existence of the film brings into sharp and inevitable focus, then, the literary problem itself. If the film had achieved this focus on the grounds of asserting jealously its true filmic rights, a separate if genuine artistry, it would be different, but what it asserts is the mere existence of the literary-filmic type of the "thriller."

One is inclined to appreciate the delicacy and underlying gravity of Mr. Warren's position in the matter. What have the Jack Burden and the Willie Stark of the screen done, in crystallizing characters less valid and interesting than their novelistic prototypes, but likewise crystallize, in Mr. Warren's direction, the pejorative elements of melodrama and journalism that, according to Mr. Bentley, inhere in the original work? In the literary perspective, Jack Burden has not only his own complexity (embodied chiefly in his ambition to write Cass Mastern's story rather than Willie Stark's) but also a special complexity in relation to his counterparts in other works of Robert Penn Warren. Mr. Warren has publicly hinted that this negative functioning of the film be disregarded in favor of something it does on its own—does for the masses who care not at all for any of his characters who live only in print, and who care just as little for the subtlety of Burden's relation to R. P. W.

I suggest—with, I confess, some timidity—that Mr. Warren may suspect that in the routine Fascist toggery with which Mr. Craw-

---

[1] Eric Bentley, "The Meaning of Robert Penn Warren's Novels," *Kenyon Review*: Summer 1948.

ford as Stark is gotten up may abide as much or more of "the truth about Huey Long" than he has put into his novel. And I suggest— with decreasing timidity—that this state of honest confusion may exist in Mr. Warren because he embarked on his project as some- thing more of an allegory than its actual guise gives one leave to assume (hence the pertinence of Mr. Bentley's comment that, as for naturalism, Mr. Warren's is "not naturalistic enough"). But if this is true, and if Jack Burden's ambivalent feeling for Stark reflects (as I should say) R. P. W.'s ambivalent feeling for what a Huey Long represents, Mr. Warren's glad hand for the movie might well be attached to an arm with a mourning band. The novelist certainly knows that where he has a thousand ways of touching off, bodying forth, the inner irrational that is Willie Stark, the film has three or four: the rest is stereotyped façade, paraphernalia, the rush of sound and matter through space.

I should identify the innate drama of the novel as based on a contest of poetic attitudes. Willie Stark's rhetoric is not the only "classical" element in his nature. As a Homer of the Rednecks' consciousness, he is also a Pisistratus, a "benefactor of the poor," and his methods are much as Pisistratus' are reputed to have been. If Huey Long was not so eloquent as Warren has made Stark, Long's personality had an inevitable cultural equivalent of mass mythology, where the legend of a Messiah, indiscriminately politico-religious, is embedded. If Jack Burden can never say outright of Willie Stark that he is a charlatan with histrionic talent, neither can Mr. Warren say it outright of the deceased Long. But why? Visualizing the premises of his novel, he cannot say it because Willie Stark is patently the incarnation of a poetic vein of politics; he engages the imagination of the people on the same basis that even Jesus engaged it, and that Napoleon and Hitler—for good or evil—engaged it: he gives them hope in the idea of a leader who shall save them in their distress, a leader who opens to them a new way of life. Perhaps the ambiguity of this political-literary legend lies, really, in a modernly vague distinction between body and spirit. When one delivers the body from want, is the spirit truly benefited through this means?

This ambiguity, on the level of a superior culture, must in- evitably be translated into more refined terms. That is, such a "humane tyrant" as Willie Stark is perhaps too much dedicated (by whatever methods!) to the relief of "the body," to the relief of the materially underprivileged. Dr. Adam Stanton's compromised position becomes entirely credible in this light. Yes, Stark's monument to personal vanity, the hospital, *will* do a great deal of common good. But there is too—as Adam knows—the soul, which also must have "common good." But when Adam Stanton says "soul," is he not a little prejudiced—doesn't he really mean the souls of a limited, privileged class who have gone to big universities in both North and South and as adults brood over the meaning of life and literature more than they concern themselves with the sufferings of the poor? When a surgeon cuts, he cuts for money, for private fame, and for science as much as he does for others and for human life. Such seems, when all is said and done, the ineluctable reality of human nature. And when Jack Burden must criticize Willie Stark for "doing good" by questionable means (though none seem so bad as the screen Willie's are made to be), doesn't he perceive that everyone who acts must, in a way, act selfishly? Burden, indeed, defined Stark's genius as interest in self (see *All the King's Men,* page 134). May we not conclude that, as Warren's mouthpiece, Burden is actually defining here a typical, even *indispensable*, characteristic of genius?

In such a case, Warren is as selfishly interested in the phenomenon of Long as Burden is, however subconsciously, in the phenomenon of Stark. And how is Burden "selfishly" interested in the phenomenon of Stark? He is—as we learn fully by the end—actually practicing for the book he has been unable to write on Cass Mastern, his ancestor, and his training in Stark's "school of research" paradoxically issues, as the novel ends, in his new-found power to go ahead with the Mastern story that long ago he laid aside. So what purpose does Stark serve for Burden? His career as savior of the people has at once disillusioned and initiated him. It becomes the old story of the man of action in relation to the man of thought. Stark combines thought *and* action in that he combines a poetry of traditional culture (the Messiah role and its accoutrement of eloquence) with successful politics. Warren observed the career of Stark's prototype, Long, and considered the *Republic* of Plato. He decided, in all honor to his class of creative intellectuals, that Long must be proven false to poetry as well as to the State. Napoleon's epigrams didn't make him a Homer. Nor did Hitler's rhetoric make him either Vergilian or quite decent. At the same time, to speak in sheer respect for reality, Long was a dynamic realization of an age-old myth and he understood the *poetry* of a life of such ambiguous dedication. Warren could not resist this inevitable poetry, even though his loyalty to it, like Burden's loyalty to Stark, led logically to the moment of downfall, to the final "criticism" of the assassin's bullet. And who is the assassin? It is the absolute, unyielding amalgam of idealist and practical man: Dr. Stanton, the surgeon. He, too, is annihilated because he *competes* with the Messiah. And one cannot compete with the Messiah.

Unless, that is to say, one is a *writer*, the man who acts not relatively, but absolutely, through words; the man who has, as Mr. Warren has had, the last word. And literature's Mr. Warren, not Hollywood's Mr. Rossen, has—make no mistake!—had it. The screen Stark's eloquence (both in words and substance) is to the original Stark's as Walter Winchell's memory picture of the grave-yard scene in *Hamlet* must be to Shakespeare's verse. I wish to emphasize here that Warren's selfishness was antithetically constructed to convey the charm and mysterious human challenge of such a person as Stark-Long, for it was against the practical man-of-words, the poet-politician, that he pitted the legend of the pure literary creator, himself, even though he stacked the plot so that the frustrated writer (Burden) should become less frustrated (Warren) precisely because of a now worm-eaten fact, Louisiana's "little dictator."

I submit that we should not evade, nevertheless, the question of the influence a priori no less than the influence a posteriori of the movies on fiction. For these influences exist apart and together—the latter when the a priori influence clicks in Hollywood. If it is a necessary humiliation to literature that, however less than perfect it be, its faults be scientifically isolated and shown up by the movies, the fact should be a lesson to all writers, especially to the epic poet that Warren is by way of being in the novel form. The lesson is perhaps that the epic quality is not to be bought at any price and that the creative writer must make his decisions more decisively, and in advance of writing his work rather than at its conclusion. It is more than three centuries since the murdered "benevolent tyrant," Julius Caesar, was made a tragic hero in great dramatic literature, and earlier in the present century a gentleman now hired by Hollywood, Orson Welles, devised a dramatic commentary which helps to make the film's Willie Stark the more credible as a "March of Time" hero. About fifteen years ago, Welles streamlined the Shakespearian text and put Caesar and the play into Hitlerian mufti. Isn't it high time either to reject or accept the socio-moral, or broad cultural truth of the contemporary dictator-type?

The question is not whether the Dictator is politically desirable. The question (in that limited sense in which the creative writer *can* be legitimately selfish) is whether the Dictator is desirable as a hero of the imagination. I don't say that Mr. Warren's novel has spoken "the last word" in the theoretical sense, but according to his view of the matter there is a contradiction between the Dictator's validity in the imagination and his validity in society—a kind of contradiction which did not exist when kings and messiahs had "divine rights"; that is, when evil as well as good was privileged. Today, because the Devil's work is supposed gradually to be yielding to the implacable advance of scientific ideas, evil no longer has its ancient privileges. It no longer entitles the hero to that very "agony of will" which Burden at last attributes, but without ethical definition, to Willie Stark. Evil shows signs of being absorbed neutrally, scientifically, into an especially stark Promethean tragedy, in which any great creative effort automatically entails both evil and good. In any case, evil is, somehow, still with us. It may be the destiny of Hollywood merely to note this fact in passing. Responsible creative art, in whatever medium, should judge it. The film, *All the King's Men,* underlines that Mr. Warren hasn't, quite, judged it. And what I mean the novelist should judge is whether political evil deserves the tragic stature.

Lionel Trilling WORDSWORTH

AND THE IRON TIME

O UR meeting here to do honor to William Wordsworth will
have its counterparts in academic centers in all the English-
speaking countries. But we can scarcely suppose that in the world
outside the universities the impulse to commemorate Wordsworth
will be felt to any significant extent. Indeed, our occasion must
inevitably be charged with the consciousness that were he not kept
in mind by the universities, Wordsworth would scarcely be remembered at all. In our culture it is not the common habit to read
the books of a century ago and very likely all that we can mean
when we say that a writer of the past is "alive" in people's minds
is that, to those who once read him as a college assignment or who
have formed an image of him from what they have heard about
him, he exists as an attractive idea, as an intellectual possibility. If
we think of the three poets whom Matthew Arnold celebrated in
his "Memorial Verses," we know that Byron is still attractive and
possible, and so is Goethe, as was indicated last year by the elabo-
rateness with which the bicentenary of his birth was celebrated. But
Wordsworth is not attractive and not an intellectual possibility.
He was once the great, the speaking poet for all who read English.
He spoke both to the ordinary reader and to the literary man. But
now the literary man outside the university will scarcely think

Delivered at Princeton University on the occasion of the 100th anniversary
of Wordsworth's death, April 21-23, 1950. This essay is included in *Wordsworth Centenary Studies*, the Princeton University Press.

of referring to Wordsworth as an important event of modern literature; and to the ordinary reader he is likely to exist as the very type of the poet whom life has passed by, presumably for the very good reason that he passed life by.

The discrepancy between the opinion of the world and the opinion, or at least the pious action, of the universities is a matter which in itself is worthy of comment and I should like to touch upon certain of its implications before I have done. But my chief intention is to ask what are the reasons for the world's present opinion of Wordsworth and in how far that opinion is justified. By trying to answer these questions I hope to arrive at an understanding of Wordsworth suitable for our time, and thus to praise him.

If we ask why Wordsworth is no longer the loved poet he once was, why, indeed, he is felt to be absurd and even a little despicable, one answer that suggests itself is that for modern taste he is too Christian a poet. He is certainly not to be wholly characterized by the Christian element of his poetry. Nor can we say of him that he is a Christian poet in the same sense that Dante is, or Donne, or Hopkins. With them the specific Christian feeling and doctrine is of the essence of their matter and conscious intention, as it is not with Wordsworth. Yet at the present time, the doctrinal tendency of the world at large being what it is, that which *is* Christian in Wordsworth may well seem to be more prominent than it ever was before, and more decisive. I have in mind his concern for the life of humbleness and quiet, his search for peace, his sense of the burdens of this life, those which are inherent in the flesh and spirit of man. Then there is his belief that the bonds of society ought to be inner and habitual, not merely external and formal, and that the strengthening of these bonds by the acts and attitudes of charity is a great and charming duty. Christian too seems his responsiveness to the idea that there is virtue in the discharge of duties that are not humble, those which are of the great world and therefore dangerous to simple peace. There is his impulse to submit to the conditions of life under a guidance which is at once certain and mysterious—his sense of the possibility and actuality of enlightenment, it need scarcely be said, is one of the characteristic things about him. It was not he who said that the world was a vale of soul-making, but the poet who did make this striking paraphrase of the Christian sentiment could not have uttered it had not Wordsworth made it possible for him to do so. And then above all there is his consciousness of the *neighbor*, his impulse to bring into the circle of significant life those of the neighbors who are simple and outside the circle of social pride, and also those who, in the judgment of the world, are queer and strange and useless.

Certainly this that I have called Christian in Wordsworth scarcely approaches, let alone makes up, the sum of Christianity. But then no personal document or canon can do that, not even the work of a poet who is specifically Christian in the way of Dante, or of Donne, or of Hopkins. When we speak of a poet as being of a particular religion, we do not imply in him completeness or orthodoxy, or even explicitness of doctrine, but only that his secular utterance has the decisive mark of the religion upon it. And if a religion is manifold in its aspects and extensive in time, the marks that are to be found on the poets who are in a relation to it will be various in kind. It seems to me that the marks of Christianity on Wordsworth are clear and indelible. It is therefore worth trying the hypothesis that the world today does not like him because it does not like the Christian quality and virtues.

But the question at once arises whether this hypothesis is actually available to us. Professor Fairchild says, and in a very explicit way, that it is not—in the chapter on Wordsworth in the third volume of his *Religious Trends in English Poetry*, he not only says that Wordsworth is not a Christian poet but he also expresses doubts that Wordsworth was ever properly to be called a Christian, even when he became a communicant of the Church and its defender, and goes so far as to tell us that as a poet Wordsworth is actually dangerous to the Christian faith. He is dangerous in the degree that he is religious at all, for his religion is said to be only religiosity, the religion of nothing more than the religious emotion, beginning and ending in the mere sense of transcendence. Naked of dogma, bare of precise predication of God and the nature of man, this religiosity of Wordsworth is to be understood as a pretentious and seductive rival of Christianity. It is the more dangerous because it gives license to man's pretensions—Professor Fairchild subscribes to the belief which is not uncommonly held by proponents of religion, or by those who defend what they call a classical view of the world, that Romanticism must bear a large part of the responsibility for our present ills, especially for those which involve man's direct and conscious inhumanity to man.

We can surely find a degree of cogency in Professor Fairchild's argument within the terms of its intention. The nineteenth century was in many respects a very Christian century, but in the aspect of it which bulks largest in our minds it developed chiefly the ethical and social parts of Christian belief and no doubt at the cost of the dogmatic part, which had already been weakened by the latitudinarian tendency of the eighteenth century. And it is probably true that when in religion the dogmatic principle is slighted, religion goes along for a while on generalized emotion and ethical intention —"morality touched by emotion"—and then loses the force of its impulse, even the essence of its being. In this sort of attenuation of religion Romanticism in general and Wordsworth in particular did indeed play a great part by making the sense of transcendence and immanence so real and so attractive.

It is certainly true that, through the most interesting and creative part of his career, Wordsworth cut himself off from a conscious involvement with or reference to the doctrinal teachings of the Church. He spoke of the virtues of faith, hope, and charity without reference to the specifically Christian source and end of these virtues. His sense of the need for salvation did not, certainly, take account of the Christian means of salvation. Of evil in the Christian sense of the word, of sin as an element of the nature of man, he also took no account. And yet, all this being true, as we look at him in the context of his own time and in the context of our own time, what may properly be called his Christian element can be made to speak to us, as it spoke to so many Christians in the nineteenth century, as it spoke to so many who were not Christians and made them in one degree or another accessible to Christianity.

"Any religious movement," says Christopher Dawson, an orthodox Christian scholar, "which adopts a purely critical and negative attitude to culture is . . . a force of destruction and disintegration which mobilizes against it the healthiest and most constructive elements in society—elements which can by no means be dismissed as worthless from the religious point of view." Romanticism in general was far from worthless to Christianity, far from worthless to that very Anglo-Catholicism which likes to be so strict with it. And this is true of Wordsworth in particular. He certainly did not in his great period accept as adequate what the Church taught about the nature of man. But he was one of the few poets who really discovered something about the nature of man. And what he discovered can no doubt be shown, if the argument be conducted by a comparison of formulas and doctrine, to be at variance with the teachings of Christianity. Yet I think it can also be shown that he discovered much that a strong Christianity must take account of, and be easy with, and make use of—it can be shown too that the Church, consciously or not, has found advantage in what Wordsworth told us of the nature of man.

Professor Fairchild understands Christianity far better than I do through having studied it ever so much more than I have; and of course he understands it far better than I might ever hope to because he has experienced it as a communicant; and he has, I am sure, tested his conclusions by the whole tendency of the Church to which he gives so strong and thoughtful an allegiance; my own reading of this tendency, at least as it appears in literature and in literary criticism where it has been so influential, is that it is not inclined to accept Wordsworth as a Christian poet. As against the force of Professor Fairchild's judgment, I cannot help feeling that there is an important element of Christianity with which Wordsworth has a significant affinity, even though this element is not now of a chief importance to Christian intellectuals. But this is not an occasion for anything like contentiousness, and I ought not to seem to be forcing even a great poet into a faith whose members do not want him there. I am not, in any case, so much concerned to prove that Wordsworth is a Christian poet as to account for a certain quality in him which makes him unacceptable to the modern world. And so, without repudiating my first hypothesis, I shall abandon it for this fresh one: that the quality in Wordsworth that now makes him unacceptable is a Judaic quality.

My knowledge of the Jewish tradition is, I fear, all too slight to permit me to hope that I can develop this new hypothesis in any very enlightening way. Yet there is one Jewish work of traditional importance which I happen to know with some intimacy and it lends a certain color of accuracy to my notion. This is the work called *Pirke Aboth*, that is, the sayings, the *sententiae*, of the Fathers. It was edited in the second century of the present era by the scholar and teacher who bore the magnificent name of Rabbi Jehudah the Prince, and who is traditionally referred to by the even more magnificent name of *Rabbi—the* rabbi, the master-teacher, the greatest of all. In its first intention, *Pirke Aboth*, under the name *Aboth*, Fathers, was one of the tractates of the Mishnah, which is the traditional Jewish doctrine represented chiefly by rabbinical decisions; but *Aboth* itself, the last of the tractates, does not deal with decisions; nor is it what a common English rendering of the longer title, "Ethics of the Fathers," would seem to imply, for it is not a system of ethics at all but simply a collection of maxims and *pensées*, some quite fine, some quite dull, which praise the life of study and give advice on how to live it.

In speaking of Wordsworth a recollection of boyhood cannot be amiss—my intimacy with this book comes from my having read it many times in boyhood. It certainly isn't the kind of book a boy is easily drawn to read, and certainly I did not read it out of piety. On the contrary, indeed: for when I was supposed to be reading my prayers, very long and in the Hebrew language which I never mastered, I spent the required time reading the English translation of the *Pirke Aboth* which, although it is not a devotional work, had long ago been thought of as an aid to devotion and included in the prayerbook. It was more attractive to me than psalms, meditations, and supplications; it seemed more humane, and the Fathers had a curious substantiality. Just where they lived I did not know, nor just when, and certainly the rule of life they recommended had a very quaint difference from the life I knew, or, indeed, from any life I wanted to know. Yet they were real, their way of life had the charm of coherence. And when I went back to them, using this time R. Travers Herford's scholarly edition and translation of their sayings,[1] I could feel that my

---

[1] I have also consulted the edition and translation of the Very Rev. Dr. Joseph H. Hertz, Chief Rabbi of the British Empire, and in my quotations I have drawn upon both versions. Sometimes, when it suited my point, I have combined two versions in a single quotation.

early illicit intimacy with them had prepared the way for my responsiveness to Wordsworth, that between them and him an affinity existed.

But I must at once admit that a large difficulty stands in the way of the affinity I suggest. The *Aboth* is a collection of the sayings of masters of the written word. The ethical life it recommends has for its end the study of Torah, of the Law, which alone can give blessedness. So that from the start I am at the disadvantage of trying to make a conjunction between scholars living for the perpetual interpretation of a text and a poet for whom the natural world was at the heart of his doctrine and for whom books were barren leaves. The Rabbis were as suspicious of the natural world as Wordsworth was suspicious of study. That the warning was given at all seems to hint that the Rabbis felt the natural world to be a charm and a temptation, still the *Aboth* does warn us that whoever interrupts his study to observe the beauty of a fine tree or a fine meadow is guilty of sin. And yet I think that it can be said without extravagance that it is precisely here, where they seem most to differ, that the Rabbis and Wordsworth are most at one. For between the Law as the Rabbis understood it and Nature as Wordsworth understood that, there is a pregnant similarity.

The Rabbis of the *Aboth* were Pharisees. I shall assume that the long scholarly efforts of Mr. Herford, as well as those of George Foot Moore, have by now made it generally known that the Pharisees were not in actual fact what tradition represents them to have been. They were anything but mere formalists, they were certainly not the hypocrites of popular conception. Here is Mr. Herford's statement of the defining principle of Pharisaism: "The central conception of Pharisaism is Torah, the divine Teaching, the full and inexhaustible revelation which God had made. The knowledge of what was revealed was to be sought, and would be found, in the first instance in the written text of the Pentateuch, but the revelation, the real Torah, was the meaning of what was there written, the meaning as interpreted by all the recognized and accepted methods of the schools, and unfolded in ever greater fullness of detail by successive generations of devoted teachers. The written text of the Pentateuch might be compared to the mouth of a well; the Torah was the water which was drawn from it. He who

wished to draw the water must needs go to the well, but there was
no limit to the water there for him to draw. . . . The study of Torah
. . . means therefore much more than the study of the Pentateuch,
or even of the whole Scripture, regarded as mere literature, written
documents. It means the study of revelation made through these
documents, the divine teaching therein imparted, the divine thought
therein disclosed. Apart from the direct intercourse of prayer, the
study of Torah was the way of closest approach to God; it might
be called the Pharisaic form of the Beatific Vision. To study
Torah was, to the devout Pharisee, 'to think God's thoughts after
him,' as Kepler said." The Rabbis, that is, found sermons in texts,
tongues in the running commentary; they conceived failure to lie
in supposing that the yellow primrose of a word was a yellow
primrose and nothing more.

And Mr. Herford goes on to say that it might be remarked
that in the *Aboth* there are very few direct references to God.
"This is true," he says, "but it is beside the mark. Wherever Torah
is mentioned, there God is implied. He is behind the Torah, the
Revealer of what is Revealed."

What I wish to suggest is that, different as the immediately
present objects were in each case, there existed for the Rabbis and
for Wordsworth a great object, which is from God and might be
said to represent Him as a sort of surrogate, a divine object to which
one can be in an intimate passionate relationship, an active relationship—for Wordsworth's "wise passiveness" is of course an activity—
which one can, as it were, handle, and in a sense create, drawing
from it inexhaustible meaning by desire, intuition, and attention.

And when we turn to the particulars of the *Aboth* we see that
the affinity continues. In Jewish tradition the great Hillel has a
peculiarly Wordsworthian personality, being the type of gentleness
and peace, and having about him a kind of *joy* which has always
been found wonderfully attractive; and Hillel said—was, indeed,
in the habit of saying: he "used to say"—"If I am not for myself,
who, then, is for me? And if I am for myself, what then am I?" Mr.
Herford implies that this is a difficult utterance, but it is not difficult for the reader of Wordsworth, who find the Wordsworthian
essence here, the interplay between individualism and the sense of
community, between an awareness of the self that must be saved

and developed and an awareness that the self is yet fulfilled only in community. How profoundly Wordsworthian too is this saying of Akiba's, which, with so handsome a boldness, handles the problem of fate and free will, of grace and works: "All is foreseen and yet free-will is given; and the world is judged by grace and yet all is according to the work."

There are other parallels to be drawn—for example, one finds in the *Aboth* remarks which have a certain wit and daring because they go against the whole tendency of the work in telling us that the multiplication of words is an occasion for sin and that not study but action is the chief thing; one finds the injunction to the scholar to divide his time between study and a trade, presumably in the interest of humility; and the warning that the world must not be too much with him, that getting and spending he lays waste his powers; and the concern with the Ages of Man, with the right time in the individual development for each of life's activities. But it is needless to multiply the details of the affinity, which in any case must not be insisted on too far. All that I want to suggest is the community of ideal and sensibility between the *Aboth* and the canon of Wordsworth's work—the passionate contemplation and experience of the great object which is proximate to Deity; then the plain living that goes with the high thinking, the desire for the humble life and the discharge of duty; and last, but not least important, a certain insouciant acquiescence in the anomalies of the moral order of the universe, a respectful indifference to, or a graceful surrender before, the mysteries of the moral relation of God to man.

This last element as it is expressed by Akiba's *pensée* has, I think, its connection with something in the *Aboth* which for me is definitive of its quality. Actually it is something not in the *Aboth* but left out—we find in the tractate no implication of spiritual struggle. We find the energy of assiduity but not the energy of resistance. We hear about sin, but we do not hear about the sinful nature of man. Man in the *Aboth* guards against sin but he does not struggle against it, and of evil we hear nothing at all. When we have observed this it is natural to observe next that there is no mention in the *Aboth* of courage or heroism. In our culture we connect the notion of courage or heroism with the religious life.

We conceive of the perpetual enemy within and the perpetual enemy without which must be "withstood," "overcome," "conquered"— the language of religion and the language of fighting are in our culture assimilated to each other. Not so in the *Aboth*. The enemy within seems not to be conceived of at all. The enemy without is never mentioned, although the *Aboth* was compiled after the Dispersion, after the Temple and the Nation had been destroyed, with what heroism in the face of suffering we know from Josephus. Of the men whose words are cited, many met martyrdom for their religion, and the martyrology records their calm and fortitude in torture and death; of Akiba it records his heroic joy. And yet in their maxims they never speak of courage.

As much as anything else in my boyhood experience of the *Aboth* it was this that fascinated me. It also repelled me. It had the double effect because it went so clearly against the militancy of spirit which in our culture is normally assumed. And even now as I consider this indifference to heroism, I have the old ambiguous response to it, so that I think I can understand the feelings that readers have when they encounter something similar in Wordsworth. For there is indeed something similar in Wordsworth. It is what Matthew Arnold notes when in the "Memorial Verses" he compares Wordsworth with Byron, who was for Arnold the embodiment of militancy of spirit. Arnold said of Wordsworth that part of his peculiar value to us arose from his indifference to "man's fiery might," to the Byronic courage in fronting human destiny:

> *The cloud of human destiny,*
> *Others will front it fearlessly—*
> *But who, like him, will put it by?*

Arnold certainly did not mean that Wordsworth lacked courage or took no account of it. He liked nothing better, indeed, than to recite examples of courage, but the Wordsworthian courage is different in kind from the Byronic. For one thing, it is never aware of itself, it is scarcely personal. It is the courage of mute, insensate things, and is often poetically associated with these things, with rocks and stones and trees, or with stars. Michael on his hilltop, whose character is defined by the light of his cottage, which was called The Northern Star, and by the stones of his sheepfold; or the Leech Gatherer, who is like some old, great rock; or Margaret, who like a tree endured as long as she might after she was blasted— of the Lesser Celandine it is said that its fortitude is neither its courage nor its choice but its necessity in being old, and the same thing is to be said of all of Wordsworth's exemplars of courage: they endure because they are what they are, and we might almost say that they survive out of a kind of biological faith, which is not the less human because it is nearly an animal or vegetable faith; and, indeed, as I have suggested, it is sometimes nearly mineral. Even the Happy Warrior, the man in arms, derives his courage not from his militancy of spirit but from his calm submission to the law of things.

In Wordsworth's vision of life, then, the element of quietude approaches passivity, even insentience, and the dizzy raptures of youth have their issue in the elemental existence of which I have spoken. The scholars of the *Aboth* certainly had no such notion, they lived for intellectual sentience. But where the scholars and Wordsworth are at one is in the quietism, which is not in the least a negation of life, but on the contrary an affirmation of life so complete that it needed no saying. To the Rabbis, as I read them, there life was, unquestionable because committed to a divine object. There life was—in our view rather stuffy and airless, or circumscribed and thin, but very intense and absolutely and utterly real, not needing to be affirmed by force or assertion, real because the object of its regard was unquestioned and because that object was unquestionably more important than the individual persons who regarded it and lived by it. To Wordsworth, as I read him, a similar thing was true in its own way. Much as he loved to affirm the dizzy raptures of sentience, of the ear and the eye and the mind, he also loved to move down the scale of being, to say that when the spirit was sealed by slumber, was without motion and force, when it was like a rock or a stone or a tree, not hearing or seeing and passive in the cosmic motion, that even then, or especially then, existence was blessed.

Now nothing could be further from the tendency of our culture than this Wordsworthian attitude or quality of feeling. We can say in general that our culture is committed to nothing so much as sentience and activity, to motion and force, and that with us the basis of spiritual prestige is some form of violence directed toward others or toward ourselves. An example comes conveniently to hand in T. S. Eliot's explanation of the decline of Wordsworth's genius from its greatness to what Mr. Eliot calls the "still, sad music of infirmity." Wordsworth, says Mr. Eliot, suffered from the lack of an eagle—that eagle which André Gide's Prometheus says is necessary for the successful spiritual or poetic life: "*Il faut avoir un aigle.*" This fierce but validating bird, this *aigle obligatoire,* suggests the status of the feral and the violent in our literature. Nothing is better established in our literary life than the knowledge that the tigers of wrath are better than the horses of instruction. We have been taught that we must give our partisanship to the fierce bulls in the ring rather than to the worn, patient, disembowelled horses. Or in the matter of horses themselves, we have been taught to prefer those of Plato's chariot which are black and wild to those which are white. We do not, to be sure, live in the fashion of the beasts we admire in our literary lives—the discrepancy is much to the point—but we cherish them as representing something that we all seem to seek. They are the emblems of that *charisma*—to borrow a word which the sociologists have borrowed from the theologians—which is the hot, direct relationship with godhead, or with the sources of life upon which depend our notions of what I have called spiritual prestige.

At every point in our culture we find this predilection which makes it impossible for most readers to accept Wordsworth. It is the predilection for the powerful, the fierce, the assertive, the personally heroic. There is manifest everywhere in our literature the search for a sort of personal, private *charisma,* the desire for the acquisition of *mana.* We find it in the liberal-bourgeois admiration of the novels of Thomas Wolfe and of Theodore Dreiser. On a somewhat lower intellectual level we find it in the popularity of the curious demonism of that curious underground work, *The Fountainhead.* On a higher intellectual level we find it in the response to certain aspects of Yeats and Lawrence, whose celebration of force will suggest a standard element in contemporary literature. It appears in our politics, for quite apart from what we actually *do* about politics, when we mix it up with our sensibility, we are convinced in our hearts that politics should be ultimate and absolute, that, at the behest of the pure, perfect, magical vision, we should finish up things once and for all. We find it in our religion, or in our conception of religion—to most intellectuals the violence of Dostoevski represents the natural form of the religious life; and although some years ago Mr. Eliot reprobated Lawrence, in the name of religion, for his addiction to this characteristic violence, yet for Mr. Eliot the equally violent Baudelaire is preeminently a Christian poet.

The other day Mr. Richard Chase reviewed the book of a notable English scholar, Professor Willey, and I cannot give a better description of the quality of our literature I am concerned with than by quoting the characterization of it which Mr. Chase finds occasion to make. Professor Willey, it is relevant to remark, deals with the nineteenth century from the point of view of the Anglican form of Christianity, and Mr. Chase is commenting on Professor Willey's hostility to a certain Victorian figure who, in any discussion of Wordsworth, must inevitably be in our minds—John Stuart Mill: his name seems very queer and shocking when it is spoken together with the names of the headlong figures of modern literature. "Among the Victorians," says Mr. Chase, "it is Mill who tests the modern mind, and in relation to him at least two of its weaknesses come quickly to light. The first is its morose desire for dogmatic certainty. The second is its hyperaesthesia: its feeling that no thought is permissible except an extreme thought; that every idea must be directly emblematic of concentration camps, alienation, madness, hell, history, and God; that every word must bristle and explode with the magic potency of our plight."

I must be careful not to seem to speak, as certainly Mr. Chase is not speaking, against the sense of urgency and immediacy, or against power; and certainly not against the great, sad figures of modern literature. Nor would I be taken to mean that the Wordsworthian way of feeling is the whole desideratum of the emotional life. We all know that there is an extension of the Wordsworthian feeling that we dread. When in *The Excursion* the Wanderer and the Poet and the Parson sit upon the gravestones and tell sad stories of the deaths of other mild old men for the benefit of the Solitary, who has had his fling at life and is understandably a little bitter, we know that something wrong is being done to us, we long for the winding of a horn or the drawing of a sword, we want someone to dash in on a horse—I think we want exactly a stallion. For

there can be no doubt about it, Wordsworth at the extreme or perversion of himself carries the element of quietude to the denial of
sexuality; and perhaps at all times he implies a non-sexuality. And
this is eventually what makes the *Aboth* seem quaint and oppressive, what, I suppose, makes a modern reader uneasy under any of
the philosophies which urge us to the contemplation of a unitary
reality which is described as being disturbed and destroyed by the
desires. Whether it be the Torah of the *Aboth,* or the Cosmos of
Marcus Aurelius, or the Nature of Spinoza or of Wordsworth, it depends upon the suppression not only of the sexual emotions but also
of the qualities that are associated with sexuality: high-heartedness,
self-assertiveness, wit, creative innovation.

But now, when we have touched upon the Wordsworthian
quality which is very close to *apatheia,* let us remember what great
particular thing it was that Wordsworth accomplished. Matthew
Arnold's statement cannot be bettered. In a wintry clime, in an iron
time, Wordsworth taught us to feel. What a statement to make,
what a thing to say! What it implies of our culture for some two
centuries, of the situation in the general life which has been expressed by the most sensitive observers as the inability to experience
the emotions which have traditionally been associated with simply
being human! The instruction in the emotions which Arnold says
was Wordsworth's characteristic work was certainly not completed
by Wordsworth. It has been taken up by almost every notable writer
of our own day. There is scarcely a contemporary writer who has
not addressed himself to the feelings as if they were a problem, who
has not tried to go back to roots and sources in order to reconstitute
the strength of the emotions. They do so, to be sure, under a necessity somewhat different from Wordsworth's, and this necessity
makes it seem to them appropriate that, with Byron, they assert fiery
life. (Blake more aptly suggests the quality of their militancy, but I
stay with the terms of Arnold's opposition.) It is not hard to understand this. Their fierce animals are partly political animals in that
sense of the word political which has to do with the quality of
being that a man is permitted to have. Their beasts, wrong-headed,
cruel, or limited in understanding as beasts often are, have been
created to assert some of the personal qualities that are associated
with an older, presumably freer and more personally aristocratic time.

As such we must regard them with ambivalence. A certain sliced-off ear which is an object of pleasure to Yeats, a certain kick given by an employer to his employee which wins approval from Lawrence—these repel us and remind us of some of the actual consequences of the *charisma* and *mana* that we desire. Yet we know that this violence can, in other aspects, serve to stand against an extreme fate of which we are all conscious. We really know in our time what the death of the word can be—for that knowledge we have only to read an account of contemporary Russian literature. We really know now what the death of the spirit means, we have seen it overtake whole peoples. And we understand that the violent animals are intended to protect us from being the gored or work-destroyed horse, or the ox, or the plucked and devoured goose.

This we must be aware of, and yet at the same time we cannot help seeing that the extreme violence and assertiveness of the great fierce beasts go along with the most profound depression of spirits, along with boredom, *ennui, noia, acedia*. The extremity of the one leads to the extremity of the other, and it doesn't much matter from which you start, the oscillation must be perpetual. What Wordsworth knew—and said, for he had his comment to make on the literature of violence—is that life does not have to be justified and feeling affirmed by that which is violent, or by that which is proud: the meanest flower is enough. What he asserted was the justification of life where no pride and fierceness is. He laid us, Arnold said, on the lap of earth—reminded us, that is, of the infant existence before the social pride had put its mark on us. He groped, not always sure of his direction but always sure of his intention, toward the images of the extremity of the will that would destroy the roots of life, and the will itself. If we bring it up against him that he negated some of these very roots, for instance the sexual ones, may it not be answered that perhaps they exactly needed to be negated for a time, so charged were they, and still are, with the tensions of the will?

Perhaps nothing could better summarize our passion for the heroic ultimate than a recent incident of our literature of which everyone seems to be aware. I refer to Mr. Eliot's description, in *The Cocktail Party*, of the two virtuous ways of life, that of daily, habitual routine—Wordsworth was particularly interested in it—and that of spiritual heroism. The two ways, Mr. Eliot tells us, are of equal value, the way of the saint is not better than that of the common householder. Yet when it comes to describing the life of "the common routine," Mr. Eliot says this of those who elect it: that they

> *Learn to avoid excessive expectation,*
> *Become tolerant of themselves and others,*
> *Giving and taking, in the usual actions*
> *What there is to give and take. They do not repine;*
> *And are contented with the morning that separates*
> *And with the evening that brings together*
> *For casual talk before the fire*
> *Two people who know that they do not understand each other,*
> *Breeding children whom they do not understand*
> *And who will never understand them.*

Well, few of us will want to say much for the life of the common routine, the life without an eagle, yet we know we can say more than this. We know that it is both more wonderful and more terrible than Mr. Eliot says it is, having its moments of unbearable pain and its moments of glory—I use the Wordsworthian word with intention. And this failure of Mr. Eliot's to conceive the pains and glories of the habitual life is typical of modern literature since, say, Tolstoy. We are drawn to the violence of extremity. In our hearts we subscribe to the belief that the more sin the more grace, or at any rate the more life. We are in love, at least in our literature, with the fantasy of death—perhaps this is not new and we now but intensify what is indigenous in our culture. Death and suffering, when we read, are our only means of testing the actuality of life; and it is impossible for us to make real the image of love unless death attend it.

Perhaps this is in the nature of life as Western culture has long been, and will continue to be, fated to see it: which may also be to say that this is in the nature of life. Perhaps it is inescapable that for us the word *tragic* must be the ultimate recommendation of a sense of life. But we, when we use the word, barely mean it, we mean something like violent and conclusive; we mean death: for us tragedy is the violent, conclusive gesture of dying. And just here lies a paradox and our point. For it is precisely the true awareness of what Wordsworth called common life, and even of common life as it exists at a very low level of consciousness, pride, and assertiveness, that validates heroism and tragedy. If we ask why the martyrdom which Mr. Eliot presents in his play seems to us somewhat factitious, however much we may respect the intention for which it was conceived, must we not answer that this is because it is presented in a system of feeling which sets very little store by the life of the common routine? And this seems to be borne out by the emphasis which is put on the peculiar horror of the death, as if only by an extremity of pain could we be made to realize that a life has been sacrificed—or, indeed, has been lived.

Wordsworth's incapacity for tragedy has often been remarked on, and accurately enough. Yet we cannot conclude that Wordsworth's relation to tragedy is wholly negative. The possibility of tragic art in any honorific sense of the word depends primarily upon the worth we ascribe not to dying but to living, and to living in the common routine. The Homeric tragedy, for example, exists in its power by reason of the pathos, which the poet is at pains to bring before us again and again, of young men dying, of not seeing ever again the trees of their native farmsteads, of not being admired and indulged by their parents, of not being permitted to live out the common routine; the tragic hero, Achilles, becomes a tragic hero exactly because he has made choice to give up the life of the common routine which all his comrades yearn for, and the pathos of his particular situation becomes the great thing it is because of the respondent pathos of Hector and Priam, the pathos of the family and the common routine, which we understand less and less and find ourselves more and more uncomfortable with. And I think it can be shown that every tragic literature owes its power to captivate us to the high esteem in which it holds the common routine, the elemental *given* of biology. So that although Wordsworth is indeed far from tragic art, we can say that he sought to nourish its very germ.

It has not been my intention to make a separation between Wordsworth and the literature of our time. The separation cannot, indeed, be made really to exist. There never was, I believe, a secular literature which so massively and so explicitly as ours directed itself to the spiritual life, for good or bad carrying the problems of life and death into the market place: Alexandria was nothing to us when it comes to a theological population. In this movement of secular exploration of the spirit Wordsworth was a founding father. And not merely because of his general preoccupation is Wordsworth part of modern literature. He initiated the attack on the problem that has involved the energies of a main part of modern literature, the problem of affectlessness, of loss of feeling and of humanness, under which we subsume all the details of our modern spiritual plight. Even in that one decisive element of his work which I have isolated to distinguish him from the tendency of contemporary literature, he has been followed as well as departed from. For when we have taken account of all that is feral and fierce and consciously heroic and charismatic in our literature, we must yet recognize how strong, if still subaltern, is the impulse to find the validation of life in its common, elemental, instinctual roots, in its enduring humility. Not only Faulkner's Negroes, of whom it is said, as it is so often said of people by Wordsworth, *they endured*, but Faulkner's many images of the significance of elemental existence; the curious, quiet dignity of Hemingway's waiters; Joyce's paternal dreamer and Joyce's preference for Bloom over Dedalus; even Dreiser's Jennie Gerhardt; Lawrence's representation of people whose pride is only that of plants and animals—out of the characteristic violence these and others come movingly to mind.

In one other respect Wordsworth is of our time—he taught us not only to feel but to remember. What role the art of memory has played in our literature needs scarcely to be spoken of. The instances of its use will occur to everyone, they are so numerous as to make an endemic condition of our thought and to suggest that something like a mutation in the nature of man has taken place. But at the same time that we observe this flowering of the faculty of memory and relate it to the great nineteenth-century movement in the study of history and to modern theories of growth and development, we must observe as well the tendency of our democratic culture to wish to forget. We of the universities can be especially aware of this tendency. We feel the pressure upon us to prove our usefulness by displaying our sense of the immediately contemporary and our power over it, and we know that the mandate of the contemporary and the instrumental brings with it the strong implication that the least useful thing the universities can do is to continue their old characteristic work of conservation, of keeping alive, in some part of the social mind, the culture of the past.

It is indeed very difficult to demonstrate that this is truly a socially useful work, yet Wordsworth taught us that some truth and strength were to be gained for the personal life by binding our days together, and we may well suppose that the same thing may be said of the communal life. I have noted the wide discrepancy that exists between the opinion of Wordsworth that is held by the modern world and the opinion that is expressed by the universities in commemorations like this one. It seems worth saying that in consenting to this discrepancy, in maintaining our own opinion, in preserving and finding interesting a spirit that the world at this moment thinks dead and done with, we do something to fulfill one of the essential functions of the university in our society.

Book Reviews

John Berryman THE LOUD HILL

OF WALES

THE unmistakable signature of Dylan Thomas's poetry, so far as we have it in his three English volumes or in the forty poems here selected from them, is certainly its diction. Here are some of the key words: blood, sea, dry, ghost, grave, straw, worm, double, crooked, salt, cancer, tower, shape, fork, marrow; and the more usual death, light, time, sun, night, wind, love, grief. Each of these appears many times and has regularly one or several symbolic values. The verse abounds in unusual epithets (the grave for example is called, at various points in seven poems, moon-drawn, stallion, corkscrew, running, savage, outspoken, country-handed, climbing, gallow), compounds (firewind, marrowroot, fly-lord, manstring, manseed, man-iron, manshape, manwax), old, new, obsolete, coined and colloquial words (scut, fibs, hank, boxy, morsing, brawned, cockshut, mitching, nowheres, pickthank, macadam, scrams, etna, rooking, hyleg, arc-lamped, contages, natron, herods, two-gunned, pickbrain). Colors are frequent, especially green, which occurs twenty-eight times and connotes origin, innocence (green Adam, green genesis, green of beginning); red is for experience, violence. The notions of halving, doubling, quartering, dichotomy, multiplicity of function, appear often, affecting the precise look of the diction; the concept of number and division organizes several poems. Some of the language is Biblical. But the principal sources of im-

A review of *The World I Breathe* by Dylan Thomas (New York: New Directions Press, 1940).

agery are the sea and sex. In ten poems the dominant imagery is marine, and marine imagery occurs incidentally in twenty-four others. A host of terms show the sexual emphasis: sucking, kiss, loin, naked, rub, tickle, unsex, nippled, virgin, thigh, cuddled, sea-hymen; metaphors extend the reach and importance of this area. All these words, and stranger others, meet violently to form a texture impressive and exciting. One has the sense of words set at an angle, language seen freshly, a new language.

The themes upon which this wealth of diction is employed are simple, but not I think so unimportant as Julian Symons calls them in a very bad article once published in the *Kenyon Review*. I have not time to notice any considerable part of Mr. Symons's nonsense; one quotation must serve. "What is said in Mr. Thomas's poems is that the seasons change; that we decrease in vigour as we grow older; that life has no obvious meaning; that love dies. His poems mean no more than that. They mean too little." Evidently it is necessary to point out to Mr. Symons what is elementary, that a poem means more than the abstract, banal statement of its theme: it means its imagery, the disparate parts and relations of it, its ambiguities, by extension the techniques which produced it and the emotions it legitimately produces. A poem is an accretion of knowledge, of which only the flimsiest portion can be translated into bromide. A poem that works well demonstrates an insight, and the insight may consist, not in the theme, but in the image-relations or the structure-relations; this is a value and a meaning which cannot appear in Mr. Symons's catalogue. Even the single lines mean more than their prose doubles:

The fruit of man unwrinkles in the stars.

Glory cracked like a flea.

Sigh long, clay cold, lie shorn.

The terrible world my brother bares his skin.

Each of these presents a perception and an attitude, even a process of sensibility. I do not find them in Mr. Symons's catalogue. Here is the short final poem:

Twenty-four years remind the tears of my eyes.
(Bury the dead for fear that they walk to the grave in labour.)

In the groin of the natural doorway I crouched like a tailor
Sewing a shroud for a journey
By the light of the meat-eating sun.
Dressed to die, the sensual strut begun,
With my red veins full of money,
In the final direction of the elementary town
I advance for as long as forever is.

The figures and their interaction cannot be expressed as "life has no obvious meaning": where is the body seen as a shroud worn on the way to the *elementary* town? where is the hovering "dressed to kill"? What Mr. Symons misses is the value of presentation, the dramatic truth of metaphor. A good poem is not as he says restatement, but statement. His catalogue, moreover, on a simpler level is seriously incomplete. Several of the poems are religious in substance and address; two poems deal mainly, and others deal in part, with the poet's gift of speech; other examples of exceptions could be adduced. It is worth emphasizing, however, that few poems describe what may be called a human situation, a recognizable particular scene. There is a subject matter, but it is general, as indeed the diction would lead one to expect. The treatment is concrete, in the language, but the conception is abstract.

Much of Thomas's inventive energy, then, goes into technique; he faces in a lesser degree than most poets the problems of a given subject. Alliteration, internal rhyme, refrain and repetition, puns, continuous and complicated tropes, are some of the devices. He works usually in rigid stanzas, six-line in the earlier poems, the lines of equal length; recently he has used very elaborate stanzas and varied the line lengths. The metrical development is from iambics to manipulation, spondees, anapests; in the short-line poems especially, the movement is expert. Certain technical derivations there are, despite one's impression of originality: from Blake (the *Songs of Experience* and *Thel*), Hopkins, Yeats (the middle and later poetry), Auden (the 1930 *Poems*); I think it likely also that he and Auden learnt, independently, something in tone, consonance, extra syllables and feminine rhymes, from Ransom. Possibly the verse has roots in Welsh poetry, folk or professional, with which I am not familiar. Hart Crane offers a parallel development, in part similar but not influential. This brings us to the question of obscurity.

That a good many of these poems are difficult cannot be denied. The difficulty has various causes, some of them being distortion or inadequacy of syntax (sometimes the pointing is responsible), compounding of negatives, mixing of figures, the occasionally continuous novelty of expression and relation, employment of a high-pitched rhetoric as in poem 29, and the use as subjects of nightmare, fantasy, as in poem 2. Personification is so frequent and is accomplished with so little ceremony that the reference of personal pronouns is now and then erratic; in general, the practice with pronouns and antecedents is careless. In many passages, insufficient control is exerted by the context on a given verbal ambiguity; the ambiguity, indeed, may be made the basis for a further, and absolutely puzzling, extension of metaphor. Development in the poem, when it exists, may be sidewise, will probably be interrupted, may be abandoned; in the difficult poems it is never straightforward. All this is unfortunate when it interferes with communication, and the trouble is found not only in the weakest poems (21, 29) but also in some of the best (11, 28, 38). But the whole matter can be, and by most of Thomas's critics has been, exaggerated. At least fifteen poems, more than one third of those in the book, present no substantial difficulty to a conscientious reader; some present no difficulty at all. Of the rest, perhaps eight are largely insoluble or only provisionally soluble. This is not a large number, and it is simply the price one pays for what is valuable and cannot be got elsewhere. One would have more reason to complain, were not much of the finest twentieth-century work difficult; Yeats, Lorca, Eliot, Stevens are sufficient reminder. Thomas's obscurity is not greater than Crane's, and their values are comparable.

This verse cannot be called "promising," however, in the ordinary way, although its author is a young man. Poets progress usually by moving to a new substance or by extending their technique to handle a new part of an old substance. But Thomas's work is so special, and his substance so restricted, that neither of these paths, if I am correct, is really open to him. This is not to say that no development can be seen in the poems. They are arranged in order roughly chronological, and the latest poems are harsher, more

closely worked; some technical changes have been noted; the subjects are more often violent. The diction has partly altered; for
instance, blood or a derivative occurs twenty-four times in the first
twenty poems, only nine times in the second twenty, and where the
concept remains it may be transformed: "my red veins full of
money." But Thomas's verse does not show the major signs, such as
a powerful dramatic sense, wide interests, a flexible and appropriate
diction, skill over a broad range of subjects, that are clear in the work
of his American contemporary Delmore Schwartz and point confidently to the future. Any large development is probably not to be
expected. This circumstance, of course, cannot affect the present
achievement, which is formidable. All the poems should be read
with attention by anyone who is interested in poetry. In a dozen
of these pieces, some of them imperfect, all brilliant—"A saint about
to fall," "Especially when the October wind," "Then was my neo-
phyte" and "Light breaks where no sun shines" may be mentioned
in their four kinds—Thomas has extended the language and to a
lesser degree the methods of lyric poetry.

Eleanor Clark THE MYTH OF

SAINTHOOD

PERIODICALLY the stream of French literature bursts its
banks, casts off all moral fetters including Catholicism, and
swings violently to the side of reason or unreason. There appears

A review of *The Star of Satan* by George Bernanos (New York: The Macmillan Company, 1940).

Voltaire, or Rimbaud. It will seem perhaps quixotic that the violent one, the fighter of this time, Georges Bernanos, should be preaching neither science nor vice nor even the "natural man," but traditionalism in every sense. Should be royalist and Catholic and a believer in knights: should passionately advocate continuity, that sense of the past which in England, he remarks, is so often confused with the sense of humor. It is a curious trick and glory of the human mind that it demands a myth, out of the need to codify its thought and to fence itself around against the infinite so that the heart can function without terror. The myth works many ways: gives form, without which there is no truth but only flashes in the pan, gives freedom of a kind. But also restricts, and in the end inevitably sanctions every littleness and crime in the effort to preserve its worldly counterpart. It is an indication of the quality of Bernanos that although utterly dedicated to the Christian Heritage, he will not accept the dotage of the Catholic myth, but prefers to howl against the storm like Lear, without even a fool beside him. One wonders then why he does not separate himself from the myth, a question that is often disposed with that old tautological gag: "He believes." The answer is I think more complicated and more to every one's credit, including Bernanos's.

It is not, of course, only the scandals of Catholicism in practice that Bernanos rejects. He is a moral writer, all moral, he is concerned with the inwardness of things. And since social and political like all other human affairs are witness to some inner truth—which may be on the order of a vacuum—he is concerned with them too. He is devoured by a sense of right, not only of Godly right but of a most human justice, and he is not stupid. Early in 1939 he wrote: "I have not the courage to face the dishonor of my country." He did face it, told what he saw, and moved to Brazil. There has been no more tormenting plea for political decency than the two books in which he laid bare the appalling maladies that have since grown into the defeat of France. Earlier, in his *Diary of My Times,* he had described the brutalities of the Spanish Civil War, specifically of Franco and his allies of the Church. All this has been a call to honor, to an honorable conception of political affairs, as against "realism," cynicism, the hollow man. It seems unnecessary to discuss at the moment whether Bernanos's own peculiar and isolated brand of royalism could ever restore, or be restored by, "*la chevalerie chrétienne française.*" What matters is that the spiritual punch is there, terribly reinforced by the facts, and the world is hungering for someone who will speak in terms other than those used by the enemy. We are in danger of being knocked over like ninepins, largely for lack of a definition of dignity. Bernanos believes in dignity. It is perhaps a Christian corollary of this, but I think it may also be taken as a human one, that he believes in saints.

The Star of Satan—which appears in this country in a stilted and in parts grotesque translation—is the story of a modern saint, dealing, as part of the stuff of sainthood, with Satan or the principle of evil. Is this literal? Is its strength inseparable from the technicalities of the myth? On the strictly human level, if it is fair for a moment to make such a vivisection, there is little obscurity. The young priest Father Donissan, clumsy, loutish, leaden-tongued, is endowed with grace: we need no catechism to recognize its marks. "He did not hesitate to do battle alone in the hardest warfare that ever a man waged against himself. Literally he felt no need of any support. . . . He fancied that he was doing no more than a simple everyday thing. He had nothing to say about himself." "He was never the dupe of words. He had really not much imagination. But the fire in his heart burnt all to ashes." The book opens with the story of the girl Mouchette, a trivial sinner, a poor thing, frantic with evil and sharpened by it beyond her years. She is a little no-account Bovary. Or she is a Hemingway character, beautifully described and weirdly out of place, seething along from one false step to another until it is quite unavoidable that she cut her throat. She is of course a foil for Father Donissan, his first great and ambiguous defeat. In the long and ghoulish night before their meeting he has been with Satan, has taken the burden of evil on himself and will never be free of it again, no matter how great his longing for simplicity and rest. This is the price of stature, or in the author's terms, the price of grace, ordinary sinners being playthings of whom no such struggle is asked. "The monster looks down at you and laughs, but hasn't got you in his grip. . . . He is to be found in the prayers of the hermit, in his fasting and penitence, in the depths of ecstasy and in the silence of the heart. . . . He lies upon the lips that are about to pronounce the truth, he pursues the just man through the

thunder and lightning of beatitude into the very arms of God. . . .
His vengeance is reserved for saints."

To the unbeliever the word "saint" carries an image of disease,
something ripe for neurological analysis, but Bernanos guards his
essential meaning very carefully. Is the man mad? Perhaps. After
the Mouchette affair he is placed by his superiors in a sanitorium.
He flagellates himself cruelly, out of the blind need "to reach and
destroy the very principle of evil in his own intolerable flesh," and
this is nothing compared to the self-inflicted torture of his soul. He
is known for his "stupid patience," which is more like the crazy
persistence of a gangster, or a lunatic, or a great artist. And, in the
end, an old man who has hurled himself against his last fabulous
temptation and suffered his last defeat, he himself cries out that he
is mad. But very slyly and quietly the author brings in here a "famous man," successful and weary and somewhat put out by the
thought of approaching death—as in *The Diary of a County Priest*
he used the isolated intellect—and the thing crumbles like dried
mud. It is the other who stands, saint or hero, who has paid in
agony for his power and his peace and has asked nothing.

The figure is tremendous. And in view of the author's belief
there is strangely little evidence offered as to the supernatural quality of the man's gift. The "unreal" night of the devil's appearance is
reminiscent of Kafka, even of Hawthorne's story "My Cousin
Major Molyneux," which was canalized by no belief at all and after
its beautiful dramatization of subconscious terror ends on a note of
jargonistic fact. Aside from that, by way of narrative, there is only
the moment when the saint is nearly able, but not quite, to bring a
dead child back to life. He does, to be sure, have an extraordinary
effect on people and this is perhaps something for which psychoanalysis has still to account, but the people are only sinners in the
mass and presumably subject to error in their choice of saints. And
his tenacity: "He gained little by little on all these folk the irresistible
ascendancy of those who go straight ahead without reckoning their
chances. For the shrewd and wary in reality only spare themselves."
This might be crime, or genius, though we are never allowed to forget that Bernanos is postulating a good far more profound than art.

Nevertheless, in spite of the amazing impact of this book on
an unbeliever, subjectively the portrait of Father Donissan cannot

be torn from the myth to which Bernanos has given his odd and
difficult allegiance. That he should have been obliged to do so, rebel
and thinker as he is, is in itself a commentary on the criminal shallowness of this time. With a shade more rebellion and more thought,
he might perhaps have concluded that the crimes of the Catholic
Church which he exposes with so little prudence are not skin-deep
but of the heart. This is one sphere, and a crucial one, in which he
has not allowed his brilliant insight to have play. But he knows too
much, at any rate, and has felt too deeply to want to stand alone in
the more than immediate sense. He knows that history is an organism and that there is no abstraction worth snatching out of the
air. The flaws in his special edifice are another matter—to the last
answer of traditionalists, after all, one can always ask: And what
about before?—but considering the philosophical hiatus in which
we now exist, and the particular quality of Bernanos's talents, it
seems safe to say that without Catholicism he might well have been,
like so many of his colleagues, a recorder of noisy little nothings,
casting no shadow at all. As it is he has plucked a great value out
of the past, and by a *tour de force* that commands more than respect,
has translated it in terms of a most bitter contemporary need.

Richard Eberhart Q'S REVISIONS

Q USED to come late to his class in Aristotle's Poetics which
met once a week in the evening across from St. John's. It
was the only official meeting in Cambridge at which one was
allowed the liberty of abandoning formal dress. The dozen students

A review of *The New Oxford Book of English Verse 1200-1918* edited by Sir
Arthur Quiller-Couch (London: Oxford Press, 1939).

waited expectantly in the large room at one end of which burned a
great fire in the old English fireplace which went up to the ceiling.
At a pleasant lateness Q's man would appear, a dutiful vanguard in
butler's togs, holding aloft a silver tray bearing port and cigars. He
would place his burden on a long rectangular table which dominated the room. About ten paces behind would come Q, in a sort
of toddle, mellow from dinner, dressed in evening clothes. He suf-
fused a certain geniality. He was amiable, old, a bit crotchety, but
obviously a man of telling charm. "Good evening, gentlemen," and
he would wave his pupils to the silver altar. They would help themselves, or be served, while Q was fussing about getting ready to sit
down, his back to the fire, at the head of the long table. Then in the
most leisurely fashion, he would begin talking about the Poetics.
It is notable that he only discussed one paragraph during each
weekly meeting; it is unforgettable that his digressions constituted
the main part of the discourse, these beginning soon, and usually
straying far from Aristotle—in fact, the course was an ambulatory
one in Q's diverting personality. That was a decade ago. I am told
the course is still given.

Memories induce a certain relaxation when one begins to discuss
Sir Arthur's new edition of *The Oxford Book of English Verse*.
The heart may accept what the mind rejects. Critical perception
demands a harsh dealing with this book; memory pays tribute to
a kindly scholar and a pleasant gentleman.

The first and famous *Oxford Book* was fairly just. This volume
is less just, and exposes painful errors of taste. The pain is greater
the more seriously you consider that this book, like its predecessor,
may determine the taste of great numbers of readers for years to
come, and fix in their minds the reputation and rank of the writers.
What excuse can one concoct for a "famous" editor who leaves out
D. H. Lawrence entirely, but includes W. H. Davies? I feel this
omission and cannot condone it. Surely Lawrence wrote at least
one worthy poem? I do not hold that he wrote many, but I do not
agree with his excision. Upon careful study of the later part of the
volume, one would like to make laconic remarks to any young poet
beginning his career. Don't follow knowledge like a sinking star (or
anything else) beyond the utmost bounds of human thought; don't
for Heaven's sake "die, or faint, or fail," be a "scorner of the ground,"

or seek "harmonious madness"; or strive "to find the uncreated light"; or espouse the prose formulation of poetry; or make it new by returning to vocal folk myth. No. Your strategy should lie elsewhere. Be a middle-minded man, be a center of the road singer, be smooth and dare not, be obvious, and above all be middle-Christian, and you will make Q's grade, were he to be spared a quarter of a century to build a later book. Thus, if you are Emily Dickinson, you will get one little poem; but if you are Oliver St. John Gogarty, you will get two. You could not afford to be Hopkins, with four poems, lacking "The Windhover" or "Carrion Comfort"; or Housman, your best poems unrepresented, even if you could not vent your spleen on the anthologist; or Hardy, flattened and thinned, without a balanced picture of your art and scope; and as unfortunate would it be to be the later Yeats, for you would not be represented at all.

Q is faulty as definitive editor of the best poetry since 1900. In addition, most readers will probably regret his admitted insecurity of judgment among the poetical works since 1918. One wishes he had cared to cope with Eliot and Pound at least, unless, unkind, one supposes his choices there would be as questionable as those in Hardy, Hopkins, and Yeats. It is only fair, however, to accept roughly a term of twenty years beyond which critical estimation should not be attempted. Was he unaware of Isaac Rosenberg, who died in 1918, but published two books in 1915? Could he not have chosen more than one poem by Owen, who died in 1918, but was not published until 1921? For the book is heavy with minor poets showing one poem each (Edward Thomas is accorded two). Harold Monro might have rated one; T. E. Hulme (even), and Herbert Read, and Richard Aldington might have rated one, where such sympathy is shown to one-poem poets of the nineteenth century; perhaps Graves more than one. This is not to exhaust the list of possibilities before 1918.

Q has resurrected notable anonymous pieces; he has corrected mistakes, as in the restoration of the severed "Ecstasy," by Donne, and in crediting to Thomas Osbert Mordaunt (1730-1809) "The Call," which he formerly gave to Sir Walter Scott. He has added poets of former times, such as Lord Herbert of Cherbury and Charles Wesley; he has added light pieces, such as the four-page addition to

Prior of "Jinny the Just," and "The Ballad of Bouillabaisse," by Thackeray. He has banned minor poets to oblivion, and raised up others from the shades: a collation of such editing makes a nice pleasure. He has juggled the entries of a good many poets, adding or subtracting, according to a critical estimation some may call whim. Clare has still only one poem; one Praed is substituted for another; a third is added to a minor like Mangan. Beddoes is cut from three to two: all cases of injustice. But a charming, delightful thing Q has done is to insert several two- or four-line poems, dug from one wonders where. May I quote No. 395, anonymous, which endears Q to the reader:

> On ELEANOR FREEMAN
> who died 1650, aged 21
> *Let not Death boast his conquering power,*
> *She'll rise a star that fell a flower.*

And there is a long stretch of the book, from Herrick through Milton and Marvell, to Vaughan, over a hundred pages, left without change. Shakespeare is not touched.

My main disappointment, for purposes of this review, is in Q's maladministration of Hopkins, Housman, Hardy, and Yeats. Hardy's five entries are insufficient, not composite. The editor would have had to add the poem on Meredith and "Channel Firing," at least. A. E. Housman receives but three poems, suffering misfortune at the hands of an editor living almost across the street. Hopkins's utmost peculiarities and values are not exhibited. Q relaxes to add a tenth to Bridges (Hopkins has four), but in this case the sentimentality of "On a Dead Child" is lost in "Elegy: on a Lady, Whom Grief for the death of her Betrothed killed," of stately formal song. Something stronger than concern is called out against the editor, however, because of his feeble treatment of Yeats. Only two pieces are added to the earlier three, "Down by the Salley Garden," and "Aedh wishes for the Cloths of Heaven," a total and ignominious disregard of the author of "The Tower" and all later works.

I conclude with a question: Would English literature be shown to greater advantage if all, or most of the one-poem poets were left out, only the major figures showing, and these with more poems?

Q has obviously paid a good deal of attention to minor poets, in the earlier part switching one for another, in the latter part discovering a considerable number for inclusion. My conclusion is that the Muse has not appeared only to her greatest servants throughout the centuries in England; that many single poems of minor writers deserve preservation; and that this whole corpus of work definitely shows to the glory (if not to the highest glory) of English poetry. One poet with one good poem preserved for centuries may be about as well off as some writer more famous in his time, dwindled to a few period poems. It is a tribute to English poetry that not all its excellent poems are written by the major figures. It is a tribute to Q that he is aware of this.

But now the class is over. "Good evening, gentlemen," and Q toddles back into the inner room.

Cleanth Brooks, Jr. THE WHOLE

OF HOUSMAN

THE appearance of the *Collected Poems* provides an occasion for making some tentative generalizations on the total value of Housman and his work, though a note so brief as this can hardly pretend to go beyond suggestion.

First, there is the matter of Housman's basic attitudes, his world view. Actually, I believe that the pessimism of Housman's poetry is pretty closely related to that of Bertrand Russell, his

A review of *The Collected Poems of A. E. Housman* (New York: Henry Holt & Company, 1940).

Cambridge contemporary—say, to that of the famous purple patch in Russell's "A Free Man's Worship": "Brief and powerless is Man's life; on him and all his race the slow, sure doom falls pitiless and dark. Blind to good and evil, reckless of destruction, omnipotent matter rolls on its relentless way, etc., etc." Here are to be found all the elements of the Romantic despair which possesses Housman's young soldiers, shepherds, and athletes: the helplessness of man in an alien universe, the stoicism, the Spartan courage, the Romantic bravado.

Frank Harris records in one of his essays that Housman protested that he had not meant "1887" to be taken as irony at the expense of Queen Victoria and Victorian imperialism. It is possible that he did not (though it will be impossible for most readers of that fine poem not to feel such irony as a necessary and valuable ingredient of the experience). If Housman's poetry seems to show a continual thrusting at Victorian optimism and conventionally held ideals, there are still other poems sufficient in number to indicate that Housman had no special animus against the commercialism and imperialism of his times. The Shropshire lad, far from teeming London, finds evil all about him, the necessary accompaniment of human life.

Yet a rereading of the mass of Housman's poetry indicates that Housman had no ambitious or even passionately held world view to set up. Intellectually, he has not moved far past an austere scepticism; emotionally, one feels that he has a special and "literary" interest in the pathos of the passing of first love, the parting of friends, the loss of youth, the unpredictable and meaningless death —he is interested in them for their own sakes. Indeed, the intellectual fabric is so slight that one feels that his impulse borders on the literary and his performance occasionally hovers on the verge of the sentimental. In any case, one can understand why his *Name and Nature of Poetry* should have turned out to be a rear-guard action fought against the modern enemies of Romanticism, with some not very carefully disguised thrusts at Cambridge contemporaries like I. A. Richards and F. R. Leavis.

The late professor of the classics is essentially a romantic poet, and no amount of talk about classic influence, classic lucidity, etc., should delude us into thinking him otherwise. It is no accident that another Cambridge contemporary, F. L. Lucas, in his *Decline and Fall of the Romantic Ideal*, should again and again put Housman's poetry within what he calls the magic triangle bounded by Romanticism, Classicism, and Realism.

It is not difficult to see why Housman should appeal to Mr. Lucas. The difficulty is in explaining why some of his poems should also appeal to us. I think that we can bound his talent with a different set of terms: (1) his irony, when it commits itself firmly as in "1887":

> *To skies that knit their heartstrings right,*
> *To fields that bred them brave,*
> *The saviors come not home to-night:*
> *Themselves they could not save. . . .*

(2) his understatement, when it does not degenerate into self-conscious smirking; (3) his use of symbolism, when timidity does not force him to label the symbol; and (4) his use of metaphor, when he will use it wholeheartedly.

Suppose we state Housman's essential method as Mr. Lucas might have stated it for him: "Housman takes the ordinary theme, and then, by a faultless choice of words and by the practice of a beautiful simplicity, makes us fasten our hands upon our hearts." Fair enough. But on what principle is the selection based? And may not the simplicity be more exactly stated as "economy" and a "sense of understatement"? The selection is "faultless" just in proportion as it succeeds in dramatizing the theme with sharp contrasts, revitalizing it with fresh perceptions (inevitably by means of metaphor). And as for economy—is not the essence of economy in poetry the exploitation of metaphor?

If these propositions are true, one is allowed to see how much handicapped was the poet who distrusted irony and wit as smacking of the unpoetic intellect (see *The Name and Nature of Poetry*), and who distrusted the obscurity of metaphor to the point of reducing it to the clarity of abstraction. That is why Housman, in his weaker poems, is flat and thin. Even so fine a poem as "Bredon Hill" is flawed by Housman's fear of the obscurity inherent in metaphor. In this poem, death is described as a bridal—and effectively. Yet even here, Housman finds it necessary to explain the metaphor to his reader:

> *They tolled the one bell only,*
> *Groom there was none to see,*
> *The mourners followed after,*
> *And so to church went she,*
> *And would not wait for me.*

It is in the bolder poems, where the poet triumphs over the restrictions of Victorian decorum, that one finds the Housman that will endure. Consider the following passages: Poem XXV of *A Shropshire Lad* ends thus:

> *Fred keeps the house all kinds of weather,*
> *And clay's the house he keeps;*
> *When Rose and I walk out together*
> *Stock-still lies Fred and sleeps.*

Poem XX of *Last Poems* ends:

> *Fall, winter, fall; for he,*
> *Prompt hand and headpiece clever,*
> *Has woven a winter robe,*
> *And made of earth and sea*
> *His overcoat for ever,*
> *And wears the turning globe.*

Both poems attempt to accommodate the grave to the commonplace and the domestic, and thus gain their irony. But in the first the explanatory "And clay's the house he keeps" comes perilously near robbing the fine "Fred keeps the house all kinds of weather" of its effect. The second passage with its full commitment to the metaphor and its triumphant assimilation of the domestic and realistic "overcoat" is rather unusual for Housman. The first passage is nearer his norm.

If Housman's desire for simplicity sometimes makes him flat and obvious, the fault is frequently of a different kind: a too self-conscious archness. But like the first, it too is an aspect of Housman's difficulty in handling the witty and the ironic. Many of

Housman's poems seem to be epigrams softened in the direction of the romantic and the "poetic." As a consequence, a number of his poems are oddly suggestive of Dorothy Parker or Edna St. Vincent Millay. This is especially true of some of the poetry which Housman did not choose to publish in his lifetime, but which has been included in this volume. Consider, for example:

> *From the wash the laundress sends*
> *My collars home with ravelled ends;*
> *I must fit, now these are frayed,*
> *My neck with new ones London-made.*
>
> *Homespun collars, homespun hearts,*
> *Wear to rags in foreign parts.*
> *Mine at least's as good as done,*
> *And I must get a London one.*

Even the poems which aim at an effect of laconic understatement sometimes fail in the same way. For all their surface hardness and toughness, they discover themselves, on second glance, to be pretty and at worst sentimental. "With Rue My Heart Is Laden" is "pretty"—in the bad as well as the good sense of this word. Or, consider "Could Man Be Drunk Forever." The poem ends thus:

> *But men at whiles are sober*
> *And think by fits and starts,*
> *And if they think, they fasten*
> *Their hands upon their hearts.*

Obviously, the poem works by insisting on a studied understatement. The men on whom the melancholy impinges are not mooning sentimentalists—they are lusty, red-blooded fellows, no strangers to "liquor, love, or fights." They betray their feelings by no outcry, no lamentation—only by the almost instinctive gesture, made before their self-possession masters their actions once more. But if the reader is not too easily beguiled, if *he* thinks, he will find the gesture not an understatement at all, but melodramatic and theatrical; and this effect is not softened by the choice of the word "fasten" and the emphasis which the poet places upon it.

Housman is not the perfect minor poet. Real poetic power he

undoubtedly possessed; and he has left us a small number of fine lyrics. But everywhere upon the body of his work is the evidence of limitations imposed upon his essential genius by a conscious aesthetic which was crippling to it. The proof of this, it seems to me, is that you cannot defend the best effects of his poetry in terms of the critical position laid down in *The Name and Nature of Poetry*. Those effects can best be described in terms of the wit, irony, and even "conceit," which Housman consciously repudiated. We must be grateful for good poetry, however it is come by. Some of the poems that Housman wrote are very good indeed. But the best of his poetry seems to me poetry achieved in spite of the immediate tradition out of which he wrote.

Delmore Schwartz NEITHER

HISTORIAN NOR CRITIC

ONE must agree that Mr. Brooks's success is perfectly justified. *The Flowering of New England* has had more than a hundred thousand readers and its sequel should have still more. Whether or not so many readers can be wrong is hardly the point. Many must enjoy this work a great deal; else why would they read it?

Yet it is the undeniable virtue of Mr. Brooks's two books which suggests what is wrong with his work. It seems unlikely that a hundred thousand readers in America are interested in literary criticism

A review of *New England: Indian Summer* by Van Wyck Brooks (New York: E. P. Dutton & Company, 1940).

or literary history. They are interested in enjoyable reading. Mr. Brooks is able to provide it with great richness because he is a wonderful reader and a fine writer himself. Or rather, say he is a most delightful anthologist both of his own sensibility and of the writings of other men. But an anthologist, however good, does not provide literary criticism or literary history.

Perhaps it is merely a question of names, though the merely nominal has started wars; and perhaps it is better to be the kind of writer Mr. Brooks now is, than to be a literary historian or critic. The most that this review intends to insist is that Mr. Brooks is neither one nor the other, though he was once both.

Mr. Brooks's method has been described and commented upon by a number of critics whose competence and knowledge far exceed that of the present reviewer; and if I venture upon one more partial synopsis of what may be very familiar, it is for the sake of a shift of emphasis and interest. Mr. Brooks chooses from his authors' lives and books the passages which seem significant to him, and fuses them, quotation marks removed, with his own impressions and comments. It becomes clear after a time that Mr. Brooks is very much interested in descriptions of landscape and countryside; and in writers' habits of work. These two concerns stem quite naturally, if excessively, from the dominant theme of Mr. Brooks's whole career, the fate of the author in America. Mr. Brooks does not like the author who did not like America enough to stay. He rejoices in the author, however insignificant, who has described the scenery and other beauties of his locales. Celia Thaxter is but one of many possible illustrations:

> Most luminous of these little moons, Celia Thaxter dwelt in her far sky-blue parlor; or, rather, on the Isle of Shoals, where the bells tolled on their rocking buoys, she moved in an orbit of her own. In the vast wooden barrack, with its long piazza, the Appledore Hotel, kept by her brothers, she lived with her poems, her music and her friends, surrounded by books, terns, flowers, shells and seaweeds. . . .

Similarly, Mr. Brooks's loving descriptions of authors' habits of work may also be the results of his obsessive concern with what it is to be a writer in America, though again one gets into so many minute and fascinating details that the general thesis, such as it is, hardly matters.

Is it fanciful, then, to suppose that this love of landscape is responsible for Mr. Brooks's use of the year's weather as the source not only of the titles of his two books, but also of the whole movement he attributes to New England culture? Perhaps it is fancy; metaphors are fine things, the hallmark of genius, according to the best authority. Somewhat as an afterthought, Mr. Brooks summons up Oswald Spengler to justify his metaphor of the cultural cycle, and D. H. Lawrence to state the pious localism which makes and marks the great writer: *Men are free when they are in a living homeland, not when they are straying and breaking away.* . . . Men are free when they belong to a living, organic, believing community. . . ." Mr. Brooks quotes more than this from Lawrence; but it is only the words I have italicized that actually concern him. They provide for him all the general insight into man and society he finds necessary.

The result is very peculiar so far as the work as a whole goes. One remarkable chapter, "The Post-War Years," describes the immediate effect upon New England culture of the growth and triumph of industrialism. Mr. Brooks presents all the relevant evidence that industrialism was the chief cause of the radical changes in the character of New England intellectual life. The causal connections seem to be clearly recognized, distinguished, and weighed. But then Mr. Brooks moves on to a thousand other matters of surface and impression, and when he once more feels the need of a large-scale generalization, he returns to his metaphor of the cultural cycle as the seasons of the year, an identification of the processes of society and the processes of nature for which there can be no serious argument. Given that metaphor, it is natural and necessary that New England culture, having had its spring and summer, should have its autumn. All the effects of industrialism, the fact that, as Henry Adams said, "Boston seemed to offer no market for educated labor," and that "the colleges were pouring out new types to meet new conditions, mining engineers and railroad experts, geologists and technicians," and that the classics were thrown overboard,— all the connections made with completeness in "The Post-War

Years" are mainly forgotten. When Mr. Brooks arrives at the year 1915, it is for him the beginning of a "second March," though all the tendencies which had brought about the end of the flowering of New England had by that time become more powerful than ever before. The issue here is not an insistence on social or economic determinism apart from much else and from many unique individual souls; the difficulty is rather with Mr. Brooks's use of the seasons, imposed on evidence which connects the individual with society in so many ways other than and more important than the year's weather.

When Mr. Brooks descends to literary criticism, he does so mainly in order to damn Henry James. Perhaps it would not seem so curious, if he did not look with so uncritical an eye on Amy Lowell, Thomas Bailey Aldrich, and other mediocrities and nonentities. James is but one example among many of the deficiencies of Mr. Brooks's method, and the intermissions. He tells us that James was interested in manners, not morals, an amazing representation of an author so hunted by the Furies. Or, turning to particular books, we are told that Isabel Archer's marriage to Gilbert Osmond, the most important event in *The Portrait of a Lady,* is presented as a matter of "higher discernment" on her part, though almost every other character in the book is presented as against the marriage and fully aware of her blindness. Mr. Brooks's method is such that, if the reader has read this novel of James's, (and the others which Mr. Brooks also condemns), he is left without the evidence which Mr. Brooks had in mind in making his judgment; if the reader has not read James, he is not likely to read him in order to find out how right or wrong Mr. Brooks is.

The same kind of difficulty crops up in the details of Mr. Brooks's writing. Of Santayana, he writes: "In Cambridge, he wore a long, picturesque cape; and, aloof as he was from the other professors, he was charmed by some of the students. Their 'animal faith' was sympathetic to him." Now some readers of Mr. Brooks will know that Mr. Santayana's animal faith is a technical term and wonder just what Mr. Brooks means. Some readers will not have read Santayana and the possibilities of their misunderstanding will be immense.

But more important than the difficulty with thousands of such details of the prose, more important than any other aspect of Mr. Brooks's work, is the way that the quality of life is made mellow, genteel, literary, full of sweetness, light, and landscapes by Mr. Brooks's method. Such are the wages of impressionism and a love of description. The difficulty, effort, strain, conflict, even the agony of his authors' lives disappear at Mr. Brooks's genial approach. Ambition, unhappiness, frustration, hatred, and mighty poets in their misery dead are aspects of life and of authorship which hardly concern the man who wrote *The Ordeal of Mark Twain*. Religious elements, as in Emily Dickinson, and the historical imagination, as in Henry Adams, get the same emphasis and the same amount of attention as dinner-party epigrams and the "trees which brushed the open windows, through which the murmuring summer sounds mingled with the voices of the speakers." Amy Lowell, Edna St. Vincent Millay, John P. Marquand, Wallace Stevens, Eugene O'Neill, and T. S. Eliot are equally significant figures from the perspective Mr. Brooks employs.

For the charming, moving, amusing, and beautiful qualities of Mr. Brooks's work, one can have nothing but admiration. If a masterpiece is a book many people read and enjoy for a long time, Mr. Brooks has produced a masterpiece. But one is profoundly mistaken, if one takes it for literary criticism, literary history, or anything close to those difficult arts. And it will be taken in that way, it will lead to a misunderstanding of great writers and a whole culture, it will mislead as well as give pleasure to many readers.

Randall Jarrell THE HUMBLE

ANIMAL

I HAVE read Miss Moore's poetry too many years and too many
times not to be afraid that both the poems and my feelings
about them will be unjustly represented by anything I write. It
might be better to say, like Graves's Augustus, "Words fail me, my
lords," and to go through *What Are Years* pointing. This is Miss
Moore's own method of criticism, as anyone who has read one of
her reviews will remember; so it would be a rude kind of justice
to make a criticism of her poetry quotations and a few conjunctions.

One critic has said that Miss Moore's poetry is not poetry at all,
but criticism—actually even her criticism is not criticism but an inferior sort of poetry. She not only can, but must, make poetry out of
everything and anything: she is like Midas, or like Mozart choosing
unpromising themes for the fun of it, or like one of those princesses
wizards force to manufacture sheets out of nettles. But actually there
is one thing that Miss Moore has a distaste for making poetry of:
the Poetic. She has made a principle out of refusing to believe that
there is any such thing as the antipoetic; her poems restore to poetry
the "business documents and school books" that Tolstoy took away.

Pound wrote one famous sentence of advice which, to judge
from the practice of most of the poets who read it, was understood
as: *Poetry must be just as badly written as prose.* Miss Moore understood it more as it was meant to be understood: her poetry, not

---

A review of *What Are Years* by Marianne Moore (New York: The Macmillan
Company, 1941).

satisfied with the difficulties of verse, has added to them those of prose. Her poems certainly have the virtues—form, concentration, emotion, observation, imagination, and so on—that one expects of poetry; but one also finds in them, in supersaturated solution, some of the virtues of good prose. Miss Moore's language fits Wordsworth's formula surprisingly well—something that will disquiet lovers of either, though not lovers of both; but I am sure Wordsworth would have looked at it with uncomfortable dislike, and have called it the language of extraordinary women. This would be true: Miss Moore, in spite of a restraint unparalleled in our time, is a natural, excessive, and magnificent eccentric. (On a small scale, of course; like all cultivated Americans, she is afraid of size.) Eccentricity has been to her a first resort, an easy but inescapable refuge.

Miss Moore's forms have the lacy, mathematical extravagance of snowflakes, seem arbitrary as the prohibitions in fairy tales; but they work as those work—disregard them and everything goes to pieces. Her forms, tricks and all, are like the aria of the Queen of the Night: the intricate and artificial elaboration not only does not conflict with the emotion but is its vehicle. And her machinery—bestiary, rather—fits both the form and final content of her poems as precisely as if all three were pieces of some extraordinary puzzle. Another of the finest American poets, Wallace Stevens, is as addicted to exotic properties; but his often get in the way of what he has to say, or hide from him the fact that he does not, this time, care to say anything. The things *are* what Miss Moore wants to say, and express her as naturally and satisfactorily as the Lamb and the Tyger did God. (Some true wit—Miss Moore, I suppose—put an index at the back of *Observations,* the early collection of her poems.) A style ought to make it easy for you to say all that you have to say, not, as most do, make it impossible for you to get free from one narrowed range of experience and expression; Miss Moore's style, whether it seems to or not, does the first—this is proved by the fact that her poetry is richer, more balanced, and more objective than her prose. Nobody else's mechanism and mannerisms come so close to being independently satisfactory—like the Cheshire Cat's smile, which bewitched one for some time after the cat was gone. (Sometimes the smile is almost better than the cat: I once read, in a college newspaper's account of a lecture, that poets put "real toes in imaginary gardens, as Mary Ann Moore says.")

It would be stupid not to see Miss Moore in all her protective creatures—"another armored animal," she once reflects, or confesses. Patience, honesty, the courage that is never conscious of itself because it has always taken itself for granted—all the qualities she distills from, or infuses into, the real pastoral of natural history books, she is at last able even to permit to man, looking at him (in the beautiful "The Pangolin") as equably, carefully, and even affectionately as she ever looked at any animal. "The Pangolin" may very well be her best poem; it is certainly one of the most moving, honest, and haunting poems that anyone has written in our century.

Miss Moore realizes that there is no such thing as the *Ding an Sich,* that the relations are the thing; that the outside, looked at hard enough, is the inside; that the wrinkles are only the erosion of habitual emotion. She shows that everything is related to everything else, by comparing everything to everything else; no one has compared successfully more disparate objects. She has as careful and acute an eye as anybody alive, and almost as good a tongue; so that when she describes something, a carrot, it is as if you had taken the carrot's words in some final crisis, words that hold in themselves a whole mode of existence. One finds in her poems so much wit and particularity and observation; a knowledge of "prosaic" words that reminds one of *Comus*; a texture that will withstand any amount of rereading; a restraint and delicacy that make many more powerful poems seem obvious. And, over and above the love and care and knowledge she has lavished on the smallest details of the poems, Miss Moore is an oddly *moral* writer, one who coalesces moralities hardly ever found together; she is even, extraordinarily enough in our time, a writer with a happy ending—of a kind.

One could make a queer economic-historical analysis of Miss Moore, as the representative of a morality divorced both from religion and from economics, of a class segment that has almost been freed either from power or from guilt—whose cultivation, because of its helplessness and poverty, is touching. One might say that Miss Moore is, fragmentarily, Henry James in pure crystalline form. (Sometimes James's morality, in its last extravagance, is one more Great Game, a species of ethical hydroponics.) In Miss Moore's

poems religion and economics are ghosts. Clergymen are spare cultivated old men, friends of your father, living scrupulously off dwin-
dling incomes, who on the lawn tell you occasionally, not without
a dry and absent impressiveness, about unfrequented hallways of
the Old Testament. Business, the West, furnish you with no more
than an odd quotation about the paper of an encyclopedia, and in
the colonies of the West there are neither workers nor hunger,
only pandas. Society is the incredible monster you inhabit, like the
whale in Lucian; for many years, long before your birth even, there
has been nothing anyone could do—so while you wait under the
shade of that great doom you do well and, whether any bless you
or not, are blessed. Alone in your civility, precariously safe and
beautiful in the enforced essential privacy of late individualism, you
are like the reed which escapes, perhaps, the storm that wrecks the
forest; or like the humble, the children and sparrows, who served
as models for salvation in the similar convulsions of an earlier
world. And what an advantage it is to be poor and humble, to have
lost your stake in the game that corrupts even if you play unwillingly
and without belief! It is you who can sit still—no need to wish to
—and keep your mouth shut, or speak so softly and dryly it is as
good as silence.

Miss Moore has great limitations—her work is one long triumph
of them; but it was sad, for so many years, to see them and nothing
else insisted upon, and Miss Moore neglected for poets who ought
not to be allowed to throw elegies in her grave. I have read that
several people think So-and-So the greatest living woman poet;
anybody would dislike applying so clumsy a phrase to Miss Moore—
but surely she is. Her poems, at their unlikely best, seem already
immortal, objects that have endured their probative millennia in bar-
rows; she has herself taken from them what time could take away,
and left a skeleton the years can only harden. People have complained about the poems, in the words of the poems: "Why dissect
destiny with instruments which are more specialized than the tis-
sues of destiny itself?" But nothing is more specialized than destiny.
Other people have objected. "They are so *small*." Yes, they are as
small as those animals which save the foolish heroes of fairy tales—
which can save only the heroes, because they are too small not to
have been disregarded by everyone else.

C. G. Wallis SATAN AND

DENIS DE ROUGEMONT

PROOFS for the existence of Satan are as integral a part of a Christian anthropology as proofs for the existence of God, of metaphysics or natural theology. For the doctrine of Original Sin, if it is formulated with any accuracy, lays down a paradox in the genesis of evil which postulates Satan as necessary for its solution. If we interpret the myth of Original Sin within the limits of human reason, it says that a man of himself always tends to act for his own private ends rather than for any reasonable good (and by the correlative doctrine of grace, that any actually reasonable and just action could not be accounted for in terms of what we know of human motives and powers—just as the poet feels that he has hit upon a good verse, or the philosopher, that he is not responsible for the insight which flashed upon him) but that this tendency to do evil has a peculiar status in human nature. For it is not any necessity of his nature which compels a man to act from private motives (as it is a necessity of his nature which compels him to think and to love) but something like a habit or second nature. He has a freedom of choice which depends upon his capacity for insight and reflection but which is limited in its fruitfulness by Original Sin. But it remains true that, considered most barely and abstractly, he could always act otherwise; for if he could not always act otherwise, no moral responsibility would attach to him, since it would be contradictory

A review of *La Parte du Diable* by Denis de Rougemont (New York: Brentano's, 1944).

281

to say that he always acts according to the necessity of his nature and yet does evil. But as he always appears to act from a mixture of good and evil motives, there are empirical grounds for saying that he acts according to a necessity of his nature. Consequently a moralist must state the paradox that the way in which a man always appears to act does not spring from his nature considered most radically. The doctrine of Original Sin is the most elaborate and successful attempt to solve this paradox and to explore, by means of a myth, in what precise sense evil is inherent in human nature and what our ultimate considerations must be in assigning moral responsibility and irresponsibility to any individual. For Original Sin is a doctrine of a moral irresponsibility for which we all remain responsible: "In Adam's fall / We sinned all." And within the doctrine of Original Sin the postulate or argument for the existence of Satan says that there is a partial responsibility for the existence of evil, which, while it cannot be assigned to God, cannot be assigned to man either.

For according to the Christian theologians, man was created in a State of Innocence, which is a very different thing from the abstraction which has been called a state of nature. For Hobbes, the state of nature is a condition of undeclared total warfare, where every man is at war with his neighbor and "life is nasty, brutish, and short," and where man is preeminently the animal which fears rather than the animal which thinks and talks. For Rousseau, the state of nature is a remotion from all social institutions, moral responsibility, and rationality: man is only potentially human. (A theologian might contend that Hobbes and Rousseau had made an abstraction of the state of corrupted nature after the fall and represented it apart from the presence of, and unredeemed by, any divine grace: consequently, the state of nature, except for the possibility of change for the better, would be a temporal Hell.) I know little discussion of a state of nature as such among theological writers. I should conceive it as being not unlike the utopian economic world of Adam Smith: where every man acts according to his self-interest, which automatically works for the common welfare; for, disciplined by experience, his choices would be dictated by prudence. And while a man would know good and evil, there would be no constant predisposition to make the wrong choice. The state of innocence, as it is conceived by theologians, is not a variant interpretation of the state of nature, but something over and above that, viz., nature perfected by grace and original justice, where man's senses, imagination, and reasoning powers are working together harmoniously; and each of his activities is without strain or fatigue. (Mr. Buckminster Fuller might argue that there would be no need at all for sleep, but that man's energies would be restored as quickly as they were consumed.) And each of man's activities produces an intense pleasure corresponding to it; indeed St. Aquinas not unreasonably argues that sexual pleasure would be more intense and in no way contrary to reason, because the senses would be purer; while, in the state of corrupted nature, no man can think of God at the moment of the orgasm. Furthermore, man has a direct perception—not, certainly, of God—but of the causality of God at work in nature, and consequently what his own relation to God is and ought to be. Now since man's will is free, it is theoretically possible for him to sin without more ado, even in the state of innocence. But since the creation is good, and his senses, imagination, and reasoning are in harmony, he knows only good. Therefore, as ignorant of evil, he must have a teacher if he is to become conscious of evil. For his intellect, in respect to individual things, is dependent upon imagination and memory, and imagination and memory upon the senses. Thus a possible evil must be introduced or suggested by means of the senses. Accordingly we have the figure of the serpent and the apple; for there is need of an extrinsic principle of evil or a Tempter; and, given man's constitution in the state of innocence, it could not work directly on the mind but only by way of the senses and the imagination. In relation to man, this is the postulate of the existence of Satan. Thus the doctrine of Original Sin is rather complex; for by the same trope it is doubtful whether there would be need of Satan on the supposition that man had been created in the state of nature, since it would be possible for him by himself to make errors in a purely prudential calculus of pleasures and pains. If we try to reduce the doctrine to rationalistic terms, it says that the tendency to evil in man's nature must be conceived not merely as if it were a bad habit inhibiting his natural powers, but as if it were a vice which corrupted or destroyed powers which were themselves better than human and as if therefore its origin could not wholly be located in the nature of man. But if we allow the fall of

Adam after temptation by Satan as a myth sufficient to account for the genesis of evil within human nature, the mystery of the origination of evil is only pushed back a step farther to Satan. Now the theologians, I take it, would say that Lucifer was created not in a state of grace like man but in a state of nature; and consequently it was possible for him to sin through pride, i.e., to will his final end (the beatific vision) through means by which it was not possible (his own powers). (On this analogy, I should like to suggest that the usual formulation of sin, viz., as the wilful choice of something created as a man's final end instead of the beatific vision seems to be metaphysically impossible. For insofar as a man knows God to be his final end [and only insofar is it possible for him to sin] how could he will or choose otherwise? It seems a self-contradiction. But he might deliberately use as a means towards this end something which is in itself incompatible with that end. The ordinary formulation of sin would make a man single-minded in relation to something created. But Kierkegaard at least would assert that a man could be single-minded only in relation to God and consequently that sin involves a double-mindedness.) Unlike man, Lucifer was a pure intelligence, without imagination and the senses; consequently the principle of his defection into moral evil must lie in his intellect. Thus the postulate of the existence of Satan says that the ultimate origination of moral evil must lie in the intellect—but in intellect conceived as abstracted from memory, imagination, and the senses. For whether the myth of Original Sin be taken as a fable or as a dogma, it is possible to make a reduction of it into rational terms. But if the postulate of the existence of Satan be interpreted substantively, it says that any act of wrong-doing bears a direct relation to another person and is not simply in relation to an impersonal moral law—like the game of chess in *Les Chevaliers de la Table Ronde* in which Sir Launcelot plays opposite an invisible diabolical antagonist.

Denis de Rougemont has written a short book on the manifestations of Satan in the modern world. He assumes the existence of Satan not merely in respect to the genesis of moral evil but also in respect to its continuance in the world, as if to say that men could not persevere in sin *nisi suadente Diabolo,* but just as God must continuously maintain the world in being (and so the act of creation is coexistent with the duration of the world) so Satan must constantly tempt man to sin, and so renew the fall of man. Viewing Satan as The Prince of this World, the Tempter, the Accuser, the Father of Lies, whose primary role is that of an *agent provocateur* and whose preeminent work in the modern world is to teach men to disavow their moral responsibility, De Rougemont finds Satan (who works always under an incognito, in order to persuade men of his non-existence) manifested ubiquitously: the idols of Race, Nation, and Class, worldly virtue, artistic productivity, psychoanalysis, the American code of success, the loss of the sense of personal responsibility, the babelization of the useful arts, modern love, sex, the rule of the mob in the democracies and in the totalitarian states, the liberal who does not believe in the Devil, and even the persuasion that "the little man in the brown shirt" is the Devil himself,—these have all been used as Satanic disguises.

De Rougemont's politics—for to some extent this work is a political tract—is that of a federal world order, which is the only "utopia" which offers a solution to the dilemma of "war and the totalitarian state, which is nothing else than the state of permanent war." De Rougemont finds it

> just and necessary to say that Satanism is not solely Hitlerite, that Hitlerism is not solely German, that here too we are more or less Hitlerized in our manners and in our thoughts. But that does not excuse Hitler. Far from it! It accuses us. . . . The solution is to attack Hitler—since he is attacking us—with tanks, planes, solid propaganda, iron discipline, and *at the same time* to attack him with a new ideal. For in this way we will not be annexed externally, and we will not be annexed internally either.

The position is—or was at the time of writing—intelligible and honest. The parts of the book devoted to Hitlerism and the democracies are what might be called De Rougemont's permanent contribution to the war effort.

I should like however to examine more closely two of the places in which De Rougemont finds diabolism manifesting itself, namely in psychoanalysis and authorship. He criticizes psychoanalysis as leading to a loss of moral responsibility or conscience.

Psychoanalysis can be defined as an attempt to reduce "sin" and "Evil" to subjective mechanisms, which medicine can learn to control. . . . In the eyes of the Freudian there is no Devil, but merely a belief in the Devil, springing from the "projection" of a guilt-complex. Heal this complex, and there won't be belief in the Devil any more, nor consequently any Devil.

And he proposes as a truth contrary to psychoanalysis that

since the action of the Devil consists in clouding over our sense of guilt and in making us believe that evil is always the fault of *something* else, the nature of things or destiny, the contrary action will alone be sanctifying. Baudelaire said that true civilization consists in diminishing the traces of original sin. Similarly, true sanctification consists in increasing our sense of being accomplices in all the evil which takes place in the world. The height of sanctity is not in the illusory certitude of being without sin. The contrary is revealed to us by Christ when he submits to death in assuming all the sins of the world.

Let us say that the major premise of De Rougemont's argument is true; for, as Father Zossima says in *The Brothers Karamazov,* each man must learn that he is responsible to all and for all. But certainly in his minor premise De Rougemont is guilty of a fallacious piece of casuistry, and is laying himself open catastrophically to the charge of theological obscurantism. For if we look at psychoanalysis theologically, then is not its proper function to heal the false feelings of guilt, which are induced by a neurotic superego—a different thing from the moral conscience even if it is related to it—and which have their source in childhood events which occurred before the age of reason in which the conscience could function properly? For if a man is obsessed with a false guilt, it is difficult for him to recognize his real responsibilities. The moral guilt of a neurotic would lie in malingering in his neurosis; for the neurotic, as distinguished from the psychotic, is still ethically responsible. Psychoanalysis should be conceived as a special discipline of self-knowledge; and in order to make a moral choice, a man must know his desires. By enabling a man to see where certain guilt feelings and anxieties are false, psychoanalysis should make it possible for him to act

morally in a fuller sense and to taste certain natural joys of the creation of which his complex has deprived him. Satan is also the Spirit
that Denies, and his work should be evident in a guilt-neurosis as
well as in a loss of moral responsibility.

Recognizing the suspicion which the topic throws upon himself,
De Rougemont discusses the devil as an author. As Gide says: "No
literary work is possible without the collaboration of the demon."
And Blake said: "The reason why Milton wrote in fetters when he
wrote of Angels & God, and at liberty when of Devils & Hell, is
because he was a true Poet and of the Devil's party without knowing it." Jacob Boehme wrote that Satan told a questioner he left
Paradise in order to become an author. Following them with some
difference, De Rougemont asserts: "In truth, the will to create, the
need to write, considered absolutely, coincides at bottom with
Lucifer's temptation: to make oneself as God, to become an author,
to create one's own authority in an autonomous world." But I think
that the diabolism to which authorship is subject may be stated
more concretely and that there is an even more radical analogue for
Lucifer's temptation in the nature of man itself. The dialectical
diabolism inherent in writing is to forget the thought in developing the image or trope in which it must be expressed, to lose
sight of what is signified and see only the symbol which one is
using. As the great poet confesses:

> *Players and painted stage took all my love,*
> *And not those things that they were emblems of.*

The moral diabolism lies in the poet's temptation to live his life
for the perfection of the written work and subordinate his universal
ethical responsibilities to his art. For in relation to a moral life, the
excellence of art is secondary and symbolic rather than essential.
The poets (and the philosophers as well, from Plato and Aristotle
on down) have been subject to this failing, and it is one of the prices
which has been paid for our classics.

But let me point out a more radical analogue for the Satanic
temptation, which De Rougemont defines as a false imitation of the
act of creation. According to the theologians, the act of creation was
the free and, as it were, arbitrary act of the will of God, in contra-
distinction to the eternal generation of the Trinity, which is anal-

ogous to a necessity of knowing and loving. But if the theological notion of the creation is that of a free act (almost a *gratuitous act,* in Gide's sense), then any human act of free choice or judgment is an imitation of the divine free act of creation and is by its nature as much subject to the Satanic temptation as the act of symbolic expression. If Satan is always with us, then, as De Rougemont observes, he may be found in the ritual of exorcism itself; and since Satan is always with us, it is also well to remember that he can only be found in something which is in itself an actual and a natural good.

As a whole, the book is earnest in its intention; and as expressing some genuine theological insights, it is edifying. But in comparison with *L'Amour et L'Occident,* which was, I think a major theological study of the relations between eros and the death-wish, it is disappointing. De Rougemont is more sophisticated in his casuistry of the modern world than most Roman Catholic apologists. But if *L'Amour et L'Occident* was Kierkegaardian in its seriousness and its inventiveness, *La Part du Diable* often suffers from the same glibness which is the defect of Maritain. De Rougemont is less a philosopher than a poet or iconographer. The best pages here are the fable (retold from Jung) of the woman who thought she was attacked by birds; the fable, *La Bastonnade,* on eros and sadism; and *Le Coup de Pistolet,* a fable on Rimbaud's "Je me crois en Enfer, donc j'y suis."

Martin Lebowitz THE

EVERLASTING MR. HUXLEY

LIKE *Eyeless in Gaza,* Huxley's new novel is a parable of his own development. The characters personify various moral alternatives and are supposed to illustrate the impossibility of any purely secular form of virtue or salvation. The main character, Sebastian Barnack, blessed at the age of seventeen with an angelic face, poetic talent, a pornographic imagination, and a nascent Huxleyan sense of the ineffable grossness of the human body, undergoes, during a week's visit to his uncle's Florentine villa, a very intensive, accelerated sort of education. In the first place he learns from Veronica Thwale, the young companion of his uncle's aged mother-in-law, that his adolescent sexual fantasies have no relation to the reality; and on another plane he discovers that his uncle, a rich, kindly, unprincipled, unfortunately gluttonous aesthete who dies of over-indulgence the night of Sebastian's arrival, is morally superior to his father, an austere socialist politician whose life is purportedly governed solely by principle, never by instinct or affection (although the distinction evades me): the point being, apparently, that inaction, although the obverse of evil, is better than action governed by a temporal ideal. But the chief lesson, not excluding the one taught by Mrs. Thwale, is communicated by Bruno Rontini, the saintly, somewhat vulpine bookseller, a Florentine avatar, presumably, of Gerald Heard.

A review of *Time Must Have a Stop* by Aldous Huxley (New York: Harper & Brothers, 1944).

Sebastian, falsely suspected of having stolen the Degas drawing his uncle had given him just before dying, obtains the aid of Rontini, who retrieves the situation although in consequence of the episode Rontini is imprisoned by the Fascists, a pet Pomeranian poisoned, and an innocent child brutally accused of theft. This is supposed to demonstrate what Rontini calls the genealogy of evil, and thus, of course, the necessity of non-attachment.

Meanwhile we are treated to something quite possibly unique in fiction: a circumstantial account of Uncle Eustace's posthumous refusal in the super-temporal realm to abdicate his humanity—his affection for ribald jokes and his recollection of sleek women, strong drinks, and Romeo and Juliet cigars—and be saved.

The skeptical reader will probably dissociate the substance of the book, which is, in the main, amusing, from the message, which is somewhat harder to take though not altogether absurd. The theme is joined to the plot so far as Uncle Eustace is more presentable than Sebastian's father and Rontini is fully identifiable by context and implication: for in fiction (and this of course is the moral quality of fiction) to be "real" is to be endearing, and the politician father seems to sustain the theme only because Huxley uses the unconscious subterfuge of failing to realize him. His austerity is not lifelike because it is not austerity so much as bloodlessness. It is not this alone that prevents the didactic success of the book, although it seems to confirm a lot of didacticism about the non-didactic nature of art, and much else, most of it quite in line with Huxley's present opinions. A novelist who expressly favors compassion should not depend upon this sort of thing:

> The other inclined his head and, in an accent which betrayed that he had not been educated at one of the more ancient and expensive seats of learning. . . .

Certainly not satire, save in reverse, for it is the sort of grossness or irresolution of feeling that is the normal object of satire. As to Eustace Barnack's posthumous struggles, one inevitably enjoys his preference for the women and cigars, and Huxley's sense of absurdity, irrepressible as it is, had not *quite* betrayed him. But the quality of pessimism that comprises Huxley's wit is not only stale, now, but irrelevant, and not even realistic; and, as always, it seems

to involve the inverse pedantry of our inclination to laugh at the
mere use of certain words:

> To make a picture others need
> All Ovid and the Nicene Creed;
> Degas succeeds with one tin tub,
> Two buttocks and a pendulous bub.

Just after the seance in which a stupid medium farcically misunderstands Eustace's thoughts, Veronica Thwale, looking upon
the roofs of Florence, reflects:

> Shamelessness at the core; but on the surface Brunelleschi and
> Michelangelo, good manners and Lanvin clothes, art and science
> and religion. And the charm of life consisted precisely in the
> inconsistency between essence and appearance, and the art of
> living in a delicate acrobacy of *sauts perilleux* from one world
> to the other, in a prestidigitation that could always discover
> the obscenity of rabbits at the bottom of even the glossiest
> high hat and, conversely, the elegant decency of a hat to conceal
> even the most pregnant and lascivious of rodents.

Thwale is perhaps a mouthpiece of the "early" Huxley, but this is
the theme of all his novels: his concern has expressly been this
contradiction between pretension and reality. But the distinction
"between essence and appearance"—the word "reality," that is—is
inevitably question-begging, or metaphysical, just as any word ultimately is. Huxley's satire is as venomous as it is, as obsessed with
the traumatic and the grotesque, precisely because it is the result of
a pervasive unconscious metaphysical conviction. Thwale's thoughts
comprise a sort of inverse Platonism, a negative duplicate, actually,
of Huxley's present belief.

The suggestive fact about Huxley's ancestry is not that his
grandfather was Thomas Huxley but that he is related through his
mother to Matthew Arnold. True, as one writer has said, in Aldous
Huxley "the great influences of Victorian art and science meet"—
they meet head on. He inherits the largely gratuitous or even
anomalous despair of Victorian materialism. The point of his early
novels is the irreparable antipathy of the natural to the ideal, of
knowledge to virtue, of truth to beauty. In *Point Counter Point* the

antithesis is between science, intellect, and civilization on the one hand and instinct and emotion on the other. Certainly it was preconceptions such as these, the habit of thinking in terms of these conventional dualities, that made Huxley so responsive to both D. H. Lawrence and Gerald Heard.

Presumably Huxley's repeated stress on unity, on the need for unification, is related to his satirical awareness of disparity and contradiction. But the incongruities that offend Huxley are the concern not only of satire but of all moral discourse. However, for the secularist, or indeed any relatively dispassionate person, ugliness and evil are not intrinsic features of anything, are not self-caused, but, rather, are aspects of the collision of morally neutral, in fact, ultimately impersonal forces. Huxley's materialism, his attitude toward sex and toward the human body, has all along, as in the case of Eliot, been a kind of truncated theology.

Since Huxley's quietism is simply an evolution of the cynicism that still pervades his work, the value of his current views depends upon their validity as negative comments upon secular ideals. Yet his critique of existing morality, though very stimulating and intelligent, is not quite successful. Why, after all, is every moral system manifestly imperfect? For one thing it has been habitual for moralists to identify virtue with the perfection of a "definite" faculty or set of faculties. The trouble, extending even to pragmatism and utilitarianism, is that this requires us to judge behavior as an index of cause, or "intention," rather than of result. Prudence, temperance, piety, humility, intelligence, love, even "good will" are all vices as well as virtues depending upon their effect in a given situation. Every "faculty" or "motive" is morally questionable, just so far as, in effect, every action is; and of course all three are conceivably ambivalent. Philosophers recognize this by applying a dialectical role to evil: evil becomes the matrix of action, or history.

In this sense, of course, it is true, as Huxley contends, that evil is integral to time. But he is confused, or, actually, undecided whether or not time should be abandoned entirely. The whole idea of virtue is for him an object of ambivalence, though this, if conscious, is, as I have suggested, to his credit. In *Ends and Means* he says that reform is self-defeating unless the means are of the same quality as the end. This may be a shrewd historical insight, but it raises certain questions. Every social idealist contemplates a society in which means are not merely of the same quality as ends but indistinguishable from them. It is an ideal of this sort that we call Utopian, for in such a society life would cease to be problematic. Huxley is right only so far as the idea of virtue is not ultimately psychological but metaphysical; and it is for just this reason, perhaps, that no moral *system* can ever be adequate.

Rontini somewhere mentions the difficulty of becoming "your inner not-self in God while remaining your outer self in the world." This of course is simply the old conflict between conscience and necessity, and an evolution, in Huxley's case, of the conflict between beauty and truth. Like every comparable dilemma, it evinces some sort of subjective failure. It is just this difficulty that makes sainthood largely a perversion, if not, indeed, a misapprehension. Innocence, which of course the Taoists stress, is perhaps the only "virtue" because it is the best moral index of growth.

Harold Whitehall LINGUISTIC

PATRIOT

THE last few months have given us several works of popular linguistic importance. First came the Hogben-Bodmer *Loom of Language*; then, Joseph Shipley's *Dictionary of Word Origins* cheek by jowl with G. B. Stewart's *Words on the Land*. Now comes the long-expected Mencken volume—by intention, the first of two

A review of *The American Language: Supplement One* by H. L. Mencken (New York: Alfred A. Knopf, 1945).

supplements to *The American Language* (4th edition), but actually a book to be read in its own right and on its own merits. Such is the intrinsic interest of the subject that even the dullest philological drudge cannot make words uninteresting. But Mencken is the first American writer since Sapir to make them dramatic.

Mencken's general position on language has been clear ever since the first edition of *The American Language* in 1919. He was (and in a nobler sense still is) a linguistic patriot, imbued with the spirit if not the smugness that prompted John Adams to propose his American Academy for Refining, Improving, and Ascertaining the English Language. His linguistic studies began in the exploitation of one of his well-known series of *Prejudices*—as it happens, the most far-reaching prejudice of them all. But Mencken has grown, as anyone having to do with language in an honest way inevitably grows. In the beginning, he was a brilliant amateur, with an amateur's enthusiasms and style, but also with an amateur's technical limitations. As *The American Language* passed through its various editions, the amateurishness, and some of the vehemence, was dissipated. In this book, little is left of earlier attitudes but the unchanged point of view which organizes it and the Mencken style, still pungent, still vigorous, and still clean. In all important respects, Mencken is now as professional as a post-doctoral research fellow at Harvard.

There is something quietly ironical about this personal transition of Mencken's. Above all else, this Supplement One is a superb example of compilative and organizational scholarship by one who, in the none too distant past, affected to gibe at scholars if not at scholarship. If; as Sapir used to say, the core of linguistics is careful bookkeeping, then Mencken ranks among the greatest linguists of our time. But, more important than that, he is a writer, and among linguists, writers, or even moderately gifted pedagogues, are rarer than hen's teeth. T. E. Lawrence once alleged to Marshal Foch that soldiers ought to be professionals; generals, amateurs. Even more certainly, the professional linguists need to be marshaled by someone like Mencken. As one of those same professionals, I am more than satisfied with his generalship.

The book falls structurally into five parts: (1) The Two Streams of English, (2) The Beginnings of American, (3) The Period of

Growth, (4) The Language of Today, and (5) American and English. Considering its subject matter, it should be regarded less as a sober treatise than a drama in five acts, in which the American David, derided by the British Goliath in the first, achieves stature through two, three, and four, and overcomes the Philistine in the fifth. Like Nathan, Mencken is nothing if not naturally dramatic, and his scenario loses nothing from being so obviously founded on fact. It is fact that British observers, most of them linguistic ignoramuses, criticized and (to use the word they scorned) belittled the nascent American language. It is fact that linguistic traitors abounded within the American camp, that Anglomania attempted what British criticism had failed to achieve, that a deal of prissiness and stuffiness on both sides of the Atlantic obscured the plain truth that a new English was amaking. It is indisputable fact that American English, long ago come of age, has already captured the outer bastions, if not the central keep, of British English tradition. Yet, after all, drama is mimesis, and selective mimesis at that. It cannot hurt, it might even amplify Mencken's case, to examine one or two aspects of this *mythos*.

The rococo English world of the late seventeenth and early eighteenth centuries was convinced that English had finally crystallized into hard-won perfection. Men like Swift, Nathanael Bailey, and Pope took it for granted, and, like the frenetic Elizabethans under threat of Puritanism, prized it more highly in that it might soon be lost—in this case to a tasteless bourgeoisie. Samuel Johnson, with his usual practical sense, set himself to record the perfection before it was too late; and the result was his *Dictionary* of 1755. Authoritarianism, particularly linguistic authoritarianism, is at best unlovely, but we must give this particular devil his due. Even the prescriptive (and restrictive) grammars of Bishop Lowth and his imitators, aimed primarily at the credulities and pocketbooks of the parvenu middle classes, had in one sense a nobler aim: they attempted to uphold the perfection of Augustan English in a period which had already lost it. Only against this background can the villains in the first part of Mencken's piece be motivated. What Swift in 1702 and Johnson in 1755 had to say about the threatened "corruption" of English, was echoed, much more moderately, by Pickering in 1815:

It is to be regretted that the reviewers have not pointed out *all* the instances which have come under their notice of our deviations from the *English* standard. This would have been doing an essential service to our literature, and have been the most effectual means of accomplishing what those scholars appear to have so much at heart—the preservation of the English language in its purity, wherever it is spoken.

Men like Pickering and Johnson, and men like Witherspoon, Gifford, Eddis, Cresswell, and Hamilton lived before the scientific study of language had penetrated, if it has ever penetrated, the popular consciousness. There were many fools among them, and some knaves. But it will weaken neither Mencken's scenario nor convictions if we realize that they were fighting, however mistakenly, for a *cause*.

But devil's advocacy is a profession whose temptations I will not here resist. Nothing in Mencken's book is more illuminating than the section of the last part which anatomizes the differences between American and British English and demonstrates how the direction of linguistic exportation has reversed from east-to-west and its west-to-east. Mencken's two theses, that British English is less word-colorful than American and that American English is making great headway in England itself, are devastatingly complete in their documentation. Yet one wonders whether a list of Briticisms and Americanisms, and even the lively, well-informed discussion that accompanies them, can sufficiently indicate the root differences between the American and British forms of the English language.

Written British English (and spoken Received Standard British) represents an attempt to achieve a national language as untouched as possible by regional peculiarities, an *Übersprache* poised as securely as possible over the welter of difficult and often mutually incomprehensible British dialects. Since the vast majority of Britons do not and never will speak this language, it is, in a sense, as far removed from the daily life of the average Englishman as Ciceronian Latin from that of a Roman fruitseller. It steadfastly turns its back on the colloquial and the dialectal merely because it is its function, as an instrument of communication, to be non-colloquial, non-dialectal—everyman's language, not anyman's. If we assume, as we must, that it loses a good deal of the spirit of rowdy life because of the empyrean in which it exists, we can underline, from another angle, Mencken's feeling that its inventive founts have dried up.

Yet there is another factor, not considered by Mencken nor, as far as I know, by anyone else. There seems to be a difference of actual stylistic spirit between written American and British English— a difference sufficiently evident, for instance, in a contrast of the *New York Times* or *Christian Science Monitor* with *The Manchester Guardian*. It is not merely a difference of vocabulary, but of the same language, with the same morphological and syntactical resources, being used in contrary ways for quite contrary ends. The best way I can express the difference is that American English functions more morphologically than British English, British English more syntactically than American English. Or, to use another angle of approach, that American English is *chromatic*, British English *achromatic*. In the most typical American writing, sentences seem to be constructs in which the key words function as isolated counters of expression even as they function as part of their syntactical *milieu*. For all that they are combined in a larger unit of expression, they are still sense-units themselves, and often colorful units at that. In British English, individual words, even the key words, seem to be far more submerged into the larger syntactical units of expression. The sense hovers over the whole phrase or sentence, not over the word, which, therefore, decreases in linguistic importance. In the best British writing, the medium itself is translucent, achromatic, self-effacing; one can forget that it exists. In poorer writing, it is merely gray and muddy. My overstatement of the case will not, I think, invalidate the kernel of truth it possesses. That kernel may go a long way towards explaining the superior word-color of American English, its penchant for verbal inventions, its often brilliant utilization of morphological resources, in short, its chromatism. It may also explain the obvious, and to Mencken quite deplorable, sterility of British English in precisely these virtues. Perhaps, after all, it is not the loss of spiritual adventurousness which makes the British verbally impoverished. If Roosevelt was American as a wordmaker, is not Churchill typically British as a phrase-maker?

Isaac Rosenfeld DRY WATERSHED

KENNETH BURKE'S criticism, from *Permanence and Change* to the present volume, has been moving toward greater generality in form while remaining more or less static in content. He has been covering the same ground, but each time around the course has cut a deeper track. The subject has remained "motives," which, as Mr. Burke uses the term, means "situation," "situation involving attribution of motives," "statements about motives," "criticism of statements about motives," etc. The term has also designated a variety and complexity of things having to do with, among others, poetic, monetary and political strategies and perspectives—the purpose of such "anatomizing" of motives being to inculcate an attitude of "linguistic skepticism" and to "purify war" by extending the area of rational intercourse. The means to this end have grown more specific; one can trace their development from the multitude of interlocking linguistic perspectives in *Permanence and Change,* through the extrapolation of dramatic or poetic perspectives as basic strategies, with the comic serving as *primus inter pares,* in *Attitudes Towards History,* to the present division of the dramatic perspective into five key terms: Scene, Act, Agent, Agency, and Purpose. The interrelationship of these key terms and their analytic function in varying ratios make up the text of *A Grammar of Motives.*

The use Mr. Burke makes of his pentad of terms and the significance he attaches to them call to mind Kant's deduction of the categories. The dream of philosophical criticism, as of critical

A review of *A Grammar of Motives* by Kenneth Burke (New York: Prentice Hall, 1946).

philosophy, is the discovery of categories which are necessarily involved in all analysis. (Mr. Burke's shift from strict Kantianism is a characteristically modern one—from categories of the understanding to categories of linguistics—a transformation exemplifying what he would call a "conversion downwards.") The key terms, then, are said to figure necessarily in all discourse about motives; and their generating perspective must be "dramatist," as distinct from "scientist," for although statements about motives may be empirical, the subject of motivation is philosophical and can be adequately treated only from a perspective that transcends the limitations of science by resisting the reduction of *action* to *motion*.

The first problem with which Burke deals is that of placement. The characterization of an act, or of any other object, in whatever way, places it with reference to an environment or Scene. Here begins the domain of the term "scene" which appears in such relationships as "container and thing-contained," an action (in drama) as related to its scene or setting, etc. By use of this term, analysis discovers the particular meanings that accrue to an object when its environmental or material background is emphasized. Ratios arise in the overlapping of terms and create a range from purely scenic ways of placement to placement in mixed modes: scene-act, scene-agent, and so on.

A specifically linguistic way of placement is shown forth in definition. Here Burke analyzes what he calls the paradox of substance. A thing is defined in terms of what it is not, and as a definition sets up an equation between *definiens* and *definiendum,* we get the paradoxical result that a thing is said to be what it is not. This paradox can lead to great confusion, especially when a thing is reduced, as in science, to terms of a different or lower perspective. The greatest danger is that we may continue to speak of a thing substantively when we claim to be doing otherwise. But because substance characterizations persist even in fields that supposedly have dissolved substance, Burke, by a curious shift, makes the antinomies of definition stand as a reason for retaining the idea of substance. We will need it particularly, says he, for dramatist purposes, since substances call for analysis in terms of act or action. Science, however, in dissolving the terminology of substance also carries away the features essential to action, leaving in their place terms of mere motion. Burke's favorite example is that of the animal psychologist, with his poor rabbits and white mice, who transfers the results of animal motion, as studied under artificial conditions in the laboratory, to the human perspective and thus reduces the philosophical problem of man's complex motivational behavior to non-philosophical terms. At this point Mr. Burke develops a lengthy critique of ways of reduction, showing the falsifications inherent in the use of simple, exclusive "God-terms." The proper study of man can be conducted only by maintaining a delicate balance of motives and meanings, sacrificing nothing to the strictures, however convenient for a limited purpose, of reductive analysis. It is the purpose of the pentad to detect such errors of reduction; and since everything that can be significantly said about motives, or about statements about motives, must be expressed in terms of the pentad, it stands guard against falsification by bringing to bear on the human scene the enlightening perspective of drama.

The second part of *A Grammar of Motives* is devoted to an interpretation of the philosophical schools with the aid of five key terms of dramatism. Thus, Hobbes, exemplar of materialism in general, represents in its purest form the predominance of the scenic in philosophy. The scenic elements of Spinozism are also analyzed, and it is shown how Spinoza, though a rationalist, stands at a crucial moment in the history of science, for his rationalism and his God-Substance-Nature equation provide the systemic groundwork for the logic of empirical science, once the metaphysical elements are cut away by the principle of Occam's razor.

Idealism features the term "Agent," because of its stress on the percipient subject. Berkeley, Hume, and Leibniz are examined with regard to Agent. Kant is shown to be dealing with a typical Agent problem in his concern with finding the grounds of freedom (action) in the world of science (motion). Hegel and Marx are also placed in the tradition of Agent-featuring, as is Santayana. The term "Act" is located in Aristotle and Aquinas, and in the nominalism-realism controversy of the Middle Ages. Pragmatism is shown to be the logical home of the term "Agensy," and the Agency-Purpose ratio typical of James is investigated in some detail. Mysticism features Purpose, as established by its concentration on ends, union with the Divine and disregard for the nature of means.

Part Three, On Dialectic, is concerned with the Dialectic of Constitutions as the most representative "anecdote" or case of the effect of men's interests and motives upon a linguistic structure, and with Dialectic in General, which returns to a development of the more abstract linguistic properties considered at the beginning of the *Grammar*.

However indispensable to the practice of criticism Mr. Burke may have found his five key terms to be, I do not see how he can maintain that they are logically necessary. The attractiveness of a Kantian deduction is obvious, and so are the advantages of possessing a set of concepts that are at once ultimately constitutive of a given part of nature and of the language in which all statements about this segment of nature must be expressed. Yet the very linguistic perspective which Mr. Burke has been developing should have guarded him against the erroneous ambition of claiming so much authority for his system. The logical necessity of the pentad holds only within Mr. Burke's language. That is to say, his terms are analytic, and their apparent necessity follows not from the nature of human motivation as such, but from motivation as defined within the dramatist perspective. Mr. Burke's own definition of his subject matter and the criterion of relevance whereby he selects its features constitute a reduction in scope, a particular, limited formulation. Since his selection, like every other possible one, is no more than partial, it follows that other selections can be made, that other perspectives can be framed and that the dramatist perspective is not exhaustive. And just as inquiry into means, motivations and their linguistic reflections remains open in the material sense, allowing the isolation of other "substances," so, too, it remains open formally. Other terms may be chosen to do the work at present performed by our five; and the work which the new terms will do will reconstitute both the object of inquiry and the language in which it is carried on. Who shall say that other perspectives are impossible? Least of all a perspectivist. The reason Mr. Burke believes his pentad to be necessarily involved in the analysis of dramatic situations is that he has fixed its meaning in advance. Its logical necessity turns out to be purely tautological or formal; materially, it possesses no priority at all.

I also fail to see what is gained by clinging, as Burke does, to the notion of *substance*. It is strange that, after presenting in some detail the various arguments which have been advanced for discarding the substance concept, Mr. Burke should show such little curiosity about the truth of these arguments. He counters the arguments against substance by calling attention to the reductive perspectives in which they are formulated and showing their inadequacy from a dramatist point of view. But this merely begs the question. What, to begin with, is his ground for asserting truth within his own perspective, when his whole development of a theory of perspectives has been to establish that linguistic frameworks give a weighted deflection to assertions made within their confines? A general theory of perspectival translation would first be necessary, whereby statements in one perspective could be adequately examined in another. Lacking this, Mr. Burke's position is a kind of linguistic solipsism. Another step necessary for the justification of the truth claims he makes for his own perspective is the construction of a "grammar of truth," a statement of what is meant by "true" and a criterion of evidence for perspectival assertions. Such groundwork is not even attempted in this *Grammar*. Moreover, Mr. Burke's linguistic analysis of substance, like so much of his criticism, generally, is linguistic only in tone and terminology. It is actually no formal doctrine, no statement about language proceeding from the logical analysis that his program should require, but itself another bit of philosophy, a substance metaphysics. That a particular philosophical perspective requires a substance concept, is no good reason for retaining "substance" as a term of linguistic analysis, especially when the truth of the perspective in which it occurs has not been independently demonstrated. There are, however, methods of linguistic analysis (of which I shall speak later) that are metaphysically neutral, that discard substance in the light of the very excellent reasons for so doing and that at the same time achieve clearer and better results than Mr. Burke's *Grammar*.

The damage Mr. Burke does his case by clinging to a non-relational, substantival logic of language can be estimated linguistically, from the following passage:

> If we quizzically scrutinize the expression, "the motivating of an act," we note that it implicitly contains the paradox of substance. Grammatically, if a construction is active, it is not passive

[and vice versa]. But to consider an *act* in terms of its *grounds* is to consider it in terms of what it is not, namely, in terms of motives that, in acting upon the active, would make it a passive. We could state the paradox another way by saying that the concept of activation implies a kind of passive-behind-the-passive; for an agent who is "motivated by his passions" would be "moved by his being movedness," or "acted upon by his state of being acted upon."

The whole "paradox" here rests in taking an act to be substantively other than its motive—hence the two can never get together again. Once the purely verbal nature of this difficulty is recognized, and it is seen that the word "other" does not generate a distinction in substance, the motive can very readily get into the act by way of an inference that selects one or more of a field of possible motives. Obviously, "motive" and "act" belong together—as Mr. Burke, up to this point, has confidently assumed; to argue that there is something suspect about their union is to reach that stage of subtlety which marks the evaporation of sense. And to insist on this paradox is all the more idle when techniques, no more recondite than the ordinary inferences of everyday life, exist for getting around it. "Inference," however, is a term that Mr. Burke zealously avoids. He clings to his paradoxes (which he converts into *recommendations* for substance!) on the ground, apparently, that to infer is to incur a loss in perspectival dignity. Inferences are for scientists (rat torturers) who would deprive man of his true essence by imprisoning him in the category of motion. Dramatism alone, faithful to action and substance, is the defender of freedom. Which seems to me little better than philosophical petulance.

As a general observation, I should say that the greatest fault with the *Grammar* is that it is not a grammar at all, but a mixture of formal and material elements, comprising a metaphysics. That metaphysical methods are ill suited to the analysis of language should, I trust, be clear from the foregoing. It remains to be shown that linguistic analysis can be conducted non-metaphysically and can attain greater generality and clarity when freed of the impediments with which Mr. Burke burdens it.

A Grammar of Motives, as a treatise on motivation, covers only one-third of the ground open to linguistic analysis. (It is certainly time to remark that there is an ambiguity in the words "linguistic analysis." The expression can mean analysis of language, or analysis by way of language. Kenneth Burke engages in both.) In the Theory of Signs, a general theory of semiosis, as developed by Charles W. Morris, motivations fall under the heading of Pragmatics. Pragmatics is in turn defined as that dimension of sign-functioning (which, for present purposes, we may restrict to language activity) that comprises the practical, or the expression of the practical: sentences in the form of evaluations, moral judgments, technological statements, imputations, etc. The two remaining dimensions of sign functioning are Syntactics and Semantics. Syntactics investigates the relations of signs to each other, as in logic, mathematics, art, etc.; semantics is concerned with the relation of signs to the objects they refer to, and pragmatics studies the relation of signs to their users. The key terms are three in number: "implies" (syntactics); "designates," or "denotes" (semantics); and "expresses" (pragmatics).[1]

In this relatively simple framework, Mr. Morris has been able to work out a fully articulated system of analysis, of which linguistics forms only a part. The advantages of this system are its range and scope (the whole field of semiosis), its clarity, economy and neutrality. The latter quality is particularly noteworthy; though Mr. Morris' theory is constructed on an anti-metaphysical bias, it is of sufficient generality to cut under specific metaphysical issues. Moreover, the selection of key terms is neutral in that it proceeds from a consideration of semiosis in general, rather than, as with Burke, from a perspective that is metaphysically deflected to begin with. There is no reason, for instance, why a metaphysician should not be able to avail himself of the purely formal apparatus of the Theory of Signs for the analysis, development and presentation of his own system. Burke, for one, could certainly profit from it; it would cut under a good deal of his unnecessary verbiage.

One may well ask, how serious are objections of the sort I have been making. A book, like a good deed, is not necessarily invalidated by the mistakes which attend its execution. To dig for contradiction, to posit formal consistency or simplicity as the sole

---

[1] Cf. Charles W. Morris, *Introduction to the Theory of Signs.* (Encyclopedia of Unified Science.) University of Chicago Press.

standard of merit, is, in a manner of speaking, like divining with entrails: *Innerlichkeit* is falsely satisfied, and the bird does not have the worth of its own offal. It is a habit encouraged by linguistics, and whoever would undertake the improvement of linguistics must first dissociate himself from its narrow regulations and replace them by the criteria—"dramatist" or simply human—by which he would judge the more representative concerns of men in society at large.

Let us therefore preserve only the essential criticism, which, as is always the case, has to do with truth. If one may apply the term to matters of logic, Mr. Burke's theses, of which I have examined only two, the claim of logical necessity and the doctrine of substance, both implying a critique of empirical science, are not true. But as even a false premise can lead to a true conclusion, one must now examine his conclusions in a broader way than heretofore.

The "purification of war," at which the *Grammar* aims, is the final public cause of all semantics, which, observing the verbal distortions caused by a clash of interests, believes that a technique of verbal clarification will serve also as a means of moderating the incompatibility of conflicting ends. I am not convinced that it can ever attain its objective; on the contrary, it seems to me that except in so far as given conflicts are *purely* verbal, semantics is a useless oil that does not affect the waters on which it is poured. Rival imperialisms, for example, will not call off their rivalries when deprived of the ideological disguise of their ambitions. Ideologies have a way of perpetuating themselves, if only because truth will also serve as a weapon of war, and ideologies (need one point out?) are sometimes true. When issues are real and important enough, when conditions of conflict are sufficiently desperate, men can even afford to be honest. At best, semantics can have only a symptomatic effect, for in overthrowing one ideology it but prepares the way for another. The cause of conflict, unaffected by purificatory rites, will continue to provide distortions. Burke's kind of semantics even becomes a technique of falsification; in its emphasis on the verbal aspects of conflict, it leads to the development of a perspective in which non-verbal causes are minimized, discounted and forgotten. At best, his purification of war yields only greater exactitude of war, and though the area of reason is spread, war is not thereby diminished. Modern war, with its tremendous rationalizations of industry and society, its systematic planning and coordination—and especially as the Anglo-American allies fought the last one, with (comparatively speaking) a minimum of ideology ("As the war progresses, it becomes less and less ideological," said Churchill), and with the majority of our soldiers not even knowing "what it was all about"—can even be called a triumph of reason. So much for a semantical peace.

Kenneth Burke's own gloomy prophecy, expressed in a single paragraph, of an age of bureaucracy that will exceed anything we have known to date and, presumably, deprive the world even of such freedom as survives our most recent war, outweighs, for sheer reality, the entire body of counter-measures that semantics can propose. How will an "attitude of linguistic skepticism" forestall the bureaucratization of the earth? It is the very political application of semantics, intended to lead criticism out of the closet, that in the end double-bars it there.

Which suggests that Burke's own criticism, at the height of its present confusion, has reached the "watershed" point. To remain meaningful, it must develop either in the direction of greater formal clarity, or greater material commitment, that is, toward pure linguistics, or a sociology of knowledge and a program of politics. Even as a work of "poetry," which, I suppose, is the justification that Mr. Burke would claim for his opus (a *Rhetoric* and a *Symbolic of Motives* are forthcoming), it lacks the commitment, the sheer espousal value, whether of essences or of doctrines, that poetry always embodies. The *Grammar* as a whole is "scenic"—it is without inwardness in its analysis of ideas. Not only does it fail, as in its treatment of empiricism, to get at the heart of an intellectual tradition and discover the structure or "meaning" of meaning contained therein, but it confines itself to the mere *logistics* of ideas (symbolically borne out by the fact that Burke first considered taking a railroad terminal as a representative case study for his section on dialectic). As such, it reduces intellectual history to matters of transformation, placement and position—in short, to the very terms of motion that the five key dramatist terms were designed to prevent.

Dudley Fitts THE HELLENISM OF

ROBINSON JEFFERS

FEW of the legends of prehistoric Greece are as suited to the peculiar genius of Mr. Robinson Jeffers as is the myth of Jason and Medea. True, the element of incest is lacking; but this deficiency is supplied by a nightmare richness of violence. The barbaric Princess of Colchis at the world's end, after betraying her father and assassinating her brother in order to help Jason get home with the Golden Fleece, is in her turn abandoned by her radiant· Hero. In revenge she horribly disposes of his new wife and royal father-in-law, and then, to leave no vein of horror unexplored, she concludes the action by murdering her two little sons. That is the skeleton of the myth which Euripides knew and from which he fashioned what many call his greatest tragedy, a poem which Mr. Jeffers has "freely adapted" for his own purposes.

A man who is making a free adaptation of an ancient play has every right to inject as much of himself as he likes. It is a perilous right, for the injection may kill; but it is his idiosyncratic way of seeing the material that can make his work valuable or otherwise. Mr. Jeffers has always seen vividly, not to say garishly, and in his rather cavalier handling of his original he is proceeding much as Euripides must have done with the myth. After all, what he perceived was not (what Aeschylos almost certainly would have) a text for a politico-theological Morality, but a chance to dramatize a

A review of *Medea*, freely adapted from the *Medea* of Euripides by Robinson Jeffers (New York: Random House, 1946).

psychological problem. In doing so, he unquestionably tampered with tradition. It is probable, for example, that he is responsible for the idea that Medea killed her children, for tradition said that they were killed by the family of King Kreon or, alternatively, stoned to death by the people of Corinth; but the myth was not sacrosanct, and the alteration produced some of the finest poetry that Euripides ever composed. Similarly, Mr. Jeffers has laid fairly violent hands upon his original; and if we agree, as I think that we must, that he has come out with something distinctly less than fine, we must consider the nature and purpose of his alterations.

Some of them are plainly in the interests of compression and of a swifter movement. The choral odes disappear almost wholly. A phrase or two from one may be juxtaposed to an echo of another, but there is no choric feeling. The great set speeches—Medea's especially, and the narrative of the Messenger—are cut down. The dialogue, especially the so frequently ridiculous stichomythy, is slashed, and what remains is often curiously transformed—witness the conversation between Medea and King Aegeus. These are largely mechanical alterations, and in a work that is avowedly not a translation they are no more exceptionable than are Cocteau's reductions of Sophocles.

Slightly different in purpose are two innovations, in both of which Mr. Jeffers seems to me to excel his original. The first of these is his treatment of the two little boys. In Euripides they appear on the stage, but they have no lines until we hear their death-cries within the house. Mr. Jeffers has provided them with speaking parts that are economical, moving, and right. Moreover, Jason's playing with them—marred only by an awkward reminiscence of Astyanax frightened by the plume on Hektor's helmet (*Iliad* VI:469)—is finely handled; and the scenes dealing with their carrying the poisoned gifts to Creüsa-Glaukê are piercing in their compassionate irony. One has only to think of small Eumelos' dirge for his mother Alkestis in order to be thankful that Euripides restrained himself in *Medea;* but that does not detract from Mr. Jeffers's artistry. The other improvement occurs at the end. Euripides has Medea appear above the house in a dragon-drawn winged chariot, the gift of Helios, thereby offending the taste of Aristotle and winning the disapproval of most critics since. Mr. Jeffers, with perfect realism, yet creating an even heightened atmosphere of sorcery—the Colchian aura—has his Medea pass through the portal, mysteriously protected by two flickering lamps which her women have placed at the base of the central pillars, lamps beyond which Jason can not penetrate and between which he falls exhausted at the end. A trick, admittedly; but a better trick than the aerial car.

So it can, and should, be done. My complaint is that Mr. Jeffers's alterations are most often not of this illuminating structural kind, but distortions of the *dynamis,* the central drive, of the play itself. And the trouble lies in his language. With few exceptions, a heightening of the dramatic tension of a situation is the signal for the shouting to begin; and the shouting, like noises heard in delirium, drowns out the meaning of the poem. The passion of Euripides becomes the Californian violence of Mr. Jeffers, and I must further particularize that violence as Hollywoodian.

This rhetoric is not easily described, for I am prepossessed by many things: the old *Medea,* for one, the Euripidean ways of thought and speech; and for another, the *luor* of the Point Sur system of tragedy, its inhumanity, its reckless self-spending. I can not be sure how the present play would have affected me if I had never read *Tamar* and *Roan Stallion,* to say nothing of *The Tower Beyond Tragedy.* Probably, being unprepared, I should have been worse bruised; but I suspect that I should not have been even as little able as I am to accept this Medea: Tamar has to a certain extent "conditioned" me. Any acceptance must be shot-gun, on Mr. Jeffers's terms: *Credo quia absurdum* in this Colchian cinema. *Credo quia* box-office.

After a rather promising prologue—a deft and graceful dilution of Euripides's lines—the Chorus enters and the trouble begins. We hear Medea some time before we see her, wailing in her house. SHE IS ASIATIC, comments a stage-direction, AND LAMENTS LOUDLY. She does, for a fact:

> Death. Death is my wish. For myself, my enemies, my children.
>   Destruction.
> That's the word. Grind, crush, burn. Destruction. Ai . . . Ai . . .

Later (SHE IS PROWLING BACK AND FORTH BEYOND THE DOORWAY, says the direction, risking a simile, LIKE A CAGED ANIMAL) she remarks:

> I will not allow blubber-eyed pity, nor contempt either, to snivel
> over the stones of my tomb,

although why contempt should snivel over a tomb I do not know. At any rate, she finally COMES THROUGH THE DOORWAY, PROPPING HERSELF AGAINST ONE OF THE PILLARS, AND STANDS STARING—thus interpreting the exhaustion of grief and symbolically) suggesting the imminent collapse of the house of Jason. Immediately she passes into one of those Aeschylean comas—there is more than a touch of Kassandra here—and emerges from it at length with very harsh words to say:

> I will look at the light of the sun, this last time. I wish
> from that blue sky the white wolf of lightning
> Would leap, and burst my skull and my brain, and like a burning babe cling to these breasts . . . [SHE CHECKS AND LOOKS FIERCELY AT THE WOMEN BELOW]

Well might she check at such a metaphor: it would have floored the Ancient Pistol himself. But it is not merely that the language is almost comically forced. What is significant is the unheard but remembered counterpoint of Euripides's heroine chanting at this same point—wildly, indeed, but with a control of phrasing and image that makes this acrobatic white wolf silly enough. The Euripidean energy—and he was not a moderate man—has been transformed into as coarse a ranting as ever fluttered the nickelodeons.

An inevitable result of this sort of thing is the shattering of focus. How can the subtle adjustments of character to character, or character to situation, be clearly observed in this tumult? Interpretation must go awry. For example: while in Euripides the chief interest is the analysis of Medea's dark mind, a secondary but by no means unimportant theme is the rehabilitation of Jason. I do not mean that we come to love him; but whereas at the outset we see in him only another Admetos, a complacent cad, at the end we can not help perceiving traces of true magnanimity, the Aristotelian goodness; and certainly we feel with him in his desolation. This is partly the result of the horrible *dénoûement,* but the ageless idea of salvation through suffering is clearly present. But Mr. Jeffers's Jason, for all his selfish cruelty, is from the beginning more appealing than he should be, simply because Medea is so much less appealing than he. Accordingly the character seems, though it actually is not, static. It is possible that in stage representation something might be done to remedy this, but on the printed page the cinema violence of Medea's language—*the poet's entire conception of Medea,* for that is what makes her language possible—disperses the finer meanings. Either Mr. Jeffers has misread Euripides, or his imagination can not encompass the tragic stature of the heroine. He was given a woman as magnificent in her way, and as touching, as Lady Macbeth; he gives us a Grand-Guignol version of an oriental Hedda Gabler with the diction of Termagant and the manners of a fishwife. Naturally we sympathize with Jason's desire to rid himself of her; it's a pity, we feel, that the Fleece involved him with her in the first place. But this is not to "adapt" Euripides, however freely. It is a kind of falsification. And it is the more annoying because one is constantly catching glimpses of what the poem might have been. In the greatest scene of all, culminating in Medea's farewell to her children, we come upon something very like the pathos of the Greek:

> *Look, their sweet lips are trembling: look, women, the*
> *little mouths: I frightened them*
> *With those wild words: they stood and faced me, they*
> *never flinched.*
> *Look at their proud young eyes! My eaglets, my golden*
> *ones! O sweet small faces ... like the pale wild roses*
> *That bloom where the cliff breaks toward the brilliant*
> *sea: the delicate form and color, the dear, dear*
> *fragrance*
> *Of your sweet breath ...*

Mentem mortalia tangunt; and if it is overdone (I do not admit that it is, up as far as the last colon) the precedent in this instance is unimpeachable.

I conclude, then, that although Mr. Jeffers can be effective, even memorably effective, at a low pitch, and can occasionally rise above himself to a genuinely eloquent pathos, he is in this poem incapable of tragic force. He lacks insight and control. His characters to him are speaking puppets, not fleshly men and women. He does not penetrate, he cannot sympathize. Jason-Medea, Medea-Kreon, Nurse-Medea: every one of the great agons goes shrill. The fact that this is not a translation, but a restatement, is irrelevant. He has chosen to retell one of the great stories of our heritage; but the result would have been as false if he had invented it all.

It is silly to talk about the Greek tragic poets as though they were bloodless golden creatures, moving with perfect poise through landscaped asphodel and bearing aloft that banner with the sad device MEDEN AGAN. We need no Aristophanes come back from the grave to tell us how often and how ludicrously they nodded. But it is equally false to treat them as though they were creatures of our own unbelieving suicidal age. *Numberless are the world's wonders,* sings Sophocles in the First Ode of *Antigonê;* and adds, *but none more wonderful than man.* It is this religious sense of the wonder of man that lifts the Medea of Euripides above the bloody fable that was its source. It recognizes the essential oneness of God and man; it represents that divine Philanthropy which informs the greatest art of Hellas.

Paul Goodman TARDY AND

PARTIAL RECOGNITION

AFTER fifty years, judging by continual revival among the literate and semi-literate, we probably must take Wilde to be the chief English general man of letters of his age. To this there is no doubt cause to sigh *Hélas* ("Hugo, hélas!") — yet there is the

A review of *Oscar Wilde* by Edouard Roditi (New York: New Directions Press, 1948).

fact, to conjure with or explain. If we consider that today Eliot and Gide, two minds far from first-rate—even, as they themselves understand, a little stupid—nevertheless rightly hold almost authoritative positions in English and French letters, we learn to expect that inconspicuous virtues and chances can combine to preeminence. The purpose of Roditi's little study of Wilde is "to indicate the central position that Wilde's works and ideas occupy in the thought and art of his age, and in the shift of English and American literature from established and aging Romanticism to what we now call modernism." This purpose he achieves, though in a schematic way, by drawing various historical lines and demonstrating his author to be in a synoptic and bestriding position, not merely an object of influence; since no one else has essayed this, his book for all its faults has value. More important than this academic purpose, however, is that Roditi takes Wilde seriously: that is, he often asks whether what Wilde says is true or false, relevant or irrelevant, tending to happiness or unhappiness. Obviously the explanation of the persistent revival of Wilde must come from such inquiries, and Roditi raises real problems. He does not solve them, he does not explain Wilde's importance to us nor, the same thing, what Wilde is and stands for. (I do not recall a book on Wilde that gives a less vivid notion of his spirit.) Partly this is because Roditi's own standards are sometimes unexamined and inconsistent and sometimes, I think, wrong, lifeless; partly it is because he does not carry out the academic job to the end, to show the peculiar creative power of his author as well as his literary-historical place—for if he would do this, he could not fail to reveal his importance to us; and also, without doing this one can never make clear, except schematically, how an author plays a central role at all. Frankly, I get the unhappy impression that Roditi dislikes Wilde, admires but dislikes him, certainly does not rejoice in him; he is offended by Wilde's popular appeal, grossly underestimates its importance, and thereby misses the center of Wilde's "central position."

I shall restrict myself to commenting on a few passages. Roditi says:

In the confusion of late Victorian criticism . . . Wilde's ingenious, imaginative, and vigorous dialectical thought appears monumental. Few critics in our own more critical age are gifted with his scholarship, his acumen, his stylistic brilliance . . . and especially his sense of philosophical structure, which places him at once in the same class as Matthew Arnold and Coleridge. . . . To prove conclusively Wilde's equality with Coleridge and Arnold would require as varied and detailed a comparative analysis of their ideas and methods as of Wilde's and this . . . would lead beyond the limitations of this book.

The encomium is just, but the last sentence is quite false. All that would be necessary, and this is where Roditi should have begun, would be to show Wilde *directly at grips* with Arnold on a single issue; and in fact the *Intentions* is a continual fight with *Culture and Anarchy*, etc., on every issue; then it would at once be seen that Wilde is much closer to social and personal reality than Arnold; that because he understands some politics he sees through the Philistinism, to its heart of violence, that Arnold only stands off from —all is not nearly so above-board as Arnold thinks; then he is able to hit the dynamic urgency and also the illusoriness (the "masks") of the imaginative and cultural life. Wilde, indeed, carries on the psychological exploration of the great early Romantics, with a new insight given by seeing the working out of industrialism, by a flair for social intercourse, an ambiguous emotional position, etc. Finally, we should see why the epigrams and paradoxes, vaguely understood by the public, and derided and called a formula by every smart aleck, still strike home.

Again, Roditi very adequately demonstrates the history and qualities of the Decadence, the exoticism, pictorialism, confusion of the senses and the genres. Oddly, but rather profitably, he equates the hypnotic evocative style with a kind of the old Sublime. But then, to one's astonishment, he fails to show how these hybrids were the appropriate engines of new subject matters and feelings— although in chapters on Wilde's ethics and politics he alludes to these subject matters very well; instead he condemns the mixtures on generic standards, and also condemns Wilde for not writing in prose, just as if he were Yvor Winters or somebody. Wilde was no vast poet, but what if one applied this method to Mallarmé? Surely the correct use of the structural method is first to feel very precisely what is conveyed by the whole and then to see what, in the parts, is essential to the conveyance, and also (if one wants to be censorious) what is inessential. Let me give a single example from the book: Roditi's mis-estimation of *Salome*. He starts with an excellent, I think quite original, analysis of the Dianoia of the *Poetics* as being not only the thoughts of the characters but the dialectic of persuasion throughout the play, explaining the character-change. Then suddenly we learn that *Salome* has no Dianoia and Salome is a "soulless doll":

> The plot of *Salome* is a mere "take it or leave it" affair, like that of a ballad or parable, and does not need ingenious devices to establish its probability or necessity; the whole play relies instead on lyrical quality. . . . Pageantry of staging and a diction where the sublime would offer a substitute for the catharsis were now the only elements capable of animating the plot. . . . And it is not surprising that one of Wilde's followers, Hugo von Hoffmannsthal, should have conceived his dramas so often as operas, and worked with Richard Strauss.

On the contrary, *Salome* is full of Dianoia and is terribly ingenious. Salome is not a soulless doll but a perverse child with a gnawing curiosity. The play has three long persuasions, but they are fruitless —this is why Roditi fails to see they are persuasions; but just the Dianoia of the play is that the persuasion *must* be fruitless because John is such a fanatic ox and this makes Salome's perversity compulsive, and Herod is an old fool who cannot pierce the rigidity. The bother with such a theme is that it threatens to be a bore on the stage, but Wilde accomplishes a miracle by means of high color and brevity. It would be grotesque to decide against the *theme* a priori, and in fact Wilde carries it off by moving a current of perverse suggestion under the entranced action. For the catharsis, when she says, "They say that love hath a bitter taste," do not the feelings flow? But how can Roditi imagine that Strauss's opera is the same play, when his Salome is a kind of neurotic Isolde, aged thirty, whereas Wilde's Salome is a child?

High praise is due Roditi's book for the importance he assigns to Wilde's political thought and to the Taoism central in it. He treats the politics as a development from an "ardent Ruskinian socialism" to a "consciously Taoist anarchism of inaction." Unfortunately he again makes certain errors, nor is it clear what his own standards are:

> In 1882 Wilde expressed sentimental and optimistic views about a Renaissance of art: industry should permit its workers to enjoy their art and produce, instead of the hideous wares of cheap and careless mass-production, beautiful objects which would satisfy their pride of craftsmanship. But his travels in America seem to have opened his eyes to the naive and other-worldly nature of this romantic socialism. . . . The discovery of Taoism made it possible for Wilde to transcend these political dilemmas.

Roditi misunderstands the nature of Taoist inaction or he would see that it does not transcend the art-socialism but makes it thoroughgoing. But even so far, is the Ruskin-Morris doctrine so sentimental and naïve? After three generations this doctrine, practically unchanged, is advanced as the only social salvation by more persons than ever believed it in Wilde's time; it has received psychoanalytical and progressive-pedagogic reinforcements; and I do not think that a reader of *News from Nowhere*, with its prelude in the chaos that must precede the acceptance of such a simple idea, would say that it was advanced optimistically, or naïvely. In an eloquent passage on Bohemia and Revolution, Roditi avers that "Most of us have become, through habit, quite insensitive to the full horror of our industrial Inferno and of the many wiles whereby Satan deceives us into believing that he does not exist." If in face of Hell, one asks in surprise, why were Ruskin, Morris, and Wilde naïve and idealistic? If in straits of despair, was it absurd for Ruskin to sell tea canisters and Wilde to display a sunflower? Then, as to the Taoism, Roditi seems to think the doctrine is individualistic and quietist; but on the contrary, it is an affirmation of basic nature, the energy of man and society both, and results often in simple direct action. The meaning of Taoist inaction is not contemplation but to "create a Void" by putting unnatural social conventions and neurotic personal wishes out of the way, in order that life can breathe. The Sage is not ineffectual but, to quote Wilde's fine review of Chuangtze, "He does not try to bring about his own good deeds"; he is "the unconscious vehicle of a higher illumination": "do nothing and everything will be done." (It is too bad, by the way, that Roditi does not take the opportunity to show the Void-creating force of some of the paradoxes, not dissimilar in kind from the paradoxes of the Way.)

Speaking of the comedies, Roditi says,

> It is almost as if these plays were the work of two authors, of Oscar Wilde writing the dialogue, so similiar in style and tone to his own conversation or Lord Henry's, and of some hack, the "spirit of the age," that supplied Wilde with the plots and all the emotional scenes and tirades. But the hack was Oscar Wilde himself, harried by his creditors and his own expensive habits, desperately anxious to achieve commercial success.

Now this judgment must occur to every cultivated reader; yet it is false. For the fact is that fifty years have passed and the "spirit of the age," the "concession to the bad taste of his own times," is still manifesting vitality, a most accomplished hack! The solution is, I think, simple and fundamental to every Wilde problem: In the center of Wilde's genius was the popular, to be a popularizer, to play with what was publicly accepted and comprehensible. Not to tell people what they wanted to hear, that is to be a hack; an artist must be himself; but that he could be himself, his peculiarly ambivalent self, most in the glancing milieu of social attention and hoped-for social approval. Or to put it another way: Wilde had a genius for showmanship, but what he was showing off was not a commercial product but a social idea of Morris', or an aesthetic idea of Pater's, some idea deeply felt in himself. Unlike a hack, or a Philistine, or a social critic, Wilde was able to give to the social forms his lively attention; and to create voids everywhere. (This was his pathos: that he could make so many little voids, but could not void his own great personal and social obstacles.) It was not by accident that he dwelt so much on clothes and furniture, or edited a fashion magazine, or that it was in reviewing trivia that he said some of his best things. Today we see how another artist-showman, Cocteau, is belatedly trying to play his theatre tricks in the fields of corn; far more inventive than Wilde, he is not so truly to the manor born.

This point, his flair to live out publicly his idea, is capital for the details of Wilde's biography. It is absurd to blame his expensive habits for conflicting with his art, when it was rather his central creative art that made him live as he did; he could not write drawing-room plays and stories without also living in the best drawing room possible. And it was the same creative impulse that pushed him into the apparently pointless trial and the singular refusal to take flight: the need to come closer to a more social, more public reality in order to be himself. When Roditi says,

> Wilde began to justify on aesthetic grounds actions which he did not have the courage to justify on the ethical grounds of a less Victorian or more revolutionary philosophy,

he turns everything upside down. To a man who, like the tattooed savage, makes his own body and clothes an art object, the aesthetic will always express the morally relevant better than the ethical; and how could such a man have a less Victorian ethics so long as he lived in a Victorian drawing room? On the contrary, Wilde tried to syncretize any action whatever into the public ethics (and even public law) just as he imported chinoiseries and japonaiseries into the drawing room, till ethics and furnishings both became a hideous chaos. But Wilde expressed his true creative good, a new simplification, when, listening to the prosecutor, he thought in a flash: "How splendid it would be if I were saying all this about myself!"

(In general in his psychological remarks, Roditi stresses the self-punishing and guilt, and he thinks that, to be consistent, Wilde should have evolved an ethics of the utility of degradation, both degradation of lusts and degradation of penalty; and surely this masochism loomed large in Wilde, as in every thwarted vital soul; also it is evident that the self-destructiveness is part of the public's fascination with the Wilde story. Yet in the end, I think not. The question turns on the meaning of Wilde's particular rationalizations (the boys are Greek athletes, etc.). Deeper than their purpose as defenses against self-degradation, these express a dumb longing for the true Golden Age of innocent sexuality from which he was cut off: the tao, the realm of childish magic. I would urge that this is the center of his whole art and thought.)

There is no space to pursue these matters further. I trust I have not been too rough with Roditi's book, for it is certainly full of real thought and experience, far more than any of the others in this series that I have read. Technically: it is not well written, I take this to be the fault of haste and excessive condensation. Its scholarship is sometimes eccentrically personal (as when he speaks of the dialogues "of St. Augustine and of Leone Ebreo"), and sometimes vastly overdone, as though he were inviting one to his particolored pavilions. On the other hand, Roditi dignifies a subject worthy of dignity by refusing to place it in the parochial setting of most such books of criticism.

Irving Howe THE COST OF

DISTRACTION

OF A. E. HOUSMAN, John Peale Bishop wrote: "What Housman told the reader is clear. But there is much that he would not, and while he lived could not, tell him. Of the suffering we have no doubt, but something, it seems, has been suppressed that it is essential to know of the particular situation of the human sufferer." Perhaps if we replaced "suppressed" by "scattered," these words could stand as the nub of one's response to Bishop's own work. There is sufficient cause for admiration in these essays: their gentle learning, quick taste and wit; but something is greatly missed—a controlling center, a motor passion or idea, to pull them into a unity. As it is, they seem less a unity than interludes between

A review of *The Collected Essays of John Peale Bishop* edited by Edmund Wilson (New York: Charles Scribner's Sons, 1948).

distraction and sometimes even the occasions of distraction. Bishop seems to have been aware of his lack of intellectual center; he called one of his more ambitious essays a dramatized dialectic on the Hemingway-Fitzgerald generation that is full of self-reference, "the Missing All." Regard that phrase in the light of his mulled relationship to Hemingway and Fitzgerald, set it off against its original context in Emily Dickinson, and you have the high profit of irony to which scrupulous self-perception can be worked.

Before having read Bishop in bulk, I had vaguely thought of him as related to the "Southern writers" and (if only through intellectual marriage) the "new critics"; but he is not so easily pegged. He wrote the expected essay on "The South and Tradition" with its fractured tribute to "a manner of living somewhat more amiable than any other that has ever been known on this continent," and its far more consequential quarrel with the conditions of modern life. The quarrel is impressive, but I must confess to finding the tribute, in good part, sentimental and desperate; how, one wonders, can a man of sensibility pass by the gnawing fact that "the somewhat more amiable" manner of living rested upon and, in the given circumstances, could only rest upon a social organization that doomed an entire people to chattel slavery? (Faulkner does not pass that fact by, and it gnaws him no end.) I raise this question not, at the moment, to stir a political quarrel but rather to inquire into a condition of compartmentalized feeling—and, yes, I know Bishop disapproved of slavery.

But as one reads further into the essay, one notices a sharp and sudden shift in its perspective; it is no longer the work of a Southerner, but of a shrewd and moralistic New Englander who points to the decline of Southern statesmanship from Jefferson to Davis. Perhaps the explanation is that it has been a West Virginian writing all along, and nobody splits himself better than a West Virginian.

In any case, the "Southern Myth" has to a large extent been willed, which is to say not a myth at all but an induced political-literary sentiment—and with Bishop far more the issue of his sense of alienation than of instinctively received feeling. The pulse of tradition does not beat as passionately in his work, metering and fortifying it, as in Tate's poetry or Faulkner's novels; one suspects that Bishop had to go hunting for what should, ideally, have been at immediate hand. But how sustaining can a sense of tradition be when it has first to be retrieved?

An analogous difficulty can be seen in his criticism. In a very fine essay, "The Infanta's Ribbon," he used Renoir's remark that "all painting is in the pink ribbon of the dress of the Infanta" as a base for some brilliant observations on the nature of art: the tensed relationship between logic and structure, meaning and sequence, language and silence. In doctrine, this essay is probably close enough to the ideas of the "new critics" to be legitimately claimed by them, but in its romantic feeling and the method of its organization is quite unlike their work. Since Bishop is far less concerned with strategies for analysis than openings for insight, his work is not dominated by a rigorous set of concepts and terms; usually he trusts to his taste, waiting with an almost pristine curiosity for a spontaneous collision between his sensibility and the work of art. His talent is for the epigram rather than exegesis, he condenses rather than exfoliates meanings; his triumphs are in phrases and sentences—and whatever the triumphs of the "new critics" they are hardly capsuled.

Bishop thinks in terms of scarcely formulated tensions and conflicts, searching for them in works of art as if driven by a need to find what is already in himself (as which critic is not?) and then to confront his sense of cultural fragmentation with the ultimate resolutions of art. He is therefore tempted to make some of his essays into mimetic surrogates of the works under discussion, carefully modelled and quasi-dramatic responses in which an essay's formal organization is as much part of the critical act as its thought. Such writing, itself a symptom of tension, might be called criticism by the sympathetic gesture.

At a number of points Bishop verges on historical criticism. The middle class, which "if it does not admire hideousness . . . can certainly stand having a great deal of it around," becomes the villain threatening the life of culture. Since this notion has been central and fertile in the criticism of the past century, it is curious that Bishop can make so little of it. He is, to be sure, heavily oppressed by a sense of history, a sense that, at least until recently, has not come easily to Americans. Like Fitzgerald, he is drawn to

Europe, seeing it both as attraction and threat. And looming over most of his work is his acute consciousness of belonging to the generation of Fitzgerald and Hemingway, which to him means being trapped at a dead end.

Now for a writer this sense of history may be a mooring of relevance or distraction's nibbling rat; it may be at his core or picked up by reading Eliot. For Bishop it is never completely any of these; it is pervasive but unformed, worrying but unusable, a wound rather than a vision. Bishop's beautiful awareness of the interaction between Europe and America is at least as acute as and far less marred by prejudice than Edmund Wilson's, but Bishop cannot use it with a fraction of the effectiveness that Wilson can. Wilson worked his sense of history into an idea of history, which could serve him both to guard sensibility and filter experience. At the other pole, Allen Tate worked his sense of history into an idea against history, a reason for madness, which served his ends as well. But Bishop, less coherent than Wilson and more reasonable than Tate, was left exposed to history as a buffet, history as a disordered and disordering affront. The more deeply he felt about it, the more it distracted him; he had no difficulty in reacting to his world, he had immense difficulty in ordering his reactions.

Through his essays there run two recurrent phrases: "intensity" and "aware of his time." He uses them as critical touchstones in pieces on Housman, MacNeice, Cummings, Arnold, a host of others. They reveal more about Bishop than about his subjects: he strained for and seldom achieved intensity, he was oppressed by his awareness of the times. It would be stacking one's cards too much in so speculative a review as this to say that it is "not accidental" that his essay on Matthew Arnold (his Jacob-figure wrestling with the angel of history) is unfinished; yet it makes for a neat if accidental symbol. The term "alienated" is now in as great disrepute as it was in favor only a few years ago, but I think Bishop must be seen as one of the most alienated American intellectuals of the twentieth century. Much came to him, little sustained him.

If, however, we take the essays as discrete performances, a great deal remains. The pieces on Hemingway and Wolfe are probably unsurpassed, for he knew them as well as he knew himself. In bullfighting Hemingway "saw his apprehension reduced to a ritual" and as a true novelist, "in searching for the meaning of his own unsought experience, he comes on the moral history of our time." Wolfe "achieved probably the utmost intensity of which incoherent writing is capable. . . ." Bishop's taste is remarkably fine; he had, to cite a simple example, enough wit and sense to admire *Moll Flanders* intensely, unlike our latter-day dons; his reviews, especially of poetry, survive as miniature essays, which is what reviews should usually be.

And then there is his gift for the aphorism and epigram, unequalled by any recent American critic. On T. S. Eliot: "One might escape his conclusions, which were singularly inconclusive, and reject his solutions, which solved none but his personal problems; but one could escape his premises only at the risk of rejecting the truth." Or: "That verse is most interesting in which the beat of the sentence runs counter to the beat of the verse; but in order to make sure of this, the beat of the verse must constantly be felt." Or: "If the critic mounts the soapbox, the garbage remains in the street." Bishop never quite reached mastery at this sort of thing, for while the aphorist can afford to be cryptic, even gnomic, he can never be uncertain.

Finally, I find myself admiring Bishop for the honesty and rigor with which he seems to have faced his own dilemma. There is no evidence that he succumbed to any of the beckoning panaceas that must have tempted him; he was in a fix, he knew it, he did the best he could. In one poem he wrote: "There was One who might have saved/Me from these grave dissolute stones/And parrot eyes. But He is dead. . . ." These are, for Bishop, words of some courage. In another poem he wrote: "The ceremony must be found/that will wed Desdemona to the huge moor." The ceremony was not found. Well, there are worse defeats, more ignoble ends. It was hardly his fault that to be a man of culture and cultivation, even as excellent a one as he, was in our age not quite enough.

William Barrett ARISTOCRACY

AND/OR CHRISTIANITY

ONE first and natural question might be: What has happened to Eliot's prose? The process, of course, has been going on for some time, and this book is no sudden lapse from its last predecessor; but one sees here what looks like the end of a process, if one compares this to a previous, very brief, but perhaps more important pronouncement on culture: the essay on Marie Lloyd (1923). The syntax of single sentences may be more precise, but the movement from sentence to sentence within the paragraph hardly exists: the concision, vigor, and crackle of the early essays is gone. There is now something cut up and pasted together about this style: it never flows. One imagines the book put together as a series of letters to the *Church Times*; and if one did not know the author, one might imagine him as some fastidious, very literate, and sorrowfully exacerbated vicar writing from the fastness of his parish study somewhere in rural England. A clergyman's stoop inhabits this prose. Alas, it also inhabits the thought. The loss of vigor in the prose reflects the loss of vigor in the mind.

The intelligence cannot be isolated from the rest of the personality; when the energy of the person declines, the intelligence can no longer push its questions far enough to lay hold of all that is implicit in its thoughts: it can, in short, no longer grasp a full

A review of *Notes Towards the Definition of Culture* by T. S. Eliot (New York: Harcourt, Brace & Company, 1949).

position but only the fragment of one. Eliot propounds what might be conveniently described as the aristocratic theory of culture, and in this respect reminds us of Ortega y Gasset. Given Eliot's intelligence, sensibility, and lifelong preoccupation with the problem of culture, one would expect from him a book comparable to *The Revolt of the Masses* (which very much bears rereading). But the present book will bear no such comparison. Where Ortega, overflowing with vigor, is the authentic aristocrat, daring to grasp his position at its source—"Life is by its nature aristocratic"—and thus communicating to us the sense of a man living within the full density of his time, we get from Eliot a kind of crabbed and narrow hesitation, perpetually boxing itself in by qualifications and provisoes. Behind Ortega, of course, there is Nietzsche, the philosopher who has dealt most profoundly with the problem of culture. Eliot's failure to make explicit use of Nietzsche's thought is a very serious deficiency, since the questions Nietzsche dared to raise lurk unasked in the background; and unless these questions are asked and answered, Eliot's views on culture do not add up to a real position but remain only a nostalgic lament for a vanished class or a Conservative's cantankerous protest at the social processes now going on in Labor England. In this review I should like to point out the precise places in Eliot's argument where these questions must be raised.

Eliot's thought on culture can be summed up very briefly as the belief that there are two necessary conditions without which a higher culture can neither arise nor continue: (1) a stable and hereditary class society, and (2) religion. Let us consider each of these in turn.

An argument may begin formally with its first premise, but behind that premise there is always some initial datum that launches the whole chain of thought and gives it its real direction. The concrete datum behind Eliot's discussion is the perception of the world-wide decline of culture during the last half century:

> We can assert with some confidence that our own period is one of decline; that the standards of culture are lower than they were fifty years ago; and that the evidences of this decline are visible in every department of human activity.

It is well that Eliot, who has not lacked for rewards at the hands of this culture, should damn it so unequivocally; when others have made this sad point, people object that it is somehow an expression of resentment. Our smug young literati, lulled in the euphoria of their last inspiration, don't want to be disturbed in their belief that they are living in the midst of a great creative renaissance. Eliot's description seems to me, so far as the artistic and philosophic parts of our culture are concerned, incontestable. There is one part of our culture, however, which he fails consistently to refer to throughout his discussion, and that is science. I do not know whether this general decline has also affected science. True, we do not hear of great theoretical minds producing new and surprising unifications of knowledge; but this may be simply a result of the progress of science itself: as science becomes more complex and specialized, the great unifying genius no longer appears or he functions within a much more restricted scope. The advance of science as an institution might entail this decline (or limitation) in individual genius. The question would have to be examined by people who are in a position to know. I bring up the question of scientific culture because it points toward two problems that Eliot gives no indication of having faced in this book. (1) The decline of our culture in certain areas may be due to the fact (noted long ago by I. A. Richards) that in our civilization the best brains are no longer drawn, as they once were, to literature and philosophy but to science and technology. (2) It may be that as science and technology dominate a given culture, the quality of art must deteriorate. The two habits of mind may be fundamentally opposed. That is, we may have to choose between a more primitive, organic, irrational culture, which will be the soil out of which great art will grow, or a more rational, less imaginative culture that produces science as its highest expression. Nietzsche posed this decisive question and made his choice; Eliot gives the impression of having chosen without having raised the question.

But granting fully this initial datum of a cultural decline, I cannot see that Eliot has explored it very concretely or profoundly. What has caused the decline? The processes of democratization, with their consequent levelling of standards, are obvious factors; but it would be important to know the precise social mechanisms and channels through which this levelling has operated. Eliot criticizes Matthew Arnold's *Culture and Anarchy* for its thinness of social background. But in fact Arnold was addressing himself to a definite social group, the middle classes at the height of their stability and prosperity, and his exhortations had thus a potentially practical reference, and therefore much more direct social relevance than Eliot's discussion. Eliot seems to think that his own thinness of social background is filled out by a few references to primitive culture and anthropology.

The central fact about the democratizing of culture is the presence of the masses themselves on the historical scene. Eliot never puts the fact (the "social background" behind his whole discussion) so bluntly; we have to go to Ortega for the frank recognition of the situation:

> Werner Sombart laid stress on a very simple fact, which I am surprised is not present to every mind which meditates on contemporary events. This very simple fact is sufficient of itself to clarify our vision of the Europe of today, or if not sufficient, puts us on the road to enlightenment. The fact is this: from the time European history begins in the VIth Century up to the year 1800—that is, through the course of twelve centuries— Europe does not succeed in reaching a total population greater than 180 million inhabitants. Now, from 1800 to 1914—little more than a century—the population of Europe mounts from 180 to 460 millions! I take it that the contrast between these figures leaves no doubt as to the prolific qualities of the last century. In three generations it produces a gigantic mass of humanity, which, launched like a torrent over the historic area, has inundated it.

Anyone who wants to meditate about the history of culture would do well to walk any afternoon in the vicinity of Times Square. Where do all these crowds come from? How do they fill their day? What is to be done with them? Technology has created these masses, but has not yet given them the leisure to acquire the disciplines of a decent or higher culture. In the historic interval (through which we now live) technology steps forward to fill this gap: it provides mechanical means to provide the masses with entertainment and culture and to conceal from them their boredom and vacuity: the radio, movies, television. But these mass media, it must be pointed out, exist because there is a *class* of clever entrepreneurs who are glad to exploit for their own profit the rest of society. Humanity would probably be better off if the radio, cinema, and television were abolished; but I doubt that this reform could be carried through without there being a literal revolt of the masses: the crowds milling about Times Square to get into the movies would tear up the pavements. The aristocratic theorist of culture must face the question of what is to be done with the masses. Here Nietzsche, frankly accepting the consequences of his position, expresses hope in the advent of a new and vigorous aristocracy to conquer the masses. Eliot is unable to push his thought this far: so far as practical means are concerned, he merely hints that perhaps we shall not hasten to extend the opportunities of education and literacy. A measure which would, at best, leave us with exactly the culture that we now have.

With all the talk in recent years about ends and means, there is one old and simple axiom that everyone seems to have forgotten: he who wills the end wills the means. Of course, the means necessary for a given end may involve evil so enormous that it outweighs all the good that the end could possibly bring. But then we have to relinquish the end altogether, and we cannot go on talking nostalgically as if we still had a real will to it. No doubt, the masses—in their sheeplike quality of masses—ask to be conquered; but they will submit only to the conquerors who are their own demagogues. The new conquering aristocracy, if it is to come everywhere in the world, will probably come in the Russian form. Eliot is obviously out of touch with things that have happened in Russia, for he does not yet know that the governing elite in Russia has solidified itself legally as a class. The cultural decrees of this new ruling class should warn us that an aristocratic and ruling class may just as well barbarize culture as refine it. Indeed, what humanity has most to fear in this historic period—and for reasons of life rather than of culture—is the emergence of a new class society.

In the meantime Eliot's thought is really turned nostalgically to an aristocratic class that is almost dead and has not made its presence felt in British culture since the first half of the eighteenth century. Hegel said, "World history is the world tribunal"—a statement which is usually reviled as a sophisticated equivalent for Might Makes Right. But there is another way of taking Hegel's statement which brings to our attention that the point of departure for all our thinking must be what is, the actual, and that the lament for lost causes becomes, after a certain point, mere self-indulgence. To put it bluntly: the aristocratic class that Eliot admires had its historic chance. It is dead, or all but dead now, because it was not strong enough to maintain itself in existence. To wish for a new class that will embody the values of a past class is another piece of very unrealistic thinking: a ruling class comes into existence historically not to provide a culture but to conquer the most primary problems of life that the previous society could not cope with. The new class, in the overflow of its energy, *may* bring a new culture to the society, but the problem of culture is posterior to the problem of power.

Eliot's argument for a class society is that a stable class structure is needed for the transmission of culture. To understand this argument one must understand the very concrete sense in which he uses the word "culture":

> It includes all the characteristic activities and interests of a people: Derby Day, Henley Regatta, Cowes, the twelfth of August, a cup final, the dog races, the pin table, the dart board, Wensleydale cheese, boiled cabbage cut into sections, beetroot in vinegar, nineteenth-century Gothic churches and the music of Elgar.

> Culture may even be described simply as that which makes life worth living.

Culture, as the totality of so many concrete habits and manners, is not something capable of being transmitted through books. Hence, the stability needed in the society in which the young person grows up. I think we can grant this much of the argument, but the further conclusion as to the necessary existence of a class structure in society does not follow. All that would be needed would be stable family groups (unless no other agencies of transmission are developed) and stable social groups (communities rather than classes) within the larger society, and of course sufficient leisure. In the aristocracies of the past one social group monopolized the leisure of the whole society. Out of this leisure they created a dignity, ease, and spaciousness in their lives, which could become material for art. The premise on which the concept of a classless society, with a high level of culture, rests is that the society is one of sufficient abundance to provide everyone with enough leisure to lead a dignified life. This level has not yet been reached anywhere in the world, and it may never be reached, but there is nothing in Eliot's argument to indicate that a classless society could not coincide with a high level of culture.

A classless society may be impossible on other grounds. At the present time it is so far in the future that one wonders why the prospect of it should give Eliot such immediate and pressing anxiety. There seems to be a curious oscillation in his thought between two chief centers of his interest: the past that ended with the middle of the eighteenth century, and a very remote, perhaps unrealizable future. In the course of this oscillation he is only rarely and remotely in touch with the present.

Pushing beyond the question of culture itself, we have to ask about the fundamental consistency of Eliot's two leading ideas: Can aristocracy and Christianity really be consistently combined? Here again, it is useful to recall Nietzsche's forthrightness: holding that culture becomes valuable as it becomes aristocratic, and that *Christianity was democratic*, Nietzsche therefore rejected Christianity. "Life itself," Nietzsche said, "is a process of exploitation, and since I am on the side of life, I am against Christianity." Eliot, however, believes that Christianity and exploitation are perfectly compatible. Now, this might be maintained for a society, like that of feudal Europe, which existed at a very limited level of material production. An equal distribution of goods and opportunity might have made impossible the achievement of certain valuable things which that society has left us. Moreover, it might be argued that the serf, contented to be a serf, had his equal rights in heaven: if the important thing is sanctity, then it may be achieved at the lowest material level of society, and the whole society is therefore Christian. Thus Christianity could fit itself into a class society like feudalism. I doubt that it can follow the same line today, when the serf has been brought to the level of consciousness and knows what he misses in life. If natural faculties exist, and it lies within the limits of the possible to cultivate them, then we are bound to do so. To discount the importance of, and the obligation to develop, natural God-given capacities is a variant of the heresy of the complete denial of the flesh. Eliot, however, seems to be willing to indulge in this heresy in a brief attack on what he calls "the mute inglorious Milton dogma"—the idea that if education is not widely available, certain natural talents may never be brought to fruition. Eliot ought to know that the word "dogma" is misused here, since it is a word intended to denote matters of faith beyond any possible empirical verification, while it is a simple biological fact that capacities appear in a species quite sporadically and without respect to human groupings. For the Christian, his life in this world may be unimportant in comparison with eternity; but, on the other hand, it is also all-important, since it is the life led on earth that determines the quality of his life hereafter; and that an individual may be brought to the level where he is aware of a life he might lead with capacities he possesses, while society at the same time does not make it possible for him to realize these capacities, may lead to such exacerbated emotions that a life sufficiently virtuous for salvation becomes impossible. The clever young man of the lower classes, resentful at his hard lot and the opportunities he has missed, should be a familiar enough figure to Eliot from the novels of D. H. Lawrence and others. What does Eliot propose to do with this young man? Push him back below the level where he would no longer even know the desire to be educated? Would that be Christian? Or would Eliot give him the opportunity of self-cultivation by expropriating a few more gentry? Would that be aristocratic? The snob and the Christian are obviously in conflict in Eliot and, though he makes no decisive choice between them, his sympathies seem to lean toward the snob.

It is unfortunate that this tone of snobbism (reminding us so often of Evelyn Waugh) should become insistent particularly when Eliot is on the subject of religion. It is time that protest was made against this morally patronizing tone with which the believer feels called upon to address the unbeliever. It seems to be assumed that anyone who is not a believing Christian is so because of irresponsibility, an unwillingness to take religion seriously. I should like to insist on the opposing fact: that there are people who have examined religion carefully, who know that their life would be much easier for them if they could adopt a belief like Catholic Christianity, but whose moral conscience forbids them to do so. As long as there are people who think and feel this way, it is doubtful whether Christianity can become what it once was and what Eliot hopes it will be again: a structure of belief binding together all members of society.

This is the aspect in which the question of religion is related to the question of culture. Viewed concretely, religion is the way of life of a people and in this sense is identical with the people's culture. It follows from this that Eliot's contention that culture cannot exist without religion is an analytic truth; and Eliot himself makes the rather remarkable admission that an "irreligiously" religious culture might exist:

> Britain, if it consummated its apostasy by reforming itself according to the prescriptions of some inferior or materialistic religion, might blossom into a culture more brilliant than that we can show today.

Elsewhere, of course, Eliot seems to forget this, and his insistence on the necessity of religion for culture is specifically connected with the continuation (or revival) of the Christian religion. It is important to stick to this concrete meaning of belief: beliefs, if they mean anything for life, must be attitudes that are lived; and when we examine, from this point of view, Christianity as it now exists among the urban populace of the world, we must entertain some doubts as to its real fruitfulness for culture. It is doubtful that Christianity in its primitive, naïve, and vigorous sense (the only sense out of which great Christian art came) can live again in a populace that is used to turning on the radio, tinkering with automobiles, or thinking of gadgets. The urban believers I know among the lower classes go to church as a matter of course, but the real center of their consciousness is elsewhere. They are further removed from the Christians of the last Age of Faith than are contemporary atheists. At the present time Christianity *lives* as a faith only among peasant populations—and some intellectuals. Thus, Eliot's quarrel turns out again to be basically with our technological civilization. In the background of his discussion is the image of a fundamentally agrarian society, with a stalwart Christian peasantry, and a very much less numerous population. But this image can be translated into a real position relevant to our problems of life, society, and culture now only if Eliot is willing to recommend (or countenance) a drastic reduction all over the world of the populations that our technological civilization supports. He who wills the end must will the means; or, as Aristotle put it, our deliberation about human affairs is significant only if confined to the practicable.

R. W. Flint I WILL TEACH YOU

MY TOWNSPEOPLE

THAT initial prejudice which sees mainly the rube or the clown behind every new irruption of provincial experience into major modes of poetry is a well-established and perhaps even a necessary phase in the complex dialectic by which good new poets are assimilated. Frost's entrance on the scene was too gentle and well-prepared to stir up a row, but it is incredible to read now about what Robinson had to contend with. Dr. Williams brought with him the scientifically trained, experimental, romantic-idealist mind *in extremis*, and the bulk of his work exerts itself, in one

A review of the following books by William Carlos Williams: *Paterson: Book III* (New York: New Directions Press, 1949); *A Dream of Love* (New York: New Directions Press, 1948); *The Clouds* (Wells College and Cummington Presses, 1948). Also a review of *William Carlos Williams* by Vivienne Koch (New York: New Directions Press, 1950).

way or another, in undermining the premises on which this mind was originally constituted. Whitman dispensed apples and candies; Williams has dealt out harsher treatments in less glamorous circumstances. He is a more sober man than Crane and a more experienced man than either Frost or Robinson in the American subject. He is also more contemporary, breathing hot down the collar of the times, than any poet before him has ever been, though Mr. Blackmur's description of him in 1939 as "the quotidian burgeoning without trace of yesterday" perhaps crowds even the conceivable.

Of the best reviews of Williams (Yvor Winters in *Primitivism and Decadence*; R. P. Blackmur in *The Expense of Greatness*; Randall Jarrell in *Partisan Review* Sept. 1946, and his Introduction to the Selected Poems; Robert Lowell in *The Nation* June 19, 1948, and *Sewanee Review* Summer 1947; Richard Wilbur in *Sewanee Review* Winter 1950) that I've seen, the first two and the last handle the poetry with more than a touch of condescension, hinting somewhat loftily of miracles and magic. Mr. Winters and Mr. Blackmur have their time-honored definition of knowledge, roughly Aristotelian and university-centered, against which Dr. Williams appears a perplexed and perplexing freak, while Mr. Jarrell, at the other extreme, starts with an *ad hominem* appeal to the poet himself, defining the poet's knowledge as his whole equipment of experience, tact, and character. The canon surely is able to accommodate both emphases. The situation which the two elder of these accounts, and those like them, provoked plays a controlling part in Williams's latest work, supplying him with his deliberately obsessive theme of "the university," a volatile abstraction which replaces the "Puritans" of his earlier work as a negative pole and generator of tension. Here is a typical diatribe from *Paterson*:

> clerks
> got out of hand forgetting for the most part
> to whom they are beholden,
> spitted on fixed concepts like
> roasting hogs, sputtering, their drip sizzling
> in the fire

Now, woe to the reader who doesn't see himself in this, who can't enjoy its rhetoric, or who takes it as an unqualified historical truth!

Examined from the perspective of an ideal academic poet like, say, Bridges, Dr. Williams appears to be groping about under a very low ceiling indeed. But none of us, fortunately, are ideal readers and only the peculiarly willful can fail to enjoy Dr. Williams's saving incoherence. Truthfully pleading his inability to handle traditional coin traditionally, Williams improvises, issues a fluid currency of his own; in *Paterson*, a set of protean, imagist-symbolist centers of force which polarize his loose, fragmentary material. By extending his lines so far into "the sticks," Williams has naturally been forced to depend more on conventionally popular responses to guide his private and poetic conduct than have either Eliot or Pound; consequently the unexamined and misunderstood more often obtrudes itself on the surface. But where Eliot and Pound are often only at the mercy of the times, Williams has been able to use them fresh and piecemeal, with that "empirical gaiety" which Mr. Jarrell aptly describes. He is perhaps the finest artistic by-product of American applied science: those who complain of his lack of order should consider how many orderly procedures, fit for sublimation into a poet's vision and technique, are involved in the work of a doctor. I would concede to Mr. Winters that Williams is a "primitive" when he has to assume, against common sense, that his protean, mythical, personified symbols are more than poetically "true." Luckily, however, his common sense is considerable and able to withstand a deal of shock.

It may be simply the effect of time, but at this writing *Paterson* I seems to me better than *Paterson* II and both of them better than *Paterson* III, though the difference is small. What cannot be enough insisted on is that in this poetry, which operates by what Crane called "metaphorical logic," the whole is always greater than the sum of parts. *Paterson is planned*, though more loosely than *Ulysses, Four Quartets*, or the Cantos. Successive books have worked fresh material into the mythic, rhythmic, and metaphorical pattern established in the first, so that the effect, though cumulative, is not oppressively so. We don't feel the clouds of a portentous Greatness gathering over us. *Paterson* is strongest when its philosophy is submerged in fact and lyric, weakest when it moves toward the Wallace Stevens of *Notes Toward a Supreme Fiction*. Williams seems to sense this instinctively; it is interesting to note the differ-

ence between his lyric from *Patterson* II, "Without invention nothing is well spaced . . ." as it moves through a danger zone of
rather flat speculation to his own style of lyric observation:

> *without invention*
> *nothing lies under the witch-hazel*
> *bush, the alder does not grow from among*
> *the hummocks. . . .*

and Pound's hyper-traditional "Learn of the green world what can
be thy place/In scaled invention or true artistry." Pound evokes
the green world through the power of abstract words to summon
up essences; Williams, with the same respect for language, projects
the green world itself; two complementary techniques.

To recapitulate: Book I, starting and ending with a meditation
by the Falls (the stream of unredeemed, overwhelming, circumstantial, multifariously active life and thought), swelled by "qualitative progression," episode vibrating against episode, into an evocation of an age of wonders in the city's youth: against which he
counterpoints a varied, elusive portrait of the poem's female antagonist, *das ewig Weibliche*, in whom the Age of Giants lives
submerged. "Rigor of beauty is the quest," as in the Cantos, but
this can only transpire in a semi-mystical "marriage" (echoes of
The Bridge). A spiralist rather than a simple cyclist in his theory
of history, Williams is committed to a candid view of what has
happened to Paterson, man and city, in the present; change *and*
recurrence.

> *the modern town, a*
>
> *disembodied roar! the cataract and*
> *its clamor broken apart—and from*
> *all learning, the empty*
> *ear struck from within, roaring.*

Book II sends the protagonist strolling through the Park
(female to the city) on a Sunday afternoon in spring, a stroll which
develops into a complex and bitter act of love. Several approxima-
tions and outright failures of love engage him along the way, notably
an amusing but sentimental caricature of "religion" in the person
of a ranting evangelist, and a running undertow of reproach

from a "lacerated and lacerating poetess" (Lowell)—which I
found movingly appropriate in its detailed Hardyesque vigor. Her
loss of love brings with it loss of poetic, though not epistolary,
language. Williams, if you like, uses the "poetry of prose" to extend his metaphors and graduate his intensity. It fails if it is simply
documentary and illustrative and not food for meditation; it must
share in the general metaphorical scheme. And Williams's metaphorical scheme is so wide and general that almost any prose
excerpt will fit, provided it is well enough placed and sensitively
written. (Parts of Book III, however, seem to toy dangerously with
mere documentation.)

Although Book III may be too "philosophical" to quite match
the other two, one has confidence in Williams's method and is
ready to suspend judgment until the pattern is complete. The
purgatorial mood of much of Book II has deepened; wind, destroying and transforming fire, and the "sullen, leaden, the silken
flood . . ." dominate the action. In a gentle episode reminiscent
of James's "The Great Good Place," Mr. Paterson retires to the
city library:

> *Spent from wandering the useless*
> *streets these months, faces folded against*
> *him like clover at nightfall, something*
> *has brought him back to his own*
>   *mind*

Soon, his perusal of old records, augmented by memories, stirs up
a mounting anger—crassness, drowned children, tortured Indians,
etc. Against the rising storm appear brief, intermittent flashes of
beauty: a woman, the thought of poetry, "the dazzled half sleepy
eyes/of some trusting animal . . . ," a roof lifted by the wind from
a burning house; all reaching its clearest focus in the "you," addressed by the poet as "my dove, my changeling," a girl encountered
in a basement, a girl in a white dress, mysteriously "unable," yet
without whom the library is a loss. Finally, the flood and fire
subside, and:

> *I cannot stay here*
> *to spend my life looking into the past:*

> *the future's no answer, I must*
> *find my meaning and lay it, white*
> *beside the sliding water; myself—*
> *comb out the language—or succumb*

If the philosophical observations and their somewhat puzzling use of Dürer, the lost poems of Sappho and the brothel-existence of Toulouse-Lautrec, their yanking into context of Artaud, now mad, of the "theatre of cruelty" (and an amusing letter from Pound telling him to stick to the classics and forget Artaud) seem a bit old-fashioned arty, they may subside into place with later readings and are, at any rate, amply redeemed by the fine kinesthetic energy of wind, fire and water. He ends on an apocalyptic note:

> *Loosen the flesh*
> *from the machine, build no more*
> *bridges. Through what air will you*
> *fly to span the continents? Let the words*
> *fall any way at all—that they may*
> *hit love aslant. It will be a rare*
> *visitation.*

A Dream of Love, the latest of three published plays, is rated next to *Paterson* by its author. Certainly it is full of Williams's obstinate wisdom and paradoxical selflessness.

DOC: Don't be profane. Every man is like me. Don't try to hand me that bunk. I know too much. I'm just the run of the farm, dull average. I'm not neurotic. That's just what I'm not. I'm just like everybody else. That's my pride. I'm proud. Hellishly proud that I'm just the core of the onion —nothing at all. That's just what makes me so right. And I know I'm right.

Yet a few scenes before, the same Doc makes the following speech:

DOC: Our relationship? Something horrible in all probability— if it isn't magnificent. Perverse. Insane—of which we shall never know anything. Murderous perhaps but inevitable . . . I love you!—the second word being an eternal lie.

Lastly, the Doctor regales the Other Woman, just before they consummate their fatal affair:

> DOC (growing more and more excited): the Greeks. Here's one of the most famous lines from their most famous poem:
>
> KAI SAY GAYRON TOW PREEN MEN HAKOIOMEN HOLBION EENAI.
>
> Sounds like a horse coughing, doesn't it? Achilles said that to Priam. Or does it, after all, remind you of Hiawatha?

So we have almost exclusively in this play the agony and bloody sweat, without the grateful compensations of *Paterson*. Here and there a turn of humor or poetry, especially in a none too relevant scene between the Negro cook and a lady evangelist, but the main action is grueling. That it illuminates Williams as a poet of the anti-poetic and a hero of the anti-heroic is incontestable. He has absorbed several devices of naturalistic-expressionistic theater, the trouble being that the play doesn't *reveal* enough for its type of theatre. A fatal incoherence at the center of the plotting forces it back on its thinness, as to a kind of penance. "Doc: 'Because I will not lie. Cost what it may, I will not lie!' " To put it bluntly, the play exploits Williams's minor vices at the expense of his major virtues; everything suffers, the language most of all.

The Clouds contains a number of Williams's best recent short poems; the title poem which successfully uses the longer line he has been developing, run over and over, sometimes using rhythmic suspense in much the same manner as Ogden Nash. (We have Toulouse-Lautrec again in section II, without which the poem would be enormously improved.) Also the fine "Lear," in his best vein; "The Visit," "The Semblables," "The Injury," and three delightfully sharp light poems, "The Savage Beast," "For a Low Voice," and "Education a Failure" (a poem in which the maddest Williams philosophy is happily absorbed into gay and vivid perception). I also liked "The Mind's Games" which, though not his very best verse, illuminates the connection between his aesthetics and his morals:

The world is too much with us? Rot!
the world is not half enough with us—
the rot of a potato with
a healthy skin, a rot that is
never revealed till we are about to
eat—and it revolts us. Beauty?
Beauty should make us paupers,
should blind us, rob us—for it
does not feed the sufferer but makes
his suffering a fly-blown putrescence
and ourselves decay—unless
the ecstasy be general.

Space lacks for more than a brief notice of Miss Koch's sturdy, painstaking book. She puts her shoulder to a mass of contradictory prejudice and makes it yield a passage. "It is clear now," she writes, "that in *Paterson* Williams is attempting one of the most adventurous and passionate assaults upon the moral structure of the American grain which the poetic imagination in this country has yet conceived." This sentence defines her sympathy and devotion. The 275 pages of her book include a careful account and exegesis of the poetry, fiction, plays and miscellaneous writings, with a bibliography and index. Her book obviously benefits from the author's talks with the poet and her access to the Williams Collection of MSS. in Buffalo.

Incoherence, then, is the principal "cost," to use a favorite word with Williams, incoherence raised to a level where it corresponds to Eliot's diffidence or Pound's tactlessness, a quirk which can sometimes reveal the poetry, sometimes conceal it, sometimes ruin it altogether, but which is also absorbed into the success of passage after passage, poem after poem.

Bibliography

AUDEN, W. H. *Yeats as an Example.* Vol. x (Spring 1948), p. 187.

BARRETT, WILLIAM. *Aristocracy and/or Christianity.* Vol. xi (Summer 1949), p. 489.

BENTLEY, ERIC. Monsieur Verdoux *as Theatre.* Vol. x (Autumn 1948), p. 705.

BERRYMAN, JOHN. *The Loud Hill of Wales.* Vol. ii (Autumn 1940), p. 481.

BISHOP, JOHN PEALE. *The Sorrows of Thomas Wolfe.* Vol. i (Winter 1939), p. 1.

BLACKMUR, RICHARD. *Parody and Critique: Notes on Thomas Mann's* Doctor Faustus. Vol. xii (Winter 1950), p. 20.

BROOKS, CLEANTH, JR. *The Whole of Housman.* Vol. iii (Winter 1941), p. 105.

CHASE, RICHARD. *The Stone and the Crucifixion: Faulkner's* Light in August. Vol. x (Autumn 1948), p. 539.

CLARK, ELEANOR. *The Myth of Sainthood.* Vol. ii (Autumn 1940), p. 485.

EBERHART, RICHARD. *Q's Revisions.* Vol. ii (Autumn 1940), p. 496.

ELLMANN, RICHARD. *Robartes and Aherne: Two Sides of a Penny.* Vol. x (Spring 1948), p. 177.

EMPSON, WILLIAM. *Emotions in Poems.* Vol x (Winter 1948), p. 579.

FITTS, DUDLEY. *The Hellenism of Robinson Jeffers.* Vol. viii (Autumn 1946), p. 678.

FLINT, ROBERT W. *I Will Teach You My Townspeople.* Vol. xii (Summer 1950), p. 537.

GOODMAN, PAUL. *Tardy and Partial Recognition.* Vol. x (Spring 1948), p. 340.

HOWE, IRVING. *The Cost of Distraction.* Vol. xi (Spring 1949), p. 336.

JARRELL, RANDALL. *The Humble Animal.* Vol. iv (Autumn 1942), p. 408.

KOCH, VIVIENNE. *The Poetry of Allen Tate.* Vol. xi (Summer 1949), p. 355.

LEBOWITZ, MARTIN. *The Everlasting Mr. Huxley.* Vol. vii (Winter 1945), p. 135.

MACAULEY, ROBIE. *The Good Ford.* Vol. xi (Spring 1949), p. 269.

MONNIER, ADRIENNE. *Joyce's* Ulysses *and the French Public.* Vol. viii (Summer 1946), p. 430.

O'DONNELL, DONAT. *The Pieties of Evelyn Waugh.* Vol. IX (Summer 1947), p. 400.

RAHV, PHILIP. *Paleface and Redskin.* Vol. I (Summer 1939), p. 251.

RICE, PHILIP BLAIR. *Existentialism and the Self.* Vol. XII (Spring 1949), p. 304.

ROSENFELD, ISAAC. *Dry Watershed.* Vol. VIII (Spring 1946), p. 310.

SCHWARTZ, DELMORE. *Neither Historian nor Critic.* Vol. III (Winter 1941), p. 119.

TRILLING, LIONEL. *Wordsworth and the Iron Time.* Vol. XII (Summer 1950), p. 477.

TYLER, PARKER. *Novel into Film:* All the King's Men. Vol. XII (Spring 1950), p. 369.

VIVAS, ELISEO. *Kafka's Distorted Mask.* Vol. VIII (Winter 1948), p. 51.

WALLIS, C. G. *Satan and Denis de Rougemont.* Vol. VI (Winter 1944), p. 150.

WARREN, AUSTIN. *Myth and Dialectic in the Later Novels of Henry James.* Vol. V (Autumn 1943), p. 551.

WARREN, ROBERT PENN. *Pure and Impure Poetry.* Vol. V (Spring 1943), p. 228.

WHITEHALL, HAROLD. *Linguistic Patriot.* Vol. VIII (Winter 1946), p. 156.